Systems and Processes

SYSTEMS

and PROCESSES

Collected Works in Sociology

Edited by

MARIO REDA

EUGENE FAPPIANO

LEON CZIKOWSKY

1968

COLLEGE & UNIVERSITY PRESS · *Publishers*

NEW HAVEN, CONN.

MANUFACTURED IN THE UNITED STATES OF AMERICA BY
UNITED PRINTING SERVICES, INC.
NEW HAVEN, CONN.

THIS WORK IS DEDICATED TO THE VARIOUS STUDENTS
AND TEACHERS WHO HAVE INFLUENCED AND ENCOUR-
AGED OUR ENDEAVORS. AMONG THE LATTER WE WISH
TO HONOR

RICHARD FRANKLIN
West Virginia University

GORDON J. DIRENZO
Indiana University

SLOAN R. WAYLAND
Columbia University

Acknowledgments

To attempt to acknowledge our debts of gratitude to the various people who have assisted us, whether directly or indirectly, is no easy task. Nevertheless, certain people do stand out for their cooperation, encouragement, and generosity. Among them we would like to list the following:

Seymour Martin Lipset, Professor of Government and Social Relations, Harvard University; Harry C. Bredemeier, Professor of Sociology, Rutgers University; J. Oscar Lee, Director of Education, The National Conference of Christians and Jews; Lawrence F. Pisani, Chairman of the Sociology Department, Southern Connecticut State College; Linda Lee Gold, for her compilation of student suggestions; Francine Beaulieu Sackett for her contribution of cover design and graphics; I. Frederick Doduck and Michael F. Morgillo, of College and University Press, for their unending patience and kindness; and, above all, our families, with a special note of gratitude to Janis Reda, whose equanimity, perseverance, and persistently pleasant disposition were a constant source of encouragement to the editors.

Lastly, the editors wish to acknowledge themselves as the ones to be held fully responsible for any of the various shortcomings that may yet be present in this volume.

M. R.
E. F.
L. C.

New Haven, Connecticut
Summer, 1968

Contents

THE FOURTH DIVISION

COLLECTIVITIES AND CHANGE

Introduction

SOCIOLOGY AS A DISCIPLINE has attempted to test a variety of hypotheses about society's organization and functions. With limited success the sociologists have created an awareness of man's social relationships, his social structures, environments, controls, and the resulting interrelationship of these components.

This text is a collection of investigations by those social and behavioral scientists. Its organization contains a basic plan that outlines broad categories which the editors intend to be much more than simply a table for grouping articles. The text design is believed to be a meaningful organizational approach in which sociological literature can be viewed.

Once the desire for a broad view of sociology became the coordinating concept of *Systems and Processes,* it was apparent to the editorial team that some functional problems about text design should also place high on the list of organizational priorities. Principally, the articles in this anthology must not only be illustrative of the title, but the title also must be an accurate organizational approach to sociological inquiry and thus illustrative of the articles. It was also believed that this work should contain elements that would make sociology lively and interesting. While this collection was being designed, there appeared to be a meta-concept constantly coming to surface in the planning: that this work be concise and the articles cited be an honest response to the call for clarity that is being sounded in sociological writing today.

With the above concepts as a guide, the works in this text have been selected as choice illustrations of readability and of the recurrence of phenomena that touch upon the universal in societies. Thus, it is hoped that the presentation of relevant historical data contained herein, by being couched within established and workable sociological theories, will assist the reader's explorative ventures in perceiving the desired unity in the field of sociology as well as the refreshing diversity of human behavior.

As one begins to examine the varieties of texts and monographs in this discipline, it becomes obvious that there are a multiplicity of approaches and definitions about the subject area. Seldom does one find an approach flexible and yet encompassing so that the subject can be viewed with a minimal amount of bias. With continued reading in sociology one can quickly compare and realize that the definitions change with the reading of each book. But all is not chaos! There are some common concepts that are found in nearly all of these definitions that weave together the components of the science of sociology. The most fundamental concept found is the individual as a unit; but the individual is usually discussed in relation to some system or social act. When the system is viewed to be static it would be referred to as a structure; and the social act when cited in process might be referred to as social interaction. Another concept that is commonly found is the idea of some recurring pattern of behavior in a social environment, be it a structure or a system, call it a culture, society, group, or collectivity. In essence, the sociologist is interested in the study of the person when he is involved in human interaction and when that process takes place in a certain system.

This work, *Systems and Processes,* has evolved into four natural divisions of organization. The first major division is entitled "The Individual and Integration." This organizational heading has been designated so that the single actor can be understood in relation to the social system. As the actor becomes involved in interaction the process of integration into an environment takes place. The second division, entitled "The Process and Structure of Socialization," is an attempt at understanding socialization from these two approaches. The social-psychological process approach is a means by which people become members of a social system and subscribe to its values. It is the process by which the new-born is brought into the family group and accepts all of the norms contained within that group. The structure of socialization and resocialization is similar to social change since both study human behavior and prepare the individual for a new set of living patterns. The structure of socialization must not only contain incentives for an individual to change, but also a framework in which one is to change. This structure facilitates the resocialization in the direction of change. "Institutions and Social Order" is the title of the third organizing division. The institutional approaches are special structures and/or systems that carry on the processes, mores, and values of a culture. The editors believed that the third organizational area needed still another dimension. Within our social system there is a pattern of recurring behavior that has many of the characteristics similar to, and yet not, an institution; the writers have called this pattern order. This anthology ends with a list of studies under the heading "Collectivities and Change." Within the sociological framework there still exist some forms of behavior that appear to be unstructured and disorganized and outside the scientific explanation. Through the perspective of sociology there can still be seen some common features that recur and are moving toward patterned collective behavior. This total work stresses the science of sociology and the organization found within the discipline. The last segment of the fourth division deals with change and the perennial question: *Sociologense Quo Vadis?*

A.M.D.G.

THE INDIVIDUAL and INTEGRATION

THE INDIVIDUAL and INTEGRATION

STORIES HAVE BEEN TOLD time and time again of individuals who chose to leave society in order to live the life of a hermit. However, society did not exactly leave them. Certain beliefs, skills, languages, and other factors accompanied them into this seclusion.

There are others who, although they have not wandered off into the seclusion of the wilderness, have chosen to abide by a set of norms, values, statuses, and roles which seem to run counter to the values of the broader system of which most of us claim to be members. To illustrate, the so-called "alienated" skid-row derelict, while deviating from some of the major norms of society, does still function in a world that has its own norms, statuses, roles, and organized group behavior. While he may be considered alienated from one system, he can be seen to be *integrated* into another system.

Individuals usually seek to be integrated into some kinds of groups or systems. If one feels himself partially or completely bereft of the meaning, values, goals, statuses, and sense of self-hood that groups provide, he will search, consciously or subconsciously, for integration. Hence there exists a variety of groups (and devoted adherents) to fill that gap. Groups serve to direct the individual amidst the heterogeneity of conflicting values or ideas; above all, many

17

groups often function to offset the feelings of loneliness or futility which can overtake an individual. Having a set of organized norms and definable patterns of interaction, they can serve to integrate the individual.

Even if our friend the hermit chooses to "go it alone," he will take with him a system of beliefs, values, language, and ways of doing things. Nevertheless, it has often been confirmed that the individual can best *maintain* his system of values if he stays within the context of the group.

While written in a humorous manner, this article significantly probes the importance of "culture" in shaping goals, values and meaning for the individual members.

I

Body Ritual among the Nacirema*

HORACE MINER

THE ANTHROPOLOGIST HAS BECOME so familiar with the diversity of ways in which different peoples behave in similar situations that he is not apt to be surprised by even the most exotic customs. In fact, if all of the logically possible combinations of behavior have not been found somewhere in the world, he is apt to suspect that they must be present in some yet undescribed tribe. This point has, in fact, been expressed with respect to clan organization by Murdock (1949:71). In this light, the magical beliefs and practices of the Nacirema present such unusual aspects that it seems desirable to describe them as an example of the extremes to which human behavior can go.

Professor Linton first brought the ritual of the Nacirema to the attention of anthropologists twenty years ago (1936:326), but the culture of this people is still very poorly understood. They are a North American group living in the territory between the Canadian Cree, the Yaqui and Tarahumare of Mexico, and the Carib and Arawak of the Antilles. Little is known of their origin, although tradition states that they came from the east. According to Nacirema mythology, their nation was originated by a culture hero, Notgnihsaw, who is otherwise known for two great feats of strength—the throwing of a piece of wampum across the river Pa-To-Mac and the chopping down of a cherry tree in which the Spirit of Truth resided.

Nacirema culture is characterized by a highly developed market economy which has evolved in a rich natural habitat. While much of the people's time is devoted to economic pursuits, a large part of the fruits of these labors and a considerable por-

* Reproduced by permission of the American Anthropological Association from the *American Anthropologist* 58: 503-507 (1956), and the author.

tion of the day are spent in ritual activity. The focus of this activity is the human body, the appearance and health of which loom as a dominant concern in the ethos of the people. While such a concern is certainly not unusual, its ceremonial aspects and associated philosophy are unique.

The fundamental belief underlying the whole system appears to be that the human body is ugly and that its natural tendency is to debility and disease. Incarcerated in such a body, man's only hope is to avert these characteristics through the use of the powerful influences of ritual and ceremony. Every household has one or more shrines devoted to this purpose. The more powerful individuals in the society have several shrines in their houses and, in fact, the opulence of a house is often referred to in terms of the number of such ritual centers it possesses. Most houses are of wattle and daub construction, but the shrine rooms of the more wealthy are walled with stone. Poorer families imitate the rich by applying pottery plaques to their shrine walls.

While each family has at least one such shrine, the rituals associated with it are not family ceremonies but are private and secret. The rites are normally only discussed with children, and then only during the period when they are being initiated into these mysteries. I was able, however, to establish sufficient rapport with the natives to examine these shrines and to have the rituals described to me.

The focal point of the shrine is a box or chest which is built into the wall. In this chest are kept the many charms and magical potions without which no native believes he could live. These preparations are secured from a variety of specialized practitioners. The most powerful of these are the medicine men, whose assistance must be rewarded with substantial gifts. However, the medicine men do not provide the curative potions for their clients, but decide what the ingredients should be and then write them down in an ancient and secret language. This writing is understood only by the medicine men and by the herbalists who, for another gift, provide the required charm.

The charm is not disposed of after it has served its purpose, but is placed in the charm-box of the household shrine. As these magical materials are specific for certain ills, and the real or imagined maladies of the people are many, the charm-box is usually full to overflowing. The magical packets are so numerous that people forget what their purposes were and fear to use them again. While the natives are very vague on this point, we can only assume that the idea in retaining all the old magical materials is that their presence in the charm-box, before which the body rituals are conducted, will in some way protect the worshipper.

Beneath the charm-box is a small font. Each day every member of the family, in succession, enters the shrine room, bows his head before the charm-box, mingles different sorts of holy water in the font, and proceeds with a brief rite of ablution. The holy waters are secured from the Water Temple of the community, where the priests conduct elaborate ceremonies to make the liquid ritually pure.

In the hierarchy of magical practitioners, and below the medicine men in prestige, are specialists whose designation is best translated "holy-mouth-men." The Nacirema have an almost pathological horror of and fascination with the mouth, the condition of which is believed to have a supernatural influence on all social relationships. Were it not for the rituals of the mouth, they believe that their teeth would fall out, their gums bleed, their jaws shrink, their friends desert them, and their lovers reject them. They also believe that a strong relationship exists between oral and moral characteristics. For example, there is a ritual ablution of the mouth for children which is supposed to improve their moral fiber.

The daily body ritual performed by everyone includes a mouth-rite. Despite the fact that these people are so punctilious about care of the mouth, this rite involves a practice which strikes the uninitiated stranger as revolting. It was reported to me that the ritual consists of inserting a small bundle of hog hairs into the mouth, along with certain magical powders, and then moving the bundle in a highly formalized series of gestures.

In addition to the private mouth-rite, the people seek out a holy-mouth-man once or twice a year. These practitioners have an impressive set of paraphernalia, consisting of a variety of augers, awls, probes, and prods. The use of these objects in the exorcism of the evils of the mouth involves almost unbelievable ritual torture of the client. The holy-mouth-man opens the client's mouth and, using the above mentioned tools, enlarges any holes which decay may have created in the teeth. Magical materials are put into these holes. If there are no naturally occurring holes in the teeth, large sections of one or more teeth are gouged out so that the supernatural substance can be applied. In the client's view, the purpose of these ministrations is to arrest decay and to draw friends. The extremely sacred and traditional character of the rite is evident in the fact that the natives return to the holy-mouth-men year after year, despite the fact that their teeth continue to decay.

It is to be hoped that, when a thorough study of the Nacirema is made, there will be careful inquiry into the personality structure of these people. One has but to watch the gleam in the eye of a holy-mouth-man, as he jabs an awl into an exposed nerve, to suspect that a certain amount of sadism is involved. If this can be established, a very interesting pattern emerges, for most of the population shows definite masochistic tendencies. It was to these that Professor Linton referred in discussing a distinctive part of the daily body ritual which is performed only by men. This part of the rite involves scraping and lacerating the surface of the face with a sharp instrument. Special women's rites are performed only four times during each lunar month, but what they lack in frequency is made up in barbarity. As part of this ceremony, women bake their heads in small ovens for about an hour. The theoretically interesting point is that what seems to be a preponderantly masochistic people have developed sadistic specialists.

The medicine men have an imposing temple, or *latipso,* in every community of any size. The more elaborate ceremonies required to treat very sick patients can only be performed at this temple. These ceremonies involve not only the thaumaturge but a permanent group of vestal maidens who move sedately about the temple chambers in distinctive costume and headdress.

The *latipso* ceremonies are so harsh that it is phenomenal that a fair proportion of the really sick natives who enter the temple ever recover. Small children whose indoctrination is still incomplete have been known to resist attempts to take them to the temple because "that is where you go to die." Despite this fact, sick adults are not only willing but eager to undergo the protracted ritual purification, if they can afford to do so. No matter how ill the supplicant or how grave the emergency, the guardians of many temples will not admit a client if he cannot give a rich gift to the custodian. Even after one has gained admission and survived the ceremonies, the guardians will not permit the neophyte to leave until he makes still another gift.

The supplicant entering the temple is first stripped of all his or her clothes. In every-day life the Nacirema avoids exposure of his body and its natural functions. Bathing and excretory acts are performed only in the secrecy of the household shrine, where they are ritualized as part of the body-rites. Psychological shock results from the fact that body secrecy is suddenly lost upon entry into the *latipso*. A man, whose own wife has never seen him in an excretory act, suddenly finds himself naked and assisted by a vestal maiden while he performs his natural functions into a sacred vessel. This sort of ceremonial treatment is necessitated by the fact that the excreta are used by a diviner to ascertain the course and nature of the client's sickness. Female clients, on the other hand, find their naked bodies are subjected to the scrutiny, manipulation and prodding of the medicine men.

Few supplicants in the temple are well enough to do anything but lie on their hard beds. The daily ceremonies, like the rites of the holy-mouth-men, involve discomfort and torture. With ritual precision, the vestals awaken their miserable charges each dawn and roll them about on their beds of pain while performing ablutions, in the formal movements of which the maidens are highly trained. At other times they insert magic wands in the supplicant's mouth or force him to eat substances which are supposed to be healing. From time to time the medicine men come to their clients and jab magically treated needles into their flesh. The fact that these temple ceremonies may not cure, and may even kill the neophyte, in no way decreases the people's faith in the medicine men.

There remains one other kind of practitioner, known as a "listener." This witch-doctor has the power to exorcise the devils that lodge in the heads of people who have been bewitched. The Nacirema believe that parents bewitch their own children. Mothers are particularly suspected of putting a curse on children while teaching them the secret body rituals. The counter-magic of the witch-doctor is unusual in its lack of ritual. The patient simply tells the "listener" all his troubles and fears, beginning with the earliest difficulties he can remember. The memory displayed by the Nacirema in these exorcism sessions is truly remarkable. It is not uncommon for the patient to bemoan the rejection he felt upon being weaned as a babe, and a few individuals even see their troubles going back to the traumatic effects of their own birth.

In conclusion, mention must be made of certain practices which have their base in native esthetics but which depend upon the pervasive aversion to the natural body and its functions. There are ritual fasts to make fat people thin and ceremonial feasts to make thin people fat. Still other rites are used to make women's breasts larger if they are small, and smaller if they are large. General dissatisfaction with breast shape is symbolized in the fact that the ideal form is virtually outside the range of human variation. A few women afflicted with almost inhuman hypermammary development are so idolized that they make a handsome living by simply going from village to village and permitting the natives to stare at them for a fee.

Reference has already been made to the fact that excretory functions are ritualized, routinized, and relegated to secrecy. Natural reproductive functions are similarly distorted. Intercourse is taboo as a topic and scheduled as an act. Efforts are made to avoid pregnancy by the use of magical materials or by limiting intercourse to certain phases of the moon. Conception is actually very infrequent. When pregnant, women dress so as to hide their condition. Parturition takes place in secret, without friends or relatives to assist, and the majority of women do not nurse their infants.

Our review of the ritual life of the Nacirema has certainly shown them to be a magic-ridden people. It is hard to understand how they have managed to exist so long under the burdens which they have imposed upon themselves. But even such exotic customs as these take on real meaning when they are viewed with the insight provided by Malinowski when he wrote (1948:70):

> Looking from far and above, from our high places of safety in the developed civilization, it is easy to see all the crudity and irrelevance of magic. But without its power and guidance early man could not have mastered his practical difficulties as he has done, nor could man have advanced to the higher stages of civilization.

REFERENCES CITED

LINTON, RALPH
    1936 The Study of Man. New York, D. Appleton-Century Co.
MALINOWSKI, BRONISLAW
    1948 Magic, Science, and Religion. Glencoe, The Free Press.
MURDOCK, GEORGE P.
    1949 Social Structure. New York, The Macmillan Co.

Have you failed a test? Are you worried about making it in college? Did you say you were dropped by your steady? Do you have trouble at home? (You have a status problem!) You are the "mark." Here's how you get "cooled."

II

On Cooling the Mark Out*

Some Aspects of Adaptation to Failure

ERVING GOFFMAN

IN CASES OF CRIMINAL FRAUD, victims find they must suddenly adapt themselves to the loss of sources of security and status which they had taken for granted. A consideration of this adaptation to loss can lead us to an understanding of some relations in our society between involvements and the selves that are involved.

In the argot of the criminal world, the term "mark" refers to any individual who is a victim or prospective victim of certain forms of planned illegal exploitation. The mark is the sucker—the person who is taken in. An instance of the operation of any particular racket, taken through the full cycle of its steps or phases, is sometimes called a play. The persons who operate the racket and "take" the mark are occasionally called operators.

The confidence game—the con, as its practitioners call it—is a way of obtaining money under false pretenses by the exercise

* Reprinted by special permission of the William Alanson White Psychiatric Foundation, Inc. Erving Goffman, "On Cooling the Mark Out," *Psychiatry* (1952) 15: 451-463. Copyright is held by the William Alanson White Psychiatric Foundation, Inc.

Terminology regarding criminal activity is taken primarily from D. W. Maurer, *The Big Con* (New York, Bobbs-Merrill, 1940), and also from E. Sutherland, *The Professional Thief* (Chicago, Univ. of Chicago Press, 1937). The approach that this paper attempts to utilize is taken from Everett C. Hughes of the University of Chicago, who is not responsible for any misapplications of it which may occur here. The sociological problem of failure was first suggested to me by James Littlejohn of the University of Edinburgh. I am grateful to Professor E. A. Shils for criticism and to my wife, Angelica S. Goffman, for assistance.

of fraud and deceit. The con differs from politer forms of financial deceit in important ways. The con is practiced on private persons by talented actors who methodically and regularly build up informal social relationships just for the purpose of abusing them; white-collar crime is practiced on organizations by persons who learn to abuse positions of trust which they once filled faithfully. The one exploits poise; the other, position. Further, a con man is someone who accepts a social role in the underworld community; he is part of a brotherhood whose members make no pretense to one another of being "legit." A white-collar criminal, on the other hand, has no colleagues, although he may have an associate with whom he plans his crime and a wife to whom he confesses it.

The con is said to be a good racket in the United States only because most Americans are willing, nay eager, to make easy money, and will engage in action that is less than legal in order to do so. The typical play has typical phases. The potential sucker is first spotted, and one member of the working team (called the outside man, steerer, or roper) arranges to make social contact with him. The confidence of the mark is won, and he is given an opportunity to invest his money in a gambling venture which he understands to have been fixed in his favor. The venture, of course, is fixed, but not in his favor. The mark is permitted to win some money and then persuaded to invest more. There is an "accident" or "mistake," and the mark loses his total investment. The operators then depart in a ceremony that is called the blowoff or sting. They leave the mark but take his money. The mark is expected to go on his way, a little wiser and a lot poorer.

Sometimes, however, a mark is not quite prepared to accept his loss as a gain in experience and to say and do nothing about his venture. He may feel moved to complain to the police or to chase after the operators. In the terminology of the trade, the mark may squawk, beef, or come through. From the operators' point of view, this kind of behavior is bad for business. It gives the members of the mob a bad reputation with such police as have not yet been fixed and with marks who have not yet been taken. In order to avoid this adverse publicity, an additional phrase is sometimes added at the end of the play. It is called cooling the mark out. After the blowoff has occurred, one of the operators stays with the mark and makes an effort to keep the anger of the mark within manageable and sensible proportions. The operator stays behind his team-mates in the capacity of what might be called a cooler and exercises upon the mark the art of consolation. An attempt is made to define the situation for the mark in a way that makes it easy for him to accept the inevitable and quietly go home. The mark is given instruction in the philosophy of taking a loss.

When we call to mind the image of a mark who has just been separated from his money, we sometimes attempt to account for the greatness of his anger by the greatness of his financial loss. This is a narrow view. In many cases, especially in America, the mark's image of himself is built up on the belief that he is a pretty shrewd person when it comes to making deals and that he is not the sort of person who is taken in by anything. The mark's readiness to participate in a sure thing is based on more than avarice; it is based on a feeling that he will now be able to prove to himself that he is the sort of person who can "turn a fast buck." For many, this capacity for high finance comes near to being a sign of masculinity and a test of fulfilling the male role.

It is well known that persons protect themselves with all kinds of rationalizations when they have a buried image of themselves which the facts of their status do not support. A person may tell himself many things: that he has not been given a fair chance; that he is not really interested in becoming something else; that the time for showing his mettle has not yet come; that the usual means of realizing his desires are personally or morally distasteful, or require too much dull effort. By means of such defenses, a person saves himself from committing a cardinal social sin—the sin of defining oneself in terms of a status while lacking the qualifications which an incumbent of that status is supposed to possess.

A mark's participation in a play, and his investment in it, clearly commit him in his own eyes to the proposition that he is a smart man. The process by which he comes to believe that he cannot lose is also the process by which he drops the defenses and compensations that previously protected him from defeats. When the blowoff comes, the mark finds that he has no defense for not being a shrewd man. He has defined himself as a shrewd man and must face the fact that he is only another easy mark. He has defined himself as possessing a certain set of

qualities and then proven to himself that he is miserably lacking
in them. This is a process of self-destruction of the self. It is no
wonder that the mark needs to be cooled out and that it is good
business policy for one of the operators to stay with the mark in
order to talk him into a point of view from which it is possible
to accept a loss.

In essence, then, the cooler has the job of handling persons
who have been caught out on a limb—persons whose expectations and self-conceptions have been built up and then shattered.
The mark is a person who has compromised himself, in his own
eyes if not in the eyes of others.

Although the term, mark, is commonly applied to a person
who is given short-lived expectations by operators who have
intentionally misrepresented the facts, a less restricted definition
is desirable in analyzing the larger social scene. An expectation
may finally prove false, even though it has been possible to
sustain it for a long time and even though the operators acted
in good faith. So, too, the disappointment of reasonable expectations, as well as misguided ones, creates a need for consolation.
Persons who participate in what is recognized as a confidence
game are found in only a few social settings, but persons who
have to be cooled out are found in many. Cooling the mark out
is one theme in a very basic social story.

For purposes of analysis, one may think of an individual in
reference to the values or attributes of a socially recognized
character which he possesses. Psychologists speak of a value as
a personal involvement. Sociologists speak of a value as a status,
role, or relationship. In either case, the character of the value
that is possessed is taken in a certain way as the character of
the person who possesses it. An alteration in the kinds of attributes possessed brings an alteration to the self-conception of
the person who possesses them.

The process by which someone acquires a value is the process
by which he surrenders the claim he had to what he was and
commits himself to the conception of self which the new value
requires or allows him to have. It is the process that persons
who fall in love or take dope call getting hooked. After a person
is hooked, he must go through another process by which his new
involvement finds its proper place, in space and time, relative
to the other calls, demands, and commitments that he has upon
himself. At this point certain other persons suddenly begin to

play an important part in the individual's story; they impinge upon him by virtue of the relationship they happen to have to the value in which he has become involved. This is not the place to consider the general kinds of impingement that are institutionalized in our society and the general social relationships that arise: the personal relationship, the professional relationship, and the business relationship. Here we are concerned only with the end of the story, the way in which a person becomes disengaged from one of his involvements.

In our society, the story of a person's involvement can end in one of three general ways. According to one type of ending, he may withdraw from one of his involvements or roles in order to acquire a sequentially related one that is considered better. This is the case when a youth becomes a man, when a student becomes a practitioner, or when a man from the ranks is given a commission.

Of course, the person who must change his self at any one of these points of promotion may have profound misgivings. He may feel disloyal to the way of life that must be left behind and to the persons who do not leave it with him. His new role may require action that seems insincere, dishonest, or unfriendly. This he may experience as a loss in moral cleanliness. His new role may require him to forgo the kinds of risk-taking and exertion that he previously enjoyed, and yet his new role may not provide the kind of heroic and exalted action that he expected to find in it.[1] This he may experience as a loss in moral strength.

There is no doubt that certain kinds of role success require certain kinds of moral failure. It may therefore be necessary, in a sense, to cool the dubious neophyte in rather than out. He may have to be convinced that his doubts are a matter of sentimentality. The adult social view will be impressed upon him. He will be required to understand that a promotional change in status is voluntary, desirable, and natural, and that loss of one's role in these circumstances is the ultimate test of having fulfilled it properly.

It has been suggested that a person may leave a role under circumstances that reflect favorably upon the way in which he performed it. In theory, at least, a related possibility must be considered. A person may leave a role and at the same time leave behind him the standards by which such roles are judged. The new thing that he becomes may be so different from the thing he was that criteria such as success or failure cannot be easily applied to the change which has occurred. He becomes lost to others that he may find himself; he is of the twice-born. In our society, perhaps the most obvious example of this kind of termination occurs when a woman voluntarily gives up a prestigeful profession in order to become a wife and a mother. It is to be noted that this illustrates an institutionalized movement; those who make it do not make news. In America most other examples of this kind of termination are more a matter of talk than of occurrence. For example, one of the culture heroes of our dinner-table mythology is the man who walks out on an established calling in order to write or paint or live in the country. In other societies, the kind of abdication being considered here seems to have played a more important role. In medieval China, for instance, anchoretic withdrawal apparently gave to persons of quite different station a way of retreating from the occupational struggle while managing the retreat in an orderly, face-saving fashion.[2]

Two basic ways in which a person can lose a role have been considered; he can be promoted out of it or abdicate from it. There is, of course, a third basic ending to the status story. A person may be involuntarily deprived of his position or involvement and made in return something that is considered a lesser thing to be. It is mainly in this third ending to a person's role that occasions arise for cooling him out. It is here that one deals in the full sense with the problem of persons' losing their roles.

Involuntary loss seems itself to be of two kinds. First, a person may lose a status in such a way that the loss is not taken as a reflection upon the loser. The loss of a loved one, either because of an accident that could not have been prevented or because of a disease that could not have been halted, is a case in point. Occupational retirement because of old age is another. Of course, the loss will inevitably alter the conception the loser has of himself and the conception others have of him, but the alteration itself will not be treated as a symbol of the fate he deserves to receive. No insult is added to injury. It may be necessary, none the less, to pacify the loser and resign him to his loss. The loser who is not held responsible for his loss may even find himself taking the mystical view that all involvements are part of a wider con game, for the more one takes pleasure in a particular role the more one must suffer when it is time to leave it. He may find little comfort in the fact that the play has provided him with an illusion that has lasted a lifetime. He may find little comfort in the fact that the operators had not meant to deceive him.

Secondly, a person may be involuntarily deprived of a role under circumstances which reflect unfavorably on his capacity for it. The lost role may be one that he had already acquired or one that he had openly committed himself to preparing for. In either case the loss is more than a matter of ceasing to act in a given capacity; it is ultimate proof of an incapacity. And in many cases it is even more than this. The moment of failure often catches a person acting as one who feels that he is an appropriate sort of person for the role in question. Assumption becomes presumption, and failure becomes fraud. To loss of substance is thereby added loss of face. Of the many themes that can occur in the natural history of an involvement, this seems to be the most melancholy. Here it will be quite essential and quite difficult to cool the mark out. I shall be particularly concerned with this second kind of loss—the kind that involves humiliation.

It should be noted, parenthetically, that one circle of persons may define a particular loss as the kind that casts no reflection on the loser, and that a different circle of persons may treat the same loss as a symbol of what the loser deserves. One must also note that there is a tendency today to shift certain losses of status from the category of those that reflect upon the loser to the category of those that do not. When persons lose their jobs, their courage, or their minds, we tend more and more to take a clinical or naturalistic view of the loss and a nonmoral view of their failure. We want to define a person as something that is not destroyed by the destruction of one of his selves. This benevolent attitude is in line with the effort today to publicize the view that occupational retirement is not the end of all active capacities but the beginning of new and different ones.

A consideration of consolation as a social process leads to four general problems having to do with the self in society. First, where in modern life does one find persons conducting themselves as though they were entitled to the rights of a particular status and then having to face up to the fact that they do not possess the qualification for the status? In other words, at what points in the structures of our social life are persons likely to

compromise themselves or find themselves compromised? When
is it likely that a person will have to disengage himself or become disengaged from one of his involvements? Secondly, what
are the typical ways in which persons who find themselves in
this difficult position can be cooled out; how can they be made
to accept the great injury that has been done to their image of
themselves, regroup their defenses, and carry on without raising
a squawk? Thirdly, what, in general, can happen when a person
refuses to be cooled out, that is, when he refuses to be pacified
by the cooler? Fourthly, what arrangements are made by operators and marks to avoid entirely the process of consolation?

In all personal-service organizations customers or clients sometimes make complaints. A customer may feel that he has been
given service in a way that is unacceptable to him—a way that
he interprets as an offense to the conception he has of who and
what he is. The management therefore has the problem of
cooling the mark out. Frequently this function is allotted to specialists within the organization. In restaurants of some size, for
example, one of the crucial functions of the hostess is to pacify
customers whose self-conceptions have been injured by wait-
resses or by the food. In large stores the complaint department
and the floorwalker perform a similar function.

One may note that a service organization does not operate in
an anonymous world, as does a con mob, and is therefore strongly obliged to make some effort to cool the mark out. An institution, after all, cannot take it on the lam; it must pacify its
marks.

One may also note that coolers in service organizations tend
to view their own activity in a light that softens the harsher
details of the situation. The cooler protects himself from feelings
of guilt by arguing that the customer is not really in need of
the service he expected to receive, that bad service is not really
deprivational, and that beefs and complaints are a sign of bile,
not a sign of injury. In a similar way, the con man protects himself from remorseful images of bankrupt marks by arguing that
the mark is a fool and not a full-fledged person, possessing an
inclination towards illegal gain but not the decency to admit it
or the capacity to succeed at it.

In organizations patterned after a bureaucratic model, it is
customary for personnel to expect rewards of a specified kind
upon fulfilling requirements of a specified nature. Personnel

come to define their career line in terms of a sequence of legitimate expectations and to base their self-conceptions on the assumption that in due course they will be what the institution
allows persons to become. Sometimes, however, a member of an
organization may fulfill some of the requirements for a particular
status, especially the requirements concerning technical profi-
ciency and seniority, but not other requirements, especially the
less codified ones having to do with the proper handling of social
relationships at work. It must fall to someone to break the bad
news to the victim; someone must tell him that he has been
fired, or that he has failed his examinations, or that he has been
by-passed in promotion. And after the blowoff, someone has
to cool the mark out. The necessity of disappointing the expectations that a person has taken for granted may be infrequent in
some organizations, but in others, such as training institutions,
it occurs all the time. The process of personnel selection requires
that many trainees be called but that few be chosen.

When one turns from places of work to other scenes in our
social life, one finds that each has its own occasions for cooling
the mark out. During informal social intercourse it is well understood that an effort on the part of one person (ego) to decrease his social distance from another person (alter) must be
graciously accepted by alter or, if rejected, rejected tactfully so
that the initiator of the move can save his social face. This rule
is codified in books on etiquette and is followed in actual behavior. A friendly movement in the direction of alter is a movement outward on a limb; ego communicates his belief that he
has defined himself as worthy of alter's society, while at the
same time he places alter in the strategic position of being able
to discredit this conception.

The problem of cooling persons out in informal social intercourse is seen most clearly, perhaps, in courting situations and
in what might be called de-courting situations. A proposal of
marriage in our society tends to be a way in which a man sums
up his social attributes and suggests to a woman that hers are
not so much better as to preclude a merger or partnership in
these matters. Refusal on the part of the woman, or refusal on
the part of the man to propose when he is clearly in a position
to do so, is a serious reflection on the rejected suitor. Courtship
is a way not only of presenting oneself to alter for approval but
also of saying that the opinion of alter in this matter is the opin-

ion one is most concerned with. Refusing a proposal, or refusing to propose, is therefore a difficult operation. The mark must be carefully cooled out. The act of breaking a date or of refusing one, and the task of discouraging a "steady" can also be seen in this light, although in these cases great delicacy and tact may not be required, since the mark may not be deeply involved or openly committed. Just as it is harder to refuse a proposal than to refuse a date, so it is more difficult to reject a spouse than to reject a suitor. The process of de-courting by which one person in a marriage maneuvers the other into accepting a divorce without fuss or undue rancor requires extreme finesse in the art of cooling the mark out.

In all of these cases where a person constructs a conception of himself which cannot be sustained, there is a possibility that he has not invested that which is most important to him in the soon-to-be-denied status. In the current idiom, there is a possibility that when he is hit, he will not be hit where he really lives. There is a set of cases, however, where the blowoff cannot help but strike a vital spot; these cases arise, of course, when a person must be dissuaded from life itself. The man with a fatal sickness or fatal injury, the criminal with a death sentence, the soldier with a hopeless objective—these persons must be persuaded to accept quietly the loss of life itself, the loss of all one's earthly involvements. Here, certainly, it will be difficult to cool the mark out. It is a reflection on the conceptions men have—as cooler and mark—that it is possible to do so.

I have mentioned a few of the areas of social life where it becomes necessary, upon occasion, to cool a mark out. Attention may now be directed to some of the common ways in which individuals are cooled out in all of these areas of life.

For the mark, cooling represents a process of adjustment to an impossible situation—a situation arising from having defined himself in a way which the social facts come to contradict. The mark must therefore be supplied with a new set of apologies for himself, a new framework in which to see himself and judge himself. A process of redefining the self along defensible lines must be instigated and carried along; since the mark himself is frequently in too weakened a condition to do this, the cooler must initially do it for him.

One general way of handling the problem of cooling the mark out is to give the task to someone whose status relative to the mark will serve to ease the situation in some way. In formal organizations, frequently, someone who is two or three levels above the mark in line of command will do the hatchet work, on the assumption that words of consolation and redirection will have a greater power to convince if they come from high places. There also seems to be a feeling that persons of high status are better able to withstand the moral danger of having hate directed at them. Incidentally, persons protected by high office do not like to face this issue, and frequently attempt to define themselves as merely the agents of the deed and not the source of it. In some cases, on the other hand, the task of cooling the mark out is given to a friend and peer of the mark, on the assumption that such a person will know best how to hit upon a suitable rationalization for the mark and will know best how to control the mark should the need for this arise. In some cases, as in those pertaining to death, the role of cooler is given to doctors or priests. Doctors must frequently help a family, and the member who is leaving it, to manage the leave-taking with tact and a minimum of emotional fuss.[3] A priest must not so much save a soul as create one that is consistent with what is about to become of it.

A second general solution to the problem of cooling the mark out consists of offering him a status which differs from the one he has lost or failed to gain but which provides at least a something or a somebody for him to become. Usually the alternative presented to the mark is a compromise of some kind, providing him with some of the trappings of his lost status as well as with some of its spirit. A lover may be asked to become a friend; a student of medicine may be asked to switch to the study of dentistry;[4] a boxer may become a trainer; a dying person may be asked to broaden and empty his worldly loves so as to embrace the All-Father that is about to receive him. Sometimes the mark is allowed to retain his status but is required to fulfill it in a different environment: the honest policeman is transferred to a lonely beat; the too zealous priest is encouraged to enter a monastery; an unsatisfactory plant manager is shipped off to another branch. Sometimes the mark is "kicked upstairs" and given a courtesy status such as "Vice President." In the game for social roles, transfer up, down, or away may all be consolation prizes.

A related way of handling the mark is to offer him another chance to qualify for the role at which he has failed. After his fall from grace, he is allowed to retrace his steps and try again. Officer selection programs in the army, for example, often provide for possibilities of this kind. In general, it seems that third and fourth chances are seldom given to marks, and that second chances, while often given, are seldom taken. Failure at a role removes a person from the company of those who have succeeded, but it does not bring him back—in spirit, anyway—to the society of those who have not tried or are in the process of trying. The person who has failed in a role is a constant source of embarrassment, for none of the standard patterns of treatment is quite applicable to him. Instead of taking a second chance, he usually goes away to another place where his past does not bring confusion to his present.

Another standard method of cooling the mark out—one which is frequently employed in conjunction with other methods—is to allow the mark to explode, to break down, to cause a scene, to give full vent to his reactions and feelings, to "blow his top." If this release of emotions does not find a target, then it at least serves a cathartic function. If it does find a target, as in "telling off the boss," it gives the mark a last-minute chance to re-erect his defenses and prove to himself and others that he had not really cared about the status all along. When a blow-up of this kind occurs, friends of the mark or psychotherapists are frequently brought in. Friends are willing to take responsibility for the mark because their relationship to him is not limited to the role he has failed in. This, incidentally, provides one of the less obvious reasons why the cooler in a con mob must cultivate the friendship of the mark; friendship provides the cooler with an acceptable reason for staying around while the mark is cooled out. Psychotherapists, on the other hand, are willing to take responsibility for the mark because it is their business to offer a relationship to those who have failed in a relationship to others.

It has been suggested that a mark may be cooled out by allowing him, under suitable guidance, to give full vent to his initial shock. Thus the manager of a commercial organization may listen with patience and understanding to the complaints of a customer, knowing that the full expression of a complaint is likely to weaken it. This possibility lies behind the role of a whole series of buffers in our society—janitors, restaurant hostesses, grievance committees, floorwalkers, and so on—who listen in silence, with apparent sympathy, until the mark has simmered down. Similarly, in the case of criminal trials, the defending lawyer may find it profitable to allow the public to simmer down before he brings his client to court.

A related procedure for cooling the mark out is found in what is called stalling. The feelings of the mark are not brought to a head because he is given no target at which to direct them. The operator may manage to avoid the presence of the mark or may convince the mark that there is still a slight chance that the loss has not really occurred. When the mark is stalled, he is given a chance to become familiar with the new conception of self he will have to accept before he is absolutely sure that he will have to accept it.

As another cooling procedure, there is the possibility that the operator and the mark may enter into a tacit understanding according to which the mark agrees to act as if he were leaving of his own accord, and the operator agrees to preserve the illusion that this was the case. It is a form of bribery. In this way the mark may fail in his own eyes but prevent others from discovering the failure. The mark gives up his role but saves his face. This, after all, is one of the reasons why persons who are fleeced by con men are often willing to remain silent about their adventure. The same strategy is at work in the romantic custom of allowing a guilty officer to take his own life in a private way before it is taken from him publicly, and in the less romantic custom of allowing a person to resign for delicate reasons instead of firing him for indelicate ones.

Bribery is, of course, a form of exchange. In this case, the mark guarantees to leave quickly and quietly, and in exchange is allowed to leave under a cloud of his own choosing. A more important variation on the same theme is found in the practice of financial compensation. A man can say to himself and others that he is happy to retire from his job and say this with more conviction if he is able to point to a comfortable pension. In this sense, pensions are automatic devices for providing consolation. So, too, a person who has been injured because of another's criminal or marital neglect can compensate for the loss by means of a court settlement.

I have suggested some general ways in which the mark is cooled out. The question now arises: what happens if the mark refuses to be cooled out? What are the possible lines of action he can take if he refuses to be cooled? Attempts to answer these questions will show more clearly why, in general, the operator is so anxious to pacify the mark.

It has been suggested that a mark may be cooled by allowing him to blow his top. If the blow-up is too drastic or prolonged, however, difficulties may arise. We say that the mark becomes "disturbed mentally" or "personally disorganized." Instead of merely telling his boss off, the mark may go so far as to commit criminal violence against him. Instead of merely blaming himself for failure, the mark may inflict great punishment upon himself by attempting suicide, or by acting so as to make it necessary for him to be cooled out in other areas of his social life.

Sustained personal disorganization is one way in which a mark can refuse to cool out. Another standard way is for the individual to raise a squawk, that is, to make a formal complaint to higher authorities obliged to take notice of such matters. The con mob worries lest the mark appeal to the police. The plant manager must make sure that the disgruntled department head does not carry a formal complaint to the general manager or, worse still, to the Board of Directors. The teacher worries lest the child's parent complain to the principal. Similarly, a woman who communicates her evaluation of self by accepting a proposal of marriage can sometimes protect her exposed position—should the necessity of doing so arise—by threatening her disaffected fiancé with a breach-of-promise suit. So, also, a woman who is de-courting her husband must fear lest he contest the divorce or sue her lover for alienation of affection. In much the same way, a customer who is angered by a salesperson can refuse to be mollified by the floorwalker and demand to see the manager. It is interesting to note that associations dedicated to the rights and the honor of minority groups may sometimes encourage a mark to register a formal squawk; politically it may be more advantageous to provide a test case than to allow the mark to be cooled out.

Another line of action which a mark who refuses to be cooled can pursue is that of turning "sour." The term derives from the argot of industry but the behavior it refers to occurs everywhere. The mark outwardly accepts his loss but withdraws all enthusiasm, good will, and vitality from whatever role he is allowed to maintain. He complies with the formal requirements of the role that is left him, but he withdraws his spirit and identification from it. When an employee turns sour, the interests of the organization suffer; every executive, therefore, has the problem of "sweetening" his workers. They must not come to feel that they are slowly being cooled out. This is one of the functions of granting periodic advancements in salary and status, of schemes such as profit-sharing, or of giving the "employee" at home an anniversary present. A similar view can be taken of the problem that a government faces in times of crisis when it must maintain the enthusiastic support of the nation's disadvantaged minorities, for whole groupings of the population can feel they are being cooled out and react by turning sour.

Finally, there is the possibility that the mark may, in a manner of speaking, go into business for himself. He can try to gather about him the persons and facilities required to establish a status similar to the one he has lost, albeit in relation to a different set of persons. This way of refusing to be cooled is often rehearsed in phantasies of the "I'll show them" kind, but sometimes it is actually realized in practice. The rejected marriage partner may make a better remarriage. A social stratum that has lost its status may decide to create its own social system. A leader who fails in a political party may establish his own splinter group.

All these ways in which a mark can refuse to be cooled out have consequences for other persons. There is, of course, a kind of refusal that has little consequence for others. Marks of all kinds may develop explanations and excuses to account in a creditable way for their loss. It is, perhaps, in this region of phantasy that the defeated self makes its last stand.

The process of cooling is a difficult one, both for the operator who cools the mark out and for the person who receives this treatment. Safeguards and strategies are therefore employed to ensure that the process itself need not and does not occur. One deals here with strategies of prevention, not strategies of cure.

From the point of view of the operator, there are two chief ways of avoiding the difficulties of cooling the mark out. First, devices are commonly employed to weed out those applicants for a role, office, or relationship who might later prove to be unsuitable and require removal. The applicant is not given a chance to invest his self unwisely. A variation of this technique, that provides, in a way, a built-in mechanism for cooling the mark out, is found in the institution of probationary period and "temporary" staff. These definitions of the situation make it clear to the person that he must maintain his ego in readiness for the loss of his job, or, better still, that he ought not to think of himself as really having the job. If these safety measures fail, however, a second strategy is often employed. Operators of all kinds seem to be ready, to a surprising degree, to put up with or "carry" persons who have failed but who have not yet been treated as failures. This is especially true where the involvement of the mark is deep and where his conception of self had been publicly committed. Business offices, government agencies, spouses, and other kinds of operators are often careful to make a place for the mark, so that dissolution of the bond will not be necessary. Here, perhaps, is the most important source of private charity in our society.

A consideration of these preventive strategies brings to attention an interesting functional relationship among age-grading, recruitment, and the structure of the self. In our society, as in most others, the young in years are defined as not-yet-persons. To a certain degree, they are not subject to success and failure. A child can throw himself completely into a task, and fail at it, and by and large he will not be destroyed by his failure; it is only necessary to play at cooling him out. An adolescent can be bitterly disappointed in love, and yet he will not thereby become, at least for others, a broken person. A youth can spend a certain amount of time shopping around for a congenial job or a congenial training course, because he is still thought to be able to change his mind without changing his self. And, should he fail at something to which he has tried to commit himself, no permanent damage may be done to his self. If many are to be called and few chosen, then it is more convenient for everyone concerned to call individuals who are not fully persons and cannot be destroyed by failing to be chosen. As the individual grows older, he becomes defined as someone who must not be engaged in a role for which he is unsuited. He becomes defined as something that must not fail, while at the same time arrangements are made to decrease the chances of his failing. Of course, when the mark reaches old age, he must remove himself or be removed from each of his roles, one by one, and participate in the problem of later maturity.

The strategies that are employed by operators to avoid the necessity of cooling the mark out have a counterpart in the strategies that are employed by the mark himself for the same purpose.

There is the strategy of hedging, by which a person makes sure that he is not completely committed. There is the strategy of secrecy, by which a person conceals from others and even from himself the facts of his commitment; there is also the practice of keeping two irons in the fire and the more delicate practice of maintaining a joking or unserious relationship to one's involvement. All of these strategies give the mark an out; in case of failure he can act as if the self that has failed is not one that is important to him. Here we must also consider the function of being quick to take offense and of taking hints quickly, for in these ways the mark can actively cooperate in the task of saving his face. There is also the strategy of playing it safe, as in cases where a calling is chosen because tenure is assured in it, or where a plain woman is married for much the same reason.

It has been suggested that preventive strategies are employed by operator and mark in order to reduce the chance of failing or to minimize the consequences of failure. The less importance one finds it necessary to give to the problem of cooling, the more importance one may have given to the application of preventive strategies.

I have considered some of the situations in our society in which the necessity for cooling the mark out is likely to arise. I have also considered the standard ways in which a mark can be cooled out, the lines of action he can pursue if he refuses to be cooled, and the ways in which the whole problem can be avoided. Attention can now be turned to some very general questions concerning the self in society.

First, an attempt must be made to draw together what has been implied about the structure of persons. From the point of view of this paper, a person is an individual who becomes involved in a value of some kind—a role, a status, a relationship, an ideology—and then makes a public claim that he is to be defined and treated as someone who possesses the value or property in question. The limits to his claims, and hence the limits to his self, are primarily determined by the objective facts of his social life and secondarily determined by the degree to which a sympathetic interpretation of these facts can bend them in his favor. Any event which demonstrates that someone has made a false claim, defining himself as something which he is not, tends to destroy him. If others realize that the person's conception of self has been contradicted and discredited, then the person tends to be destroyed in the eyes of others. If the person can keep the contradiction a secret, he may succeed in keeping everyone but himself from treating him as a failure.

Secondly, one must take note of what is implied by the fact that it is possible for a person to be cooled out. Difficult as this may be, persons regularly define themselves in terms of a set of attributes and then have to accept the fact that they do not possess them—and do this about-face with relatively little fuss or trouble for the operators. This implies that there is a norm in our society persuading persons to keep their chins up and make the best of it—a sort of social sanitation enjoining torn and tattered persons to keep themselves packaged up. More important still, the capacity of a person to sustain these profound embarrassments implies a certain looseness and lack of interpenetration in the organization of his several life-activities. A man may fail in his job, yet go on succeeding with his wife. His wife may ask him for a divorce, or refuse to grant him one, and yet he may push his way onto the same streetcar at the usual time on the way to the same job. He may know that he is shortly going to have to leave the status of the living, but still march with the other prisoners, or eat breakfast with his family at their usual time and from behind his usual paper. He may be conned of his life's savings on an eastbound train but return to his home town and succeed in acting as if nothing of interest had happened.

Lack of rigid integration of a person's social roles allows for compensation; he can seek comfort in one role for injuries incurred in others. There are always cases, of course, in which the mark cannot sustain the injury to his ego and cannot act like a "good scout." On these occasions the shattering experience in one area of social life may spread out to all the sectors of his activity. He may define away the barriers between his several social roles and become a source of difficulty in all of them. In such cases the play is the mark's entire social life, and the operators, really, are the society. In an increasing number of these cases, the mark is given psychological guidance by professionals of some kind. The psychotherapist is, in this sense, the society's cooler. His job is to pacify and reorient the disorganized person; his job is to send the patient back to an old world or a new one, and to send him back in a condition in which he can no longer cause trouble to others or can no longer make a fuss. In short, if one takes the society, and not the person as the unit, the psychotherapist has the basic task of cooling the mark out.

A third point of interest arises if one views all of social life from the perspective of this paper. It has been argued that a person must not openly or even privately commit himself to a conception of himself which the flow of events is likely to discredit. He must not put himself in a position of having to be cooled out. Conversely, however, he must make sure that none of the persons with whom he has dealings are of the sort who may prove unsuitable and need to be cooled out. He must make doubly sure that should it become necessary to cool his associates out, they will be the sort who allow themselves to be gotten rid of. The con man who wants the mark to go home quietly and absorb a loss, the restaurant hostess who wants a customer to eat quietly and go away without causing trouble, and, if this is not possible, quietly to take his patronage elsewhere—these are the persons and these are the relationships which set the tone of some of our social life. Underlying this tone there is the assumption that persons are institutionally related to each other in such a way that if a mark allows himself to be cooled out, then the cooler need have no further concern with him; but if the mark refuses to be cooled out, he can put institutional machinery into action against the cooler. Underlying this tone there is also the assumption that persons are sentimentally related to each other in such a way that if a person allows himself to be cooled out, however great the loss he has sustained, then the cooler withdraws all emotional identification from him; but if the mark cannot absorb the injury to his self and if he becomes personally disorganized in some way, then the cooler cannot help but feel guilt and concern over the predicament. It is this feeling of guilt—this small measure of involvement in the feelings of others—which helps to make the job of cooling the mark out distasteful, wherever it appears. It is this incapacity to be insensitive to the suffering of another person when he brings his suffering right to your door which tends to make the job of cooling a species of dirty work.

One must not, of course, make too much of the margin of sympathy connecting operator and mark. For one thing, the operator may rid himself of the mark by application or threat of pure force or open insult.[5] In Chicago in the 1920's small businessmen who suffered a loss in profits and in independence because of the "protection" services that racketeers gave to them were cooled out in this way. No doubt it is frivolous to suggest that Freud's notion of castration threat has something to do with the efforts of fathers to cool their sons out of oedipal involvements. Furthermore, there are many occasions when operators of different kinds must act as middlemen, with two marks on their hands; the calculated use of one mark as a sacrifice or fall guy may be the only way of cooling the other mark out. Finally, there are barbarous ceremonies in our society, such as criminal trials and the drumming-out ritual employed in court-martial procedures, that are expressly designed to prevent the mark from saving his face. And even in those cases where the cooler makes an effort to make things easier for the person he is getting rid of, we often find that there are bystanders who have no such scruples.[6] Onlookers who are close enough to observe the blowoff but who are not obliged to assist in the dirty work often enjoy the scene, taking pleasure in the discomfiture of the cooler and in the destruction of the mark. What is trouble for some is Schadenfreude for others.

This paper has dealt chiefly with adaptations to loss; with defenses, strategies, consolations, mitigations, compensations, and the like. The kinds of sugar-coating have been examined, and not the pill. I would like to close this paper by referring briefly to the sort of thing that would be studied if one were interested in loss as such, and not in adaptations to it.

A mark who requires cooling out is a person who can no longer sustain one of his social roles and is about to be removed from it; he is a person who is losing one of his social lives and is about to die one of the deaths that are possible for him. This leads one to consider the ways in which we can go or be sent to our death in each of our social capacities, the ways, in other words, of handling the passage from the role that we had to a state of having it no longer. One might consider the social processes of firing and laying-off; of resigning and being asked to resign; of farewell and departure; of deportation, excommunication, and going to jail; of defeat at games, contests, and wars; of being dropped from a circle of friends or an intimate social relationship; of corporate dissolution; of retirement in old age; and, lastly, of the deaths that heirs are interested in.

And, finally, attention must be directed to the things we become after we have died in one of the many social senses and capacities in which death can come to us. As one might expect, a process of sifting and sorting occurs by which the socially dead come to be effectively hidden from us. This movement of ex-persons throughout the social structure proceeds in more than one direction.

There is, first of all, the dramatic process by which persons who have died in important ways come gradually to be brought together into a common graveyard that is separated ecologically from the living community.[7] For the dead, this is at once a punishment and a defense. Jails and mental institutions are, perhaps, the most familiar examples, but other important ones exist. In America today, there is the interesting tendency to set aside certain regions and towns in California as asylums for those who have died in their capacity as workers and as parents but who are still alive financially.[8] For the old in America who have also died financially, there are old-folks homes and rooming-house areas. And, of course, large cities have their Skid Rows which are, as Park put it, ". . . full of junk, much of it human, i.e., men and women who, for some reason or other, have fallen out of line in the march of industrial progress and have been scrapped by the industrial organization of which they were once a part."[9] Hobo jungles, located near freight yards on the outskirts of towns, provide another case in point.

Just as a residential area may become a graveyard, so also certain institutions and occupational roles may take on a similar function. The ministry in Britain, for example, has sometimes served as a limbo for the occupational stillborn of better families, as have British universities. Mayhew, writing of London in the mid-nineteenth-century, provides another example: artisans of different kinds, who had failed to maintain a position in the practice of their trade, could be found working as dustmen.[10] In the United States, the jobs of waitress, cab driver, and night watchman, and the profession of prostitution, tend to be ending places where persons of certain kinds, starting from different places, can come to rest.

But perhaps the most important movement of those who fail is one we never see. Where roles are ranked and somewhat related, persons who have been rejected from the one above may be difficult to distinguish from persons who have risen from the one below. For example, in America, upper-class women who fail to make a marriage in their own circle may follow the recognized route of marrying an upper-middle class professional. Successful lower-middle class women may arrive at the same station in life, coming from the other direction. Similarly, among those who mingle with one another as colleagues in the profession of dentistry, it is possible to find some who have failed to become physicians and others who have succeeded at not becoming pharmacists or optometrists. No doubt there are few positions in life that do not throw together some persons who are there by virtue of failure and other persons who are there by virtue of success. In this sense, the dead are sorted but not segregated, and continue to walk among the living.

NOTES

1. Mr. Hughes has lectured on this kind of disappointment, and one of his students has undertaken a special study of it. See Miriam Wagenschein, " 'Reality Shock': A Study of Beginning School Teachers," M.A. thesis, Dept. of Sociology, Univ. of Chicago, 1950.

2. See, for example, Max Weber, *The Religion of China* (H. H. Gerth, tr.); Glencoe, Ill., Free Press, 1951; p. 178.

3. This role of the doctor has been stressed by W. L. Warner in his lectures at the University of Chicago on symbolic roles in "Yankee City."

4. In his seminars, Mr. Hughes has used the term "second-choice" professions to refer to cases of this kind.

5. Suggested by Saul Mendlovitz in conversation.

6. Suggested by Howard S. Becker in conversation.

7. Suggested by lectures of and a personal conversation with Mr. Hughes.

8. Some early writers on caste report a like situation in India at the turn of the nineteenth century. Hindus who were taken to the Ganges to die, and who then recovered, were apparently denied all legal rights and all social relations with the living. Apparently these excluded persons found it necessary to congregate in a few villages of their own. In California, of course, settlements of the old have a voluntary character, and members maintain ceremonial contact with younger kin by the exchange of periodic visits and letters.

9. R. E. Park, *Human Communities;* Glencoe, Ill.; Free Press, 1952; p. 60.

10. Henry Mayhew, *London Labour and the London Poor;* London, Griffin, Bohn, 1861; Vol. II, pp. 177-178.

The effective integration of the individual into the group is a problem to be faced at all levels. Semantic and other problems separate social scientists from one another as well as from laymen. This article indicates the reasons for the tensions existing among the various social sciences. In essence, the author is saying that the social scientist's heightened awareness of the motivations, consequences, and complexity of human behavior will only serve to plunge him deeper into the "ambiguities and agonies of life." Nevertheless, the author affirms the positive worth and compatibility of humility, involvement, and objectivity as necessary components of the social scientist's temperament.

III

Social Psychology, Self, and Society*

JOHN R. SEELEY

Stresses, Strains, and Distresses

SOCIAL PSYCHOLOGISTS FIND IT HARD ENOUGH to talk to one another. The languages they use range from something that looks and sounds like the writing and talk around the launching of the Venus-bound spacecraft to something that looks and sounds like what must have been the spectator-talk after the first presentation of a play by Sophocles or a Shakespearean drama. How then can a social psychologist speak to people? I do not even faintly exaggerate. On one wing, we would find a discussion in almost pure mathematical terms; on the other wing, material that taxes human range, empathy, and dramatic insight—capacity for appreciation, if you will. In the middle we would be subject to strains comparable to those called for in mastering Newtonian physics or elementary chemistry or any semistrange way of talking about semifamiliar material.

If these strains attend communication within the profession,

* Reprinted from *Journal of Applied Behavioral Science*, Vol. 1, No. 4: 311-326 (December 1965), by permission of the author and publisher.

what must be the strains of attempting to communicate with an audience outside the (divided) "mystery"? Not only *how* should one tell, but *what* should one tell?

The easiest thing perhaps would be to follow the pleasure principle: to tell the audience what it would like to hear so that it might be gratified; for if gratified, it will applaud the speaker so that he in turn will be pleased. This course is very tempting, more particularly since what audiences in general like to hear is something that assures them that something useful (to them) is being produced. By "something useful," they usually mean in reference to the social sciences something that will alleviate their miseries or increase their psychic or material incomes.

I think I could (in a technical sense) follow this course. It would be possible to point to the multiplication and proliferation of social psychologists, social psychological books, journals, articles, or associations which follows rather exactly the rate at which fruit flies multiply in a bottle: in technical jargon, what looks at first like an exponential curve, becoming rapidly visible as a logistic one. If this multiplication were not, by itself, reassuring, I think I could point to the educative effect of all this by demonstrating (by word count or "content analysis") the growing use in novels, in talk about practical affairs, such as education or race relations, of social psychological terms or views. I think I could convince you that social psychology is finding increasing use and should hence be regarded as increasingly useful. If you are too sophisticated for that, I could introduce you to some desirable uses of the stuff: I guess prisons are less patently brutal in some places; mental hospitals, less obviously inhuman; schools, less directly child-destroying; family life, less pervasively or nakedly mutually exploitative—and so on. Whether or not social psychology is the cause of these things, it does figure largely in their explanation and justification, and hence enters into their support. (Affluence and safety can also be great engenderers of debrutalization, perhaps not by themselves, but obliquely in terms of the other things they permit.)

I should be happy to do all this, except that if I allow the argument one way I have to allow it the other: the very things of which we are wont to complain most in American society find, no more and no less, their justification—if not their cause—in social psychology. The Madison Avenue conference—the aim of which is to part you from your money by making you feel that

X's soap or Y's automobile is indispensable to your femininity or masculinity—is founded in the selfsame social psychology. The aim is piratical, but out of Freud via Dale Carnegie. The method is out of Freud (on group psychology) and Cooley (primary or face-to-face groups) via R. Lippitt and Lewin and the Human Relations Training Laboratory of Bethel, Maine.

It may appear that I have said only that while social psychology shows great growth and grasp, it is, like any other science, "ethically neutral" and has hence been productive so far of great good as well as high harm. What men do with a science, say chemistry—whether, for instance they make cheap, sure equivalents for mother's milk or whether they devise nerve gas or truth serum—is something that it does not fall within the province of that science to explain (let alone affect or control). This habitual stand, relevant for chemistry, is commonly uncritically carried over to social psychology. But surely it will not hold. If men put the first deliverance of social psychology to use to destroy (or support) one another, then surely this is social behavior, and surely it is thus within the realm of social psychology and incumbent upon social psychology at least to *explain* this use in its second deliverance. Failure to take this view is itself a curious piece of social behavior and must itself come in, I should presume, for a social psychological explanation.

What I want to do here is to exhibit, as far as I can, some of the difficulties and distresses within the house of social science rather than demonstrate the achievements already won and the promises (prematurely, I think) held out. I prefer to pursue this thornier path not simply because I believe that a public is entitled to a proper reply to a well-posed question but also because I think the only sure defense against the public danger posed by a pseudoscience of human affairs is a superior understanding on the part of the public as to what is at issue.

I am thus driven to write of remote and abstract and perhaps difficult matters instead of near and concrete and easy and reassuring things. I am driven to speak, at least briefly, of the philosophy, politics, psychology, and sociology of social psychology. Not everything is so safe and settled in the social psychological house that the experts are united and must know what they are doing. As a matter of fact, I think the opposite holds: roughly, where they are united they do not know what they are doing, and where they know what they are doing they are disunited.

What "Is" Social Psychology?

The first problem is doubtless to agree on what social psychology "is." In the *Handbook of Social Psychology,* Professor Allport of Harvard, who is about as wise a man in these matters as anyone, takes about seven hundred and fifty words to tell us he has not a clue. First he says it has no sharp boundaries; then, that in many respects it is indistinguishable from general psychology. Then he speaks of its "apparent" (sic!) "lack of autonomy," finally giving it a "focus of interest" in "the social nature of the individual person." He then makes a bolder stab by saying that most social psychologists regard their discipline as "an attempt to understand and explain how the thought, feeling, and behavior of individuals are influenced by the actual, imagined, or implied presence of other human beings."

I do not know how most social psychologists view their craft, but there are some very tender points in the Allport definition. First, even before we begin, we are committed to *assuming* an "individual human being" in the actual or virtual presence of other "individual human beings," and simply asked to explain the influence of this presence on the thought, feeling, and behavior of one of them. But what influences the one is not the presence of the others but rather their thought, feeling, and behavior—which is the very thing to be explained. Moreover, their thought, feeling, and behavior is influenced by his, so that it is not a datum, not an independent variable, not something that can be used *either* to understand or explain.

Let us say that a social psychology is an attempt to account for behavior insofar as it is social (which is what makes it social) in terms of meanings (which is what makes it psychological). What is excluded is a very narrow range of happenings: if a stone "accidentally" (that is, in a meaningless way) falls upon my kneecap producing a reflex jerk directed toward no one, we are outside the realm of social psychology. When the "same" effect is produced by a doctor to whom I am a patient, part of the behavior (the naked reflex jerk) is outside, but a much greater part of the behavior—my unspoken comments, how I represent my feelings to self or others, indeed what I apprehend to have happened—is social psychological matter.

But the very words qualifying the behavior—"insofar as it is social"—is a far cry from Mr. Allport's relation of the individual to other, actual, imagined, or present individuals. It seems so close to common sense to postulate such individuals that it is very hard to shake the sense of it from scientific discourse, let alone everyday account. But shake it I must. The individual he speaks of is not only social in his origin—so that we would have to inquire into his origin before we so blithely take him as a datum—but he is social in his present nature. By "social in his present nature," I mean two quite different things, both of which leave little of Mr. Allport's individual as a datum. I mean, first, that psychologically he lives in society as, organically, he may be said to live in action. His relation to society is not to be viewed as similar to that of an island in a sea or an island in an archipelago. I mean "in" in the same sense as Jesus' observation of God: "I live in my Father and He in me." If we say analogically, with Dewey, that community exists in communication, we do not mean that the two can be abstracted from and viewed as mutually influencing each other, but that they are one and the same thing in different manifestations. Indeed, they constitute each other, without separability or residue. When we say men live in society, *that* is what we mean. The wave is not to be related to a perturbation in the medium: it is not only a perturbation of the medium, it is the medium perturbed.

The second sense in which man is social is not in relation to that "them" in whom (psychologically) he lives and moves and has his being, but in relation to that which he sets naïvely over against that them, whatever he refers to as "I." For to this object, if such it be, he sustains a *social* relationship. He talks to himself, in thought, and he may even talk to himself about himself talking to himself. He also feels about and responds to himself, and he may have feelings about his feelings for himself, which in circular fashion affect the primary set of feelings. But a system that works like that is what we *mean*, when we are at all clear, by a "society"—so that the self not only lives in a society of others but *is* a society of selves. Moreover, what he will regard as self and what he will regard as other will fluctuate from stage to stage of "his" development and from moment to moment at any stage. The "genuine voice of self" at this instant was once taken for the alien voice of other, and may yet later be felt to be ego-alien (even though coming from within); and *per contra,* the voices the others use may speak in the very tones of self at an earlier day. The self that approves and rejects the innumerable other selves of the self-same self is but one self in the company of selves, giving and withholding friendship and recognition just as, on Mr. Allport's model, the "individuals" are figured as doing between them—except that, unlike him, we recognize that they do not exist apart from the company they keep.

Something in Western thoughtways makes this line of thought extremely difficult, and it may be that the very sickness of Western society—exaggerated pride and shame, self-esteem and guilt, ulcer-pregnant sense of responsibility—stems from it. Somehow, in Western thought, as in that of a small child, society is set outside and over against the self, with some ridiculous and indefensible boundary drawn at the anatomical (and hence irrelevant) skin. It is intolerable that science should reinforce such views. Anyone who has lost a loved one—a supposed other—should know better.

It is not merely as Donne has it "that no man is an island unto himself"; the very way of thought, and with it what makes Donne's reminder necessary, is a first-order misconception that permits little thereafter to be rightly conceived. Does anyone doubt that at this moment he is in life, and life is in him; that he is simply not he intelligibly apart from life; that the terms cannot be counterposed or used to explain each other; that life does not exist apart from him and his like? Self and society are similar terms. I am in the society that is in me—as I am and can only be in that grace (small though it be) that is in me—and the very conception of a counterposition of the two shows, to my mind, so poor a socialization as to make its proponent a good spokesman neither for himself nor his society. The magnitude of the self—if one can speak of such things—is measured by the society it incorporates; the magnitude of the society—if one can speak of such things—is measured by the selves that it unites. "The society" is the name for the "unity"; but "the selves" are that in which the unity is seen as multiple. There are as many societies as there are selves, and as many selves as there are societies. It is as idle to ask which is prior or preponderant or which influences the other and how, as to ask the same questions of the life and the living, the breathing and the breath.

It may seem that I am making too much of a single point. After all, it may be said, what we do in such cases is to take the rival conceptual schemes—say, wave theory and particle theory in all-but-recent physics—draw deductions from them, test the deductions, and qualify the one and disqualify the other. I fear that in most cases, or most cases that matter, we cannot so test theories about human beings. (Such a view of the relation of theory to actuality in reference to human beings does not test but begs any question as to the soundness of the views I have just set forth.)

If we exist in one another, then it cannot be other than the case that we are affected in what we are by what others think of us—their hypotheses or theories regarding us. Thus the hypothesis to be tested affects the data that are to make the test. We are not, in my vocabulary, merely "affected" or "influenced"; we are altered as a region in a field of forces by a change in a line of force passing through it. It is not, again, that either *causes* the change in the other but that the single event may be referred, indifferently, to the line or the region.

Again, a theory about human beings if widely held tends to bring about its own confirmation. (The only value that money has, for instance, lies in our belief that others believe it to be valuable.) So a theory that picks up from the widespread Western intellectual belief in a postulated (and thereby instituted) individual as over-against society is not testable against a contrary theory. If a theory starts out from a naïve preconception in physics, the data repudiate the theory if the theory is wrong. If a theory starts out from a naïve preconception in social psychology, not only do the initial data tend to confirm it (since men are largely what they think themselves to be) but the preliminary confirmation, once published, tends to reinforce the inadequate self-conception and society-conception, and hence on subsequent tests to lend ever greater plausibility to error.

How can I maintain, it may be asked, at one and the same time that men *are* largely (or worse, wholly) what they think themselves to be—and that, nevertheless, they are in error and are really something quite other? The difficulty sounds more formidable than it is. Imagine yourself coaching a child to pitch a baseball. He makes several wild throws, is discouraged, and says *in virtue of his discouragement,* "I can't pitch!" A true report of the state of affairs. One coach may say (on hypothesis): "No, you can't," and, depending on his relation to the child, make him angry enough so that all of a sudden he can; or discouraged enough so he "really" cannot. Another may say (on hypothesis): "Sure you can, Jimmy," and in a sudden access of strength as the counterpart of faith, Jimmy may really be able to. So the hypothesis *constitutes* the new fact (not merely "causes" it), and it *is* simultaneously true that (a) Jimmy cannot really pitch, except (b) on the hypothesis that he can.

Now not just anything the coach said, no matter how close his relation to the boy, would be realized. What he can assert must not only be within the realm of the possible but must reflect accurately *and* call out a latent fact about the boy, a fact that only requires accreditation to make it manifest. The company of the coach, insofar as the boy lives in it, effects a reorganization of (more strictly, reconstitutes) the company of selves in the boy, shifting executive possibility from one to another.

The central fact that emerges is that the test of fit of a hypothesis is, in social psychology, not so much the selection of a scientific guide to study as the actual embarkation on a program of action. It is not, as in physics, so much a question of hard fact to which the hypothesis conforms, ill or well, according to well-known intellectual tests. In social psychology, the data (people, society) fit themselves, ill or well, to the hypothesis; and the tests of "goodness of fit" are not merely scientific but ethical and aesthetic as well. It is not only how closely do hypothesis and data conform to each other, for in time no doubt they may conform quite well to each other. (Parents who believe ill enough of their children long enough may finally come to have children it were well to think ill of.) The question is whether the data are *constrained* on the hypothesis; and this judgment requires canons of goodness and beauty that are not to be derived from what is manifest in man, since *ex hypothesi* it deals with what is latent, what the hypothesis may call into actualization.

On this view, a social psychological theory is in appearance an opinion on the facts but in reality a *fiat,* good or bad. No less than a statement of the rights of man, it is a proclamation: an attempt to institute what ought to be in the form of a statement as to what is. If on either ground (moral appeal or assumed factuality) it is taken to be acceptable, what it "says" comes to be true by the "data's" conforming themselves to what was hypothesized about them.

I will not go on, for it is clear that the social psychology which hoped to bring good into the world by first divorcing itself from ethics and becoming "scientific" merely succeeds in being ethically blind. That it paints for us pictures of the world and that these pictures negate and deny one another is not to be wondered at. Shall we live in the world of radical pessimism of Sigmund Freud, as in *Civilization and Its Discontents* (where the sacrifice of pleasure which is all that we *can* value is the price to be paid for civilization and culture and all that we *should* value)? Shall we live in the halfway house of Anna Freud, the revisionists, the new ego-psychologists, where a sort of precarious light of human hope filters onto and throws into bolder relief such ego-functions as we would like to identify with? May we inhabit with impunity the nearly light-filled house of a Maslow or a Fromm? As the record shows, what we dwell on we shall dwell in. Where should we like to dwell?

Or do we have a choice? If a social psychology is a science that deals exhaustively with the cause-and-effect relations in the mental or meaningful life of persons seen now severally and now as a system, then surely it must account in cause-and-effect terms for beliefs. And the beliefs to be accounted for are not just political or religious or magical beliefs, nor are they the beliefs of distant and alien others in far times and distant places. The beliefs to be accounted for include our social psychological beliefs.

Account To Be Rendered

So the social psychology must surely account for itself, explaining its own deliverances in much the same terms in which it explains its first-order subject matter. For whatever the social psychologist says or does is also a product of a society, a social system, a role playing, an attempt to maintain or alter specific personal and social balances or patterns. The ground upon which the social psychologist is to stand—presumably uninfluenced or little influenced by the actual, imagined, or implied presence of other human beings while he explains how all this works—has never been defined. I venture to suggest that, on his own hypothesis, it cannot be defined.

If it were otherwise, I am not sure that, given the social scientist's heaven, we should want to enter in. If the result were one kind of science, like astronomy, I suppose we should merely be enabled to stand by, watching with awe or horror while those stellar bodies, ourselves, rushed toward spectacular cataclysm or brilliant boreal display. If the result were the other kind of science, say, like chemistry, where control of the conceptual scheme leads to mastery of the material, the consequences would seem to be even more catastrophic. For if the knowledge leads to genuine control of the process, the question of who is to have this knowledge becomes crucial. If it is to be some select social group, then some problems of enslavement for the others arise, even if the knowledge is used for their good. On the other hand, if the knowledge is everyman's possession, are the consequences much less disastrous? For what is this within you that is to have the mastery over that that? Are master and slave relations in the psyche or among the selves any better than in the external world? (Incidentally, I believe that when we do welcome the one it is because we also would welcome the other.)

There is a still more curious consequence to be anticipated before we start to dream of self-mastery. What is mastered is generally doubly dead. It is dead to itself, but also it is dead to its master. It is without interest. The mastered *is* the lifeless. Even a slave, a prisoner, a victim, a dog is of interest only insofar as it is not mastered.

So the counterpoint to mastery is apathy—in master and mastered. On the astronomical model, we *might* retain a spark of lively interest as we observed ourselves bombinating through historic space. On the model of chemistry, we should, I presume, have much to care for and nothing to care about. Which is perilously close to where we are.

Social Psychologist and Society Psychologized

When, as social psychologists, we come upon men as a subject of interest we are already men ourselves. They and we are members of groups; neither we nor they have ever encountered an individual. We and they are in the life that is going on, the common life, the society, and it is in them and us, and we in one another. The life is ongoing, bearing us with it, as it is itself also nothing but the movement in us. In *medias res,* in the middle of the battle, someone bethinks himself (or is bethought) a little. What he thinks is given by the turmoil and is a part of the turmoil, as the bubble is in the river and part of the river. It is, as it were, an eddy, damping out the effect of a motion here, contributing to another there. One of these eddies is social psychology.

If I have firmly located social psychology in the social process itself—*in* history, *in* the culture, *in* the politics—it remains to say what differentiates it from the undifferentiated social swirl.

What differentiates it as a special sort of social activity is the company, the society in which it occurs. It—or rather the social psychologist—is deeply implicated in the society of his day. But he is also intimately implicated with other social psychologists. And, beyond this, he is implicated with an unseen company. An analogy with the religious person comes to mind: he too participates in the world, with his likes in the militant and present church, and with them in the church triumphant, both the saints departed and that effectively present future that assumes the full flowering of what is now but seed and soil.

The difference between the social psychologist and the religious person is that the former looks forward to no day of judgment, no apocalyptic transformation of the states of affairs. He looks not to solutions, let alone total solutions, but resolutions, *ad hoc*, and for now. His problems are not analogical to the discovery of how to split atoms but to the discovery of how to further justice. Concretely, justice is furthered *in a given case*. The problem arises afresh in the next and every new case. Methods may carry over from case to case, but even this cannot be counted upon. The doing of justice alters the capacity to do justice and therewith even the method.

It is in such an enterprise that the social psychologist is located. Even when he does not teach, even when he thinks himself most a scientist, he is first and last an educator: a person whose profession and pride is the enlargement of other persons —and therewith himself. The means of enlargement are quite literally those of revelation. Revelation and exposé are not synonyms but polar opposites. Revelation occurs in a relationship and has a matter or subject. The relationship is necessarily social, but more than that, ideally social—that is, loving or caring. The subject, for social psychology, is just such relations. On this view, the social psychologist, if he is an expert about society in psychological perspective, is a *society-maker:* he brings into being a society more dedicated to seeing itself now detachedly (for the sake of its commitment), now committedly (for the sake of its detachment). To put it another way: the task—and in any case the effect—of the social psychologist is not to bring into being a body of knowledge that stands apart and describes the society in some static fashion. He enters into history for the sake of making it. He does not just social psychologize. He social psychologizes *something:* the society. For better or for worse he inevitably renders it other. As he engages thus with the society out of which he has (momentarily and in part) differentiated himself, he is altered and made over by the consequences of his own acts. And this in turn means a new social psychologist facing a new society and a new social psychology.

The same dangers, as well as the same potentialities of benefit, attend social psychologizing as attend the private psychologizing we call psychotherapy. The major difference is that the social psychologist can rarely observe and almost never so quickly correct for the effect he has on his patient. Otherwise, point for point, social psychologists and psychotherapists may not aimlessly heighten awareness. Each must select what is cogent from among a potential infinity of "true" statements respecting the "patient" or subject and place these in a selection from among another infinity of contexts or under one of an indefinitely large number of constructions. What is cogent is given not only by the state to be described but by the general character of the state which is sought. The context in which material is to be seen or the construction that is to be put upon it is governed likewise by these aims. But the aims are not given. They emerge with clarity only at each reconstructive step to shape the next step.

This is not to say in the one case, any more than the other, that what is to be done is determined by the situation: such a critique would once again make a machine of the actual society. But it is obvious that the psychotherapist appeals from what is patent in his patient to what is latent; he intervenes, and his intervention involves discrimination. From among latent potentialities, he *selects;* and he selects in terms of an implicit agreement which he and the patient share, the unspoken social contract that constitutes the two a society. What he develops in the patient, when he is successful, is an added ability to complete some commitment which both accept. The completion of this commitment is the full development of the two-man society. Initially, the physician sees so much more clearly than his patient what is at stake that in a sense he leads and seems almost to control the process. Gradually this control comes into the possession of the patient. Processes the physician fathered can go on in the patient in his virtual presence without its actuality. They two are an enduring society—like the Christian forever in the company of the saints. Psychotherapy is at an end.

For all points save this last, the relation of social psychologist to society is an analogue (without the sick overtones here of Larry Frank's "Society as the Patient"). In the interaction between social psychologist and society psychologized, there is a heightening interchange without necessary terminus or canonical end. What is to come out of the interchange is the development of the society in the direction of its immanent but latent *best*. (Mere development of the society as a criterion would have led the social psychologist of that day to further Nazism had he lived in Germany, and us to sanction his actions whether we lived there or not.) The notion of the best as central implies that we know either what is best, or what is better, *and* that successive moves toward the better do cumulate in a movement toward the best. The first is, I think, improbable. I do not know whether the second is true or not. But I believe so. And I believe the belief has the quality of many such beliefs: a tendency to bring its warrantability into being as a consequence of belief itself.

The position is full of risk. Even taking it for granted that the social psychologist has steeped himself in his culture without losing himself in it, that it is a culture which does not of its very nature blind him to its own potentialities or blunt his creativity or intuition, the margin for error is immense. But the alternatives are worse. The alternatives are (a) no social psychology, which is not now possible, or (b) a random process that merely heightens oscillation to the point of upset, or (c) a social psychology of inbuilt bias that develops the existent society to its logical conclusion, which is to say its devitalization and death.

I think we have thus no choice but to go forward in fearful boldness.

Whence We Came

My position is really very simple. It is, I think, the direct implication of the central message of the great names in social psychology. From W. I. Thomas' recognition of the centrality in social action of "the definition of the situation," I derive my view of the social psychologist: the redefiner *par excellence*, hence the supreme social *actor*. From George Herbert Mead's insistence on Mind, Self, and Society as co-emergents, I derive my view that the social psychology is and can be only a co-emergent with a new personal and social self—that is, with the continuous making over of self and society. From Freud, the man who most clearly in "thinking" about men made himself (and them) over, I derive my view as to the unity, the mutual and reciprocal co-constitution, of personal and social psychology. (If I am in error, do not blame them; what I say I "derive," I might have said I imposed as construction, but then it is just that kind of act that social psychologizing is.)

A social psychology thus founded has not even, I believe, been well begun. The view, like the mystical experience, makes all things new. It brings the social psychologist and the social psychology within society. It makes of social science a value problem. It makes teaching, preaching of a quite peculiar kind. It entails the taking of a value-position, not merely in the dedication to truth or science or what-not, but in each particular scientific act: a thoroughgoing political position. It implies more of the stance of the warrior and less of the attitude of the entomologist than we wish to admit. It recommits us to the battle from which, in the belief of many, science was to provide the escape. It returns us to the ambiguities and agonies of life. It robs us of a precious—because psychopathic—defense. It makes us men among men and not demigods above them. It returns us to humility. It restores mutuality: social psychologist and social psychologized dwell in each other and have no existence *as such*, apart from their so doing.

I think such views are implicit in the warmest, gentlest, clearest of them all, Charles Horton Cooley. We have a long way to go back, I think, before we can again move forward. To that retreat for the sake of such sound advance as is possible, I invite alike my colleagues and theirs—the society of which they would like merely to speak, but which they must choose whether to hinder or help. The nirvana, the neutral ground, does not exist. Once more what is brought from the heights is not peace but a sword. Once more we hear ". . . he that is not with us is against us, and he that gathereth not with us, scattereth abroad."

*This article contains revealing comments concern-
ing the existence, or non-existence, of "alienation"
among skid road (or skid row) derelicts. Of significant interest in this regard is the authors' cogent
application of the concept known as "sub-culture."*

IV

The Skid Road "Wino"*

W. JACK PETERSON and
MILTON A. MAXWELL

SKID ROAD[1] IS A DESCRIPTIVE TERM which elicits a stereotyped picture of homeless men with no ambitions and no hopes; of drunks
content to live in the filth of the flop house, bumming meals and
drinks along the water fronts and railroad tracks of our American
cities. This stereotype is constantly reinforced by observations
of men slumped in doorways, staggering along sidewalks, and
sleeping in parks and railroad stations. The impression is furthered by popular articles in our newspapers and magazines.

The stereotype has had two significant misleading effects. On
the one hand, it has been accepted by many persons as descriptive of alcoholics in general. But the vast majority of alcoholics
are not found on Skid Road (perhaps 90-95 per cent are not) and
most of these, as recent studies have demonstrated (6, 8), do
not even show a significant degree of marital and occupational
disorganization. Thus, when alcoholics are seen through the
Skid Road stereotype, the important identifying symptoms of
the vast majority of alcoholics remain unrecognized.

The popular Skid Road stereotype has had the effect, on the
other hand, of obscuring important facts about Skid Road life.
Chief among the realities obscured are (a) the differences to
be found among the men on Skid Road, and (b) the degree to
which Skid Road life is group-centered and dominated by group

* Reprinted from *Social Problems*, Vol. 5, No. 4: 308-316 (1958).

norms. The latter will be the focus of this paper. But, first, the differences deserve mention.

There are, for example, such different types as the pensioner, the steady worker, the seasonal worker, the character, the tramp, the wino, the bum, chiseler or lone wolf, the dehorn or rubbydub, the petty thief and small-time racketeer. Men of these types belong to categories and groups which are neither mutually exclusive nor clearly differentiated.

Recently, attention has been focused on the alcoholic problem of Skid Road men. But, here also, important differences are found. While excessive drinking is characteristic of the vast majority of men on Skid Road, not all excessive drinkers can be classified as uncontrolled, addictive drinkers. Straus and McCarthy (7) found in a study of 444 Bowery men that only 43 per cent could be called addictive drinkers. The heavy but "controlled" drinkers constituted over one-fourth (28 per cent) of the total sample. Furthermore, they classified 17 per cent of the men as "moderate" drinkers, and found that 11 per cent were nondrinkers (although some of the last had been heavy drinkers at one time).

Not only has the Skid Road stereotype been found wanting, but there has also been a growing realization of the expense[2] and the futility of the usual modes of handling and attempting to rehabilitate these men. This, in turn, has led to studies of homeless men with sociologists taking a leading role.

A major contribution was made by Straus in his concept of "undersocialization" which he believed applicable to "nearly all homeless men." (5)

> Undersocialization can be considered a syndrome which includes a wide variety of atypical conditions and relationships with normal society. . . . Deficiently socialized persons are usually deprived of the opportunity of sharing experiences with others, of belonging to social groups and participating in social activities. They are deprived, also, of certain important satisfactions, such as affection, prestige, the feeling of security, the rewarding aspects of identifying with others and the like. The satisfaction of these personal needs usually comes only through association with other people. . . . Such associations are normally found in the parental home, in the marital family, in schools,

in employment situations, in church participation and in community life. These are the very institutional situations in which the experiences of homeless men are incomplete and unsatisfying and which are, therefore, the criteria of his undersocialization. . . . (5, p. 363)

But no matter what his early experiences, by the time a man is separated from the normal community by his "homelessness," he ". . . is not reached by the normal everyday sanctions of society, positive and negative, which tend to hold men in line and prescribe limits for certain types of behavior, and to determine other types of behavior which must be performed." (5, p. 364)

From the viewpoint of participating in the larger society, Straus's analysis seems irrefutable. Undersocialization can account in the majority of cases for the affinity to, or the drift to, Skid Road where the expectations and demands are minimal, where there is freedom from the pressures of the normal world, and where the anxiety which normal society arouses in the undersocialized is no longer experienced.

But no matter how cut off from the main stream of society, it does not follow that the persons on Skid Road lack a community of their own. This was the important contribution of Jackson and Connor (2) who found life on Skid Road to be group-oriented, with a describable culture to be learned, folkways and mores to be lived by, and a web of expectations and obligations which provide economic and emotional support to the members of these groups.

Jackson and Connor identified six social segments into which Skid Road excessive drinkers fall: "older alcoholics," "bums," "characters," "winos," "rubby-dubs," and "lushes." Their paper, however, concentrated on what they chose to call the "lush" segment, though the term is not so applied by Skid Roaders themselves. They describe this segment as being the "prestige group" of alcoholics, ". . . tending to be composed of temporary residents of Skid Road." (2, p. 470) They describe the group life and the culture of this segment and the learning process by which men become accommodated to, and assimilated into, this subculture. They point out the mutual aid, companionship, and psychological support which this subsociety and small group membership provide. But they also make it clear that, "To reap the benefits of membership in such a group, the alcoholic must adhere to group standards and accept obligations imposed upon him. Violation of group standards means not only rejection from a particular group but also isolation from the lush segment as a whole." (2, p. 471)

Jackson and Connor have satisfactorily demonstrated that this upper segment of Skid Road alcoholics is not composed of isolates but is a subsociety with a culture of its own.

The present study set out to discover whether or not the "wino" segment has similar social characteristics. Even though "wino" is a term of contempt, and even though "winos" are rejected by the non-wino prestige segment, does it follow that the despised "winos" are rejected isolates? Or do they also form groups of their own in which they live as social beings, responsive to group norms which are standard for the entire wino segment?

The study was conducted in Spokane and Seattle, Washington, in the spring of 1955. Beginning with a few exwinos in Alcoholics Anonymous in Spokane, the study expanded to include men in the Spokane City Jail and the Seattle Police Farm. The informants included 19 men who were known on the Skid Roads of the two cities as "winos," and another 14 persons who had been closely associated with winos and were familiar with their behavior patterns. All were used as informants.[3]

Wine Drinking

It became clear very quickly that winos do have a group life and a culture which prescribes their behavior. But before analyzing that culture, a descriptive definition of the wino and a consideration of his wine drinking are in order.

Winos are identified not only because they habitually drink wine, with a consequent unpleasant, characteristic odor, but also by a generally rundown appearance (even by Skid Road standards) both in dress and physical condition. In this dual observation there is the suggestion that wine drinking is both cause and consequence of the total situation in which they find themselves.

First, it should be noted that even though the wino primarily drinks wine, he would not do so if he had his choice. Only 4 of the 19 winos interviewed expressed an actual preference for wine. Why, then, do the men drink wine? This choice is clearly a function of their economic situation. The wino drinks wine because his situation has made it important for him to buy the cheapest form of beverage alcohol which he can buy. Many winos in the State of Washington buy apple wine (known as "apple," "apple jack," or "Wenatchee bourbon") containing 20 to 22 per cent alcohol. In 1955, it could be purchased for 55 cents a pint in almost any tavern. The cheapest 80 proof whiskey, on the other hand, sold for $2.36 a pint. In other words, in wine an ounce of absolute alcohol cost only 17 cents as compared to 37 cents an ounce in whiskey. The differential is even greater in some cities at the present time, with cheap wine retailing at 50 cents a pint and Puerto Rican wine at 35 cents in certain Eastern cities.

Wine is not only the cheapest alcoholic beverage, but it was believed by the wino informants to have the additional advantage of providing longer lasting effects. "Whiskey hits you faster and knocks you out." "It is possible to maintain a level of drunkenness with wine." These answers exemplify what Newman and Abramson (3) call the high "buffer" capacity of wines. Because the wine is absorbed more slowly, the blood-alcohol curve of the wine drinker does not reach the high peak it would if he were drinking other types of liquor; and once a peak is reached, the concentration does not decrease as rapidly. The winos felt that this effect of wine was important in determining the pattern of their drinking. As one of them put it:

> A lot of times after a hard night I would get up in the morning not feeling very good. I knew I needed a drink. . . . I'd look around for one of my old buddies. I'd usually find someone I knew down on the street and two or three of us would go in on a pint of apple. After taking a couple of good jolts we could nibble on it all morning until there were more people in the streets and we could bum money for another bottle. It wouldn't make us feel high or anything, but I wouldn't feel as sick as I had when I got up.

Wine was also believed to have a more deadening effect. Common were such expressions as "it makes you rum dum," "dense," "dopey," "stupid." Others said it "numbs you" or "puts you in a stupor."

It was also believed that wine hangovers last longer and make the person more ill, but that when ill, wine is the easiest on the stomach—easiest to keep down.

It was also believed that wine, more than other alcoholic beverages, kills the appetite. An interesting reciprocal belief was that the appetite could be restored by a "pink lady," a drink made from canned heat. In fact, this was the procedure recommended by wino folklore for a wino who had been on a bout for some time, who had no appetite but knew that he should eat some food.

It was also generally believed that "wine sores," open sores beginning on the legs and gradually extending up the body, are also a consequence of wine drinking. These may be a dual consequence of the avitaminosis attendant upon any extended drinking and the general uncleanliness to which the wino is reduced. But wino folklore blames it on the wine.

The Wino Way of Life

In his life on Skid Road, the wino has many associations with small groups of men. These associations, generally of three or four men, tend to be very informal and frequently of short duration since their primary function is the procurement and consumption of wine. While an individual may have close friends in the same group as he, and even though some groups persist over a period of time, permanence is not a prevailing characteristic of these groups. The size and duration of a small group is often governed by the price of a bottle, the time it takes to raise this amount of money, and the time spent drinking it. But no matter how transitory the specific groups may be, almost all wine drinking is done in such groups, and groups tend to be formed within a range of acquaintances. Furthermore, the sense of obligation toward all wino companions with whom a man has associated is great.

This brings up the most imperative of the mores in wino culture: the obligation to share. The wino will share his money and his wine with another wino and unquestioningly expects the same treatment in return. Reciprocity is a must. It is the "Dick Smith" or "chiseler" who will accept a drink and not give one, or who, when he has a bottle of his own, will go off and drink by himself. Such a person is shunned by winos and such behavior is severely condemned, for sharing is a matter of survival. As one of the wino informants pointed out:

For a wino to survive as a wino he needs someone to get him something to drink when he is sick and broke. Where it would be difficult for an individual to keep enough money for liquor coming in, two or three men bumming together can usually manage to keep enough money coming in for wine.

Winos have two main sources of money: work and bumming. By the time a person becomes a wino, his earning capacity is generally not very great. It tends to be confined to short term and "spot" jobs, and work is undertaken with only one purpose in mind: to earn money for wine. But no matter how determined an effort he makes, or how careful he is to work the minimum time during the year so that he has unemployment compensation ("rocking chair money") during the winter, such money never lasts long. Obligations have to be paid back, drinks shared, and loans for "flops" provided. But he knows that others will do the same for him when he is broke. By sharing what little they earn, winos can make that little go a long way.

The other method of obtaining money is "bumming"—either by straight-out panhandling or some indirect method on the street, or by approaching "live ones" (workers or others who have money) drinking in Skid Road bars. Because these "live ones" are in a different stratum and have no sense of obligation toward winos, there is a risk of being turned down. But often enough the winos succeed.

Not only are the little groups which winos form relatively temporary, they are also relatively unstructured. Only two group roles could be identified: the "promoter" and the "runner." Anyone can approach another to start a group. Two or three may be asked to join in "piecing out a bottle." If between them, they do not "hold" the price of a bottle, they will have to "promote" the difference. A man skillful in bumming money is known as a "promoter," and is sought out by groups. The worth of a good promoter to a group is evident.

As soon as a group is piecing out a bottle, "the baby is born." Now comes the selection of a "runner" to be sent to buy the bottle. A great deal is at stake, by this time, and the runner must be selected with care. A person who is too dirty, too poorly dressed, or who shows obvious signs of intoxication is a poor risk, for he is likely to be picked up by the police. But of all considerations, the prime one is trustworthiness—someone who will not "go south" with the money or the bottle.

Next in importance to obtaining wine is finding a place to sleep, and winos will help each other in this. In summer, any sheltered nook where he can get out of sight of the police will serve his needs, but in cold weather, he has a problem. One form of help is for a wino who has just come in from an outside job and is staying in a Skid Road hotel to offer hospitality to some of his buddies. If they can manage to get by the night clerk, three or four men may sleep on the floor of his room. Or again, a wino who has some money (who is "stakey") will give or loan his buddy the price of a flop. But if a wino has found no place to sleep by nightfall, he must start bumming for a "flop" in earnest.

The price of a flop may range from 25 to 75 cents. The flop house is usually a room as full of beds or cots as the health inspector will allow. The beds will be much the worse for wear, with a poor excuse for a mattress, and a dirty blanket. But at least a man can lie down and not freeze.

In some cities, a wino can sit up all night in a movie house. But if all else fails and the wino cannot find a warm place to sleep or stay, he may be forced "to carry the banner," that is, walk the streets all night, hoping to catch some sleep the next day in a bus or railroad station or any place where he can keep warm and not be picked up by the police.

Two other problems which winos help each other meet are protection from the police and illness. First of all, they share their knowledge about the local police, judges and jails, and the grapevine quickly warns of unusual police activity in the area. They help each other take protective measures and they pull their incapacitated buddies out of sight of the police. They take care of each other in minor illnesses, and when the illness is greater, they try to get the man to whatever medical help is available to them, often at the jail. In the latter case, they may place their buddy where the police will be sure to pick him up. The city jails in the two cities studied do provide some medical care. Frequently, all a man needs is to be kept "off the wine" for a while by confinement in jail and to eat regularly until his health is built up again.

If sharing in these various ways is a basic requirement, certain other expectations are better stated as negative mores, or taboos. The most stringent taboo on Skid Road is that against "going south" with the money for a bottle. This is the surest way of getting the reputation of being a "chiseler," and the grapevine will spread the news that a man is a "chiseler"—even from one city to another.

Breaches of honor somewhat less important but still serious enough to classify the culprit as a chiseler include "breaking into a pitch." When a wino has found a "live one" to buy him drinks or food, no other wino is to capitalize on the same individual at the same time.

There is also a taboo against becoming dependent upon missions. Winos have little respect for the majority of Skid Road missions and will exploit them frequently; yet, they look down on the wino who hangs around them all the time. Such a person is a "mission stiff."

Nor dare a wino become too dirty. As one wino informant expressed it, "It's no disgrace to get lousy, but there is no excuse for a man to stay lousy." Furthermore, a man who gets too dirty cannot be successful in bumming and is therefore a sheer liability to other winos.

A final and interesting taboo is that against talking about their troubles. Winos can tell sad stories about their lives, stories told many times to policemen, judges, mission workers, and "live ones" who may have listened. Winos are not, however, to bother each other with these stories. Every wino has had enough troubles of his own. Anyone who persists in spinning a tale of woe will be shunned.

Men guilty of violating the mores and taboos of the wino culture will be avoided by other winos—excluded from wino association. It must in all honesty be observed, however, that such a situation is not absolutely irreversible. All it takes for a man suddenly to regain a host of "friends" and an elevated status is to come into some money and be willing to share it. His grievous faults suddenly evaporate. He may even be permitted to tell his troubled life story and his beneficiaries will pretend to lend an ear. For anyone is a "good guy" if he has a dollar, and a prince of a fellow if he has five.

This paper has already included a sampling of the colorful words and expressions, drawn from many sources, which constitute the wino's distinctive language. Many more examples could be given. Learning this language is a part of the assimilation process. Its chief function, perhaps, is to indicate that a person "belongs," that he is an insider. It provides for quick acceptance in a new city, for the language is widely used with but relatively minor regional differences. The man who speaks the language indicates thereby that he shares the wino "universe of discourse," not just the words but also a common background of experience, similar assumptions and viewpoints.

The major institutions of the wino are the tavern, the flophouse, the mission and the jail. They play indispensable roles in the wino way of life. The tavern is his social center, providing in addition to a bar a large area for card playing. On fight nights, the television is popular. In the tavern he contacts his fellow winos, taps the grapevine, rubs shoulders with men of other strata, and here he is most apt to find "live ones." As for the flophouse, mission, and jail, some indication of their function in his life has already been presented.

For a complete description of the wino way of life, of course, much greater detail regarding his language and institutions would be in order. But the present purpose has been to sketch enough of his life to show that the wino does not belong to a category of rejected isolates, but that he does live as a social being in a subsociety of his own. Furthermore, his groups are generally not cold, impersonal arrangements dictated solely by necessity. The men become persons to each other. There is some sense of human fellowship to assuage loneliness and a sense of defeat. The men may be homeless but here is a community of their fellows in which they do find some emotional sustenance, minimum though it may be from the viewpoint of the larger society.

Relationship of Winos to Other Skid Road Alcoholics

A final consideration is the relationship of winos to the other men on Skid Road; and the relationship of the wino subculture to the alcoholic subculture of Skid Road itself.

It has been pointed out that winos do not enjoy so high a status as the non-wino, temporary alcoholics. Nevertheless, winos find comfort in standing higher than two other categories of men: the "chiselers" and the "rubbydubs" or "dehorns."

Chiselers. Chiselers are also wine drinkers but, as noted, they are men who do not abide by the wino rules. By this rejection of the wino cultural norms, they place themselves beyond the pale. From the wino point of view, they are "bums," undependable, unethical, and neither safe nor fit for wino association. It is perhaps indirect evidence of the vitality of the wino culture that the per cent of persons willing to defy that culture is very small.

Dehorns or rubbydubs. Dehorns or rubbydubs are habitual drinkers of nonbeverage alcohol, chiefly bay rum ("bay horse") and canned heat. A man on bay rum is referred to as a "bay horse jockey." These men may also resort to shaving lotion, paint thinner mixed with water ("smoke"), and rubbing alcohol. All the wino informants had drunk nonbeverage alcohol at some desperate moment or other, but the habitual user of such alcohol is considered to be the lowest of the low.

Workers. The wino informants seemed to view all of the Skid Road men of higher status as "workers." Obviously included in the "worker" classification are the men who hold steady or seasonal jobs outside and who, except for drinking and having their recreation on Skid Road, are not really "on Skid Road." This category would include pensioners and others who have been workers but are now living in adjacent hotels. The category also includes the non-wino prestige segment described by Jackson and Connor, for these men tend to be seen as "workers," who are temporarily "on the bum."

Similarities and differences. In thinking of the non-wino alcoholics as "workers temporarily on the bum," the wino reveals what he conceives to be the main difference between himself and the Skid Road alcoholics of higher status.

To the objective observer, it is clear that the differences between these two segments of alcoholics do not lie in their subcultures. A reading of Jackson and Connor's description of the higher segment's way of life is sufficient to impress the reader with the social and cultural similarity of this segment to that of the wino segment in terms of grouping, mutual aid requirements, taboos, language, etc. It seems safe to conclude that both segments have a common alcoholic subculture.

More could be made of the outwardly visible characteristics which are held to distinguish the winos, such as wine drinking, a rundown appearance, and the fact that they have to "scratch" harder for wine and shelter. But the higher status alcoholics frequently end a period on Skid Road with behavior and appearance scarcely different from that of the wino. They too may be reduced to the economies of wine drinking, may be rundown in appearance, and may have to bum their drinks and flops. But even in such straits, they do not think of themselves as winos. Nor, for that matter, are they considered to be winos by the winos themselves. The crucial differences lie elsewhere.

As previously suggested, the wino gets to the heart of the matter when he classifies the higher status alcoholics as "workers temporarily on the bum." This brings into clear relief the two factors which basically separate the wino from the others. The others are still primarily *workers*. The others are *temporary* residents of Skid Road. Which is to say, the wino can no longer look upon himself as primarily a worker. True, the wino will still work, but only to drink. Drinking, not working, is primary in his life. Nor can the wino view himself as a temporary resident of Skid Road. True, the wino may still try to delude himself by saying and half-believing that he is on Skid Road temporarily (even after 10 years), but he has little or no real hope that he can ever make the break.

Thus it seems that there are, in addition to the two low status strata of chiselers and rubbydubs, two main classes of men participating in the alcoholic subculture, differentiated from each other by the degree to which they have become assimilated into the Skid Road alcoholic subsociety. Because the assimilation process is continuous, the division of the men into two strata is an arbitrary classification not quite so neatly seen when trying to place individual men. This continuum aspect also accounts for the frequently observed relativity with which the wino designation is applied by one Skid Road alcoholic to another. The label is often hung on anyone who, from the observer's point of view, seems to be in a hopeless position. But even this relativity does not obscure the criteria by which the two strata are differentiated. Men in the upper stratum still have some confidence that they can again work and reside in the outside world. Men in the wino stratum have more or less resigned themselves to permanence on Skid Road and their work is designed to support this way of life.

Conclusion

This study leaves a number of interesting questions unanswered. One of these is the number and proportion of the men to be found in the various Skid Road groupings. Another is the question of regionalism. The authors have reasons, based upon the literature and informal observation, to assume that the *essential* findings of this study will apply to the other Skid Roads of the United States. But the fact remains that the study was made in the Pacific Northwest and that other studies are required to determine national applicability.

But the question which stimulated this study has been answered. Winos are not isolates. Instead they are found to live as social beings in a society of their fellows. It is a society which prescribes and provides mutual aid in meeting the problems of survival: food, drink, shelter, illness and protection. But more than that, it is a society which also provides the emotional support found in the acceptance by, and the companionship of, fellow human beings.

NOTES

1. Even though the term Skid Row is widely used, it is derived from Skid Road, a term which originated in Seattle, Washington, where a homeless man area developed alongside a prominent skid road—a logging skid—in early Seattle days.

2. For example, 30 per cent of San Francisco's Police Department budget, in 1946, was spent for the arrest and jailing of drunks. (1)

3. For details as to methodology and other descriptive details not included in this paper, see the unpublished thesis. (4)

REFERENCES

DALEY, E. A., "A Report on the Pilot Alcoholism Rehabilitation Clinic at San Francisco," *Quarterly Journal of Studies on Alcohol*, 13 (June, 1952), 345-355.

JACKSON, JOAN K. and RALPH CONNOR, "The Skid Road Alcoholic," *Quarterly Journal of Studies on Alcohol*, 14 (September, 1953), 468-486.

NEWMAN, H. and M. ABRAMSON, "Absorption of Various Alcoholic Beverages," *Science*, 96 (1942), 43-44.

PETERSON, W. JACK, *The Culture of the Skid Road Wino* (Unpublished M. A. Thesis, Pullman, Wash., State College of Washington, 1955).

STRAUS, ROBERT, "Alcohol and the Homeless Man," *Quarterly Journal of Studies on Alcohol*, 7 (December, 1946), 360-404.

STRAUS, ROBERT and SELDEN D. BACON, "Alcoholism and Social Stability. A Study of Occupational Integration in 2,023 Male Clinic Patients," *Quarterly Journal of Studies on Alcohol*, 12 (June, 1951), 231-260.

STRAUS, ROBERT and RAYMOND G. McCARTHY, "Nonaddictive Pathological Drinking Patterns of Homeless Men," *Quarterly Journal of Studies on Alcohol*, 12 (December, 1951), 601-612.

WELLMAN, WAYNE M., MILTON A. MAXWELL and PAUL O'HOLLAREN, "Private Hospital Alcoholic Patients and the Changing Conception of the 'Typical' Alcoholic," *Quarterly Journal of Studies on Alcohol*, 18 (September, 1957), 388-404.

THE PROCESS and STRUCTURE of SOCIALIZATION

THE PROCESS and STRUCTURE
of SOCIALIZATION

THE CHILD'S BASIC HEREDITARY COMPONENTS are established at the moment of conception. From this moment, other changes are brought about by either the physical or social environment. At various times in the Western World, the child has been viewed as either innately "evil" or innately "good." However, because of a lack of empirical evidence to substantiate either position, and in order to avoid philosophical controversy, most sociologists at the present time view the child basically as being born a raw individual into a waiting culture.

Numerous groups and institutions have an impact on the socialization of the child. The family "gets" the child first, and at this time the personality is most plastic. The child is soon exposed to play groups, often of a background similar to that of the parents. Before the early formative years are over, the child enters school, a milieu that may be a drastic change for some children. Community groups such as scouts, clubs, little leagues, Sunday schools, and gangs all influence the socialization process. In the total picture, this is part of an on-going process that continues into adolescence and adulthood. As it occurs, additional socialization or resocialization structures, such as the military or work groups, are incorporated into the person's experience.

Each institutional structure has its norms (even if vaguely defined), exerts controls and sanctions, conveys status with role expectations, and has goals, sentiments and belief systems. Thus, the entire process and structure of socialization operates to create a world of meaning, an opportunity to

77

develop one's potentials and a motivation to pursue certain goals. The primary goal of socialization, then, is to create a world devoid of emptiness! However, such developments as competing and conflicting role expectations and incomplete socialization may lead to deviant behavior and the utilization of sanctions. Generally, the process continually moves people within the bounds of the norms, thus leading to the development of the category called social persons.

Inkeles views the business of socialization as the preparation of children so that they will be able to fulfill required social obligations. The twig is bent early, one can say. However, for minority groups, discrimination and disadvantage may deprive the individual of competence which the author feels is essential to free competition for opportunities.

V

Social Structure and the Socialization of Competence*

ALEX INKELES

I WILL DEFINE COMPETENCE as the ability effectively to attain and perform in three sets of statuses: those which one's society will normally assign one, those in the repertoire of one's social system one may appropriately aspire to, and those which one might reasonably invent or elaborate for oneself. In contrast to socialization, then, the concept of competence stresses the end-product, the person as he is *after* he has been socialized, rather than the formative process itself. This conception is also broader than that of socialization in that the latter usually is defined with reference to a fixed repertoire of roles provided by a given socio-cultural system, whereas competence is here defined to include an individual's capacity to move to *new* statuses and to *elaborate* new roles. Despite these differences, however, the concepts so-

* Alex Inkeles, "A Note on Social Structure and the Socialization of Competence," *Harvard Educational Review*, 36, Summer 1966, 265-283. Copyright © 1966 by President and Fellows of Harvard College.

Prepared for a Conference on the Socialization of Competence sponsored by the Committee on Socialization, Social Science Research Council, meeting in Puerto Rico April 29-May 1, 1965. M. Brewster Smith summarized the results of the Conference in *Items*, published by the Social Science Research Council, Vol. XIX, (June, 1965). The work of the Committee on Socialization is supported by the National Institutes of Mental Health (Grant # MH4160), whose aid is gratefully acknowledged.

cialization and competence are intimately linked. In general, the objective of socialization is to produce competent people, as competence is defined in any given society. It aims to develop a person who can take care of himself, support others, conceive and raise children, hunt boar or grow vegetables, vote, fill out an application form, drive an auto, and what have you.

As soon as we specify some of these qualities, it becomes evident that the research on socialization in our scientific literature has little to say about these matters. Research on socialization addresses itself predominantly to understanding how the child learns to manage his own body and his primary needs. It inquires mainly how the child is guided in learning to manage the intake of food, the discharge of waste, and the control of sexual and aggressive impulses. Except for the rather isolated, even if highly interesting, forays in the direction of studying modes of moral functioning,[1] little is done in socialization research to study the acquisition of a broad array of qualities, skills, habits, and motives, which are essential to the adequate social functioning of any man or woman and in fact occupy the great bulk of the time of all socializing agents. A discussion of competence provides an opportunity to correct that imbalance in some small degree. I propose, therefore, to emphasize some of the qualities of individuals which are of most interest to society (and, incidentally, the focus of a good part of its socialization effort after infancy) but which seem largely to have escaped systematic study by students of socialization.

Two paths are open to me. One would be to list demands on the individual typically made by society, followed by specification of the requisite personal qualities these demands assume and of the socialization patterns presumed to engender these "socially demanded" personality dispositions. While this might be manageable if I were dealing with a particular stratum of a single society, it is otherwise too large and diffuse a perspective for the limited space at my disposal. I have therefore chosen to follow a second path, that of presenting a model of the personal system, essentially an accounting scheme of the elements of personality, broadly conceived, which I have found highly serviceable in all my efforts systematically to relate personality to social structure. The elements of this scheme will then serve me as indicators, pointing to more specific personal attributes I consider relevant to a discussion of competence.

A *Model of Personality and Its Implications for Research*
on the Socialization of Competence

In this section, I will present a model of the personality, one which represents essentially an accounting scheme rather than a theory.[2] I make no claim for originality in this scheme, but rather emphasize its practical usefulness as a framework for the discussion of personality in those researches in which interest is centered not in intra-personal dynamics but rather on interaction between the person and the socio-cultural system. I have used the scheme here, as elsewhere, mainly as a way of organizing the discussion of a social issue which we assume cannot be dealt with adequately unless we take systematic account of personality.[3] In this case, the theme is competence to perform social roles. Each element in the scheme will serve as an opportunity to point up an aspect on the "social demand" side of the equation which requires certain personal system attributes in the incumbents of social statuses. Further, to keep the discussion focussed, I approach competence mainly as a requirement for participation in contemporary and "modern" urban industrial settings. And rather than attempt any thorough coverage of the relevant issues, I have concentrated my energies on pointing to what seem to me important neglected opportunities in socialization research.

One of the virtues of the model is that it encompasses, in a decidedly limited set of some twelve to fifteen major headings, a great deal of what is ordinarily included in "personality." Even within that restricted frame, space limitations require that I forego altogether discussion of most elements of the model. My objective here is not to be exhaustive, but rather, by suggestion and illustration, to open up a discussion. The following list presents the scheme in full, and asterisks indicate those elements of the model which are actually taken up in the subsequent presentation.

The scheme, I repeat, is arbitrary, meant to serve as an accounting device. This applies not only to the main entries but also to the subsystems into which I have suggested they may be grouped. But I hope that in the discussion which follows, the utility of the scheme will nevertheless be manifest. As already indicated, because of space limitations I have in the section which follows undertaken to discuss only five of the sixteen main entries.

An Accounting Scheme for Personality Study

Psychomotor System {
 Temperament
 *Aptitudes
 *Skills

Idea System {
 *Information
 Opinions and Attitudes

Motivational System {
 Values
 *Motives and Needs

Relational System {
 Orientation to Authority Figures
 Orientation to Intimates and Peers
 Orientation to Collectivities

Self System {
 Conceptions of Self
 Modes of Defense
 Modes of Moral Functioning

Modes of Functioning {
 *Cognitive Modes
 Affective Modes
 Conative Modes

* Indicates an element discussed in the text.

Aptitudes

By an aptitude I mean an innate capacity or potential capacity to perform exceptionally well specific and difficult acts of sensing, muscular coordination, or the like. I include this heading more for the sake of completeness than out of a conviction that it has a definite relevance to the study of social competence. At the present time we are not at all sure which, if any, qualities meet the test of biological distinctiveness as special rather than general aptitudes characterizing all men more or less equally. Musical ability very likely does, manual dexterity and coordination may. Intelligence seems to be the clearest case, although some will question all the evidence yet available. Of course, at the extremes of the distribution, there may be nothing very problematical here. A child with impaired brain functioning is clearly not competent to learn more than the most rudimentary forms of social behavior and can never become a full participant in his society. Such a person may be defined legally as incompetent and therefore may be barred from exercising any of the formal rights allowed to most individuals in our society, such as rights to hold property, to vote, to conduct vehicles on the public thoroughfares, or to choose one's place of residence or occupation. Yet an adult male moron or imbecile may be perfectly competent to impregnate some female. So the *physical* capacity, drive, and coordination aspect of competence—the aptitude if you wish—must be clearly discriminated from the social and legal definition of competence.

Large numbers of our citizens have been and are defined, by the powers that be, as legally incompetent to participate in society on the basis of their alleged lack of aptitude. I have in mind not only the 600,000 who occupy our mental hospitals, but also much of the Negro population of the American South and a great many of the American Indians. Not unlike many tribal and colonially dominated people in other parts of the world, they have often been deemed by authorities as incompetent to exercise the rights of citizenship and in other ways conduct their own affairs. This legal definition of incompetence has frequently been justified on the grounds that mentally and psychologically, the Negroes affected are incapable of managing their own affairs, presumably because endowed by our maker with insufficient innate intelligence or social maturity. But in our Northern cities, the argument takes a rather different form. There we can encounter many social workers, often motivated by the highest ideals, who believe that the disadvantaged minorities are basically equipped by nature as are other men. Yet large numbers of these social workers in Harlem and Brooklyn have come to the conclusion that many of their clients are not able to manage their own lives and will likely be more or less permanent wards of the State or of private welfare agencies. If we hold fast to the belief that this is not due to *innate* defects, i.e., to lack of aptitude, then we must ask: what is lacking in their clients and what produced this condition? Presumably we may find the clue in some other aspect of the personal system.

Skills

Skills are aptitudes which have been trained or developed in accord with some cultural pattern. In other words, a skill is a socialized aptitude. Skills may therefore be based on the special aptitudes such as musical or mathematical ability, or on the more general aptitudes for muscular coordination, or for learning and using language, which virtually everyone possesses. The essential condition of the social groups and individuals who perform at a disadvantage in our society is their lack of the primary social skills. Our disadvantaged minorities are disadvantaged not only in winning so small a share of the available goods, services, and psychic rewards, but precisely because they so often lack the specific skills which could enable them to win a larger, or at least more adequate, share.

The main facts are today so well known that they have become almost clichés. While the end results, as reflected in low IQ scores, abysmal performance on aptitude tests, and consistent failure in the classroom, are well known, we must admit that students of socialization have done little to study the process which presumably yields this low capacity, especially as the process unfolds in the home, on the street, and in the primary grades of the classroom.

Of course, as we begin to explore these antecedent conditions, we may be led to re-examine our impressions of the actual pattern of skill deficiencies. The Harlem boy and girl may have an extremely meager vocabulary and very little ability to manipulate concepts—but are they also less well coordinated muscularly? Is the little Indian girl less able to cook or care for a younger sibling? And is the little Puerto Rican boy less able to bat a ball, to put it through a basket, or to sew on its torn cover? These questions, which unhappily we cannot pursue here, point to the important distinction between the social desirability of skills and their intrinsic difficulty, rarity, or aesthetic value. Some of the skills one must possess in minimum degree to participate in one society might be totally irrelevant or even outright disadvantageous in another.

Yet it does not do much good to mourn the fact that the other skills men *do* have are fine, even exquisite. The problem is painfully evident in the developing countries. There, the demands of the industrial order and urban living insistently undermine the relevance of venerable and often exquisitely developed skills which were highly important in the past; and they elevate to great importance *new* skills which, to the citizens of more developed countries, seem most elementary, yet which may seem difficult to master, even occult, to those in the developing nations.[4] It is notable, at least to me, that many of these skills are precisely those which *also* seem to be seriously underdeveloped in those groups in American society which are most disadvantaged, i.e., our ethnic minorities, including those in our Indian population and in our pockets of Protestant white poverty such as Appalachia and the South. Among the more obvious skills which are relevant to adaptation to modern life and insufficiently mastered by these disadvantaged groups I note, for illustrative purposes:

The telling and management of time: I know of no simpler or better indicator of a man's desire to show himself as modern than the acquiring and *demonstrative* wearing of a wrist watch. Of course, what is involved here is a value as well as a skill. However we may *feel* about the coercion of the clock, we must recognize the ability to tell time and to order one's affairs in relation to the clock as a critical skill for participation in the modern world. From social workers in the more deteriorated slums, and researchers who have worked with juvenile delinquents, one hears the frequent complaint that "they *never* keep appointments." Although my search is probably not exhaustive, I have not come upon a single article comparing children of different backgrounds in their ability to tell time and to meet the exigencies of the clock. This is all the more striking since the literature on developing countries gives the problem so much attention, and long ago Lewis Mumford argued that the industrial revolution and the modern world were ushered in not by the steam engine but by the elaborate organization of time in Christian monasteries.

The command of language, especially in its written form: The point certainly needs no elaboration, but perhaps I may be permitted to inquire what light our numerous studies of socialization can throw on the persistent failure of our Negro slum children to master language in a way appropriate to adequate performance in our schools? We cannot be satisfied with the usual reference to "poverty," not only because it is so global but also because it seems hardly to explain the extraordinary richness of the language and the elaborateness of the spoken style of Oscar Lewis' poor Mexican families.[5] And poverty can hardly explain the late readers and language cripples who bloom so profusely in some of our most favored suburban communities. Here again, then, we would like to see fuller study of those practices of child rearing, those patterns of interaction between parent, environment, and child, which lead to greater or lesser degree of command over spoken and written language.

The research cupboard is not so bare in the case of studies of the acquisition of language skills as it is of those involving management of time, but neither are we presented with a bursting granary. We may eagerly await the second volume of *The Review of Child Development,* which is to give us a chapter on "Language Development and its Social Context." If we are to judge from advance reports on the studies of Martin Deutsch and Irving Taylor at the Institute for Developmental Studies, we may yet meet some surprises in discovering that it is not the number but the use of words that distinguishes the underprivileged child.[6] For them, apparently, words stand for objects and objects for action. One word does not elicit another word, but rather elicits the *image* of action. This would seem to be highly congruent with the findings of Miller and Swanson.[7] It could also serve somewhat to explain not only the disadvantaged minority groups' performances on our typical word tests, but also the problems of later incorporating these groups into environments where one word leads to another word and not to an action.

Arithmetic: I suppose I cannot mention the language of words without also mentioning the language of numerical and mathematical symbols. On a four-item arithmetic test we gave to thirty-seven miners and ex-miners in Appalachia whose education averaged three to four years, we found that two "occupational" groups—the physically disabled and those now employed on relief jobs—could collectively answer only 6 per cent and 17 per cent of the problems, respectively. In the physically disabled group, for example, only three of the twenty men could correctly subtract 9 from 23! Two of these three could also multiply 8×9. So two men got half the problems right, one man got a quarter right, and the remaining seventeen men missed all four. We must note not only the appalling average lack of skill, but the individual variation. The group employed on relief did better, collectively, but the difference is due largely to individual variation. Two of the seventeen could answer all four questions, one could do three, another man one, and the remaining thirteen could answer none!

We had a very similar experience with tests of verbal ability. Using a larger sample from the same region of Appalachia, now augmented by groups with an average of seven or eight years of school, we asked the respondent to give the opposite of each of fifteen words. Before the fifteen words were presented, the interviewee was given an example such as "black" and "white." Many of the men simply could not grasp the task, that is, they could not dominate the *concept* of a word's opposite. By contrast, there were some who could give twelve correct answers, including words as difficult as "intelligent," "modest," "corpulent," and "affluent." Although education played a large role in this outcome, the variation within groups of the same education was very wide.[8] Again we are led to wonder what are the precise qualities of intelligence, of home environment, or of later experience which yield these differences.

Getzels and Jackson have presented some highly suggestive research relevant to these issues as they apply at a quite different educational and cultural level.[9] In their research they distinguished between adolescents with a high IQ on standard tests and those with the special skill to use ideas and information creatively. Perhaps this is matter not merely of basic skill, but rather of cognitive style, which will be discussed below.

Information

The cognitive element of the personality may be divided into two broad categories—levels of information and styles of thinking. I refer to the former here. Almost every public opinion poll ever conducted has shown great differences in the sheer quantity of fact known by middle and upper class individuals as against those in the lower classes. Such differences are not restricted to news events and public figures, but include as well all sorts of practical and useful information, such as how to get your gas turned on or your garbage collected, how to get permission to conduct publicly controlled activities, how to organize a meeting, and so on. We may assume that this kind of knowledge about getting along in the everyday world is an important pre-condition to effective and independent participation in the modern social order.

The difference in information among various social class

groups is generally attributed to the differences in their average education. While acknowledging the importance of education, I am rather of the opinion that these differences are already quite marked by the time children enter grade school, and that a great deal of the variance is to be explained as a result of the different early socialization experiences which the children of the several groups receive.

I am further strengthened in this belief by the clear evidence of great individual variation in information levels among persons with equal education. Thus, when we asked former Soviet citizens what they could do if some bureaucrat were taking an action injurious to them, the most common response among workers was "nothing," whereas most members of the intelligentsia cited at least two sources to which they might turn for help.[10] But there were ordinary workers who named four, five, six, and more agencies they would write to—the Communist party, the trade union committee, the factory manager, the newspapers, and finally Stalin himself! These different levels of information undoubtedly reflect the influence of motivation to know and perhaps also of a sense of efficacy—but that does not make it any less interesting to inquire what are the mechanisms of socialization which lead to these differences both in the desire to know and the resultant knowing.

The topic of language skills and information provides an opportunity to highlight the conceptual problems of relating major social-structural factors to a socialization problem such as "the development of competence." Again I emphasize the necessarily schematic form which must characterize my discussion. The points I can make within these limits are rather obvious, but perhaps they will serve to provide a starting point for future discussion.

Let us consider the command of language, including the size and content of vocabulary and the capacity to form sentences and larger units of speech in grammatical and culturally acceptable ways, thus enabling one to bring his language capacity effectively to bear on situations of action.[11] Assume we deal with a Negro boy in Harlem with normal intelligence and no more than the average number of situational disabilities which affect residents of that area. How would the hypothetical "self-sustaining vicious circle" we so often hear about be apparent in his case? In the home, we may identify the following inputs:

Low capacity models: From a sheer learning point of view, the total vocabulary available to be learned in the home is likely to be quite small because of the limited education and experience of the parents or others in the household. Each incumbent of the home probably adds very little that is not already in the vocabulary of others, so that the total word pool is likely to be small and restricted. Since many homes are broken and one parent absent, the available pool of models is further reduced. Inevitably, fewer words will be learned than actually are available in the limited total potential vocabulary of even this group. The prognosis is for a very limited vocabulary.

Interaction effects: Whatever the pool of potential words to be learned, they cannot be learned if those who know them do not use them in situations in which the child can learn them. If mother and father are gone most of the day and/or leave the child alone a great deal, effective learning is greatly reduced. Mother and father may be there, but not communicate much with each other. Thus, in my current cross-national research I found in all countries marked social group and individual differences in the frequency with which men indicate any interest in communicating with their wives on a variety of themes, such as work, educating the children, running the house, and sex.

Content and tone: Interaction effects are felt not only in that they make words "available" for learning. The quality of the interaction clearly will affect the relative frequency of words and, beyond that, the emotional tone associated with verbal exchange in general. If the parents talk to each other mainly to complain, grumble, or quarrel, the words in that realm will obviously be learned sooner and more fully. Perhaps more important, the unconscious conception of what language is mainly "about" or "for" will be affected. With parental communication mostly demanding or quarrelling, the likelihood is greater that, unconsciously, language and verbal expression will be associated mainly with unpleasant experiences and hence be something more or less avoided.

Social valuation: The interest or motivation for involvement in language will be affected not only by unconscious association with situation and content, but also by the more explicit cultural valuation put on relative degrees of skill and interest in the use of language. If the most common evaluations are generally negatively toned, as I believe they are in Harlem, the effect will most likely be to induce the child to view language skills as relatively undesirable qualities to cultivate in oneself. I cannot establish the point as a matter of fact, but I feel fairly certain that in Negro Harlem, the most common evaluations of language facility are negative: "big talker" and "talking big" are clearly negative. "Loudmouth," "shooting off the mouth" speak for themselves. "Preaching" is not too good. "Nagging" is, after all, mainly verbal behavior, and "talking foolish like a woman" reflects a similar feeling. There may be some positive associations to the facile use of language, but they seem fewer and less strongly toned than the negative associations.

The brief sketch of the Harlem boy's start in language in the home could be extended, but I trust I have made my point. The same mode of analysis could be applied as well to later stages in his language training, but I had better forbear. Let me merely note a few salient points. In the peer group, again, the pool of words collectively shared will be small and each boy will add little new. New vocabulary may be amply introduced, but mainly in areas relating to sex, aggression, and the law, and of such nature that the words cannot be carried over for use in polite society. On the streets, the skills valued and encouraged will be mainly physical, and indeed, the verbal may be actively disvalued.

When the boy later arrives at school, interesting new elements are introduced. In contrast to the rewards the school offers the middle class child for what he already *knows*, it is likely to greet our Harlem boy with horror for what he does *not* know and *cannot* do with language. The result, on his part, will be more avoidance of words and language. Much of the language he does know will be unacceptable, and if expressed will produce more negative reactions. The mode of expression of which he is most capable, the physical, will likely find no valued outlet at school, or may even be punished.

This analysis could be carried further in the life cycle, to the first job and beyond, but I suspect everyone can tell it for himself. Whether the story is accurate or not is unfortunately not as well documented as it might be, but I doubt that it qualifies as a "just-so" story.

Motives

The preceding discussion points to the importance of motives as an underpinning for the acquisition of information, and thus alerts us to the relevance of motivation for a discussion of competence. Certainly at first blush, motivation would seem to have little to do with competence, since competence refers to the *ability* to do something whereas motivation deals with the *desire* or wish to do it. But if we recognize skills and information as contributing to competence to perform social roles, then we must recognize the *motive* to attain socially valued status positions as a necessary, even if not sufficient, requirement for competence in social action.

It might be argued that the point is trivial, on the grounds that little if anything socially desirable, yet relatively scarce, will be acquired without motivation to do so. The more challenging question is whether there are any motives which in and of themselves can be seen as more adaptive, and in this sense contributing more to one's competence to attain and perform in available and respected social roles. I am rather of the opinion that this question cannot be answered if it is put in general terms, as applying to any socio-cultural system. Every sort of motivation, including aggression and hostility or extreme dependency and passivity, has been found to be relevant and adaptive in some culture somewhere. If we specify performance in a particular type of social system, however, then we can identify more or less precisely motives which are differentially adaptive. For example, cross-cultural anthropological research indicates that hunting and gathering societies are more likely to train youngsters for autonomy and independence, while pastoral societies give more emphasis to inculcating compliance and dependence.[12] In the context of modern industrial society, we might expect the need for achievement to be more adaptive than the need for affiliation, the need for autonomy more productive than the need for dependence, at least for those competing for middle class positions. Studies of the adult population of the United States indicate that there is some such pattern in the distribution of motives,[13] and studies of child rearing in the different class and ethnic groups suggest that these adult differences most likely rest on differences in socialization practices.[14]

Cognitive Modes of Functioning

When we considered the theme of information, we were concerned mainly with the amount and type of knowledge possessed by the individual. The cognitive modes refer to the forms of thinking and to the "style" characterizing the individual's mental processes. We ask: Is thinking abstract, concrete, or both? Is it slow and deliberate, or quick and mercurial? Is interest focussed or diffuse? Is the language of emotion more elaborated than is the conceptual apparatus for dealing with objects or material relations?

Cognitive functioning, at least in the realm of concept formation, has certainly been of interest to students of child socialization, but the interest has been mainly the usual developmental one of fixing the ages at which different conceptual skills emerge, with little systematic attention paid to individual, and even less to group, differences.[15] The work of Miller and Swanson and their students in establishing the stronger tendency to conceptual expression in the middle class child and of motoric expression in the working class child points the way. Unhappily, this path has been little followed by other workers in the field.

The modes of cognitive functioning clearly influence the child's initial performance in meeting the demands of the school and other social agencies; his later preferences for academic work, trade school, or practical apprenticeship; and his eventual choice and performance in his occupational and other adult roles. The boy who feels inadequate or is made uncomfortable in an environment which gives much emphasis to manipulating symbols instead of things will soon be drifting out of school to a world in which experience is more immediate and concrete. And this applies not only at the level of primary school and in disadvantaged neighborhoods. The problem is also very real for those who are already in college and choosing their professional careers. Thus, Stern, Stein, and Bloom report how great a role cognitive styles played in the adjustment of freshmen at the College of the University of Chicago. The College program stressed and rewarded "abstract analysis and relativity of values and judgment rather than fixed standards." (p. 191) Teachers introduced a good deal of ambiguity and often departed from conventional standards of judgment. It was precisely those students whose cognitive style inclined them to concrete thinking, to an insistence on one "correct" answer, who made up the bulk of the academic casualties at the end of the year. And this was true despite close matching of the students on measures of intelligence and scholastic aptitude.[16]

Unfortunately, Stern, Stein, and Bloom did not systematically explore the home environments which produced these different types. Indeed, we have very little knowledge about the socialization experiences from which stem one or another style of cognitive functioning. Rokeach, for example, tells us almost nothing of the home environment of those with "open" and "closed" minds. He does suggest, however, that ambivalence toward parents which is not permitted expression generates anxiety and narrowed possibilities for identification with persons outside the family. Rokeach sees both of these conditions, in turn, leading to the development of closed belief systems.[17] The point seems closely paralleled by the observation of Getzels and Jackson with regard to the home environments producing more creative adolescents.[18] The creative family, they concluded, "is one in which individual divergence is permitted and risks accepted." Those which produced a mere high IQ without "creativity" seemed more conventional, with the mothers stressing cleanliness, good manners, and studiousness. Miller and Swanson help us to see that physical punishment is more intimately tied to motoric than to conceptual expression, whereas psychological discipline, such as the threatened withdrawal of love, more often yields conceptual expression.[19] Hoffman's research also contributes to isolating the style of training he calls "inductive discipline," referring to efforts to explain to the child the effects of his action on others. The outcome which interests Hoffman, however, is less a mode of cognitive and more a mode of moral functioning.[20] We should, of course, here recall the explorations into the origins of the authoritarian personality, one component—some would argue the main component—of which is a certain cognitive style. Adorno *et al.* suggest a series of antecedents in the home environment of those who display prejudice and authoritarianism, but their evidence is mainly clinical and has not been more systematically tested on large samples.[21]

Cognitive styles emerge as an extremely important component of the individual's equipment for coping with the demands of society and a critical element in determining what kinds of roles he may seek out and successfully play. Cognitive style will evidently play an early role in school performance; it will channel —and limit—the choice of occupations, and will affect the nature of one's political participation. The evidence seems unmistakable that the observed adult differences in cognitive style have their origins in childhood experience. Unfortunately, very little has been done by specialists on socialization to follow these insights in programs of systematic research. The implications for future research seem clear.

Conclusions

This presentation of a comprehensive conception of the elements of personality may have led the reader astray, and may leave me exposed to the charge of neglecting my announced subject. Admittedly, I have not discussed as fully as I perhaps should have social structure and the socialization of competence. If this is so, I beg indulgence on the ground that it seemed to me the main topic could not be properly understood unless we first dealt with matters more fundamental. In my discussion of the elements of the personal system, I have in effect sought to establish the basis on which—and in a sense the language in which— a more meaningful discussion can be presented. But it has taken so long to compile the vocabulary and explain the grammar that little space remains for telling the tale I meant to recite.

The message is very simple. Like so many obvious things, it is not only fundamental but also much overlooked. The main business of socialization is the training of infants, children, adolescents (and sometimes adults) so that they can ultimately fulfill the social obligations that their society and culture will place on them. Implicit in this statement is the expectation that, in meeting these societal demands, the individual will not be placed under so much strain as to fall apart psychologically. And not excluded is the thought that the term "social obligations" includes elaborating and acting effectively in roles not commonly assigned by the given socio-cultural system. Indeed, we do not by any means exclude the possibility that the most creative way of meeting the demands of a given social situation may be to reject that situation as it presents itself, to insist on a new deal, and to forge new roles and new styles of life.

I am firmly convinced that concern about the ultimate playing of social roles is the decisive element in the child-rearing behavior of most parents or chief parent-surrogates. This is not meant to deny that at some periods in a person's life—especially in early infancy and perhaps again at puberty—the problems of sheer management of physical need or the facts of physiological change may not come briefly to dominate the concerns of the socializers. Yet, I believe that even in dealing with such ulti-mately physiological needs as the hunger drive, socializers never lose sight of the long-run adaptive significance, both of the sheer mastery of this drive and of the *way* in which it is mastered. Evidence for this can be found in the common speech of every mother. Nor do I mean to deny that there may be periods in the child's development when what is done to him more expresses the psychic needs and desires of the parent for giving or with-holding, for restraining or indulging, than it represents any con-scious or subconscious thoughts about the social roles the child will ultimately play in society. The issue is clearly one of relative emphasis. My chief point is that the degree to which, and the ways in which, socialization is a relatively conscious process of training in anticipation of future social roles, have been neg-lected relative to the conception of socialization as mainly a process in which adults cope with the challenge of the infant and child as *organism*. The same criticism applies to those who approach the study of socialization as mainly expressive of the parents' needs and dispositions.

So far as competence is concerned, some children face a situ-ation in which almost everything conspires to insure that most of the more favored positions in society will be closed to them. They will grow up ill-equipped to compete for entrance into the more advantaged roles, and those desirable positions they may acquire they will be unable to hold successfully. This is what we mean by competence—the ability to attain and perform in valued social roles. In our society this means, above all, the ability to work at gainful and reasonably remunerative employ-ment, to meet the competition of those who would undo us while yet observing the rules for such competition set down by so-ciety, to manage one's own affairs, to achieve some significant and effective participation in community and political life, and to establish and maintain a reasonably stable home and family life. We should not for a moment forget the massive and cruel formal obstacles our society has devised to prevent the disad-vantaged minorities from sharing equally in the opportunities inherent in the level of wealth and civilization we have attained. But we must also recognize that these obstacles—such as overt discrimination, segregated schools and communities, color-bar hiring practices, and even legal disfranchisement—are not the *only* barriers to effective functioning on the part of disadvantaged minorities. The most cruel aspect of discrimination and disadvantage lies in its ability to deprive the individual of that competence which is essential to effective functioning once the formal barriers to free competition have been breached. Lack of competence effectively to take advantage of new opportunities in a competitive system can make the attainment of nominal legal equality a hollow victory, and make a self-fulfilling prophecy of the bigots' claim that minority members are unable to perform effectively even when not formally discriminated against. To deny people the means for attaining competence while yet granting them technical equality under the law is the contemporary equivalent of saying that the majesty of the law confers on the rich as on the poor alike the right to sleep under bridges.

To perform effectively in contemporary society, one must acquire a series of qualities I believe to be developed mainly in the socialization process. Effective participation in a modern industrial and urban society requires certain levels of skill in the manipulation of language and other symbol systems, such as arithmetic and time; the ability to comprehend and complete forms; information as to when and where to go for what; skills in interpersonal relations which permit negotiation, insure protection of one's interests, and provide maintenance of stable and satisfying relations with intimates, peers, and authorities; motives to achieve, to master, to persevere; defenses to control and channel acceptably the impulses to aggression, to sexual expression, to extreme dependency; a cognitive style which permits thinking in concrete terms while still permitting reasonable handling of abstractions and general concepts; a mind which does not insist on excessively premature closure, is tolerant of diversity, and has some components of flexibility; a conative style which facilitates reasonably regular, steady, and persistent effort, relieved by rest and relaxation but not requiring long periods of total withdrawal or depressive psychic slump; and a style of expressing affect which encourages stable and enduring relationships without excessive narcissistic dependence or explosive aggression in the face of petty frustration.

This is already a long list, and surely much more could be added. My purpose here is not to strive for an exhaustive list. I want simply to indicate the *kinds* of personal attributes which I feel a modern industrial society requires in significant quantity of substantial numbers of its citizens. Without most of this array, one is not competently prepared for life in our society, and must sink into some form of dependency or deviance. There is no great difficulty in demonstrating that these qualities are very unevenly distributed in the several strata of our society—educational, occupational, ethnic, and regional. The challenge for the students of child-rearing is to show whether, and explain how, these differences came about as a result of differential socialization practices and experiences. My assessment of recent work in the field of socialization research is that very few of these issues have been the object of much systematic study on a significant scale. More than that, I incline to the conclusion that this situation is not now rapidly changing. The cause, I believe, lies in the scientific "culture" of those doing socialization research; they are beginning at the wrong end.

The master key to understanding socialization, in my opinion, lies not in further deepening our involvement in the innate propensities of the child and the situation of action this defines for the parent. The key lies rather in a redefinition of the problems of socialization research which starts with a clear statement of what are the massively evident observed *differences* among adults which appear socially important enough to be worth the trouble of explaining. I have tried to show through a brief and limited discussion of competence what a few such differences may be. But any other social issue—mobility, political participation, delinquency and crime, or occupational performance—could have served the same purpose. I applaud the fact that the six-culture study sponsored by the Laboratory of Human Development at Harvard included, in the nine standard behavior systems to be observed, not only the old and tried themes of nurturance, succorance, aggression, and obedience, but also responsibility, sociability, achievement, and self-reliance.[22] Even in this case one may ask: If you have not first defined what is the quality of the adult you wish to understand, how do you know what to look for in the disciplining of the child when you study "responsibility" and "achievement"? And beyond responsibility, sociability, and achievement, we still want to know about information, values, motives, skills, moral functioning, self-conceptions, cognitive, conative, and affective modes; about the ability to trust others and enter into enduring relationships of cooperation or undestructive competition; about images of and relations to authority figures, and the sense of membership in, and feeling of obligation to, the community.

Before concluding, I should clarify some issues not necessarily important to the student of socialization, but nevertheless fundamental to the functionalist perspective on social structure, a perspective which my analysis in this paper represents.

The first issue concerns the appropriateness of a *general* model of competence, such as I have presented, for the analysis of performance in what is inevitably a highly differentiated social structure. Another, and blunter, way of making the point is to claim that I have presented a model of competence as defined by the middle class in American society. The charge is correct. The aspects of competence I have sketched above are precisely those which one requires either to continue as part of, or to attain to a position in, middle class America. Every model of competence is, in large measure, specific to some culture, and often even to some stratum of a particular society. The elements of competence, as I have sketched them above, would not necessarily loom equally important for a man who was hoping to be the world's heavyweight champion. And they might be quite beside the point for a Trobriand Island fisherman or an Arctic Eskimo. The point I mean to make in this way, again, is that socialization research generally begins from the wrong end. In my opinion, the starting point of every socialization study should be a set of qualities "required" by, i.e., maximally adaptive in, a given sociocultural system and/or manifested in a given population. The task of students of socialization should be to explain how these qualities came to be manifested by individuals, thus rendering them competent, or why individuals failed to manifest these same qualities, thus being rendered less competent to perform in the given social setting.

The very form of my last sentence raises the second and last issue on which I wish to touch briefly—the issue of "competence for what?" or "adjustment for whom?" A functional perspective always runs the risk of leading one to assume that what is good for society is good for the individual, and vice versa. Those interested in encouraging competence, or excellence, or whatever desirable quality, run the same risk. If we define competence as the capacity to organize one's life and to strive so as to achieve some degree of social stability or desired mobility, it means that many individuals, in seeking to meet the competence requirements of their society, may in that very act also be inviting more or less certain frustration. The Negro in Harlem who is quite comfortably able to accept his dependence on welfare authorities, to be passive in the face of middle class society's expectation of constant effort and striving, and to find release from his tensions through extreme physical and vocal expression in his storefront church, may be making a more appropriate adjustment to the realities of his situation, and to that degree be more *competently* managing his life than is his neighbor who has all the white middle class virtues, which will in turn increase the probability that he will run up against a solid wall of frustration and futility.

Everywhere today—by continent, by nation, by region, by class—there is a vast process of social change exerting its force. To manage their lives in a satisfying way, men need new information, skills, motives. New problems and situations everywhere constantly challenge their competence. Tragically, men find that the skills and talents which formerly made them models of competence in their community are of no value or are even demeaned and degraded in the new scheme of things. In this turbulent sea, we often glimpse some remarkable people who seem especially equipped to navigate freely and easily through conditions which are tumbling most people overboard. Are there then some qualities of man which give him a general competence useful in all places and times, qualities especially suited to adapt a man to all waters no matter how fast the current or sudden its changes? What are these qualities and what are the special forms of socialization which bring them into being? Here is a challenge to the student of socialization worthy of *his* competence.

NOTES

1. See the review by Lawrence Kohlberg, "Development of Moral Character and Moral Ideology" in Martin L. and Lois W. Hoffman, *Review of Child Development Research* (New York: Russell Sage Foundation, 1964), Vol. I.

2. The model is as much Daniel J. Levinson's as it is mine. Although we have used it extensively in our work, we have never published a full and systematic account of the scheme. We sketched some of its elements in the article "National Character" in Gardner Lindzey (ed.), *Handbook of Social Psychology*, Vol. II, 1954, and later in "The Personal System and the Sociocultural System in Large Scale Organi-

zations," *Sociometry*, Vol. XXVI (June, 1963). I used the scheme systematically in empirical research reported in A. Inkeles, E. Hanfmann, and H. Beier, "Modal Personality and Adjustment to the Soviet Socio-Political System," *Human Relations*, Vol. XI (1958). The conception is outlined in schematic form most fully in A. Inkeles, "Sociology and Psychology" in Sigmund Koch (ed.), *Psychology: A Study of a Science*, Vol. VI (New York: McGraw-Hill, Inc., 1963).

3. For a fuller statement of this issue see: A. Inkeles, "Personality and Social Structure," in Robert Merton, *et al.* (eds.), *Sociology Today* (New York: Basic Books, 1959).

4. One of the most sensitive accounts is offered by Erik Erikson in his remarks on the Dakota Indians, in *Childhood and Society* (New York: W. W. Norton & Company, 1950), whom he describes as no longer having a socially satisfying mode of using either their skill as riders and hunters or the character traits of cruelty and generosity, which were apparently meaningful, rewarding, and encouraged when their culture was whole.

5. The richness of the vocabulary and the fluency of expression of his Mexican subjects has so struck readers of Lewis' accounts that many wonder to what extent these qualities are the product of translation and editing. But those who have heard the tapes in Spanish say they are often quite poetic. And Lewis says: "Despite their lack of formal training, these young people express themselves remarkably well. . . ." (Oscar Lewis, *The Children of Sanchez* [New York: Random House, 1961], p. xii.) Of course, one might well retort: "So do many Harlem Negroes." Has Lewis been unusually selective? In any case, we may ask how two environments so much alike in their poverty and related conditions can produce groups of individuals so different in their command of language. Surely socialization practices played some role.

6. These have been briefly summarized by Frank Riessman in *The Culturally Deprived Child* (New York: Harper & Row, 1962).

7. I have in mind their finding, reported in *Inner Conflict and Defense* (Holt-Dryden, 1960), that middle class boys more often adopted a conceptual mode of expression, whereas the motoric mode was more typical for working class boys.

8. These results are presented in an unpublished senior honors thesis by William W. Lawrence, Department of Social Relations, Harvard College, April, 1965.

9. Jacob W. Getzels and Philip W. Jackson, "Family Environment and Cognitive Style: A Study of the Sources of Highly Intelligent and of Highly Creative Adolescents," *American Sociological Review*, XXVI (1961), 351-59.

10. See Alex Inkeles and Raymond Bauer, *The Soviet Citizen* (Cambridge: Harvard University Press, 1959).

11. Any discussant of this topic is necessarily heavily indebted to Basil Bernstein's pioneering work in the development of socio-linguistics. See "Some Sociological Determinants of Perception: An Inquiry into Sub-Cultural Differences," *British Journal of Sociology*, Vol. IX (1958) and "Language and Social Class," *British Journal of Sociology*, Vol. XI (September, 1960).

12. Barry Herbert, A. Irvin Child, and Margaret Bacon, "Relations of Child Training to Subsistence Economy," *American Anthropologist*, LXI (1959), 51-63. Also see David Aberle, "Culture and Socialization," in F. H. Hsu (ed.), *Psychological Anthropology* (Homewood, Ill.: Dorsey, 1961).

13. See Joseph Veroff, *et al.*, "The Use of the Thematic Apperception Test to Assess Motivation in a Nationwide Interview Study," *Psychological Monographs*, Vol. LXXIV (1960).

14. See B. C. Rosen, "The Achievement Syndrome," *American Sociological Review*, XXI (1956), 203-11; F. L. Strodtbeck, "Family Interaction, Values, and Achievement," in D. C. McClelland, *et al.* (eds.), *Talent and Society* (New York: Van Nostrand, 1958); D. R. Miller and G. E. Swanson, *op. cit.*

15. This should be readily apparent to anyone who consults the review by Irving I. Sigel, "The Attainment of Concepts," in *Review of Child Development Research*, Vol. I, M. L. Hoffman and L. W. Hoffman (eds.) (New York: Russell Sage Foundation, 1964).

16. G. Stern, *et al.*, *Methods in Personality Assessment* (Glencoe: Free Press, 1956).

17. M. Rokeach, *The Open and Closed Mind* (New York: Basic Books, 1960).

18. Getzels and Jackson, *op. cit.*

19. Miller and Swanson, *op. cit.*

20. Martin L. Hoffman, "Report of Research Sponsored by N.I.M.H." (Merrill-Palmer Institute, October, 1964). (Mimeographed.)

21. Adorno, *et al.*, *The Authoritarian Personality* (New York: Harper & Row, 1950). Also see Else Frenkel-Brunswik and J. Havel, "Authoritarianism in the Interviews of Children," *Journal of General Psychology*, LXXXII (1953), 91-136.

22. Beatrice B. Whiting (ed.), *Six Cultures* (New York: John Wiley & Sons, 1963).

*The author recounts for the reader an interesting
number of empirical observations about a minority
(ethnic) group and refers to these observations as
"largely a matter of colored words." The work
serves as an everyday reminder how scientist and
layman alike can unconsciously succumb to the acceptance of oversimplifications about groups.*

VI

The Question of Personality Traits*

LAWRENCE F. PISANI

ARE THERE TRAITS of personality which are more common to
Italians than to other groups? If there are, how can we explain
them? And if there are not, how can we explain why they are
so often said to be?

The author, who is Italian-American, has had occasion to be
on the receiving end of assertive statements about the Italian
character made to him by Italians and non-Italians alike. When
he points out individual Italians whom these statements will
not cover, he is always assured that these are individual exceptions who do not conform to the true pattern. "It isn't that folks
don't know anything," said the old Yankee storyteller; "it's that
they know so many things that ain't so."

It is some people's idea that nationality traits follow the globe.
Starting at the north is the practically emotionless Eskimo. Moving toward the center of the sphere we come across the enig-
matic Russian and the dour Scot. A little further south the Dutch
and Germans are more open but still keep themselves under restraint. But it is thought that in the Latin nations the people
almost consume themselves with the intensity of their fiery
passion.

Even today the notion persists that a man's nature can be

* *The Italian in America* by Lawrence Frank Pisani ©, Exposition-Uni-
versity Press, 1957; reprinted with permission of the author and publisher.

told merely by knowing where he came from. Fifty and sixty years ago, when the theories of national characteristics held sway, it was the accepted thing. Some peoples loved liberty; others wanted to be governed by rigid authority. Some were imaginative and creative; others dull and placid; some leaders, others followers.

Which people demonstrated which attributes was not always agreed upon, however. In the nineteenth century, British travellers in the United States commented that the Americans were a sluggish, slow-moving people, and offered all sorts of reasons for this, ranging from the climate to the national habit of drinking ice water. Today the reputation of Americans is for hustling and bustling to the point of unreason.

Theodore Roosevelt, who in addition to being President of the United States was a distinguished scholar, could write that the Germans were an individualistic people while the French lacked individual enterprise and looked to the state for the initiative. This morning's paper tells us that French individualism almost to the point of anarchy threatens that nation's stability, while Germans' love of order and willingness to sacrifice their individual fates in the common enterprise, almost second nature to them, has restored the country's balance. One concludes that either the nations have switched attributes in the last half century or it is more difficult to generalize about national traits than one would suppose.

Such generalizations persist, however, assuring us that Italians are all cut from the same mold and that, except in trifling matters, individual differences do not exist. This is a remnant, perhaps, from the racial pseudo-science of the late nineteenth century which measured heads to determine intellectual superiority, and saw all good as emanating from one racial stock. The science may now be exploded but some of its tenets are still unconsciously believed, partly because they had been believed before anyway.

Although the notion that nationality traits are in the blood of each people may be summarily rejected, the claim that they have traits, at least to an extent commonly held among themselves and different from others, inculcated by social teaching, must be taken more seriously. The way people behave is determined not only by their native ability but also by what they learn by observing other people's behavior, and by being taught what the elders of their society believe. To the extent that communities are isolated from each other, the members tend to develop the same broad beliefs, customs, even gestures and ways of speaking.

There are some characteristics which hold true for Italians. Too much has been said at one time or another about them that has had little relation to the truth, however, or which was true about Italians only to the extent that it was true of all people. As Italians adjusted to the American society, either deliberately or unconsciously many changed their supposedly ingrained traits, showing that these were environmental rather than congenital.

What was commonly said about the Italians? It should be remembered, to begin with, that a great distinction was made in the popular mind between the North Italian and the South Italian, a grouping which erred both in lumping together men from different communities with different customs, and in attributing characteristics too universally to one and excluding them too greatly from the other.

The men of the North were pictured somewhat in the same stereotype as the American Yankee, as more shrewd and enterprising, cold in nature, and a little too concerned with money, but, nevertheless, the source of monumental movement and progress. The men of the South were viewed as more genial and easygoing, more in love with life and with nature, in disposition good-natured and sunny.

The United States Immigration Commission used to keep separate figures for North and for South Italians, although they made no such divisions in the case of people from any other country. Although it would have been difficult to gather records according to each province of origin, there was no real reason to make any division in the first place. Others joined them in their error, however, and the remark was often heard that, whatever faults the speaker might attribute to Italians in general, the North Italians, who "were all right," were exempted. Some North Italians were generally earlier immigrants, so this may have been a matter of greater assimilation, for they themselves sometimes made the distinction.

The friends of the Italians, as well as their enemies, were a little too glib in generalizing about them. Almost all favorably inclined were cheerfully impressed by a certain *joie de vivre* they claimed to see in all the sons of Italy. "They come from a land of beauty and fame, song and sunshine, and bring a sunny temperament not easily soured by hardship or disappointment," declared a writer at the beginning of this century, seeking to explain Italians to native Americans. They needed this sunny temperament, he went on, or otherwise they could never have survived their ordeals in America. They did not restrain themselves, but expressed their emotions and their quick and lively imaginations. They were of quick wit and intuition, with good humor and gusto, getting a little honest fun where others saw only gloom.

Much the same opinion had been expressed in a national periodical shortly before the Civil War, when the Italian immigrant was perhaps still something of a novelty and therefore a subject for discovery by the *littérateur*, as today he will discover an out-of-the-way restaurant or authentic native music. The writer of the article, evidently having made the acquaintance of such an Italian shortly before, reported his delight in the warm, open ways of his friend, so different from what he had been used to. He contrasted his friend's belief that "there was an absolutely enjoyable vein in the mere act of living, a possible art of being happy" with "my elders of the austere community [where the author lived], anxious plodders who did everything by rule; a thrifty, grave set, whose ideal was respectability—who lived with little apparent emotion, and in a perfectly decent but extremely uninteresting way." Italian behavior, on the other hand, was "such a violation of the current (drab) philosophy of life, such a free, irresponsible, genial exception to the general rule." Withal, there was no vulgarity involved, but a kind of "refined enjoyment."

The observant reader may perhaps have noted the similarity of these sentiments to those expressed by many social thinkers, from Rousseau to Tolstoy, about the superior happiness and nobility of the simple peasant as against either the aristocrat or the urban money-maker. Only the humble worker close to the earth, ran the theory, knew how to live properly. One would never suspect from articles like these that Italians ever grew angry, or dispirited, or weary from long and unrewarding toil. Only a picture of a smiling *papier-mâché* Italian was painted.

The less favorably inclined looked at the same people and saw a startlingly different picture. The Italians were not delightfully carefree, they were irresponsible. They were not fun-loving, they were thriftless. They were not people who knew how to enjoy unhurried life, they were lazy. How all this could account for the hard labor most adult Italians were at one time engaged in, or their passion for saving even from incredibly low salaries, was not explained.

In line with the statements about the Italians' natural tendency to live life better were others describing him as a colorful personality, living a life not of quiet desperation but of noisy enjoyment. They loved display in festivals, loved garish costumes, and would seize the slightest excuse to interrupt the humdrum routine of existence with a parade featuring colorful floats and loud bands. "The Latin," said an Italian magazine, "believes in expressing himself, all that he feels, all that he wishes, all that his senses urge him towards, without restraint or embarrassment." Unlike the cold Yankee of Puritan strain, he refused to repress himself or to feel that anything enjoyable was *ipso facto* sinful. Therefore he loved flowers, not only to grow in his backyard but to have around his home and to carry around with him. He loved music to be dramatic, either violently sentimental or heroic, rather than sweetly symphonic.

He was a born actor, too, because of his innate temper, supplemented by his histrionic ability. "Italians," said the editor Arthur Brisbane, "the Southern Italians particularly, are natural actors, and will make themselves felt in politics more than any of our nationals." They could appeal to a political gathering in the same way they could to a theatrical audience. The dramatic way in which the Italian father, at an evening gathering of his family, would regale the members with stories of his experiences was put forth also as evidence of his flair for the drama.

But there was a darker side to this warm nature too, the analyzers sombrely warned. Since he lived life to the full, the Italian was also proud and high-spirited, and his "hot blood" quick to resent a slight or a fancied insult. The hot climate from which he came made him prone to crimes of passion and violence. The spur of revenge led him as a quick resort to the knife.

Even the guidebook which welcomed him to the country seemed convinced these attributes were truly characteristic, for it counseled him, "Italians are too ready to have recourse to violence in quarrels. If this habit could be given up, Italian immigrants would at once find themselves more welcome in America. Throw away all weapons you may have. Speak in a low voice. Try not to gesticulate, and do not get excited in your discussions. . . ."

The newcomer who did not assert himself at once was taken advantage of, sometimes by officials, or by criminals who preyed on his ignorance, or by his own less scrupulous countrymen. Little cry for his protection was heard, but when at last he rebelled, others were quick to call him lawless.

It has been suggested that the so-called violent emotionalism of the Italians is a matter of misinterpretation by outsiders. Many Italians were accustomed to gesturing excitedly when they spoke (as did many non-Italians), and to arguing heatedly even on matters about which they may not have had especially strong feelings. The participants themselves were aware of this, and would be discussing another matter amiably a few moments later. To the uninitiated, however, the arguers mistakenly appeared to be on the point of blows.

If the Italians had a gift for acting, as some of their analyzers felt, they had also a gift for art and music. If not all were creative in this respect, all were appreciative. "Even the Italians of the working class," we are assured, "possess an almost inborn aesthetic sense and an intellectual idealism, a spirituality of mind which consists of a certain sensitiveness to the finer values of life and appreciation of all things intellectual and beautiful." They are the most gifted nation in Europe, said others, as why should they not be, coming from a country with so glorious a history in literature and the arts?

It was claimed for the Italians, indeed, that the glories of Italy were in the blood of all of them, that they were the heirs of more than two thousand years of civilization. "The poorest Italian immigrant," it was said, "is by blood and language linked with conquerors and rulers, artists, musicians, and poets." It was this belief, that any prominent Italian who performed some noteworthy feat was somehow proving the worthiness of all Italians and that his glory permeated them also, that perhaps explains the fervor with which the news of Marconi's wireless discoveries was hailed in the Italian-American community. It was further proof that Italy was the land of Galileo and Galvani, and, by extension, that Italians were scientifically minded.

By the same principle, the achievements of Verdi and Puccini in music, of Leonardo and Michelangelo in art, of Dante and

Tasso in literature, were held to reflect glory on all Italians, to show that all had the touch of genius in their blood. Art and music were said to be second nature to them. (Undoubtedly the argument was also used to refute the contention that somehow only Anglo-Saxon nations produced superior individuals.)

It is somewhat a contradiction, after noting the beliefs about their romanticism and warm expressiveness or the beliefs about their "hot-blooded" lawlessness, to relate that the Italians were also held to be peculiarly realistic and logical, a characteristic they possessed in common with all Latin nations. Two thousand years of civilization had presumably taught them not to go overboard for every promising plan that was proposed, but to examine ideas through to their logical consequences, from the viewpoint of those who had much experience with which to compare them. Without losing their feeling for life, they did not lose themselves in visionary schemes which would not work, but retained their practicality. They were of the earth, not of the clouds.

Their experience had taught them also to be conservative. Love for the old ways of doing things which tied them to the family still in Italy, love for the old country itself with so many familiar scenes they would never see again, kept them from becoming too excited about everything new to which they were introduced. They had seen many new things arouse great enthusiasm only later to prove not workable. Decades of struggling for economic security, with the threat of starvation in a bad year always present, had impressed them with the grim necessity of digging their roots firmly in the ground and holding on to what they had. It induced in them as well a passion for saving.

It was also said about the Italians that they were overly clannish. They retained their affection for the old country, sending money overseas, communicating with relatives still in Italy, keeping up their interests in Italian affairs. Moreover, they kept to themselves, living in their own quarters of the city, reading newspapers in their own language, forming their own clubs and societies. They intermarried and had mostly Italian friends. The complaint, in short, was that the Italian-Americans refused to stop being Italians.

The Italians were called naturally gregarious. They liked to dwell in the midst of many people, to establish communities rather than settle in isolated outposts of civilization. This overlooked the scarcity of such areas available to attract them at the time they came over, and the individual Italians who earlier had lived in just the isolated manner they were said not to prefer.

In their behalf it was said that there was a native politeness about the Italians, an Old World respect for the rights of others and a desire for their good opinion. Their naturally unhurrying ways were contrasted with the rudeness of people always on the move. They were modest and given to self-deprecation, undemanding, and responsive to kindness. The hope was expressed that their Old World ways might have a favorable influence on the supposed American characteristics of boastfulness and swaggering, and that undue insistence on personal rights and privileges without regard for the rights of others.

How should all these views be evaluated?

It is not impossible that an Italian could be found of a sunny, expressive, unrestrained disposition, whose background led him into extreme resentments of unintended slights and into lawlessness, an artist who nevertheless was realistic with a strong conservative streak, who was exclusively clannish and yet possessed of Old World charm and politeness. It is not impossible—but highly improbable. It is more likely to find most Italians having a few of these characteristics.

Assuming for the moment that most of these generalizations about Italians were correct, it would take more than that to tab them as Italian characteristics. It would have to be shown as well that these were traits that did not hold equally well for others. But what other people could not claim the same attributes? If the Italian peasant had an enjoyment of life, so did the Russian peasant. The French were as nonpuritanical, and as coldly logical. Rumanian Gypsies were as colorful. Spaniards were as proud and as "hot blooded." The heritage of Greek civilization was older. A bent for art and music was equally strong in the Germans. Viennese were as polite. Jews were as clannish. Irishmen were as strongly tied to the home country. And a country which housed the Daughters of the American Revolution might certainly be expected to pause before accusing others of being excessively bound up with their ancestors.

In addition to this consideration, it would be possible to quote exactly opposite declarations also made about Italians. It is largely a matter of colored words. Frontiersmen who depended on their own justice in preference to civil authority were self-reliant; Italians who did the same were lawless. Native Americans who could trace their ancestors to these shores three hundred years back understood the continuity of history; Italians who kept up their interest in the affairs of their native town were hidebound ancestor worshippers. What is admirable in ourselves may be condemned in others.

How then will the investigator solve this enigma? Perhaps he will get out of the world of commentators and magazine articles, and take a trip for himself through the streets of any Italian-American community. If he does, he will see some people with the joy of living shining on their faces, and some reserved with little display of emotion. He will see some who are high spirited and other who are humble, some who carefully nurtured flowers and some who could not abide them, some who argued in heated discussions and others who spoke but little above a whisper. To put it another way, he will not see the stereotype of any one Italian who sets the pattern for all of them. For Italians are *individuals,* and therefore differ greatly among themselves.

Obviously when some Italians rose to great wealth while others remained forever bogged down, when some achieved fame and high position while others remained in obscurity, one may generalize about Italians only with extreme caution. Beyond the social graces, which may be untaught in a new social surrounding, it was individual, not inherited, traits which were important. Mark Twain was once asked his opinion about a social group. To paraphrase his response, "Italians are human beings. Worse than that I cannot say about them."

Or better.

The youthful idealism of the student nurse is cooled by increased exposure to, and acceptance of, the calculating rationalism characteristic of the socialization process of this formal organization. The technique known as Role Projective Test is used herein to shed light on "the fate of idealism in nursing school."

VII

The Fate of Idealism in Nursing School*

GEORGE PSATHAS

ENTRANTS INTO SUCH TRAINING PROGRAMS as nursing or medicine may be expected to show the idealism and optimism that characterize new entrants in any field. Becker and Geer,[1] in describing the fate of idealism among medical students, find that the expression of idealism varies with the objects of the attitudes (e.g., specific situations or role relationships) and the audiences the individual has in mind when the attitude is adopted (e.g., other students, instructors, or the lay public). Certain aspects of idealism are found to be irrelevant in the school situation and as Becker *et al.*[2] describe, realistic attitudes concerning "getting

* Reprinted from the *Journal of Health and Social Behavior*, Vol. 9, No. 1, March, 1968, by permission of the author and the American Sociological Association.

I am grateful to Marilyn Frank Price for her many contributions to this study. Others who gave valuable assistance were Sandra Gold and Jon Plapp. This is a partial report of a research project, Role Differentials and Nursing Ideology, supported by Public Health Service Research Grant NU00050 from the Division of Nursing, Bureau of State-Services-Community Health, and administered by the Medical Care Research Center of Washington University.

I also wish to express my thanks to the students and faculty of the General Hospital School of Nursing (pseudonym) who contributed so generously of their time and effort to make this research possible. A complete report of this research is presented in Psathas, G., *The Student Nurse and the Diploma School of Nursing*, New York: Springer, 1968.

through school" become more salient than idealistic attitudes concerning the future practice of medicine. However, as the students reach the end of medical school, their original idealism about the practice of medicine is once again expressed.

In the present study, expressions of idealism, optimism and realism are viewed as situationally specific attitudes whose degree of intensity and expression vary with the role relationships in which the student nurse is involved. The relevance of the attitude is expected to vary according to the student's perception of the situation and with her perception of the setting and the interaction occurring within it. Further, the student is expected to show changes in her perceptions of situations as she gains experience, acquires skills and knowledge, and successfully copes with the realities of nursing. What may be termed "youthful" or "naive" idealism becomes tempered with experience into more realistic perceptions and outlooks.

In this paper, we chose to explore the student nurses' perceptions and attitudes in relation to specific roles and situations. Since this was an exploratory study, we did not adopt a hypothesis testing model but present data as illustrations and examples of the students' perceptions. By constructing stories about situations depicted in a series of photographs, respondents could project themselves into the situation. The social self we are concerned with is the student nurse who is either a freshman or senior and still in nursing school. We expect that respondents will attempt to "normalize" the perception of events and construct "typical" events occurring in "typical" sequences. The construction of the scene can then be taken to represent the students' typification of reality, i.e., how they perceive reality, despite the fact that this reality is in "fictitious" scenes. If their stories show patterns related to their year in school, then it will be possible for us to construct ideal typical descriptions of their typifications. These may then be used to assess changes that occur during their years in nursing school. As we will note shortly, there is a pattern of typification that can be called "idealism" for freshmen students. It changes over time with different patterns emerging for seniors. The characterization of these patterns and an interpretation of their theoretical significance is the task of this paper.

Method and Procedure

The method used to collect data concerning student nurses' perceptions of various interaction situations *vis-à-vis* particular others was an instrument called the Role Projective Test (RPT).[3] It consisted of a set of 10 photographs or slides depicting a number of hospital situations. The photographs were taken in a hospital, but actors rather than real patients or nurses were posed. A brief description of each of the nine slides included in the analysis presented here is given in Figure 1. Students were instructed to write a brief story about each picture, "using their imagination" to describe (1) what led up to the situation, (2) what is happening, and (3) what will be the outcome.

Seventy-six freshman nursing students, class of 1965, at a large midwestern hospital-based diploma school of nursing answered the RPT in January, 1963, when they were freshmen. They had entered in September, and had been exposed to approximately 11 weeks of clinical experience in the hospital. They were compared, in a cross-sectional comparison, with a senior group of 29 students of the class of 1963 who took the RPT in August, 1963.

FIGURE 1.—*Descriptions of the Slides*

Patient

Slide 1. Student nurse giving drink to patient.
  Male patient is reclining in hospital bed. Student nurse is bending over the patient holding a glass of clear liquid (water) extended toward the patient's mouth.

Slide 9. Student nurse entering room, patient has buzzer in hand.
  Student nurse is entering open door to patient's room. Her back is to the camera. Patient is raised up in bed looking and leaning toward the doorway. He holds the call buzzer in his right hand.

Student Nurse Alone

Slide 6. Student nurse in open doorway, hand over mouth.
  Student nurse is standing in open doorway. Her right hand is raised to her mouth. Her mouth is open thus giving her an expression of either shock, surprise, fear, amazement, etc.

Slide 7. Student nurse looking at light on wall.
  Student nurse is standing or walking in hospital corridor and looking up at what appears to be a light on the wall between two doors.

Doctors and Interns

Slide 3. Student nurse and doctor near nurses' station.

Student nurse and doctor (in street clothes) are standing in front of the nurses' station. Two nurses are in the background.

Slide 5. Student nurse and intern in front of nurses' station.

Student nurse stands in front of nurses' station with her back to the station. She's looking into the eyes of an intern who is standing in front of her holding a bottle half filled with some liquid.

Other Nurses

Slide 2. Two students—utility room.

Two students are standing in a utility room. One nurse has her back to the camera. The other nurse is facing the camera and holding a cup and saucer in her left hand.

Slide 10. Student nurse and R. N.

Nurse is seated behind nurses' station. Student nurse holding a tray is standing at the side of the station looking at the nurse who is seated.

Slide 8. Student nurse in supervisor's (or clinical instructor's) office.

Student nurse is in supervisor's office standing in front of desk at which supervisor (age about 50) is seated.

The stories of the remaining group of 49 seniors from the class of 1965 who took the RPT for the second time, just prior to graduation in June of 1965, were compared with the stories they wrote when they were freshmen.

The dimensions used to classify the content of the stories were not developed on an *a priori* basis but instead grew out of the content of the stories themselves. They therefore represent themes that are common to several slides. The major dimensions that were developed and used to classify the stories were the following: who initiated the interaction; the roles attributed to persons shown in the slide; the reasons for occurrence of the interaction; the specific type of interaction which occurred; emotional expressions attributed to others and the reasons for these; statements which indicated model, appropriate, correct or ideal behaviors, thoughts, or feelings for nurses and which were attributed to the student nurse (or expressed in the third person) by the respondent; statements which indicated inappropriate, inadequate, or incorrect behaviors, thoughts, or feelings for nurses and which were attributed to the student nurse or expressed in the third person by the respondent; and, finally, the outcome of the interaction.

Each slide was examined separately. The story, or protocol, was taken as the unit of analysis. A response that could be classified as falling on one dimension was tabulated only once under one of the sub-categories of that dimension, i.e., multiple coding was not done.[4]

Some of the dimensions and their sub-categories were cross tabulated in order to determine thematic patterns in the stories.

Because of the exploratory nature of the analysis we did not deem it desirable to develop a set of categories with the cross-sectional groups that could then be checked or tested for stability with the longitudinal group comparisons. Ideally, two independent samples of freshmen and seniors would be needed, the first to be used in the development of the categories and the second in the testing of any hypotheses concerning freshmen-senior differences.

In the analysis, the cross-sectional freshman-senior comparisons and the longitudinal comparisons were tabulated and examined separately. If the observed differences were not consistent, i.e., not in the same direction, or no difference greater than 10 per cent was found, then the results were disregarded. If both comparisons showed differences between freshmen and seniors greater than 10 per cent, then they could be used in developing the description of a pattern. When percentages are reported, cross-sectional comparisons are given for illustrative purposes. Since the study is exploratory and we are more concerned with describing and then suggesting possible interpretations of the patterns discovered, the percentages were useful in the development of the description. Rather than report such preliminary calculations here and mislead the reader into thinking they represent significant and quantifiable differences when freshmen and seniors are compared, they are omitted. The most significant data are represented by the quotations from the stories written by respondents.

The stories which are quoted appear exactly as the respondent wrote them, i.e., grammar, spelling and punctuation were *not* corrected. We chose to do this rather than undertake to edit all stories and, by editing, introduce distortion. Stories are identified by the class of the respondent.

We classified the stimulus photographs according to the cate-

gory of the role portrayed by the other person (as validated by
the student's perception) i.e., if the other person was intended
to be an intern by the actors posed in the photograph, but was
seen as an orderly by the student, then this response was removed from those classified under the heading of "seen as intern." Although the slide was then called the "intern slide," responses which did not conform to this perception were excluded.[5]

Patients (Slides 1 and 9). Freshmen tend to write stories in
response to slide 9 in which both positive and negative emotional
characteristics of the patient were mentioned, e.g., the patients
were "lonely," "worried," "afraid," "angry," "demanding," "crabby," "cooperative," "grateful," or "happy." More freshmen than
seniors see the student nurse as responding to these emotions
and feelings in a manner indicative of concern and in an effort
to give emotional support. The stories of freshmen have an
idealistic quality in that the nurse is seen as effective in responding to the emotional needs of the patient which means that she
not only knows what to do but she does it and achieves, as an
outcome, the resolution of the patient's problems.

Seniors more typically see the situation as one involving simple
technical or physical problems such as providing a glass of water
for the patient. The nurse meets these easily. Similarly, for slide
1, the seniors merely describe what is occurring in the slide and
mention simple procedures.

The differences between freshmen and seniors can be characterized as showing a shift from the freshman's description of
the student nurse as a "model" student engaged in "appropriate,"
"correct," "Florence Nightingale-ish" behavior, thoughts or feelings who idealistically felt that situations ultimately end for "the
best" or in a "better" way, to the senior's description of the nurse
as one who was negligent or inadequate in her patient care, who
engaged in unprofessional conduct, thought, or feelings and who
was "negative" or "pessimistic" in picturing the outcome of situations. One indicator of this shift seemed to be revealed in the
attitudes, feelings and specific traits which characterized the student nurse.

In response to slide 9, the freshmen were more likely than the
seniors to describe the student as a "model" nurse by portraying
her as "kind," "tactful," "understanding," "sympathetic," "effi-

cient," "pleasant," and other such descriptive words or phrases which connoted a "good" or "model" nurse. Examples from the stories are:

> "This man is very upset. . . . He is the kind who wants a lot of attention. . . . The nurse is understanding and kind and patient. . . ."
> (Freshman)
> "The student has come to answer this man's call light. He is unable to get out of bed. . . . He feels like a pest having to call for such a small thing, but the nurse assures him with her smile and her manner that she is glad to help him & she . . . leaves the room leaving her cheerful spirit to stay in the room long after she leaves."
> (Freshman)

In particular, the freshmen were more likely than the seniors to exhibit this "model" behavior when confronted with the difficult patient who was "demanding," "crabby," "irritable," "angry," "bored," "lonely," "disobeying orders," etc. Occasionally this would involve an adaptation of what may be termed a "professional attitude," i.e., the inclinations of the nurse would be to avoid the patient or show irritation toward him, but, realizing that she is a nurse with certain professional duties and obligations, she would suppress this tendency and fulfill her professional responsibilities. This professional attitude was expressed somewhat more frequently by freshmen than seniors. For example:

> "This patient is very mad because he has been pushing his call-light for five min. And he was waiting to jump on the first person who walked in which happened to be this student nurse. He telling her off because it took her so long to come. And all he wants is a fresh pitcher of water & he just got one an hour ago. She will go get the pitcher of water and keep saying to herself that she must remember people are diff. when they are ill. . . ."
> (Freshman)

Finally, with regard to outcomes depicted, freshmen are more "idealistic" than seniors whereas seniors more frequently presented a "negative" outcome than the freshmen.

In slide 9, this "idealism" of freshmen was revealed in the tendency for a greater proportion of outcomes constructed by freshmen to extol the accomplishments of the student nurse as adequately and successfully giving care to her patients. The freshmen were not only "idealistic" in believing that situations in general turn out favorably, but they had enough faith in their ability to believe that even they could cope with the more difficult patients.

The seniors, on the other hand, more frequently than the freshmen constructed an outcome with "negative" overtones in response to slide 9. In these stories the student nurse was portrayed either as being unsuccessful in coping with emotional or physical aspects of the patient; or the patient would die; or the nurse would be engaged in unprofessional conduct, thoughts, or feelings with regard to the patient.

Student Nurse Alone (Slides 6 and 7). Because the stories written in response to these slides often involve interaction with patients we will consider these next.

The freshmen are more likely than the seniors to portray the student as reacting emotionally to the situation witnessed in slide 6. Because many of these situations are the same as those constructed by seniors but without mention of an emotional response, the implication is that seniors treat these incidents in a more "matter-of-fact" way and no longer react emotionally when confronted with these situations. The following examples demonstrate this freshman-senior difference in portraying the emotional reactions of the student:

Situations Involving a Patient Who Had Died

"This nurse's patient has just died as she was going in to check on him. This is the first such case for this young nurse and she doesn't know what to do or where to turn. She seems to be quite taken in and frightened by it. . . ."
(Freshman)

"The call-light went on and the nurse ran to the room. Upon reaching the room, the nurse found the patient half-in the bed and partially on the floor. She saw much blood in the bed and on the patient. It was then determined that the patient had begun hemorrhaging and tried to get out of bed for help but had fallen and expired before he could get help."
(Senior)

Situations Involving a Patient Who Has Fallen Out of Bed or Been Involved in Other Mishaps

"The nurse in this picture has been asked to come to a patient's room. The picture shows her standing shocked at the door —she is shocked because the patient on complete bedrest is lying sprawled on the floor. . . ."
(Freshman)

"A student nurse stops almost in the doorway of a patient's room. As she looks inside she sees him fall on the floor. She immediately thinks of a possible injury & also the accident report that she will have to fill out."
(Senior)

Situations Involving a Patient Who Is Disobeying the Doctor's Orders

"Apparently the nurse is returning to her pt. that she had just left a few minutes ago. It looks like she is horrified at what she sees.

"The pt. probably wasn't supposed to be out of bed and has gotten out of bed and doing something he isn't supposed to be doing. . . ."
(Freshman)

"(1) Nsg. stud is taking care of a patient on complete bedrest who has a cardiac problem.

(2) As she enters room she finds him climbing over side rails.

(3) She quickly puts him back to bed, restrains him, reports incident, & taken vital signs."
(Senior)

In response to slide 7, the freshmen more frequently than the seniors describe the student as experiencing "fear" or "confusion," or as being "timid" and "unsure." These "negative" emotions are expressed when confronted with the following situations: a patient who has died, a nude patient, or a patient who has fallen out of bed or has been involved in some other mishap while in the hospital.

Freshmen tend to depict the student as possessing the attributes of a "model," "dedicated" and "idealistic" nurse. In contrast the seniors were more likely than the freshmen to portray the student nurse as more oriented to the "world outside of nursing," and as less "idealistic."

In response to slide 6, the freshmen wrote more statements which could be categorized as expressions of "idealized nursing role behavior" some of which read like normative statements from textbooks. Others present a more personal portrayal of their own conception of "good" or "successful" nursing behavior. In some instances, the student was either portrayed as a "model" nurse in the present situation or there was an "idealistic" belief that she would become one. The following quotes will demonstrate more clearly the specific nature of these statements:

> "The nurse walks up to a door of a room & looks in before entering. She sees a sight that startles & shocks her. She stops and gasps. Undoubtedly she will recover hurriedly and enter the room. If the situation needs correcting she will do so in a calm, correct, formal & polite manner. . . ."
> (Freshman)
> "This student has just lost her first patient. She is upset. She wants to cry. But soon this will wear off. The sight of death will no longer bother her she will become hard like all the other nurses in the world. This is the fate of all nurses after a while they lose all contact with human feelings and become iron-clad nurses. The only way a nurse can be a good one is to let these things bother her. Become involved with the pt. worry about him. Don't let your feelings turn to stone."
> (Freshman)

The seniors, on the other hand, were more likely than the freshmen to construct stories in response to slide 6 which specifically dealt with the non-nursing situation of heterosexual relationships. Examples from the protocols are:

> "Student goes in to assist doctor & another student for a procedure. They didn't know she was coming. He was kissing the other student. Result girl at the door was surprised & upset. She likes him too."
> (Senior)
> "The student has been having an affair with a married intern. She just walked into her room at the dorm and found him in bed with her roommate. They'll both give him up and find someone else."
> (Senior)

Other data we have obtained corroborate this pattern of increased interest in heterosexual activity on the part of seniors. The results from an analysis of personality need scores, based on the Edwards Personal Preference Schedule (EPPS), administered to the same freshmen and seniors in a longitudinal study, showed that need Heterosexuality increases significantly and to an extent greater than non-nursing age-control groups. The stories seniors construct are consistent with this pattern of changing interest in heterosexual activities. This interest also appears in the doctor and intern slides to be discussed below.

The outcomes depicted in these stories show that freshmen are more likely than seniors to construct what was categorized as a "positive" outcome. Positive outcomes included such statements as: "the patient recovers," "the student will do a good job," "the student gains confidence in her own ability," "the student will learn how to handle the situation in the future," "fortunately no harm developed from the student's error," "the student enjoys her work and is in good spirits." In other words, positive outcomes are manifestations of an optimistic orientation which expresses the belief that situations turn out for the best in the end.

Negative outcomes included such statements as: "the patient dies"; "the student will not give adequate or proper patient care"; "the student is unhappy"; "the student nurse is angry at, or dislikes the patient." In these stories, the closure to the story is, therefore, either pessimistic in its orientation, is representative of an "unprofessional" attitude of the student, or indicates that the student is not a successful or model nurse. Examples are:

Slide 6

"Student has just come on duty & is yawning. Outcome is that she works the entire day thinking of an excuse to get off."
(Senior)

"The student has just had a shocking experience. She does not have control of her emotions because of this she gives poor nursing care. She will be asked to leave because of this."
(Senior)

Slide 7

"A pt. puts on the call light. The student sees it but doesn't think it's important so she doesn't answer it. The pt. dies of resp. distress."
(Senior)

"The pts. light has been on frequently. The patient is in critical condition so the nurse is concern & running to answer it.

"The man will be in cardiac arrest & she'll call the Dr's *stat.* The man will recover but die later that week."
(Senior)

Doctor and Intern (Slides 3 and 5). The freshmen are more likely than the seniors to view their "professional" contact with physicians as placing the student in the role of an "information-giver." In most instances, they indicate that the physician, because he "knows" that nurses and even student nurses have frequent contact with his patients, approaches her seeking information about his patient's condition:

"This student's patient is also the doctor's patient. He is getting ready to go see his patient. He wants to know how his patient is getting along. When he asked the head nurse she referred him to the student who is taking care of the patient. The student is telling him that his patient feels much better this a.m. . . . ."
(Freshman)
"Nurses are supposed to report observations to the doctors because the nurses are with the patient a lot more than the doctor, that led up to this situation.
"The nurse is telling the doctor the observation she has made like caring for the patient. . . ."
(Freshman)

Seniors on the other hand are somewhat more likely than freshmen to view the physician as teaching the student about his patient's condition, teaching her some aspect of patient care, or other medically related matters. In most of these "teaching" situations the student, being curious or concerned about her patient or some aspect of his care, will initiate the interaction by directly approaching the physician:

"This student is quite concerned about her patient's prognosis —She has a chance to find out for she has spotted his doctor. She is asking about her patient. . . ."
(Senior)
"I had been taking care of Mrs. M. all morning now, but I couldn't understand why she continued to run a Temp. I approached her doctor and asked if he would explain this to me. . . ."
(Senior)

The stories by freshmen place themselves in a position subordinate to that of the physician whereas the seniors describe interaction which reflects a narrowing of the status gap.

The freshmen are more likely to point out the importance of the role of the nurse in the patient-nurse-physician relationship. The function of a nurse as an "information giver" is seen as "essential" or "important" because of the resultant increase in the physician's knowledge which "enables him to give better care to his patient." A few freshmen also see the role of student nurse as "essential" or "important" because she may serve as a "check" on the physician by "catching his mistakes"; or because "he will work better with the nurse at his side." An example is:

> ". . . He has a patient on her division & is now questioning the nurse on how the patient has been feeling and if anything of outstanding importance has developed. . . . She finishes her report & the Dr. now goes into the patient's room with a picture of how the patient will be feeling from the report of the nurse. Maybe she has observed something in the patient that the Dr. has not."
> (Freshman)

Statements like these are rarely found among the seniors.

Freshmen also see the outcome of the contact with physicians as resulting in an ultimate improvement in the ability of the physicians and nurses to administer care to their patients. This improvement is seen as a result of the student's functioning as an "information giver," thereby contributing to the physician's knowledge of his patient's condition.

The "professional" relationship which students have with interns (or residents or medical students) differs from their "professional" relationships with physicians.[6] Very few freshmen or senior nursing students portrayed the intern as a "teacher," and only a few freshmen portrayed the student as an "information giver." Freshmen primarily viewed the intern as someone who "asked" the nurse to perform some simple technical activity for him—frequently this would consist of taking a specimen bottle to the laboratory—while seniors saw him as asking for assistance in more complicated nursing procedures.

Finally, some seniors and freshmen portrayed the "intern" as having less experience in the particular hospital setting (i.e., the intern was new on the ward) than the student and as asking for her guidance. In contrast, data from the "doctor slide" indicated that physicians were never portrayed as asking for guidance from the students.

"(a) New intern on the floor—he is holding bottle of irrigation saline.

(b) Intern is going to use saline to irrigate cath. of male patient. He asks nurse to come c̄ him since she knows patient and he does not. Intern seems somewhat unsure of himself. Nurse finds this semi-amusing for doctor to rely on her as a buffer agent between her & patient.

(c) Nurse knows that in a month, this intern will need no buffer and will know his way around the hospital."

(Senior)

Their stories reflect the realities of hospital life. Interns come and go and when "new" need to find out where things are and what the routine is. The staff physician has generally been there longer than the student nurse.

Several kinds of "social" interaction appear in the stories. One was the description of a "platonic" relationship such as would exist between "friends" who were of the opposite sex. In other words, there would be no implication that the two people had a "romantic" interest in or a dating relationship with each other.

Another is what might be described as a non-reciprocated "crush." Occasionally, the explanation for his lack of reciprocation would be the discovery by the student that he was already married. In other stories, there would be no reciprocation, but the mere fact that he would say "hello" or speak to her would be satisfying to the student.

Another type is a "reciprocal" romantic relationship, whereby either the student was dating or had an opportunity to date the intern or physician, or the implication was given that the "romantic" interest was (or would become) a mutual feeling.

This reciprocal relationship is normally restricted to an actual or eventual dating relationship. A few seniors, however, explicitly or implicitly incorporated an element of "promiscuity" in their reciprocal relationship with the intern and with the physician. This "promiscuity" consisted primarily of going out or "having an affair" with the intern or physician even though he was married.

Doctor Slide

"(1) Nurse had date c̄ this married Dr. two nights ago.
(2) They are sneakeley trying to make another date.
(3) Nurse gets kicked out of training—Dr. gets divorce."
(Senior)

Intern Slide

"The student and the intern are discussing what time she can
sneak into his room tonight. They are both married (not to each
other) so that makes it difficult. But the affair will crystallize."
(Senior)

There is an important difference in the perception of the role
of the other in the intern slide. Only seniors described the other
as an orderly or technician and mentioned some kind of social
relationship. In these stories, two-thirds (6 of 9) saw the relationship as romantic rather than platonic. This can be interpreted
as a more realistic approach on the part of seniors concerning the
possibility for romantic relationships with men on the hospital
staff. It has been hypothesized that opportunities to meet and
eventually marry men in the medical profession are expectations
that many girls who enter nursing have. (Studies show that 20%
of interns are married to nurses.) Girls from lower socio-economic backgrounds without college education (as is true for the
students in a diploma program) may expect to be able to achieve
upward social mobility by marrying physicians. However, by the
time one becomes a senior, such relationships with orderlies and
technicians, who are of lower or equal status, is a more realistic
expectation. The frequency with which their relationships with
doctors and interns are described as "affairs" with married men
also reflects the reality of the age and status difference between
doctors and student nurses.

Further evidence of the seniors' more realistic views are revealed in the manner in which the student's interest in the young
man was stated. Freshmen were more likely to depict the student
as experiencing emotional feelings which resembled the "typical
high school crush," and were more likely to depict the student
as experiencing satisfaction by merely being around or being
noticed by him. The seniors, however, were more likely to depict a romantic or dating relationship as actually being con-
summated.

"The student nurse assisted the intern with starting I.V. fluids.

"Now there in the corridor talking and he is thanking her for helping him.

"The patient will receive his fluids the nurse will be flying on a cloud being able to assist the most handsome intern and the intern will be busy about his other duties."
(Freshman)

"This intern is conversing with the S. N. They are both working nights. They are planning a date for the next Saturday night, since they have that day off. They are going dining (cheaply) & either dancing or playing cards with a few other couples. They will both enjoy themselves."
(Senior)

Other Nurses (Slides 2, 10 and 8). In the supervisor-instructor and R. N. slides, the freshmen were more likely than the seniors to portray the student as encountering clinical and/or academic problems. In the fellow student slide, both freshmen and seniors described nursing problems but the nursing problems described by the freshmen were more complex and technical than those described by seniors.[7] The observed patterns seem to be consistent with the interpretation that both freshmen and seniors are oriented to status but in different forms. The freshmen are more likely to carefully distinguish the head nurse from the nurse and to see themselves as being called in by the clinical instructor, someone with whom they frequently interact. The seniors, probably because of their own higher status, are more likely to see themselves as having contact with the director of nursing and are less concerned about drawing distinctions between head nurse and nurse. The seniors show a typical strategy in hierarchical status systems of enhancing one's own status by "misperceiving" the other's status, classifying higher status persons as more nearly like oneself or seeing oneself associating with higher status persons.

The fellow student slide revealed that the freshmen often see the student as having difficulty with procedures, e.g., setting up equipment, passing medications, etc., and in coping with patient problems—of either a specific or undefined nature.

"In this situation the freshman student was suppose to set up a tray for a doctor however being a student in the first year she hadn't been trained in what should be on the tray therefore she

had to rely on a junior student to have her set up the tray for her. . . ."
(Freshman)

The seniors, on the other hand, depict the type of assistance needed as being of a less complicated, less technical nature—e.g., request for information concerning where equipment was located, help in completing work more quickly with the assistance of the other student.

The freshmen see the student nurse as encountering a qualitatively different type of difficulty . . . a difficulty which reflects their relative inexperience in "doing procedure, handling patients, etc." A larger percentage of the freshmen who construct stories in which one student is seen as helping the other mention that the girl who seeks (or is given) help is a "freshman" and the girl who gives (or offers) help is a "senior."

In interacting with the supervisor-instructor (slide 8) the freshmen are more likely than the seniors to say the student was called in to discuss her clinical or academic work—primarily a difficulty she is experiencing in her work or a mistake she has made.

> "This student has had consistent trouble in managing one of her patients and it disturbs her very much. Today things were so bad that her instructor called her in to discuss the matter. . . ."
> (Freshman)

Furthermore, the freshmen are more likely to specifically mention that the instructor attempts to help, or succeeds in helping the student overcome her clinical and/or academic difficulties.

> "This is a familiar scene every student nurse goes through at one time or another.
> "The older woman in the picture is this girls instructor. She is explaining to the girl the things that she did wrong and how she can improve them.
> "The girl listens respectfully to her instructor and benefits from her advice. . . ."
> (Freshman)

In response to this slide, the seniors depict interactions which pertained to topics other than clinical or academic work—primarily concerning their future career in nursing.

"The student is about to end her training period and is now
ready to make application for a job. She has gone into her hospital director of nursing for final conference and application of a
position at her home hospital."
(Senior)

These findings indicate that the orientation of the freshmen
and seniors to the supervisor-instructor is very different. The
freshmen, being new to the school and to clinical experience,
are not yet sure of their ability to perform on the wards and in
classes. Many actually were having difficulties in their studies
and hospital work but had not yet dropped out of nursing school.
(Of this freshman class, some 27 girls dropped out within the
first two years, 17 in the first year, many classified as academic
failures.) Given the academic problems that develop in the first
year, a topic to discuss with their teachers and directors of nursing service would be their performance in the clinical or academic area. Among seniors, those who initially had scholastic
problems or difficulties adjusting to their clinical experience
would, in all probability, either have overcome these problems
by now or have dropped out of nursing school. The seniors now
present themselves as more knowledgeable, experienced and con-
fident. They are also oriented to their future after nursing school.[8]
In all the slides freshmen were more likely to describe the
student's thoughts, feelings or behavior as corresponding to what
the ideal nurse might be like. This includes statements which
indicate that (1) the student is willing and eager to perform
well and to learn correct nursing procedures and behavior, (2)
she actually does her work well or learns how to do so, (3) she
demonstrates a great deal of concern for her patient and may
even give him care which is "above-and-beyond the call of duty."
In discussing outcomes, freshmen make statements which indicated "an increased professional knowledge on the part of the
student," "good or successful performance" by the student in
her work, successful solving of problematic nursing situations,
good or better working relations with other staff members, improvement in the patient's condition, etc. There was also a slight
tendency in all the slides for the seniors to close the encounter
with statements which had a "negative professional connotation."
These outcomes consisted of statements which indicated that

the student disliked or was hostile toward the nursing profession or members of the nursing staff, that she blatantly deviated from the hospital or dormitory rules or that the student was doing her work poorly. Other "negative" outcomes with a professional connotation were patient oriented, e.g., the student would become upset about a patient in critical condition, or the patient's condition would become worse. Examples from the stories are:

Fellow Student Slide
"(1) Nurse c̄ back to us heard other nurse talking about her.
(2) She has confronted said nurse in med room to find out what she has been saying.
(3) They will argue, stop speaking to each other and not work in harmony."
(Senior)

Instructor-Director Slide
"The student broke a rule.
"The instructor is reprimanding her. The instructor is a most unpleasant person who is poor in her teaching and instruction on the divisions as well as having little tact c̄ her students.
"The student heard very little of what was said to her & left resenting the instructor."
(Senior)

R. N. Slide
"The student has worked hard all day. She is now ready to report off duty & giving the head nurse report. The head nurse informs the student of all the mistakes she has made during the day. The student leaves work disgusted with nursing. All she wanted was a simple 'thank you' for a hard day's work of trying to do everything to the best of her avail."
(Senior)

The finding that seniors not only write fewer stories with outcomes which are positive in their professional connotation, but also tend to write more stories which are negative gives additional support to the notion that changes occur in what has been termed idealism.

Conclusion and Discussion. These results in general show that in the variety of role relationships and situations depicted in the Role Projective Test, freshmen express a degree of idealism and optimism which is not found among seniors. Freshmen also show greater concern with the problems and difficulties of nursing practice, relationships with patients and problems faced in nursing school. However, their optimism pervades such encounters and their stories depict outcomes in which progress, satisfactory results, and favorable outcomes occur.

In relation to patients, seniors give more "technique oriented" than "patient centered" care, see patients more as "disease entities" than "whole" people with distinct personalities and devote less energy toward meeting patient needs in a creative and distinctive fashion.

In situations that are relatively undefined, i.e., student nurse alone, the less experienced freshmen see themselves as frightened, nervous, upset, embarrassed and unsure of themselves in performing and experiencing what eventually become normal nursing tasks. However, despite their insecurities they not only aspire to succeed but describe outcomes in which problems are resolved.

In relation to physicians and residents some of the stories reflect the growth of interest in heterosexual activities on the part of seniors. Seniors are less likely to have "crushes" and more likely to have "affairs." The realities of the status differences between themselves and physicians and residents enter into the perception by seniors of social interaction with orderlies and technicians, the same person who was previously seen as an intern.

With increased experience in the hospital, the senior is less likely to describe herself as a valuable contributor to the physician in providing better patient care.

In their interaction with fellow nurses seniors become better able to cope with the difficulties that freshmen sought help for, see themselves as more nearly equal in status to staff nurses, and become oriented to the future after nursing school.

The patterns observed are relevant for understanding the nursing student's perception of nursing. In learning to perform as a nurse, the student learns to vary her behavior in relation to particular others who are members of the role-set. She perceives others and herself in a manner appropriate to the performance of the role—as perceived in the particular situation—and, presumably, expects that others will validate that perception by producing acts that are consistent with her own perception. The neophyte, entering school and performing the nursing role for the first time, has as models the idealized versions depicted in literature, mass media, recruitment brochures and formal didactic materials such as textbooks. She perceives that nurses behave properly, are guided by the call of duty, make mistakes but recover, provide effective care to patients, serve as the physician's informant, learn to work with their fellow nurses and continue to develop skills and acquire knowledge that will make them more effective role performers. What is the meaning of these idealistic expressions? How are they modified by actual experiences?

Idealism has been regarded as functional for the recruitment of the student, and for sustaining him in the educational experience. The loss of idealism is problematic, then, if it serves to sustain motivation. What sources of sustaining motivation replace this? Becker *et al.* argue that a present orientation to making grades, learning what the faculty regards as important, in short, passing the course and formal requirements, substitute for the idealistic outlook found at time of entry.

However, a question can be raised concerning the motivational significance of these attitudes. Is it possible that idealistic views represent perceptions of the role which outsiders, because they cannot know what it is "to be" in the role, bring with them? Experience *in* the role rather than didactic teaching *about* the role, produces changed perceptions and, in a sense, a restructuring of the phenomenal world of the actor. The freshman or neophyte has only the definition of the role as presented in didactic teaching or popular attitudes as the basis for his perception; however, with experience, things are not the same as they were because the actor is no longer the same. He cannot perceive things in the same way because he has changed. He has come to "know" what it means to be an actual self, not a merely imagined self in the situation. Only after much experience does he achieve the internal re-organization of perception and understanding of the world-as-it-is. Obviously, if only a few experiences were all that it takes to achieve this, the teaching of adequate role-performance and the re-organization of a self in relation to that role would be easily done. But even longer term incumbents of a role do not necessarily perceive the world (i.e., the particular role-set in question) in identical fashion.

Formal training and education do not in and of themselves operate to produce such changes. Our understanding of the reshaping of the individual, of the production of a new self, is not adequate yet to permit us to say *how* this is achieved. We know that it does occur for some students in the course of their training and for others it may never occur to the extent that "experts" in the socialization of the neophyte would say "Now, there's a real ...." (substitute in the blank space the name of whatever role is being taught).

In short, we are proposing an alternative interpretation of the expression of "idealistic" or "realistic" attitudes concerning the role. Rather than assigning them motivational significance or assigning them values as attitudes or orientations which affect performance, we can view them as indicators of the extent of socialization, i.e., the learning of the role. The learning we have in mind includes a cognitive orientation to the world of nursing which involves treating that world as it is, seeing in it what is in fact in it, and developing a perspective that is congruent with the perspectives of other relevant actors in the situation such that they can, in fact, successfully interact with one another.[9]

Idealism can be interpreted to mean that the neophyte is aware of her present limitations and can only express the hope and expectation that these will be overcome. Such stories may also serve a wish-fulfillment and anxiety-reduction function. But we prefer to interpret their significance for socialization as meaning that the emerging self is seen as competent rather than incompetent, that a belief exists that events can be normalized and that "what to do" will become known and routine although it may not be so at the moment.

This interpretation can be extended to the several slides described here. The realism, and what sometimes appears to be "cynicism," concerning the nurse's tasks and duties and her interaction with patients, doctors and nurses, represents an awareness of events that do occur in the situation depicted. The senior shows that situations that were formerly difficult, disturbing or described as containing considerable diversity of activity become routine, understandable and easily dealt with. Novelty has also worn off and the only area in which it seems to remain is that involving sexual activities. As the work situation becomes routine it may also become less attractive to the practitioner. That this result could occur within three years and while the girl is still in school does not speak well for the development of an academic or professional interest or for an increased dedication to the role. The training program is, as Becker observed for medical school, something to "get through." For seniors, an orientation to the world of work and to life-after-school begins to offer the new experience and novelty which was originally associated with entering school. The re-assertion of a new idealism, oriented toward the practice of nursing and the world of work and marriage, rather than school, can be expected, much as Becker found for the senior medical student.

Viewed in this way, a succession of new experiences, scheduled sequentially and step-wise such that successful achievement in one is a necessary prerequisite for entry into another may be an effective way of maintaining the challenge that new situations and the awareness of a need to develop skills to cope with them sustain.[10]

In our view, these typifications which student nurses make of nursing or hospital scenes indicate a need for more attention to what the role is "really" like. If seniors' accounts are normalizations and routinizations of what were formerly difficult, uncomfortable, and challenging scenes, then the world as it is, for nurses, may need to be studied more closely. If their typifications are reflections of the degree of role-learning and the perception of life-as-it-is for those who perform the role as a daily activity then there may be a problem for nursing.

It is our conclusion that the "realistic" perception of life-as-it-is by these respondents and by other nurses and medical students who have been studied is problematic for the profession only to the extent that the features of the world perceived by the student are judged to be undesirable. The student's perception cannot be localized as a phenomenon internal to the student which is determined solely by individual characteristics. Such a judgment would lead to efforts to change the perceiving individual. Instead, the world-perceived may need to be re-structured so that the "undesirable" perceptions of it may also change. The dilemma with regard to strategies of change is that the individual's perceptions may harden into a set which affects subsequent perceptions of situations, even after they are changed, or which affects interaction in such a way as to lead the individual to "produce" the reality which he expects to find. Further, even subsequent efforts to re-socialize the individual may be difficult. With specific reference to nurses, the implication is that the effective point for change is during the initial formal socialization period, i.e., while they are still in nursing school. To the extent that the typifications discovered here are based on the students' experiences in the hospital as well as the nursing school, change would require modifications in both institutions.

NOTES

1. Becker, H. and Geer, B., "The Fate of Idealism in Medical School," *American Sociological Review*, 23 (1958), pp. 50-56.

2. Becker, H., *et al.*, *Boys in White*, Chicago: University of Chicago Press, 1961.

3. This test was developed by Albert F. Wessen and is described in Barber, W. H. and Wessen, A. F., "Perspective and Strategy in Nursing Role Research," unpublished manuscript. The numbers assigned to the slides represent the order in which they were presented. One slide (No. 4) given at the same time is omitted here because it could not be paired with any other. It depicted the student nurse with a visitor.

4. For example, assume that one dimension had five sub-categories. A protocol would be scored for only one of these sub-categories even though other sub-categories also appeared in the story. The decision as to which of the categories to score was made in terms of the following criteria: (1) if one of the sub-categories was, in the judgment of the scorer, the predominant theme or focus of the story, it would be scored; (2) if no one sub-category could be judged as a major theme or focus of the story, then the first mentioned category would be scored. For some dimensions, problems such as these did not occur because the sub-categories were mutually exclusive. For example, for the dimension, "who initiated the interaction," four sub-categories were used: (1) the student, (2) the other person in the slide, (3) someone not shown in the slide, and (4) no mention of who initiated the interaction or unable to determine.

5. For purposes of this analysis, all respondents who identified the young man as an orderly or technician were not included, since their position in the hospital status hierarchy was lower than interns, residents and medical students.

6. The differences between the professional relationships students have with physicians, on the one hand, and with interns (or residents or medical students), on the other hand, must be interpreted with caution due to the nature of the two slides. The fact that the intern had a laboratory bottle in his hands, while the physician had a stethoscope in his pocket but was holding nothing in his hands may have influenced the content of their "professional" interaction.

7. It must be noted that although all respondents described the

position of the person in the fellow student slide as a student nurse, there was some variation in the description of the nurse in the two other slides. On the supervisor-instructor slide the seniors are more likely to assign a higher status position to the nurse whereas on the R. N. slide it is the freshmen who more frequently describe the nurse as a head nurse or clinical instructor.

8. In response to the R. N. slide there were no major freshman-senior differences in the portrayal of the student as needing assistance in her clinical and/or academic work. However, as was true in the supervisor-instructor slide, the freshmen were more likely to specifically mention that the nurse attempted to help or succeeded in helping the student.

It may be noted also that the nature of the difficulty or problem experienced by the student is described as being of a more serious nature in the supervisor-instructor slide than in the other two. This is probably due to the fact that the scene takes place in the office of a superior rather than being one on the ward setting which is a more routine situation. To see a superior in her office is viewed as a special situation.

9. In some respects, this is consistent with the view of Becker *et al., op. cit.*, who hold that the perspective of the actor must be viewed in the context in which it appears. It differs in emphasis in that expressions of realism or "cynicism" are seen as indicators of successful socialization and of the adoption of relevant perspectives rather than as situational adaptations. These perspectives *are* the actor's view, i.e., the real self, though that self may later change.

10. I am grateful to Daniel V. Caputo for this suggestion.

The social invention called bureaucracy is probed and weighed by the author. His analysis does not stop here. Bennis proceeds to forecast organizational life in the next 25 to 50 years.

VIII

Beyond Bureaucracy*

WARREN BENNIS

MOST OF US SPEND ALL OF OUR WORKING DAY and a great deal of our non-working day in a unique and extremely durable social arrangement called "bureaucracy." I use the term "bureaucracy" descriptively, not as an epithet about those "guys in Washington" or as a metaphor *a la* Kafka's *Castle* which conjures up an image of red tape, or faceless and despairing masses standing in endless lines. Bureaucracy, as I shall use the term here, is a social invention, perfected during the industrial revolution to organize and direct the activities of the business firm.

It is my premise that the bureaucratic form of organization is becoming less and less effective; that it is hopelessly out of joint with contemporary realities; that new shapes, patterns, and models are emerging which promise drastic changes in the conduct of the corporation and of managerial practices in general. In the next 25 to 50 years we should witness, and participate in, the end of bureaucracy and the rise of new social systems better suited to twentieth century demands of industrialization. (Sociological evolutionists substantially agree that 25 to 50 years from now most people in the world will live in industrialized societies.)

Corsica, according to Gibbon, is much easier to deplore than to describe. The same holds true for bureaucracy. Basically, bureaucracy is a social invention which relies exclusively on the power to influence through rules, reason, and law. Max Weber, the German sociologist who developed the theory of bureaucracy around the turn of the century, once described bureaucracy as a social machine:

> Bureaucracy is like a modern judge who is a vending machine into which the pleadings are inserted together with the fee and which then disgorges the judgment together with its reasons mechanically derived from the code.

The bureaucratic "machine model" Weber outlined was developed as a reaction against the personal subjugation, nepotism, cruelty, emotional vicissitudes, and capricious judgment which passed for managerial practices in the early days of the industrial revolution. The true hope for man, it was thought, lay in his ability to rationalize, calculate, to use his head as well as his hands and heart. Thus, in the bureaucratic system social roles were institutionalized and reinforced by legal tradition rather than by the "cult of personality"; rationality and predictability were sought for in order to eliminate chaos and unanticipated consequences; emphasis was placed on technical competence rather than arbitrary or "iron whims." These are oversimplifications, to be sure, but contemporary analysts of organizations would tend to agree with them. In fact, there is a general consensus that the anatomy of bureaucracy consists of the following "organs":

- a division of labor based on functional specialization.
- a well-defined hierarchy of authority.
- a system of rules covering the rights and duties of employees.
- a system of procedures for dealing with work situations.
- impersonality of interpersonal relations.
- promotion and selection based on technical competence.

It does not take great critical imagination to detect the flaws and problems in the bureaucratic model. We have all *experienced* them:

- bosses without (and underlings with) technical competence.
- arbitrary and zany rules.
- an underworld (or informal) organization which subverts or even replaces the formal apparatus.

- confusion and conflict among roles.
- cruel treatment of subordinates based not on rational or legal grounds but upon inhumanity.

The tremendous range of unanticipated consequences provides a gold mine of material for comics like Charlie Chaplin and Jacques Tati who capture with a smile or a shrug the absurdity of authority systems based on pseudo-logic and inappropriate rules.

Almost everybody, including many observers of organizational behavior, approaches bureaucracy with a chip on his shoulder. It has been attacked for many reasons: for theoretical confusion and contradictions; for moral and ethical reasons; on practical grounds such as its inefficiency; for methodological weaknesses; for containing too many implicit values and for containing too few. I have recently catalogued the criticisms of bureaucracy and they outnumber and outdo the ninety-five theses tacked on the church door at Wittenberg in attacking another bureaucracy. A small sample of these:

(1) Bureaucracy does not adequately allow for personal growth and the development of mature personalities.
(2) It develops conformity and "group-think."
(3) It does not take into account the "informal organization" and the emergent and unanticipated problems.
(4) Its systems of control and authority are hopelessly outdated.
(5) It has no adequate juridical process.
(6) It does not possess adequate means for resolving differences and conflicts between ranks, and most particularly, between functional groups.
(7) Communication (and innovative ideas) are thwarted or distorted due to hierarchical divisions.
(8) The full human resources of bureaucracy are not being utilized due to mistrust, fear of reprisals, etc.
(9) It cannot assimilate the influx of new technology or scientists entering the organization.
(10) It modifies personality structure so that people become and reflect the dull, gray, conditioned "organization man."

Max Weber, the developer of the theory of bureaucracy, came around to condemn the apparatus he helped immortalize. While he felt that bureaucracy was inescapable, he also thought it might strangle the spirit of capitalism or the entrepreneurial attitude, a theme which Schumpeter later developed. And in a debate on bureaucracy Weber once said, more in sorrow than in anger:

> It is horrible to think that the world could one day be filled with nothing but those little cogs, little men clinging to little jobs and striving towards bigger ones—a state of affairs which is to be seen once more, as in the Egyptian records, playing an ever-increasing part in the spirit of our present administrative system, and especially of its offspring, the students. This passion for bureaucracy . . . is enough to drive one to despair. It is as if in politics . . . we were deliberately to become men who need "order" and nothing but order, who become nervous and cowardly if for one moment this order wavers, and helpless if they are torn away from their total incorporation in it. That the world should know no men but these: it is such an evolution that we are already caught up in, and the great question is therefore not how we can promote and hasten it, but what can we oppose to this machinery in order to keep a portion of mankind free from this parcelling-out of the soul, from this supreme mastery of the bureaucratic way of life.

In what ways has bureaucracy been modified over the years in order to cope more successfully with the problems that beset it? Before answering that, we have to say something about the nature of organizations, *all* organizations, from mass production leviathans all the way to service industries such as the university or hospital. Organizations are primarily complex, goal-seeking units. In order to survive they must also accomplish the secondary tasks of (1) maintaining their internal system and co-ordinating the "human side of enterprise"—a process of mutual compliance here called *reciprocity*—and (2) adapting to and shaping the external environment—here called *adaptability*. These two organizational dilemmas can help us to organize the pivotal ways in which the bureaucratic mechanism has been altered—and found wanting.

Reciprocity primarily covers the processes which can mediate conflict between the goals of management and the individual goals of the workers. Over the past several decades a number of interesting theoretical and practical resolutions have been made which truly allow for conflict and mediation of interest. They revise, if not transform, the very nature of the bureaucratic mechanism by explicit recognition of the inescapable tension between individual and organizational goals. These theories can be called, variously, *exchange, group, value, structural, situational*—depending on what variable of the situation one wishes to modify.

The *exchange* theories postulate that wages, incomes, and services are given to the individual for an equal contribution to the organization in work. If the inducements are not adequate, men may withdraw and work elsewhere. This may be elaborated upon by regarding "payments" to individuals as including motivational units. That is to say, the organization provides a psychological anchor in times of rapid social change and a hedge against personal loss, as well as position, growth and mastery, success experience, and so forth—in exchange for energy, work, commitment.

Management tends to interpret motivation in economic terms. Man is logical; man acts in the manner which serves his self-interest; man is competitive. Elton Mayo and his associates were among the first to see human *affiliation* as a motivating force, to view industrial organization as a *social* system as well as an economic-technical system. A manager, they stated, should be judged in terms of his ability to sustain cooperation. In fact, once a cohesive, primary work group is seen as a motivating force, a managerial elite may become obsolete, and the work group itself becomes the decision maker. This allows decisions to be made at the most relevant point of the organization, where the data are most available.

Before this becomes possible, however, some theorists believe that the impersonal *value* system of bureaucracy must be modified. In this case the manager plays an important role as the instrument of change in interpersonal relations. He must instill values which permit and reinforce the expression of feeling, experimentalism, and norms of individuality, trust, and concern. Management, according to R. R. Blake, is successful insofar as it maximizes a "concern for people"—with "concern for production."

Others believe that a new conception of the *structure* of bureaucracy will create more relevant attitudes towards the function of management than formal role specifications now do. If the organization is seen as organic rather than mechanistic, as adapting spontaneously to its needs, then decisions will be made at the critical point and roles and jobs will devolve on the "natural" organizational incumbent. The shift would probably be from the individual level to cooperative group effort, from delegated to shared responsibility, from centralized to decentralized authority, from obedience to confidence, from antagonistic arbitration to problem-solving. Management centered upon problem-solving, that assumes or relaxes authority according to task demands, has most concerned some theorists who are as much interested in an organization's success and productivity as in its social system.

However, on all sides we find a growing belief that the effectiveness of bureaucracy should be evaluated by human *situation* as well as economic criteria. Social satisfaction and personal growth of employees must be considered as well as the productivity and profit of the organization. The criticism and revisions of the bureaucratic organization tend to concentrate on the internal system and its human components. But although it appears on the surface that the case against bureaucracy has to do with its ethical-moral posture and the social fabric, the real *coup de grace* has come from the environment.

Bureaucracy thrives in a highly competitive, undifferentiated and stable environment, such as the climate of its youth, the Industrial Revolution. A pyramidal structure of authority, with power concentrated in the hands of a few with the knowledge and resources to control an entire enterprise was, and is, an eminently suitable social arrangement for routinized tasks.

However, the environment has changed in just those ways which make the mechanism most problematic. Stability has vanished. As Ellis Johnson said, ". . . the once-reliable constants have now become galloping variables."

The factors accelerating change include:

- the growth of science, research and development activities, and intellectual technology.

- the increase of transactions with social institutions (and their importance in conducting the enterprise)—including government, distributors and consumers, shareholders, competitors, raw material and power suppliers, sources of employees (particularly managers), trade unions, and groups within the firms. There is also more interdependence between the economic and other facets of society, leading to greater complications of legislation and public regulation.

- competition between firms diminishing as their fates intertwine and become positively correlated.

My argument so far, to summarize quickly, is that the first assault on bureaucracy arose from its incapacity to manage the tension between individual and management goals. However, this conflict is somewhat mediated by the growth of a new ethic of productivity which includes personal growth and/or satisfaction. The second and more major shock to bureaucracy is caused by the scientific and technological revolution. It is the requirement of *adaptability* to the environment which leads to the predicted demise of bureaucracy and to the collapse of management as we know it now.

A forecast falls somewhere between a prediction and a prophecy. It lacks the divine guidance of the latter and the empirical foundation of the former. On thin empirical ice, I want to set forth some of the conditions that will dictate organizational life in the next 25 to 50 years.

- THE ENVIRONMENT. Those factors already mentioned will continue in force and increase. Rapid technological change and diversification will lead to interpenetration of the government—its legal and economic policies—with business. Partnerships between industry and government (like Telstar) will be typical. And because of the immensity and expense of the projects, there will be fewer identical units competing for the same buyers and sellers. Or, in reverse, imperfect competition leads to an oligopolistic and government-business controlled economy. The three main features of the environment will be (1) interdependence rather than competition, (2) turbulence rather than steadiness, and (3) large scale rather than small enterprises.

- POPULATION CHARACTERISTICS. We are living in what Peter Drucker calls the "educated society," and I think this is the most distinctive characteristic of our times. Within fifteen years, two-thirds of our population living in metropolitan areas will have attended college. Adult education programs, especially the management development courses of such universities as M.I.T., Harvard, and Stanford, are expanding and adding intellectual breadth. All this, of course, is not just "nice," but necessary. For as Secretary of Labor Wirtz has pointed out, computers can do the work of most high school graduates—cheaper and more effectively. Fifty years ago education used to be regarded as "non-work" and intellectuals on the payroll (and many of the staff) were considered "overhead." Today, the survival of the firm depends, more than ever before, on the proper exploitation of brain power.

One other characteristic of the population which will aid our understanding of organizations of the future is increasing job mobility. The lowered expense and ease of transportation, coupled with the real needs of a dynamic environment, will change drastically the idea of "owning" a job—or "having roots," for that matter. Participants will be shifted from job to job and even employer to employer with much less fuss than we are accustomed to.

▪ WORK VALUES. The increased level of education and mobility will change the values we hold about work. People will be more intellectually committed to their jobs and will probably require more involvement, participation, and autonomy in their work. (This turn of events is due to a composite of the following factors: (1) positive correlation between a person's education and his need for autonomy; (2) job mobility places the educated in a position of greater influence in the system; (3) job requirements call for more responsibility and discretion.)

Also, people will tend to be more "other-directed" in their dealings with others. David McClelland's studies suggest that as industrialization increases, "other-directedness" increases; so we will tend to rely more heavily on temporary social arrangements, on our immediate and constantly changing colleagues.

▪ TASKS AND GOALS. The tasks of the firm will be more technical, complicated, and unprogrammed. They will rely more on the intellect than muscle. And they will be too complicated for one person to handle or for individual supervision. Essentially, they will call for the collaboration of specialists in a project or team form of organization.

Similarly there will be a complication of goals. "Increased profits" and "raised productivity" will sound like oversimplifications and cliches. Business will concern itself increasingly with its adaptive or innovative-creative capacity. In addition, *meta*-goals will have to be articulated and developed; that is, supra-goals which shape and provide the foundation for the goal structure. For example, one meta-goal might be a system for detecting new and changing goals; another could be a system for deciding priorities among goals.

Finally, there will be more conflict and contradiction among diverse standards of organizational effectiveness, just as in hospitals and universities today there is conflict between teaching and research. The reason for this is the increased number of professionals involved, who tend to identify as much with the supra-goals of their profession as with those of their immediate employer. University professors can be used as a case in point. More and more of their income comes from outside sources, such as private or public foundations and consultant work. They tend not to make good "company men" because they are divided in their loyalty to professional values and organizational demands.

▪ ORGANIZATION. The social structure of organizations of the future will have some unique characteristics. The key word will be "temporary"; there will be adaptive, rapidly changing *temporary systems*. These will be "task forces" organized around problems-to-be-solved. The problems will be solved by groups of relative strangers who represent a set of diverse professional skills. The groups will be arranged on organic rather than mechanical models; they will evolve in response to a problem rather than to programmed role expectations. The "executive" thus becomes a coordinator or "linking pin" between various task forces. He must be a man who can speak the diverse languages of research, with skills to relay information and to mediate between groups. *People will be differentiated not vertically, according to rank and role, but flexibly and functionally according to skill and professional training.*

Adaptive, problem-solving, temporary systems of diverse specialists, linked together by coordinating and task evaluating specialists in an organic flux—this is the organizational form that will gradually replace bureaucracy as we know it. As no catchy phrase comes to mind, let us call this an *organic-adaptive* structure.

As an aside—what will happen to the rest of society, to the manual laborers, to the less educated, to those who desire to work under conditions of high authority, and so forth? Many such jobs will disappear; other jobs will be automated. However, there will be a corresponding growth in the service-type occupations, such as those in the "war on poverty" and the Peace Corps programs. In times of change, where there is a discrepancy between cultures, when industrialization and especially urbanization proceeds rapidly, the market for men with training and skill in human interaction increases. We might guess that approximately 40 per cent of the population would be involved in jobs of this nature, 40 per cent in technological jobs, with a 20 per cent bureaucratic minority.

▪ MOTIVATION. Our above discussion of "reciprocity" indicated the shortcomings of bureaucracy in maximizing employee effectiveness. The "organic-adaptive" structure should increase motivation, and thereby effectiveness, because it enhances satisfactions intrinsic to the task. There is a harmony between the educated individual's need for meaningful, satisfactory, and creative tasks and a flexible organizational structure.

Of course, where the reciprocity problem is ameliorated, there are corresponding tensions between the individual's involvement in his professional community and his involvement in his employing organization. Professionals are notoriously "disloyal" to organizational demands.

There will, however, also be reduced commitment to work groups, for these groups, as I have already mentioned, will be transient and changing. While skills in human interaction will become more important, due to the growing needs for collaboration in complex tasks, there will be a concomitant reduction in group cohesiveness. I would predict that in the organic-adaptive system people will have to learn to develop quick and intense relationships on the job, and learn to bear the loss of more enduring work relationships.

In general I do not agree with Clark Kerr, Harold Leavitt, and others in their emphasis on a "New Bohemianism" in which leisure—not work—becomes the emotional-creative sphere of life. They assume a technological slow-down and leveling off, and a stabilizing of social mobility. This may happen in a society of the distant future. But long before then we will face the challenge of creating the new service-type organizations with an organic-adaptive structure.

Jobs in the next century should become more rather than less involving; man is a problem-solving animal and the tasks of the future guarantee a full agenda of problems. In addition, the adaptive process itself may become captivating to many. At the same time, I think that the future I described is not necessarily a "happy" one. Coping with rapid change, living in the temporary work systems, setting up (in quick-step time) meaningful relations—and then breaking them—all augur social strains and psychological tensions. Learning how to live with ambiguity and to be self-directing will be the task of education and the goal of maturity.

In these new organizations, participants will be called on to use their minds more than at any other time in history. Fantasy, imagination, and creativity will be legitimate in ways that today seem strange. Social structures will no longer be instruments of psychic repression but will increasingly promote play and freedom on behalf of curiosity and thought. I agree with Herbert Marcuse's thesis in *Eros and Civilization* that the necessity of repression and the suffering derived from it, decreases with the maturity of the civilization.

Not only will the problem of adaptability be overcome through the organic-adaptive structure, but the problem we started with, reciprocity, will be resolved. Bureaucracy, with its "surplus repression," was a monumental discovery for harnessing muscle power *via* guilt and instinctual renunciation. In today's world, it is a lifeless crutch that is no longer useful. For we now require structures of freedom to permit the expression of play and imagination and to exploit the new pleasure of work.

THE THIRD DIVISION

INSTITUTIONS and SOCIAL ORDER

INSTITUTIONS and SOCIAL ORDER

MAN INTERACTS IN THE MOST BASIC of groups called a dyad. Within that miniature social system the individual acts and is acted upon with the other members. These interactions are conditioned by the self, the group, and the total social environment. These patterned behavioral responses are formed from and are forming a system of rules called the normative system. Contained within this interactional system are roles and statuses. This total patterned interaction is called culture. The word culture refers to the basic "stuff," namely, the beliefs, values, and material products transmitted to the individual during the continuous process of socialization. The content of culture (i.e., the different types of values, beliefs, or priority attached to them) varies from culture to culture. Nevertheless, each culture, if it is to endure, must contain some unique values and beliefs of its own, which are not necessarily shared with other cultures.

Such a system of values and beliefs, together with its associated normative system, provides powerful support to the formation and perpetuation of certain social entities. These entities, through which all societies transmit their culture, are defined as social institutions. They are enduring phenomena in the social order, and weave socialization and culture inextricably together that they might continue to infuse a world of meaning and sense of self to each newly arrived "guest."

*The effect of educational attainment on adult oc-
cupational status is often exaggerated, but higher
education is nonetheless an important route to a
good job. The middle class have always made disproportionate use of this tool for self-advancement,
and the gap is not narrowing. The role of tuition
charges and academic tests in maintaining the middle-class advantage is not as great as many suppose;
class differences in motivation probably play the
decisive role. Even if access to higher education
became more equal, however, this would not necessarily make American life more satisfactory. The
central problem seems to be inequality, not immo-
bility, and while the two are closely related, measures intended to achieve one may not promote the
other.*

IX

Social Stratification and Higher Education*

CHRISTOPHER JENCKS

THE RELATIONSHIP BETWEEN EDUCATION and the American social
structure poses two distinct questions. The first is the effect of
mass education on the relative size of various social strata and on
the social, cultural, and economic *distances* between these strata.
The second is the effect of education on the *rate of mobility*
between social strata, both within a single lifetime and over
several generations. This article is almost entirely concerned with
the effects of higher education on social mobility, but such an

* Christopher Jencks, "Social Stratification and Higher Education," *Harvard Educational Review*, 38, Spring 1968, 277-316. Copyright © 1968 by
President and Fellows of Harvard College.

An earlier draft of this article will appear in *The Academic Revolution*,
written by myself and David Riesman and scheduled for publication in
May, 1968. I am enormously indebted to my co-author for painstaking comments and editorial suggestions, and also to the editors of the *Harvard Edu-*

151

analysis is necessarily predicated on certain assumptions about
the changing size and distance between social strata. A brief
summary of these assumptions is therefore necessary.

Distribution of Education and Income

There are virtually no statistics on the distribution of education before the Civil War, and statistics for the period between
the Civil War and World War I are full of puzzling inconsisten-
cies.[1] Nonetheless, some trends are fairly clear. According to the
1940 census, the typical individual born in 1860 had completed
the eighth grade, while the typical individual born forty years
later was still not quite a ninth-grade alumnus. The annual increase in median attainment for those leaving school between
1875 and 1914, in other words, averaged 0.25 per cent. During
the next two decades the annual increase in median attainment
was *ten times as fast:* 2.5 per cent per year. Whereas those leaving
school during World War I had not typically finished the ninth
grade, those leaving at the end of the Depression typically had
a high school diploma. After the outbreak of World War II the
rate of increase in median attainment reverted to its pre-1918
level, at about 0.25 per cent per year. The typical American today completes only about half a year more school than his father
who finished his schooling during the 1930's. This may seem
somewhat surprising in view of the much publicized expansion
of higher education since 1945, but this expansion has not yet
affected anything like the same proportion of the population as
did the expansion of secondary education during the 1920's and
1930's.

cational Review for help in cutting the earlier draft to its present
size. Alexander Astin of the American Council on Education, C. Arnold
Anderson of the University of Chicago, Samuel Bowles, André Daniere,
and Humphrey Doermann, all of Harvard University, Bruce Eckland of the
University of North Carolina, Abbott Ferriss of the Russell Sage Foundation,
John Folger of the Commission on Human Resources, Seymour Harris of
the University of California at San Diego, Charles Nam of Florida State
University, Frederick Rudolph of Williams College, Charles Silberman of
Fortune, William Spady of Harvard University, Sidney Spivak of Princeton
University, Arthur Waskow of the Institute for Policy Studies, and Finis
Welch of Southern Methodist University made indispensable criticisms of
earlier drafts of the manuscript. The Carnegie Corporation and the Samuel
Rubin Foundation both supported part of my work on these problems, but
they are of course in no way responsible for my conclusions.

The jump in median attainment between 1920 and 1940 may or may not have been accompanied by a redistribution of educational resources and results.[2] But it does seem to have been accompanied by a significant change in the shape of the American class structure. I use the word "seems" advisedly, for there is no general agreement about how to measure such changes. My conclusion is based on the assumption that every social stratum continually tries to maximize its share of the national income. I therefore view a group's success in this competition as a crude index of its power relative to other groups. Not only is income a good *index* of a group's power, it is also the *basis* for many kinds of power and privilege. Hence, if a society is becoming more egalitarian—if the distance between social strata is declining, or if the top and bottom strata are shrivelling up while the middle strata expand—one would expect the distribution of income to become more equitable. If, on the other hand, a society is becoming less egalitarian—if the distance between various social strata is becoming greater, or if the top and bottom strata are expanding at the expense of the middle—one would expect the distribution of income to become less equitable. Little reliable data is available on the income distribution in America before 1929, but the available evidence suggests that the distribution was about the same in 1914 and 1929.[3] Between 1929 and 1945 there was an apparently permanent redistribution away from the upper towards the middle strata. The share of national income going to the richest 5 per cent of the population fell from about 30 per cent to about 20 per cent in this period. On the other hand, the share of the national income going to the poorest 20 per cent of the population does not appear to have changed significantly between 1929 to 1945. Since 1945 there has been no significant redistribution at any level.[4]

Educators may incline towards the belief that there was a causal relationship between the jump in median educational attainment during the 1920's and 1930's and the redistribution of income away from the rich during the 1930's and 1940's. Others would probably prefer to view redistribution as a by-product of the Depression and World War II. So little is known about the determinants of income distribution that this argument cannot now be settled. Fortunately, however, the cause of the change is not centrally important to the discussion of *higher* education. The changes in educational attainment in the 1920's and 1930's were largely at the secondary level. Dramatic changes in the proportion of youngsters entering college came later, and they have had no apparent effect on the distribution of income. (The proportion of all young people entering college increased an average of 1 per cent each year between 1945 and 1965, yet the distribution of income was quite stable in this period.) For analytic purposes I will therefore assume that mass higher education has *no* significant effect on the size of various social strata.[5] Beginning from this premise I will look at the relationship between higher education and individual mobility between strata. The analysis includes both a review of quantitative evidence and discussion of some relationships which either have not been or cannot be examined empirically.[6]

Higher Education and Adult Social Status

The relationship between college attendance and adult social status is often somewhat exaggerated. A significant fraction of those who go to college do quite poorly in economic terms. In 1960, for example, about a fifth of the adult male labor force had completed one year of college. Less than half of this *best-educated* elite was also in the *best-paid* fifth of the labor force. A quarter of this educational elite earned less than the national average. At the other end of the scale, many of those who never enter college do quite well for themselves, especially in business. About a quarter of the adult male labor force had not completed even elementary school in 1960. Yet a fifth of these semi-literates were earning more than the national average.[7] The relationship between education and occupation is equally loose, with only about half the occupational elite also being part of the academic elite. (Three-quarters of those holding "professional, technical, and kindred" jobs in 1960 had finished a year of college, but only a third of all "managers, officials, and proprietors" had done so.[8]) This relationship can be summarized by saying that if we know men's educational attainment (i.e., the number of years of school they have completed) we can account for about 35 per cent of the variation in their occupational statuses.[9]

These gross estimates are, of course, based entirely on the *quantity* of education men have had. They ignore *quality*. Yet the two tend to be quite closely associated. Men who attended good suburban high schools have in most cases also gone to college, whereas men who attended poor rural schools seldom have done so. Similarly, attending a "good" college is usually associated with attending some sort of graduate school, while attending a "poor" college usually means dropping out or at most settling for a BA. The net result is that quantity and quality are probably quite highly correlated. Still, the multiple correlation of occupation with *both* quantity *and* quality of education would inevitably be higher than the simple correlation between occupation and quantity of education alone.

The major question, however, is not whether education really explains, say, 40 per cent of the variance in men's occupational statuses rather than 35 per cent, but whether this statistical "explanation" is also a causal one. We know, for example, that well-educated men tend to have relatively affluent parents. We must therefore assume that the occupational advantage of the well-educated derives partly from the fact that they are also well-connected. Fortunately, we have data which allow us to estimate the magnitude of this distortion quite precisely. The typical man who finishes college but does not enter graduate school today stands about one standard deviation above the national mean for educational attainment. Such a man can be expected to end up six-tenths of a standard deviation above the occupational mean. But this archetypal BA comes from a family whose educational and occupational level is almost half a standard deviation above the national mean. In order to isolate the effect of education we must look at atypical BA's: men whose families stood in the middle of the *national* pecking order and hence well *below* the mean for college graduates. Such men typically end up 0.52 deviations above the occupational mean instead of 0.60 deviations. Almost a seventh of the apparent effect of education thus turns out to be an effect of parental background.[10]

Many other factors may also inflate the statistical association between education and occupation far above the causal relationship. Genetic differences between individuals, for example, affect health, physical strength and energy, intellectual competence, and perhaps even personality. Family experience also affects these and many other human differences. Assets or liabilities of this kind presumably affect both educational attainment and subsequent occupational status. Indeed, factors of this kind presumably explain most of the variance in both occupational status and educational attainment. We do not, however, have any data which allow us to partial out the effect of these factors as we did the effect of socio-economic background.

Even if we were to isolate the unique causal effect of educational attainment on occupational status, we would still not be sure *why* attainment was important. Educational attainment has two distinct kinds of impact on life chances. The first can be called the "socialization effect" and involves actual changes in the student's skills, attitudes, interests, and so forth. The second can be called the "certification effect" and consists not of changing the student but of certifying to the world that the student already has certain skills, attitudes, or whatever.[11] For present purposes, however, these two effects need not be distinguished.

The foregoing discussion suggests that education in general, and higher education in particular, play a limited role in determining men's adult social positions. Nonetheless, educational attainment is by far the most powerful *measurable* determinant of occupational status. It explains more than twice as much of the variance in men's occupational status as family background, for example.[12] While we should be wary of assuming that access to higher education has a decisive causal effect on a man's chances of upward or downward mobility, it seems fairly likely that it does have some effect.[13] There is also some inconclusive evidence that the relationship between educational attainment and occupational status may be slowly tightening.[14] Furthermore, even if education in general is no better correlated with occupational status than in the past, college graduation may be growing more important in securing a good job. High school used to be the great sieve separating the well-educated from the poorly educated. Those who earned high school diplomas had a decisive advantage over those who lacked a diploma in securing white-collar jobs. Today almost everyone finishes high school, and college has come to play a somewhat larger role in sorting and sifting.[15] Yet even this trend may be more apparent than real, reflecting rapid expansion of nominally professional jobs like teaching, which have fairly strict educational prerequisites but modest status and income. When we examine the relative *earnings* of different educational groups at various times, we find little evidence that higher education is becoming more important.[16] Whatever the trend, it is clearly slower than most people suppose, and is not likely to affect the basic character of the relationship dramatically in the foreseeable future.[17]

We can sum up the relationship between higher education and adult social status in a metaphor. Academicians are often called the gatekeepers of the upper-middle class. This is a useful *half* truth. The straightest and best marked paths to affluence and influence undoubtedly pass through academic institutions. There are, however, more than two thousand of these institutions in America, so that a man who gets rejected by one set of gate-keepers has a pretty good chance of finding another set who will let him by. Not only that, but the walls on either side of the gates are quite low, and those who have a reasonable amount of stamina and cunning can usually scale them even if they do not have the gatekeepers' approval.

Selection for Higher Education

America is not supposed to have a fixed class-structure such that only a limited number of people can make it up the ladder. It is supposed to be a land of unlimited opportunity, in which anyone can make it if he "has what it takes." Everyone is sup-posed to have an opportunity to follow the road to the top as far as he can, falling by the wayside only when he loses heart or his footing. This mythology serves an important purpose. It implies that if a man does not make it to the position he wants it is his own fault, not the fault of "the system." If colleges are to serve as gatekeepers, they must play their role in a way which is consonant with such mythology. They cannot refuse to admit large numbers of students or flunk them out and tell them never to return. If they did, the rejects would feel that their ambitions had been blocked by a particular identifiable group, namely the academicians who judged them inadequate, and they might mo-bilize politically to alter the system. To avoid this, selection must be carried on in a low-key way which gives the student at least the illusion of making his own choices. In Erving Goffman's terminology, the student must be "cooled out," not flunked out.[18]

The American attempt to make students leave the system "vol-untarily" has been quite successful. Most high school seniors, for example, see a BA as a passport to the good life, and most would like to have one. Yet only half the nation's high school graduates ever enter college. Some of the rest would like to go but do not meet the academic requirements of any college they know. Oth-ers cannot find a way to meet the cost of such a college. Some students in both these categories doubtless feel that they have been denied a fair chance and that the system is rigged against them. But as I will try to show in due course, students of this sort are exceptional. Most high school graduates who fail to enter college do not really want to go. They find schoolwork difficult and disagreeable, or they find the social life associated with schooling unpleasant. They assume college will be more of the same, or worse, and they are willing to revise their career goals downward in order to avoid four years of presumptive misery. Such students may later regret the fact that they cannot get the kind of job, the kind of income, or the kind of social position they would like, and they may blame this on their lack of schooling. But they also tend to feel that it was their own fault they did not persevere. Since they think their lack of education reflects their own inadequacy, they are slow to attack the system for rationing good jobs on the basis of academic credentials. They mostly just tell their children to work harder and "amount to something."

Voluntarism looms even larger in selection after students enter college. Roughly half those who enter never finish. Some, of course, are "dropouts" only in the technical sense, having entered two-year colleges without expecting to earn a BA. But most start out planning to earn a BA and then lower their sights.[19] Yet these students almost never fail in the literal sense of getting too many F's and being told to withdraw. They are almost all eased out rather than thrown out.[20] The most direct way of doing this is for the college to tell the student that he is doing badly, that he is unlikely to survive the course, and that he would be wise to drop out or transfer now, while his record is still clean, rather than waiting until he has a collection of F's on his transcript. In many cases, however, no college official needs to tell the student this; the student figures it out for himself and acts accordingly, transferring into an easier program (such as Education), an easier college (often a public institution near home), the job market, the army, or the arms of the first prospective husband who comes along. In other cases the student may be doing fairly well academically but may find the psychological pressures of a relatively competitive, unsupportive, or unfriendly institution so great that he prefers to drop out rather than soldier on. Or the student may simply be bored by academic routines and unwilling to do work that means nothing to him simply to advance his career or placate his elders. Whatever the reasons for his departure, however, they are likely to be his own creation, not somebody else's. He may end up resenting a college for having made him feel miserable or inadequate, but he will not end up with the kind of grievance that can be readily translated into a direct political attack on the system. (Such resentment can, of course, be indirectly exploited for all sorts of political ends.)

All this emphasis on voluntarism helps blunt political attacks on the gatekeepers, but the fact remains that some people end up with a college's stamp of approval while others do not, and that the BA's have a significant socioeconomic advantage over the non-BA's. Not only that, but this voluntaristic selection system bestows its benefits on young people raised in prosperous and well-educated homes considerably more often than it does on young people raised in impoverished or poorly educated homes. If it did not, it probably would not be allowed to endure.

When we look at the relationship between paternal status and the number of years of schooling a son gets, we find that the fathers' occupations and education explain about 20 per cent of the variance in their sons' attainments. Or to put it another way, a man normally passes along about 44 per cent of his educational or occupational advantage to his sons, in the form of better-than-average education. This means, for example, that a father who stands in the 84th percentile of both the educational and occupational distributions will typically find that his sons end up in the 67th percentile of the educational distribution. (A father also passes along about 44 per cent of his disadvantage to his children, so that if the father stands in the 16th percentile of the educational and occupational distributions his sons typically end up in the 33rd percentile of the educational distribution.[21] These relationships did not change significantly between the generation born 1897-1906 and the one born 1927-1936.

Using these basic parameters we can estimate the socioeconomic background of college graduates at any particular moment over the past forty years. If we begin with men who graduated from college in the 1920's, we find that they represented the best-educated 8 per cent of their generation. This means that the typical college graduate's father should have stood in the 78th percentile of the educational and occupational distributions. If we then turn to men graduating from college in the 1950's, we find that they constituted the best-educated 17 per cent of their generation. Being a less elite group they should have had somewhat less elite fathers, typically standing at the 73rd rather than the 78th percentile in the educational and occupational distributions.[22]

These predictions assume the relationship between social background and educational attainment is not only stable over time but linear. If, for example, the proportion of men entering graduate school today is comparable to the proportion finishing college a generation ago (which is roughly true), this formula automatically equates the social background of today's first-year graduate students with the background of yesterday's college seniors. Similarly, if the proportion of young men entering college today is comparable to the proportion graduating from high school a generation ago (which it is), this formula presumes that today's college freshmen are neither more nor less advantaged than yesterday's high school seniors. Is this really true? We have indicated that the simple correlation between a father's social status and the number of years of school his sons complete has been stable since the 1920's. But this overall finding could mask important changes. Suppose, for example, that we imagine a society in which "the masses" control the secondary schools while "the classes" control higher education. The masses would presumably take steps to democratize the secondary schools (e.g., by keeping them tuition-free and eliminating academic requirements for promotion). But if these policies led to everyone's finishing secondary school, "the classes" would presumably respond by making selection for higher education *more* class-related. These two changes would make the relationship between background and attainment less linear, but they might not affect the regression coefficient of attainment on background. It is therefore important to check our predictions against actual background data for college students at specific periods of history.

When we do this, we find that the general formula predicts specific findings quite accurately. The typical BA in the 1920's had a father in the 78th percentile of the education distribution, just as we predicted. The typical BA in the 1950's had a father in the 75th percentile of his generation, whereas the formula predicted the 73rd percentile.[23] When we turn to the occupational distribution of fathers of BA's, our findings are also consistent with the general formula.[24] Given the crudity of the data involved, the results are very close to what we would expect if there had been no basic change in the relationship between family background and educational changes over the past forty years.[25]

Certain implications of these findings deserve particular attention, for taken in isolation they can easily be misinterpreted. If, for example, we were to ignore changes in the class background of high school graduates and simply ask how class affects the typical graduate's chances of getting to college, we would conclude that class was much more important than it used to be. There has also been a dramatic increase in the relation between class background and a given freshman's chances of graduating.[26] But this fact must be viewed in the context of changes in the relative importance of high schools and colleges as agencies of social selection. As high schools become nearly universal, graduation from them automatically becomes less class-related; and as colleges draw from this unselected pool, their recruitment and sifting process must become more class-related if the overall relation between class background and attainment is to remain stable. If the high school does not screen out or deflect the ambitions of a fair number of upwardly mobile boys, and if employers continue to look to education to do this job, the burden will fall on the colleges. If they refuse to carry it and instead offer BA's to all, the burden will shift to the graduate schools. (I assume here that any meritocratic screening system will also be class related—an assumption discussed in more detail later.)

A second point which must be emphasized is that class background has far less effect on educational attainment than other factors. If, for example, we look at the best-educated tenth of the boys born 1897-1941, less than 30 per cent of these boys started out among the most culturally advantaged tenth of their generation (as indicated by the number of years of school their father had finished). The other 70 per cent moved up from less advantaged positions, displacing 70 per cent of those who had started with "all the advantages."

This kind of turnover requires some explanation. Colleges, after all, are largely controlled by the rich and powerful. We must ask ourselves why these men have not used their positions to ensure that their children and their friends' children would get BA's and that "outsiders" would not. Several answers are relevant. First, some of the men who serve on the governing boards of colleges have had quite disinterested and self-denying temperaments. They have really believed that if their children or their friends' children could not compete academically, they should not get special treatment. Another important consideration, especially in recent years, has been faculty pressure for strictly meritocratic selection. Faculty opposition has often been a decisive factor in reducing favoritism towards alumni (though not faculty) sons and daughters, and it has sometimes led college administrators to raise scholarship money for poor but talented applicants and to recruit more such applicants. Together, these influences have kept a number of elite colleges fairly open to students from all classes and conditions.

Yet if the openness of higher education depended exclusively on the self-denying morality of the educational elite, the rate of turnover in that elite would undoubtedly be far lower than it is. The main key to this turnover is America's willingness to let groups which have been excluded from established institutions go into business for themselves. Even when the men who controlled a leading college were not willing to open it on equal terms to the academically talented children of outsiders, they had neither the political power nor (in most cases) the ideological conviction to block creation of competitive colleges which would serve such students. The initiative for such ventures has, it is true, usually come from people who would be formally classified as upper-middle-class. But these initiators and leaders, unlike those of older and more eminent institutions, have often held their position by dint of the fact that they served the interests of lower-middle and working-class parishioners or voters. The old Catholic commuter college, the municipal "streetcar" college, the rural teachers' college turned state college, and the two-year "community college" have all played this role to some extent—though they have also been havens for the less competent children of the affluent and well-educated.[27] While the alumni and trustees of older and more distinguished institutions have seldom welcomed such competition and have sometimes fought against it quite actively, they have always acquiesced in due course.

This acquiescence requires an explanation, especially when contrasted with the situation in Great Britain. Britain has not encouraged independent entrepreneurs to establish new colleges and universities. Such enterprises have been allowed only under the auspices of the state and of longer established universities. New kinds of institutions with unorthodox goals or standards have been rare. In America, on the other hand, central authority has been weaker and more distrusted than in Britain, and this has made it harder to restrain any private venture, including a college. Not only that, but the American mythology of unlimited room at the top and of universal opportunity has supported the assumption that there is an unlimited need for college graduates, regardless of competence or social background.[28] The American upper-middle class seldom saw the expansion of what it deemed mediocre lower-middle or working-class colleges as a direct threat to its own interests.

Whether the upper-middle class was right in its relatively benign view is an open question. The establishment of new sorts of colleges has probably led to a slightly higher rate of both upward and downward mobility than would otherwise have prevailed, and has in this sense threatened established privilege. At the same time, new institutions have opened to the less privileged certain callings for which the demand has exceeded the supply of competent applicants. These institutions have thus played an indispensable role in the overall economic growth of the country and perhaps also a modest role in the maintenance of the established social and political order.

It can be argued that such colleges have helped co-opt talented outsiders who might otherwise have been driven into opposition to established social institutions and arrangements. But it can equally well be argued that such colleges helped equip outsiders with sufficient competence and expertise to oppose and hence alter the system which excluded them, and that the absence of revolutionary movements in America (except for the Southern secessionists) derives from other sources. Certainly there is no historical evidence from other countries that educating selected members of the lower strata is the best way to de-fuse revolutionary demands. On the contrary, educated outsiders seem to be the enzymes without which revolution is almost impossible.

The real political importance to America of educating such individuals may not have been preventing revolution or radical reform but preserving the internal viability of established institutions. The management of large corporate and governmental empires, for example, requires leaders who can deal with extremely diverse personalities and social species. Without such peacemakers, mediators, and synthesizers at the top, large organizations tend to degenerate into mutually antagonistic fiefs, working at cross purposes, unable to serve the external world, and largely uninterested in doing so. The survival of a given institution and ultimately the survival of the whole system depend on finding and promoting individuals with a broad span of social responsiveness and control, who can keep established institutions at least minimally serviceable. Yet such individuals are relatively rare—perhaps especially so in homogeneous upper-middle class suburbs. Those leaders who were born into lower-middle class or small-town families have often come to the top by way of nonelite colleges. Whether they would have found their way into positions of power without such colleges is problematic, just as it is problematic whether the overall American system could have won its present degree of popular support if such managers had not been found.

Having said all this about the reasons for moderately equal opportunity and high rates of mobility, we must nonetheless return to the fact that opportunity is by no means completely equal and that mobility is by no means perfect. The remaining sections of this article will look in more detail at the reasons for this and at some possible remedies for it.

(1) The most obvious explanation is *money*. Attending college is expensive, and all other things being equal a student who can count on getting a lot of help from his family is more likely to attend than a student who expects little or no help. The implications of this are taken up in the next section.

(2) A second reason for class differences in enrollment rates is *environment*. All other things being equal, children with rich, well-educated, and clever parents seem to develop greater intellectual powers than children from impoverished homes.

(3) A third factor is *motivation*. Children from the upper social strata seem to be under more pressure from home both to do well in school and to go to college. They also seem to be under more internal pressure to stay in school. For a privileged child not to go to college implies downward social mobility and eventual loss of the privileges he has been raised to take for granted. Some working-class families, on the other hand, actively reject the idea of a son's going to college, on the grounds that

this would separate the son from his family.[29] Even when this is not a problem, many working-class and lower-class children feel little internal pressure to go to college when—as is often the case among children of all classes—the prospect seems intrinsically disagreeable. It is true that not going to college may restrict their chances for upward mobility, but in contrast to middle-class students, it does not imply downward mobility.

(4) A fourth reason for class differences in college entrance and graduation rates is *genetic*. This is an extremely sensitive subject. It has long been an article of liberal and radical faith that there are no genetic differences between groups, and that even genetic differences between individuals are irrelevant in explaining most differences in their actual behavior or competence. This assumption is very useful politically, for it implies that inequality and inequity result entirely from environmental factors and thus denies predestination and reinforces dreams of progress. The converse position, namely that human differences are genetically based, has been associated with conservatism in general and Southern racism in particular. Nonetheless, genes *are* important. All other things being equal, a clever child born in a particular class and family will tend to rise further in the world than a dull child from the same class and family. If the upwardly mobile tend to be more genetically favored than the downwardly mobile, this cannot but have some effect over time. Unusual people tend to have unusual children—not generally as unusual as themselves, it is true, but still unusual. This makes it almost inevitable that children born into the upper social strata will have a slightly more favorable gene pool than children born into the lower social strata.[30] We do not, however, have any basis for estimating the magnitude of these differences. I will therefore assume that they are relatively small and that class differences in measured intelligence, physical and mental health, stamina, and so forth, are mainly the result of the environment to which children of different classes are exposed. The topic is not discussed further in this article.

Financial Obstacles to Meritocratic Recruitment

While the lack of money is by no means the most serious problem confronting children from the lower strata seeking high-level education and certification, it is the most commonly discussed, the most easily analyzed, and the most readily eliminated. It is therefore important to say something about the changing relation between family incomes and college costs.

During the first half of the twentieth century the combined cost of room, board, and tuition rose considerably more slowly than family incomes.[31] This meant that a substantially larger proportion of the population could afford to attend college in 1950 than at any previous time. This was true of both public and private colleges, for both commuting and residential students. In the early 1950's this encouraging trend slowed, and by the late 1950's it had been reversed for some colleges. Between 1956 and 1964, for example, real per capita gross national product rose 16 per cent.[32] The total cost in constant dollars of going away to a public college in one's home state also rose about 15 per cent, suggesting that public residential colleges were as accessible in 1964 as in 1956. The cost of going away to college may, however, be less relevant than the cost of commuting, for commuting is the only option many lower-income students even consider. While the impact of recent increases in tuition on affluent families has been largely offset by the lag in subsistence expenses, lower-income families have benefited only indirectly from this lag.[33] Between 1956 and 1964 real private tuition rose four times as fast as per capita income (60 as against 15 per cent) while public tuition rose more than twice as fast as income (37 as against 15 per cent).[34]

Does this mean that the proportion of young people who can afford higher education is declining? Almost certainly not. Yet the question cannot be definitively answered, because there is no generally accepted definition of what families at different income levels ought to be willing to spend on higher education. Certainly there is no agreement among parents themselves on this score. Many rich parents are unwilling to spend very much, while many poor ones make enormous sacrifices. Indeed, when the University of Michigan's Survey Research Center tried to develop an empirical formula for predicting how much a given family would spend on a child's higher education, it found that family income was by no means the most important factor.[35] Well-educated parents with low incomes evidently spend more than poorly educated parents with high incomes.

Under these circumstances it is hardly surprising to discover that parental income has relatively little influence on a child's

actual chances of attending college. A study by the Bureau of
the Census in 1960, for example, found a zero-order correlation
of 0.29 between family income and a child's college chances.[36]
This is a *maximal* estimate of the influence of parental income
on a high school graduate's college chances. The relationship
would be much weaker if parental education, occupation, and
other relevant factors were controlled. The relative unimportance
of family income in determining college chances is also indicated
by Table 1, which compares parental income distributions for
various sorts of colleges to the distribution for all families in the
relevant age group.

TABLE 1.—*Income Distribution of Families and Unrelated Individuals with
Principal Earner between 45 and 54 in 1965, and of Families with
Children Entering Three Kinds of College, Fall 1966*

INCOME	All Families	All College Families	Public 4-year Colleges	Private Uni- versities
Less than $4,000	15.5	6.6	10.0	3.3
$4,000 to $5,999	14.6	12.9	17.8	7.3
$6,000 to $7,999	17.9	17.3	20.8	11.9
$8,000 to $9,999	15.6	16.9	18.3	13.6
$10,000 to $14,999	24.0	25.2	22.0	25.0
$15,000 to $24,999	9.8	14.0	8.7	20.9
$25,000 and over	2.7	7.1	2.5	17.9
TOTAL	100.1	100.0	100.1	99.9

Sources: *Current Population Reports*, Series P-60, No. 51, and Alexander
Astin, Robert Panos, and John Creager, *op. cit.* The public four-year colleges have the lowest income distribution of the nine categories for which
Astin, Panos, and Creager present data—lower, it should be noted, than the
public two-year colleges. The private universities have the highest income
distribution. (Supplementary data for Negro colleges show that the parental
income distribution at these colleges is much lower than that cited above,
but so too is the income distribution for Negroes as a group.) The income
distribution for the general population would be slightly higher if only
families and not unrelated individuals were included. Such data were not
available by age for 1965, however. On the other hand, the distribution
would be lower if older and younger family heads were included. Both
errors are small and probably offset one another. A more serious problem
is that the income estimates for freshmen were obtained from the students,
not their parents, and students tend to understate their parents' incomes.
Table 1 indicates, for example, that the median income of all college freshmen was about $9400. The actual figure was almost certainly more than
$10,000.

Another sort of evidence indicating the limited importance of family finances in determining who goes to college comes from a 1959 Census study which showed that 45 per cent of the men and 30 per cent of the women enrolled in college said they got no support from home.[37] While most of these students were undoubtedly part-time, married, enrolled in graduate school, or exaggerating their independence, a study of full-time unmarried undergraduates in the same year found that 13 per cent of their parents reported spending less than $50 a year to support the child in question.[38] While some of these self-supporting students had scholarships, of which there are only a limited number, many did not. And while some had the good fortune to live near a cheap commuter college, others had moved there in order to get an education. It seems clear, in short, that if a student is reasonably talented and wholly committed he can get through college no matter how little money his parents may have. This is even more true today than it was in 1959, for federal scholarships, loans, and subsidized jobs have become available to large numbers of students since then.

If substantial numbers of students are getting through college without help from home, why aren't more students doing so? In part, no doubt, the answer is that getting through college on one's own depends to a large extent on living near a public commuter college, on being able to enroll part-time, or on other external circumstances which apply to some students but not others. Equally important, however, is the fact that getting through college without help from home requires more interest in college than most students feel, and perhaps more ability too. An apathetic youngster who hates words and books may go to college when all his friends are going, when his parents foot the bill, and when collegiate social life seems comparatively familiar and congenial. He is hardly likely to go if few of his friends go, if college life strikes him as alarmingly different from anything he has experienced to date, and if he is going to have to work long hours after school and live in penury to make it. Money, in short, is seldom an insuperable problem when taken in isolation, but it may be decisive for the student who is ambivalent anyway. For this reason considerable caution is required when interpreting surveys which show that "lack of money" has kept large numbers of students from college. Between 15 and 20 per cent of the nation's high school graduates say they are not going to college because they lack money.[39] But what one boy sees as insufficient money, another boy sees as a down payment on his education, which he augments by borrowing, working, and hoping. "Lack of money," in other words, is as much a subjective as an objective condition.

Similar conclusions seem warranted when we turn from the influence of money on college entrance to its influence on college completion and on obtaining a graduate degree. Substantial numbers of students say they quit college because they are short of money.[40] Yet these same studies generally fail to find a correlation between parental income and a college freshman's chances of earning a degree.[41] These two findings are probably not contradictory. We know that dropouts, while coming from homes as affluent as graduates, have more poorly educated parents than graduates.[42] We also know that well-educated parents at any given income level are much more willing to spend money on sending their children to college than are poorly-educated parents in the same income group.[43] Hence, while dropping out is not related to parental income, it probably *is* related in some cases to parental parsimony. Students who drop out are probably getting slightly less financial help from home, even though their parents have no less money.

Students' own efforts to solve their money problems may also be influenced by these same background factors, though we have no hard evidence on this score. If a student finds himself short of money he can respond in several different ways. One is to borrow and/or take a part-time job. Another is to drop out. Those who drop out are perfectly correct in saying that they did so for lack of money. But an outsider, noting that many other students got through under similar circumstances, is equally correct in saying that dropouts also lacked commitment. It seems reasonable to assume that parents with professional jobs and higher degrees make their children feel that staying in college is worth considerable sacrifice, since dropping out permanently would probably mean downward mobility. Poorly educated parents, on the other hand, often seem to make their children feel that dropping out, while unfortunate, is no disaster. This suggests that a school teacher's son or a clergyman's daughter who runs out of cash may be more willing to borrow or work to stay in college than is a steel worker's child.

America could eliminate all economic obstacles to higher education by paying all students subsistence and tuition allowances. This would not be cheap, however. There were six million students in American colleges and universities in 1966-7. They were charged almost $3 billion for tuition—or an average of $500 apiece. If we allow another $40 per week for subsistence during the thirty-eight nonsummer weeks, we get an average total cost of $2000 per student, and a national outlay of $12 billion. Even by American standards that is a good deal of money. If the public assumed full responsibility for financing higher education, enrollment would presumably rise—at least that is one of the primary arguments for such a program. Barring Draconian restrictions, tuition charges would also skyrocket. Even assuming no increase in enrollment, no increases in tuition, and no students transferring from cheaper to more expensive colleges, such a program would still have meant quadrupling tax support of higher education in 1966-7.

Such a program has European and Soviet precedents, and it seems like a natural extension of free elementary and secondary education. Its virtues are, however, problematic. Table 2 shows a hypothetical distribution of costs and benefits from such a scheme. The projections may be off a bit either way, but they suggest that a program of this kind would have had very little effect on the distribution of income *between* classes. Instead, it would have served mainly to redistribute income *within* classes. It would have reduced the living standards of those whose children did not go to college (by increasing their taxes) while increasing the living standards of those whose children did go (partly by cutting their expenditures for higher education and partly by providing them with more higher education than they would otherwise have gotten). In addition, it would have redistributed resources within each group away from newlyweds and the aged (who pay taxes but have no college-age children) towards the middle-aged (who now spend a significant fraction of their incomes supporting children in college).

Those who urge free higher education would say that this sort of redistribution is a good thing, since it rewards socially desirable behavior, namely attending college, and punishes undesirable behavior, namely dropping out. Skeptics may wonder whether increasing the number of marginal students in America's colleges *is* socially desirable. Even if we assume it is, the question remains whether it is *sufficiently* desirable to justify asking those

TABLE 2.—*Sources and Allocation of Hypothetical Tuition-Subsistence Allowances by Income Classes for 1960*

INCOME GROUP	Distribution of Tax Burden	Reported Distribution of 1961 BA's	Corrected Distribution of 1961 BA's	Projected Distribution of 1961 BA's
Under $5,000	18	20	18	23
$5,000-$7,499	23	29	22	23
$7,500-$9,999	18	19	23	23
$10,000-$14,999	18	15	16	13
$15,000 and over	22	17	21	18
TOTAL	99	100	100	100

Sources: Column 1 was derived from the Bureau of the Census, *Statistical Abstract of the United States: 1965* (Washington: U.S. Government Printing Office, 1966), Table 467, on the fairly realistic assumption that the overall burden of taxation in the United States is neither progressive nor regressive but proportional to the share of pre-tax income going to families in various income groups. Column 2 was taken from reports of parental income by a representative sample of 1961 BA's. See James A. Davis, *Great Aspirations* (Chicago: Aldine, 1964), Table 1.2. Column 3 was derived from Column 2 on the assumption that the 1961 BA's typically underestimated their parents' incomes by 10 per cent. Column 4 was derived from Column 3 on the assumption that roughly half the students who said they could not afford to attend college would have done so and would have graduated if they had received a $2000 tuition-subsistence allowance, and on the further assumption that of this 20 per cent increment in the Class of 1961, half would have come from families earning less than $5,000, 30 per cent from families earning $5,000 to $7,499, and 20 per cent from families earning $7,500 to $9,999. It was also assumed that every college student would have received the same payment, regardless of where he chose to attend college. If students who lived at home or who attended low-tuition colleges had received less, the rich would have gotten a larger share of the benefits and the poor would have gotten a smaller share.

who do not get the benefits of higher education, either for themselves or for their children, to subsidize those who do. Proponents of free higher education insist that "we all benefit from higher education," and that therefore we should all help pay for it. The first half of this argument is fair enough. We do all benefit from higher education. But we also all help pay for it, by paying a premium for the services of those who have degrees. Few would deny, for example, that society as a whole benefits from the presence of engineers in its midst. But society also pays handsomely for this benefit—to the tune of about $10,000 per engineer in 1965. If these men became shop foremen we would pay them only about $7500 a year.[44] If $2500 is a realistic estimate of the difference in value between the services an engineer renders society and those a shop foreman renders, we must ask why society should pay additional tuition-subsistence allowances to help future engineers enhance their income. Why should not the engineer himself pay, if he will later be compensated fully for the services he renders society?

There are two possible answers to this question. One is that $2500 per year is *not* a fair estimate of the extra benefits society gets when a man decides to become an engineer instead of a shop foreman. A more realistic estimate might be, say, $5,000 per year. It would then follow that society was getting $2500 per year in "free" services from engineers, which would add up to more than $100,000 over a normal working lifetime. If that were the case, it would seem perfectly reasonable for society to put up $2000 a year for four years to help future engineers get through college. But those who make this argument have a heavy burden of proof on their shoulders. College graduates as a group have a very substantial voice in setting social priorities and determining who will be paid how much for his time. It may be that they undervalue the services they render one another and overvalue the services less-educated people render, but this does not seem very likely. On the contrary, it seems quite likely that the labor market, with its imperfect devices for judging men and its consequent tendency to look at credentials rather than competence, actually *overvalues* the services of college graduates relative to other workers. If this is true, college graduates are already getting larger wage differentials than they "deserve," and they surely have no claim to further subsidies.

More sophisticated advocates of tuition-subsistence allowances admit that existing wage differentials probably provide as good an estimate as we can get of the value contemporary America places on different kinds of services. They therefore conclude that if every individual youngster were economically rational, striving only to maximize his lifetime earnings, society would on the average get the maximum possible amount of useful work from him. But, they say, young men and women are *not* economically rational. If they were, more of them would borrow money against future earnings to go to college. Since this is atypical, the argument runs, we must find covert devices for making the young behave more rationally. One such device is to subsidize their higher education. This will induce them to do what they should do anyway. Society will recoup at least part of the money later, first through taxing their extra income and, second, by expanding the number of college graduates so that it does not have to pay such a premium for their services. This would be a plausible economic and social theory if it were clear that everyone *should* go to college. If, on the other hand, the value of attending college depends on the individual student's ability and/or motivation, then across-the-board financial inducements may be a mistake.

Realistically, there is no foreseeable prospect of America's moving very far in the direction of universal tuition and subsistence allowances. Given the problematic benefits of such a scheme, both for the poor and for society as a whole, perhaps it is best forgotten.[45]

The two possible modifications of tuition-subsistence allowances deserve more serious attention. First, a program which included a means test would cost less, achieve more per dollar spent, and have a more benign effect on income distribution than an across-the-board effort. The federal government now has a small program of "Educational Opportunity Grants" modeled along these lines. Unfortunately, political support for such ventures seems to be largely limited to the more liberal Northern Democrats. This reflects the fact that the driving force behind public support of higher education has almost always been the middle-class parent eager to send his child to college at less than cost. A program which provides no subsidies for such parents, but instead increases the number of working-class and lower-class students who can compete for scarce college places, has relatively limited political appeal to the middle classes. Those whose interests it would serve regard higher education as a low priority item, while the bulk of the college-oriented population does not think it stands to gain much and may even lose something.

An alternative scheme for eliminating the financial obstacles to higher education has recently been put forward by the Panel on Educational Innovation of the President's Science Advisory Committee. This calls for the creation of a federally sponsored but self-financing Educational Opportunity Bank which would lend, rather than give, students as much money as they needed for subsistence and tuition at the college of their choice. Repayment would be contingent on subsequent earnings as well as on the amount borrowed, so that no student would have to fear being saddled with a debt he could not pay.[46] Yet given the present political climate, even this relatively modest scheme is likely to get a cool reception in Congress. Nor is it clear how many lower-strata students would take advantage of such a Bank even if it existed.

Home Environment, Academic Standards, and College Recruitment

There is abundant evidence that class background influences cognitive development, even in the earliest years of childhood.[47] Indeed, the correlation between class background and verbal ability is roughly the same as the correlation between class background and educational attainment: about 0.40.[48] Since tests of verbal ability are among the best available predictors of academic performance and play an important role in determining who gets admitted to certain colleges, some observers have concluded that the apparent class bias in these tests is a primary cause of the class bias in college recruitment and selection. This interpretation is, however, probably even further from the mark than the one which emphasizes the importance of family finances in determining young people's academic destiny.

Variations in measured intellectual ability account for less than a sixth of the variation in children's college chances. A 1960 Census study, for example, found that a student's chances of entering college correlated 0.34 to 0.37 with high school grades and 0.35 to 0.40 with aptitude scores.[49] It seems fairly safe to take these zero-order correlations as a *maximal* estimate of the causal relationship between aptitude and college entrance.[50] If we then take 0.40 as a maximal estimate of the causal relationship between class background and aptitude, we get a net correlation by this causal route of about 0.14. This means that the effects of class on academic ability explain less—perhaps considerably less—than 2 per cent of the variance in an individual's college chances. Since class in general explains something like 10 per cent of the variance in college chances, it seems clear that only a small part of the relationship is mediated through academic ability.[51] The rest of the "class effect" must be attributed to other factors: class differences in economic resources, children's personalities and ambitions, and so forth.

While academic aptitude has a rather modest relationship to college entrance in general, it clearly has a very significant relation to a student's chances of entering certain selective colleges. The genesis of the current round of questions about academic standards was the "discovery" in the early 1960's that there were virtually no Negroes in most supposedly integrated Northern colleges. Once the civil rights movement, student activists, and conscientious administrators had made an issue of this, college admissions officers, especially at the more selective institutions, scurried off to predominantly Negro high schools looking for choice prospects. Within a year or two they were back with the news that there were very few Negroes in these schools (or anywhere else) with verbal and mathematical skills comparable to those of successful white applicants to selective colleges. If these colleges wanted more than a handful of black faces it was clear they would have to take students with relatively low aptitude scores and/or high school grades. An appreciable number of selective colleges did just this. The results varied. Where the presumptively unqualified students got a lot of academic and extracurricular support, a substantial fraction usually survived. In other colleges the mortality was often very high. Armed with the results of a few such experiments, however, some civil rights militants began demanding wholesale reductions in admissions requirements, on the grounds that these requirements were little more than a screen for perpetuating white supremacy.

In a sense this is true, at least if "white supremacy" is taken to mean "middle-class supremacy" or something similar. But wholesale reduction of college entrance requirements, unlike the selective reductions made up to now, would hardly achieve the revolution the militants want. Such changes would open the colleges in question to white children of middling ability as well as black children of middling ability. And there are more of the former than the latter. The same argument applies to class as well as race differences. A general reduction of college admissions requirements might easily *reduce* the mobility rate, for it would make it easier for the middle classes to get the credentials they need to hang on to power and privilege. Once merito-

cratic criteria were eliminated, insiders among the older generation would find it even easier than today to make sure their
children got in, while outsiders would have less basis for demanding access.

If this seems an idle fantasy, consider the case of the junior
college. These colleges are in many respects the embodiment
of what advocates of social mobility should want. The public
ones usually cost little more to attend than high school, and
very few require their students to demonstrate such "middle-
class" skills as literacy. They offer a variety of curricula, including some designed for the academically apathetic or inept student. Yet the existence of these colleges has not improved the
competitive position of the poor in any dramatic way. Tables 3
and 4 show the chances that a high school senior in any given
ability and socioeconomic quartile will go to various sorts of

TABLE 3.—*Probability that a High School Senior in a Given Ability and
Socioeconomic Quartile Entered Junior College the Fall
after Graduation: 1961*

Socioeconomic Quartile	Ability Quartile			
MEN	Lower	Lower-middle	Upper-middle	Upper
Lower	.04	.06	.06	.13
Lower-middle	.05	.07	.11	.07
Upper-middle	.08	.09	.10	.08
Upper	.12	.16	.11	.05
WOMEN				
Lower	.01	.05	.08	.08
Lower-middle	.06	.04	.09	.08
Upper-middle	.04	.06	.08	.08
Upper	.17	.10	.17	.05

Source: Flanagan *et al., One-Year Follow-Up Studies* (Pittsburgh, Pa.:
University of Pittsburgh, Project Talent, 1966), Table 5-1. The authors do
not report the N's for each cell, but given the correlations reported in the
text, they are certainly quite unequal. This makes it impossible to estimate
marginal totals. For descriptions of the indices of ability and status used to
classify individuals (total N = 38,106), see Flanagan *et al., op. cit.*, Appendix E. The above data are for all junior colleges, but 80 per cent of
junior college students are in public institutions, and parental incomes are
about the same in private as in public institutions. (See Astin, Panos and
Creager, *op. cit.*)

TABLE 4.—*Probability that a High School Senior in a Given Ability and Socioeconomic Quartile Entered a Four-Year College the Fall after Graduation: 1961*

Socioeconomic Quartile	Ability Quartile			
MEN	Lower	Lower-middle	Upper-middle	Upper
Lower	.06	.13	.25	.48
Lower-middle	.12	.15	.34	.70
Upper-middle	.13	.29	.45	.73
Upper	.26	.36	.65	.87
WOMEN				
Lower	.07	.08	.18	.34
Lower-middle	.07	.09	.23	.67
Upper-middle	.05	.20	.36	.67
Upper	.20	.33	.55	.82

Source: Flanagan *et al., op. cit.*, Table 5-1.

colleges. Two possible interpretations of these basic distributions are shown in Tables 5 and 6.

Table 5 shows the percentage increase in the proportion of high school seniors from various groups entering college that is attributable to the existence of two-year institutions. Reading across the rows suggests that the dullest students benefit the most from two-year colleges, while reading down the columns suggests that in general lower-strata students also benefit. This appearance results, however, primarily from the fact that there is so much more room for improvement among the duller and more impecunious students. Table 6 therefore approaches the problem in the opposite way and shows the proportion of "eligible" students in each group taking advantage of two-year colleges. It yields a very different picture. If we define any student who is not enrolled in a four-year college as being "eligible" for a two-year one, we find that there are relatively few eligible students in the brighter and richer groups. But among those who are eligible, advantaged students are far more likely to seize the two-year option than are disadvantaged students.

One way of interpreting Table 6 is to compare it to Table 4. Table 4 can be interpreted as showing the proportion of the eligible population choosing the best available option (i.e., a

Table 5.—*Percentage Increase in Proportion of High School Seniors Entering College the Fall after Graduation Attributable to the Existence of Two-Year Colleges: 1961*

Socioeconomic Quartile	Ability Quartile			
MEN	Lower	Lower-middle	Upper-middle	Upper
Lower	66	46	24	27
Lower-middle	41	47	32	10
Upper-middle	62	31	22	11
Upper	46	44	17	6
WOMEN				
Lower	14	63	44	23
Lower-middle	86	44	39	12
Upper-middle	80	30	22	12
Upper	85	30	31	6

Source: Tables 3 and 4. The probabilities in Table 3 have been divided by the probabilities in Table 4 and converted into percentages.

Table 6.—*Proportion of "Eligible" Students Attending Two-Year Colleges: 1961*

Socioeconomic Quartile	Ability Quartile			
MEN	Lower	Lower-middle	Upper-middle	Upper
Lower	.04	.07	.08	.25
Lower-middle	.05	.08	.17	.23
Upper-middle	.09	.08	.18	.30
Upper	.16	.25	.31	.38
WOMEN				
Lower	.01	.05	.10	.12
Lower-middle	.06	.04	.12	.24
Upper-middle	.04	.08	.13	.24
Upper	.21	.15	.38	.38

Source: Tables 3 and 4. An "eligible" student is defined as any student not enrolled in a four-year college.

four-year college). Table 6 indicates the proportion of the remainder who choose the second-best option. Reading across the rows we find that the ability gradient is slightly greater for four-year than for two-year colleges, indicating that ability plays a larger role in the first round of selection than in the second. When we read down the columns, however, we see that in most cases the socioeconomic gradient is greater in the second round than in the first. This suggests that the middle classes are more tenacious than the lower classes. If middle-class children don't get to a four-year college, they often go to a two-year college instead, whereas a poor boy who does not get to a four-year college seldom gets to a two-year college either. Table 5 suggests that on balance the two-year college still works to the advantage of the lower social strata, but the picture is clearly a mixed one.

If manipulating or eliminating cutting points on existing tests will not improve the competitive position of lower-class students, what about new tests? It is relatively easy to devise tests on which lower-class students do as well or better than middle-class students. If, for example, vocabulary tests were based on the language of the streets instead of the library, the competitive advantage of middle-class youngsters would be greatly reduced. If colleges selected students on the basis of their capacity for abstract as against verbal reasoning, or on the basis of their capacity to visualize in three dimensions rather than their capacity to grasp numerical relationships, this too would improve the competitive position of the lower strata. If they selected students on the basis of how much they knew about hunting and fishing, rural (and hence generally poor) boys would have a positive (though probably temporary) advantage.[52] So too if students were selected entirely on the basis of athletic ability, the competitive position of the upwardly mobile might be improved.

The difficulty with this strategy is obvious, however. Admitting students to college entirely on the basis of their football prowess might be a first step towards increasing the rate of upward mobility, but it would only be of real value if students admitted in this way could survive academically after admission. Athletic ability is not particularly helpful in such competition unless one is a major star for whom a college is willing to provide special tutoring. Nor will an intimate knowledge of deer hunting or familiarity with the argot of the Negro underworld carry a freshman very far. The best predictors of college success remain the traditional tests of verbal and mathematical ability. And of forty-nine different tests administered by Project Talent, these are the ones that correlate most closely with class background, at least among boys.[53]

Some radicals would answer that a college's choice of its curriculum is essentially arbitrary, and that the present curriculum could easily be replaced with one in which success was less related to class background. Yet this is not an easy case to prove. Certainly colleges do not think they cling to the legacies of Guttenberg and Newton simply to limit social mobility. They cling to them because they believe them both intrinsically important and instrumentally useful. College professors value verbal skills, for example, because they themselves have such skills and enjoy using them. Not only that, but the larger society reinforces college professors' natural tendency to believe that these skills are useful. It is easy to scoff at this view; it is not so easy to prove it wrong.[54]

"Middle-class values" have come in for a good deal of abuse lately, much of it justified, but they cannot easily be repudiated *en masse*. It is relatively simple to argue, for example, that middle-class anxiety about children's using four-letter words or middle-class insistence on "standard" grammar in public utterance creates as many problems as it solves. It is much harder to argue that the middle-class preference for a large vocabulary over a small one is wholly unproductive, or that a syntax which allows sentences to mean many different things is as good as a syntax which restricts the number of possible alternative interpretations. More generally, it is easy to argue that verbal and mathematical representations of the world are not our only tools for grasping what goes on around us and that colleges should place more emphasis on other ways of learning and knowing.[55] But it is by no means clear that changes in this direction, desirable as they might be in their own right, would significantly increase the rate of social mobility.

It is true that verbal and mathematical skills seem slightly less equitably distributed between classes than most other measurable cognitive skills or kinds of information. But this may simply reflect the fact that verbal and mathematical skills seem more relevant to adult success, so that middle-class parents concentrate their attention on developing these skills in their children.

If the curricula of elite colleges were reorganized so as to reward upwardly mobile farm boys who knew about the outdoors or Negroes who knew about the ghetto, middle-class parents would probably find ways to ensure that their children mastered these things instead of acquiring big vocabularies. Within a few years the middle-class advantage on these new indices of competence might easily be as great as the middle-class advantage on tests of verbal and numerical ability is today. Given the modest relationship between aptitude scores and college chances, and the likelihood that this relationship would persist even if new aptitudes were emphasized, reformers probably ought to concentrate their energies elsewhere.

Motivation, Mobility, and Equality

The discussion up to this point suggests that while both the elimination of financial obstacles and revision of the curriculum might have a marginal effect on the proportion of lower-strata youngsters getting higher education, neither step would dramatically increase the mobility rate. What, then, is the cause of the class bias in college entrance rates? And what is its cure, if any? The familiar summary answer is "motivation." Large numbers of children from the lower-social strata have only limited interest in upward mobility, whereas virtually all children from the higher strata have an intense interest in avoiding downward mobility.

For the lower-class or working-class child, going to college is a step up in the world, a way of improving on the conditions in which he or she was raised. Many lower-class children seem to feel this would be desirable, but few seem to regard it as absolutely essential. Children who have endured seventeen impoverished years in Harlem or eastern Kentucky mostly seem to feel they can endure another fifty if they have to—though few welcome the prospect and many make considerable effort to avoid it. Similarly, a child whose father is a Pittsburgh steel worker knows that such a life, while hardly what he might wish, is at least a conceivable and endurable alternative. Such a youngster may be under considerable verbal pressure from home to do better than his parents did, and in particular to do well at school and go to college. Yet even this is by no means universal. Substantial numbers of lower-strata families seem to be relatively content for their children to occupy the same position they do, and even those who would like to see their children get ahead sometimes see no connection between this and going to college.[56] Even lower strata parents who would like their children to go to college often exert little psychic pressure on them to do so. The child may sense that his entering college would make his parents happier than his taking a job or joining the army, but he is also likely to sense that if he chooses one of these latter options his parents will hardly be heartbroken. Life will go on as before, perhaps with a few recriminations but without real bitterness.

For the upper-middle-class child, on the other hand, the pressure to go to college and earn a degree is far more intense. Here we are dealing not with an aspiration but an expectation. College-educated parents simply take it for granted that their children will go to college. To do anything else would be to step onto the down escalator which leads to a poor job, low income, the wrong friends, and a generally unacceptable way of life. As already indicated, downward mobility seems to hold far greater terrors than the mere frustration of upward mobility. Indeed, it can be stated as a general law of political life that parents and children will struggle far more fiercely to hold onto what they have than most outsiders will struggle to take it away from them.[57]

It is important to remember that attending college *is* a struggle for most young people, regardless of class background. Those who examine the problem too often forget that most children find schoolwork difficult and unpleasant. They have no taste for irregular verbs, quadratic equations, the five principal products of Venezuela, or the five reasons for the end of the Middle Ages. (Things might be rather different if schools were run differently, but even then the proportion who found study exciting or even satisfying would probably remain limited.) Those to whom schoolwork comes easily often acquire a taste for it, especially if they find other activities more difficult and value the adult approval they can win by doing well in school. Able children therefore tend to do quite well in school and to go on to college no matter what their background.[58] But those who find schoolwork fairly difficult—which means the great majority even among the upper-middle class—keep at it only so long as the price of quitting seems even higher than the price of sticking with it. And as we have indicated, children from the lower strata are likely to feel they have passed the point of diminishing returns much earlier than children from the upper strata. The street cleaner's son who hates schoolwork can take a job, go on living at home, keep dating his girl-friend, and hope for the best. The doctor's son who decides not to go to college will end up with an ulcer if he stays at home and allows his parents to make him feel guilty. So he goes to college —somewhere, somehow—and more often than not he even manages to graduate.

Reformers must somehow deal with the fact that, popular mythology to the contrary notwithstanding, the poor outsider is not usually "hungrier" than the rich insider and is not usually willing to make greater sacrifices to achieve the same objective. On the contrary, it is the children of the upper-middle classes who are most likely to be "hooked" on power and privilege, and who are most willing to do what must be done to feed this addiction. (Like many other addictions, of course, this one involves genuine pleasures and rewards.)

Schools and colleges make only halfhearted efforts to alter this pattern. A suburban school, for example, will sometimes try to persuade an upper-middle-class family not to push its sub-normal, nonacademic son towards college. But parents usually take such advice very badly, and many schools are reluctant even to offer it. At the opposite end of the ability spectrum, teachers and counsellors usually make some effort to push their most talented students into college preparatory curricula and then into college itself, even if the student comes from a family where this is not expected. But here again the efforts are usually too little and too late. The school itself, moreover, may be only half-heartedly devoted to academic values. Many teachers and counsellors regard a "nice," well-spoken, but rather dim middle-class child as a better college candidate than a more sullen and less-controlled working-class child who does good work but seems like a "troublemaker." So the former is pushed into a program which will allow him to attend an unselective college, while the latter is given a hard time, made even more rebellious, and often eventually pushed out onto the street.[59] These nonacademic standards of merit almost inevitably tend to favor the middle-class student over the upwardly mobile, though one occasionally sees the opposite sort of bias too.

The heart of the problem is not, however, in the educational system. So long as the distribution of power and privilege among adults remains radically unequal, and so long as some children are raised by adults who have "all the advantages" while others are raised by adults who have all the disadvantages, children will inevitably turn out unequal. This may be partly because parents with time, money, and the respect of their fellows can do a better job raising their children than parents who lack these things. But children raised in different circumstances will also acquire different hopes, expectations, and compulsions. I suspect that these subjective differences account for more of the class variation in college chances than objective differences in financial resources, intellectual competence, or even character structure.

Such differences can be eradicated. America could commit itself, for example, to a kibbutz-like system of child-rearing, in which biological ancestry would count for relatively little. In its most extreme form such a system could virtually equalize life chances, making every child's future dependent on his genes. Such a proposal would not win much popular support in America, however, even among those whose children would presumably benefit. Rightly or wrongly, most Americans are convinced that a child needs to have someone who is irrationally and passionately devoted to it, someone who will love it not in the collective way that a good preschool teacher loves her charges but in the individual way that parents love their children. The experience of the *kibbutzim* suggests that this premise is probably oversimple and perhaps just wrong, but it is not likely to be abandoned for that reason.

So long as we cling to the family system, efforts to increase the rate of social mobility are likely to have limited impact. Not only that, but their social value is also problematic. If wealth and power remain as unequally distributed between families as they now are, and if child-rearing remains family-based, increasing the rate of social mobility substantially could easily be a formula for misery. A fluid, mobile, society in which men move up and down is also a competitive, insecure, and invidious society. The more we have of the one, the more we will have the other. This truth is often forgotten—nowhere more often, indeed, than in higher education. But it is fundamental. If, for example, colleges were to attract as many applicants from the lower strata as they now do from the upper strata, the admissions rat-race would become even more hectic than it is. There would be no more room at the top of the academic system, because the amount of room at the top is by definition limited. The "best" colleges are "best" precisely because they are competitive and exclusive. If they got more applicants they would not expand appreciably to accommodate demand, for that would jeopardize their elite standing. They would raise standards even further than they have already done, making it even harder for those who apply (including the already upwardly mobile) to get in. Most professors would no doubt welcome such a development, on the ground that it was another step towards a "really first-rate student body." Corporate recruiters and professional schools would probably also be pleased, since such changes would facilitate their efforts to sift and screen talent. But if downward mobility is in fact more painful than blocked upward mobility, such a change might not do much for individual happiness.

On the other hand, the case for a competitive, meritocratic society with a great deal of vertical mobility has never rested on individual fulfillment but rather on collective advantage. We do not give clever men power because we suppose they get more satisfaction from its exercise than do dimwits, nor do we confine incompetents to menial jobs for their own good. It is the general welfare that supposedly benefits from competition and mobility. Thus we saw earlier that the amount of room at the top of American society had remained fixed in recent times, and that social mobility was therefore a zero-sum game. But this is only a half truth. The *relative* amount of room at the top has remained fixed, but at least by some indices the *absolute* amount has increased. The skills required of the labor force grow greater annually, for example, and the incomes received by workers grow even faster. This means that most people are better off than their parents were, even though their position vis-à-vis their neighbors has not changed.

The driving force behind this sort of economic expansion is seldom the established elite, which has little incentive to take risks or disrupt established patterns of business. The pressure for growth tends to come from the upwardly mobile, who for the most part cannot hope to displace the first families from their traditional positions, but who can hope to create a new parallel elite. The upwardly mobile can do this if—and only if—they can find a way to increase the overall size of the pie, and can thus avoid any direct attempt to reduce the absolute amount going to those who currently get the lion's share. It is true that such developments make the old elite downwardly mobile in a relative sense, for their hegemony is no longer complete and their relative position no longer unchallenged. But so long as their absolute power and income remains stable or even improves, they are not likely to resist the rise of outsiders as fiercely as they otherwise would. Efforts to maintain the position of old elites while simultaneously accommodating new ones force continual transformation of the occupational structure and require continuing economic growth. If opportunities for upward mobility or the fear of downward mobility were to diminish, this kind of pressure for expanding and upgrading the overall system would diminish correspondingly. Indeed, expansion might stop altogether. Growth, after all, is strenuous and sometimes painful. It is much easier for those who are already well off just to let things go on as they are. Complacent elites which feel their position secure tend to do just that. It is the hot breath of the upwardly mobile which keeps them running.

Nonetheless, there is a point of diminishing returns beyond which the advantages of meritocracy and mobility to society as a whole may no longer offset their disadvantages to individuals who fail to meet the test. I know no way of telling when a given society has reached that point. From the top there always seems to be a shortage of talent, and hence an argument for encouraging still more youngsters to compete for elite jobs and life styles, even though relatively speaking no more can make it to the top than in the past. From the bottom, there always seems to be a shortage of opportunity, and hence a reason for being even more ruthless in weeding out incompetents who owe their privileges mainly to ancestry. Both views are correct, and one of the great virtues of meritocratic competition is that it fuses them in such a way as to keep the system as a whole expanding. Yet there seems to be something basically perverse and sadistic in trying to make America more competitive and status-conscious than it already is. If there are talented boys who do not want to go to Harvard, and if there are also mediocre ones who do, is any useful purpose really served by recruiting the former and excluding the latter? It is one thing to say that when a particular privilege is in short supply it should go to the most competent.

It is something else to say that the demand for such privileges (and admission to a selective college is among them) should be deliberately intensified.

What all this suggests is that America's emphasis on mobility may have been too single-minded. What America most needs is not just more mobility but more equality. So long as American life is premised on dramatic inequalities of wealth and power, *no* system for allocating social roles will be very satisfactory. Genes may be somewhat better than parental status, but damning a man for having a low IQ is not in the end much better than damning him for having a black skin or a working-class accent.

Furthermore, unless discrepancies in parental influence and life styles are reduced, the practical possibility of increasing mobility will remain remote. If the elite knew downward mobility could not involve falling very far, it might tolerate the probability that its children would do a little less well than itself. If it believes that downward mobility can involve an enormous fall, it will struggle far more desperately to make sure that its children stay on top. Not only that, but if the elite were only a little better off than the rest of society, its *ability* to pass on its privileges to its children would be relatively limited, simply because it would not have a dramatic economic, political, or cultural advantage to exploit. If, on the other hand, the elite is enormously more powerful than the poor, the poor will have no chance whatever of forcing elite children to compete on equal terms with poor ones.

But if increasing mobility depends on reducing inequality, the converse is probably also true: we will move towards equality of results if we have greater equality of opportunity. There are, after all, only two ways to make men equal: we can reduce the privileges of the elite or we can increase the privileges of the nonelite. The former course would probably require a violent revolution, and despite the current ferment in the ghetto this seems unlikely. The only practical way to move towards equality, then, is to help those at the lower levels of society. This does not actually imply more social mobility, since those at the top will help themselves at the same time. But the programs required to improve the position of the poor seem much the same whether we say we are working for more mobility or less inequality. It may also be that the established elite will only support social programs aimed at putting a floor under the downwardly mobile and ensuring that they do not drop out of society entirely if it feels that it is protecting its own children and grandchildren, or at least its cousins. This means the fear of downward mobility must be kept alive.

Equalizing opportunity turns out, then, to be inextricably tied up with creating a classless society. Yet this latter ideal is not one to which America has ever devoted much effort, nor is there much sign that it will begin to do so in the near future. We have eschewed rigid class distinctions, but we have not worried much about equalizing power or privilege. The past few years have seen a modest revival of demands that we move in this direction, particularly among student radicals who believe in participatory democracy, but there is no sign of substantive progress. Until such progress is made, however, the level of social mobility will probably remain at about its present level, and class differences in recruitment to higher education will probably change very little.

NOTES

1. For more detailed discussion, see Christopher Jencks and David Riesman, *The Academic Revolution* (New York: Doubleday, 1968), Chapter III.

2. *Ibid.*

3. See Simon Kuznets, *Shares of Upper Income Groups in Income and Savings* (New York: National Bureau of Economic Research, 1953), and Gabriel Kolko, *Wealth and Power in America* (New York: Praeger, 1962).

4. Herman P. Miller, *Income Distribution in the United States* (Washington: U.S. Census Monograph, 1967).

5. This whole issue is treated in more detail in Jencks and Riesman, *op. cit.*, and a bibliography of relevant evidence appears there.

6. Women reading the following discussion will find very little discussion of their distinctive problems. Social mobility among women has not been much studied, and most of the data I have located apply only to men.

7. Bureau of the Census, *U.S. Census of Population 1960*, Vol. 1, Part 1 (Washington: U.S. Government Printing Office, 1964), Table 223.

8. Bureau of the Census, *U.S. Census of Population 1960*, PC(2) 5B, *Educational Attainment* (Washington: U.S. Government Printing Office, 1964), Table 8.

9. Peter Blau and Otis Dudley Duncan, *The American Occupational Structure* (New York: John Wiley & Sons, 1967), p. 170. The

simple correlation between education and occupational status is 0.596. This means that a man one standard deviation above or below the educational mean will typically be 0.596 standard deviations above or below the occupational mean. For these purposes, occupations were ranked on a scale derived from the mean education and income associated with the occupation. For a persuasive justification of this seemingly circular procedure, see Blau and Duncan, *op. cit.*, Chapter 4.

10. Estimated from Blau and Duncan, *op. cit.*, p. 170.

11. The distinction can be illustrated by an example. A lawyer's income derives partly from his skills and partly from his credentials. We can measure the pure socialization effect by seeing how much additional income a man can expect if he studies law for three years but never earns a degree. We can measure the pure certification effect by seeing how much additional income he can expect if he never studies law and buys a degree from a diploma mill. The sum of the income increments associated with these two procedures in isolation is almost certainly smaller than the increment associated with both together. An equation for estimating the combined effect of socialization and certification would therefore probably be multiplicative or exponential rather than additive.

12. The simple correlation of fathers' occupational statuses with sons' occupational statuses is 0.40, whereas the simple correlation of sons' educational attainments with their occupational statuses is 0.60. The standardized partial regression coefficient of sons' statuses on fathers' status is 0.18, whereas the partial coefficient for education is 0.52. See Blau and Duncan, *op. cit.*, pp. 169ff. (The partial coefficients are estimated from a simplified version of Blau and Duncan's path diagram, eliminating first job and collapsing father's education and occupation.)

13. Some students of the relationship between education and occupation have focused on *mobility* rather than *status*. They have argued that while education is not necessarily especially important in *maintaining* high status, it is important in *achieving* it. This would be possible if, for example, upward mobility depended on getting credentials and joining a profession, while corporations mainly hired men with upper-middle-class parents, even when these men had no college experience. There is, however, no evidence to support such hypotheses. Blau and Duncan, *op. cit.*, p. 195, provide a formula for calculating the relationship between educational mobility and occupational mobility which shows a stable correlation of 0.32 for men born in the years 1897 to 1936. C. Arnold Anderson, "A Skeptical Note on the Relation of Vertical Mobility to Education," *American Journal of Sociology*, LXVI (May, 1961), 560-70, also reaches the conclusion from different data that education plays a modest role in mobility.

14. The best data on changes over time in the correlation between educational attainment and occupational status are probably those in Blau and Duncan, *op. cit.*, pp. 177ff. These investigators found no significant change in the relationship between educational attainment and first job between the age group born 1897-1906 and the one born 1927-1936. They did, however, find a small but steady increase in the correlation between educational attainment and occupational status as of March, 1962, as they moved from the older to the younger groups. (The simple correlation rose from 0.58 for those who were aged fifty-five to sixty-four at the time of the survey to 0.66 for those who were twenty-five to thirty-four.) At first glance this increase may seem quite natural, since one might expect education to exert maximum effect when a man looked for his first job and to have a declining effect thereafter. But that is not the case. On the contrary, education has *more* effect on men's "mature" occupations than on their first occupations. This suggests that the correlation for the twenty-five to thirty-four group may eventually be even higher than 0.66. Additional evidence for an increasingly close relationship between education and occupational status is found in sons' reports of their fathers' education and occupations at the time their sons were sixteen. The correlations for fathers were substantially lower than for sons. This may only reflect, however, the fact that sons made more mistakes when reporting on their fathers than when reporting on themselves. This assumption is supported by the fact that twenty-five- to thirty-four-year-old sons' reports on their fathers show a substantially lower correlation than the fifty-five- to sixty-four-year-old men's reports on themselves, even though the two groups should be roughly similar. Nor is there any clearcut trend over time in the correlation for fathers as there is for sons.

Unfortunately for scholarly peace of mind, Blau and Duncan's findings are at odds with findings in some other studies. Duncan and Robert Hodge, "Education and Occupational Mobility: A Regression Analysis," *American Journal of Sociology*, LXVIII (May, 1963), 629-44, found that there had been little change in the correlation of educational attainment and occupational status between the 1940 and 1950 Censuses in Chicago.

John K. Folger and Charles B. Nam, "Trends in Education in Relation to the Occupational Structure," *Sociology of Education*, XXXVIII (Fall, 1964), 19-33, found a *decline* in the correlation between education and occupational status between 1940 and 1960. This may be a by-product of their system for classifying occupations and their measure of association, which was gamma rather than a standardized correlation coefficient.

15. For evidence of a small increase between 1950 and 1959 in the relative importance of college as against high school graduation

in determining occupation, see James A. Davis, "Higher Education: Selection and Opportunity," *The School Review,* LXXI (Autumn, 1963), 249-65.

16. Herman P. Miller, "Annual and Lifetime Income in Relation to Education," *American Economic Review,* L (December, 1960), 962-86, shows little change in the overall pattern of income distribution between high school and college graduates from 1939 to 1959. The high school graduates gained on collegians from 1939 to 1949, then slipped back from 1949 to 1959. The gap in lifetime earnings, while greater in absolute terms because of general income rises, also remained fairly stable in relative terms. But Miller's analysis in *Income Distribution in the United States,* Table VI-2, suggests that this seeming stability concealed important changes. College graduation became considerably more important for the young between 1950 and 1960. This trend was concealed by the fact that older college graduates got a disproportionately small share of the fruits of economic growth.

17. If we were to assume that the trends reported by Blau and Duncan for those born 1897-1936 would continue for those born 1937-1966, the simple correlation of educational attainment and occupational status for those born in 1966 would be 0.72, compared to 0.66 for those born 1927-36. Considering the other changes likely between now and 1995, this must be reckoned a fairly stable pattern.

18. See "On Cooling the Mark Out: Some Aspects of Adaptation to Failure," [pp. 25-46] . . .

19. On expectations and reality about attaining degrees, see Robert Panos and Alexander Astin, "Attrition Among College Students," *American Council on Education Research Reports,* II, No. 4 (1967), and Alexander Astin, Robert Panos, and John Creager, "National Norms for Entering College Freshmen, Fall 1966," *American Council on Education Research Reports,* II, No. 1 (1967).

20. For a discussion of this phenomenon with particular reference to the junior colleges, see Burton Clark, "The 'Cooling Out' Function in Higher Education," *American Journal of Sociology,* LXV (May, 1960), 569-76.

21. Estimated from Blau and Duncan, *op. cit.,* pp. 169-74.

22. The basic data for the educational distributions were taken from "Educational Change in a Generation: March 1962," *Current Population Reports,* Series P-20, No. 132 (Washington: U.S. Government Printing Office, September 22, 1964). Additional tabulations of the data are found in William Spady, "Educational Mobility and Access in the United States: Growth and Paradoxes," *American Journal of Sociology,* LXXIII (November, 1967), 273-86. The regression coefficients were taken from Blau and Duncan, *op. cit.,* pp. 169-70. (Blau and Duncan used the same basic data as *Current Population Reports* and Spady.) The simple correlations of fathers' education and

occupation with sons' education are 0.453 and 0.438 respectively, so that a single value of 0.44 distorts the results very little.

23. *Current Population Reports,* Table 1. The estimates depend on interpolation, so small discrepancies between actual and expected percentiles are to be expected.

24. The data published in *Current Population Reports* only divide fathers into "white collar," "manual and service," and "farm." These divisions are even cruder than those for education and force even greater reliance on interpolation. Nonetheless, the over-representation of white-collar sons among BA's was somewhat less in the 1950's than in the 1920's, and the decline was almost exactly what one would expect if the regression coefficient for the relationship of father's occupation to son's education were constant.

25. There are a variety of other ways of analyzing whether selection for higher education is more class-related than in the past, but all produce about the same conclusion as that given in the text. One can, for example, ask to what extent the best-educated sixth (or quarter) of a given generation is composed of children whose fathers were in the best-educated sixth (or quarter) of the previous generation. Among men born 1897-1906 who ended up in the educationally most advantaged sixth, 37.8 per cent started there (judging by their father's education). The comparable percentage thirty years later was 39.4, which hardly represents a significant change. If we look at top quartiles, on the other hand, we find a somewhat greater increase in educational inheritance, with the relevant percentages rising from 42.4 to 49.4. (I am indebted to William Spady for the latter calculation, and for help in thinking through some of the theoretical issues involved in this kind of analysis.)

26. See Spady, *op. cit.,* Table 3.

27. For evidence on the relative importance of these two groups in various sorts of colleges see Alexander Astin, Robert Panos, and John Creager, "National Norms for Entering College Freshmen—Fall 1966," and "Supplementary National Norms for Freshmen Entering College in 1966," *American Council on Education Research Reports,* Vol. I, Nos. 1 & 3, 1967.

28. There have been occasional prophecies that the supply of BA's would outstrip demand, especially during the 1930's and 1940's. These have been wisely ignored.

29. See Joseph Kahl, "Educational and Occupational Aspirations of 'Common Man' Boys," *Harvard Educational Review,* XXIII (Summer, 1953), 186-203.

30. For a review of the issues and the literature on this subject, see Bruce K. Eckland, "Genetics and Sociology: A Reconsideration," *American Sociological Review,* XXXII (April, 1967), 173-93. See also Arthur R. Jensen, "Social Class, Race, and Genetics: Implications for

Education," *American Educational Research Journal,* V (January, 1968), 1-42.

31. In the analysis which follows I have ignored the "cost" of income foregone by undergraduates. It is rather difficult to estimate the potential earning power of able seventeen to twenty-one-year-olds in college. Even if this could be done, "costs" of this kind would have to be weighed against later increases in earning power. The limited evidence available from Census reports suggests that cost-benefit ratios calculated in this way would prove fairly stable over time, but a systematic investigation of this problem has yet to be attempted so far as I know.

32. Other indices of income trends suggest a more favorable trend. Median pre-tax family income rose 20 per cent in this period, and 80th percentile family income rose 28 per cent. For a variety of reasons, however, per capita GNP seems a better index of overall public capacity to pay.

33. It is not easy to estimate the cost of room and board for a commuter living at home. Many families, used to supporting a child at home, may reckon these costs close to nil, since they expect to save nothing on rent and little on food if a child goes away. If, however, we take account of the fact that an increase in family income usually means a decline in the percentage of income spent on food and rent, we can argue that the burden of supporting a child who commutes to college fell from 1956-64, perhaps at roughly the same rate as the burden of room and board charges for those living away from home. This argument is a variant on the general thesis that discretionary incomes rise faster than total incomes, and hence that ability to pay for college is rising faster than total incomes. This theme is discussed in more detail in Jencks and Riesman, *op. cit.*

34. On income trends see *The Economic Report of the President* (Washington: U.S. Government Printing Office, 1967), Tables B-16 and B-17. Estimates of college costs were derived from The American Council on Education's *Fact Book of Higher Education* (Washington: The Council, 1965), converted into constant dollars on the basis of consumer price indices given in the *Economic Report,* Table B-42. Room and board charges reported in the *Fact Book* were assumed to represent 60 per cent of total subsistence expenses in both 1956 and 1964.

35. See John B. Lansing, Thomas Lorimer, and Chikashi Moriguchi, *How People Pay for College* (Ann Arbor: Survey Research Center, 1960).

36. Charles B. Nam and James D. Cowhig, "Factors Related to College Attendance of Farm and Non-Farm High School Graduates: 1960," Series Census-ERS (P-27), No. 32 (Washington: Bureau of the Census, June 15, 1962), Table 16.

37. James D. Cowhig and Charles B. Nam, "Educational Status, College Plans, and Occupational Status of Farm and Non-Farm Youths: October 1959," Bureau of the Census, Series Census-ERS (P-27), No. 30 (Washington: U.S. Government Printing Office, August, 1961), Table A.

38. Lansing, Lorimer, and Moriguchi, op. cit.

39. Cowhig and Nam, op. cit., p. 9. For a more complete bibliography, see Norman C. Crawford, "Effects of Offers of Financial Assistance on the College-Going Decisions of Talented Students with Limited Financial Means," National Merit Scholarship Corporation Research Reports, III, No. 5 (1967).

40. The most recent and comprehensive data are reported by Robert Panos and Alexander Astin, "Attrition Among College Students," American Council on Education Research Reports, II, No. 4 (1967). Table II shows about 23 per cent of all students blaming their withdrawal from the college they first entered on money problems. For a bibliography of other literature on this subject, see John Summerskill, "Dropouts from College," in Nevitt Sanford (ed.), The American College (New York: John Wiley & Sons, 1962).

41. Panos and Astin, op. cit., evidently did not obtain data on parental income, but they did find that parental occupation had virtually no relation to completing four years of college. Their findings are supported by Eckland's study of the University of Illinois which showed a moderate relationship between college graduation and class background, but no relation between graduation and parental income taken in isolation. See "Social Class and College Graduation: Some Misconceptions Corrected," American Journal of Sociology, LXX (July, 1964), 36-50.

42. Panos and Astin, op. cit. See also Eckland, op. cit., on the reasons why many studies of single institutions fail to confirm this finding, and Spady, op. cit., for evidence that this is a fairly recent development.

43. Lansing, Lorimer, and Moriguchi, op. cit.

44. Current Population Reports, Series P-60, No. 51, Table 25.

45. The discussion in the text is directed at massive scholarship programs. Many advocates of subsidies instead place primary emphasis on institutional grants which keep tuition low. Since there are legal and political problems in supporting private colleges this way, and since institutional grants do nothing to defray subsistence costs, I prefer support of students. The economic arguments in the text apply equally to either approach, however.

46. Educational Opportunity Bank (Washington: The Panel, 1967). This idea is not original, having been urged at various times and in various forms by economists such as Charles Killingsworth, Allan Carter, William Vickrey, Seymour Harris, and others.

47. See Gerald Lesser, Gordon Fifer, and Donald Clark, "Mental Abilities of Children from Different Social Class and Cultural Groups," *Monographs of the Society for Research in Child Development*, XXX, No. 4 (1965), for an exemplary study of six- and seven-year-olds. See Marion Shaycroft, *The High School Years: Growth in Cognitive Skills* (Pittsburgh, Pa.: Project Talent, 1967), pp. 6-4 to 6-19, for data on fourteen- to seventeen-year-olds. Lesser *et al.* give a quite full bibliography of other similar studies.

48. See Shaycroft, *op. cit.*, and Blau and Duncan, *op. cit.*

49. See Nam and Cowhig, *op. cit.* The correlations must be squared to estimate the percentage of variance explained. The intercorrelation between aptitude scores and grades in this study was 0.52, but given the restriction of range from attrition before 12th grade, the fact that the data are reported only for quartile intervals, and attenuation because of misclassification of diverse tests, the actual correlation of grades with standardized test scores is probably closer to 0.60.

50. Measurement errors tend to attenuate the correlation, but such errors are almost certainly more than offset by the fact that various other causal factors like class and individual character influence both aptitude and college chances.

51. See Nam and Cowhig, *op. cit.* The correlation between fathers' occupational statuses and their children's college chances was 0.25-0.32.

52. Shaycroft, *op. cit.*, provides a correlation matrix showing the relation between the forty-nine different tests used by Project Talent (including those cited in the text) and a composite index of socioeconomic status. For evidence on the relationship between various indices of class background and different achievement tests, see John C. Flanagan *et al.*, *op. cit.*, Appendix E. Shaycroft, *op. cit.*, chapter 8, demonstrates that socioeconomic status has little independent effect on intellectual growth between the ninth and twelfth grades. There may, however, be some changes between the first and ninth grades. Lesser, Fifer, and Clark, *op. cit.*, demonstrated that among first-graders in metropolitan New York there was almost exactly as much difference between lower-class and middle-class scores on tests of reasoning and spatial perception as on tests of verbal and numerical ability. This was not true among the ninth- and twelfth-graders tested by Project Talent, where class had a significantly stronger relationship to verbal and mathematical scores ($r=0.40\pm$) than to abstract reasoning scores ($r=0.30\pm$) or ability to visualize in two or three dimensions ($r=0.20\pm$). These apparently discrepant findings for different age groups may or may not indicate real changes in the class distribution of mental abilities between the first and ninth grades. Lesser *et al.* made a meticulous effort to eliminate cultural bias from their tests, and this may have reduced class differences on vocabulary

and numerical tests somewhat more than on reasoning and spatial relations tests. Had Project Talent sought to eliminate class influences in the same way, it might have found much the same pattern that Lesser *et al.* did. Comparison is also complicated by differences in the statistical procedures used to decribe findings.

53. Shaycroft, *op. cit.*

54. One piece of evidence suggesting that it *may* be wrong, or at least much exaggerated, is the low correlation between college grades and adult success found by Donald Hoyt, "The Relationship between College Grades and Adult Achievement: A Review of the Literature," *American College Testing Research Reports* (Iowa City, 1965).

55. See, for example, Christopher Jencks, "An Anti-Academic Proposal," *The Educational Record*, XLVII (Summer, 1967), 320-26, and Jencks and Riesman, *The Academic Revolution*, chapter 12.

56. On the absence of college aspirations among lower strata parents see Kahl, *op. cit.* See also Herbert Hyman, "The Value Systems of Different Classes," in Reinhard Bendix and Seymour Lipset (eds.), *Class, Status, and Power* (Glencoe, Ill.: The Free Press, 1953). Aspirations to college have become more widespread since these studies were made, but are still nothing like universal.

57. Those with an empirical bent may want to consider how this "law" could be verified or quantified. Measuring the intensity of subjective feelings is one of the trickiest problems in social science, and the problem is compounded when one tries to measure fear of hypothetical events. Some indices are, however, relevant. In the present context, for example, one might investigate the relative willingness of students whose parents have the same income but different levels of education to take NDEA loans.

58. See Tables 4 and 5. In 1961, 61 per cent of the students in the top ability quartile and bottom socioeconomic quartile entered some sort of college the year after graduating. The proportion *eventually* entering college probably reached 75-80 per cent. (For data on the proportion of high school seniors delaying college entrance, see Cowhig and Nam, *op. cit.*, Table 3.)

59. For evidence that somewhat similar nonacademic biases are also at work in colleges, see Junius Davis, "What College Teachers Value in Students," *College Board Review* (Spring, 1965), pp. 15-8.

Old assumptions about the school system are considered here in a new perspective. A major concern of the author is his questioning of current criteria used to measure student growth, and the degree to which this concept is functional or dysfunctional for the goals of the educational system.

X

Schools and Student Growth*

HARRY C. BREDEMEIER

THERE SEEM TO BE TWO MAJOR WAYS of conceiving the social function of schools, not counting the baby-sitting and labor force-reducing functions. One is to regard them as sifting mechanisms; the other is to regard them as nurturing structures.

As sifting mechanisms, schools expose each generation of children and adolescents to a standard set of curricular mazes to run, examine them periodically, and sort them into several piles: those who had run very well (college-bound); those who had run fairly well (bound where?); and those who had run poorly (poverty-bound). The purpose of tests in this view is to sift and sort; and the relevant questions about tests are their reliability and validity in predicting performance against some criterion such as college grades, or occupational success, or ability to master the material in some other "track." School tests in this context are like medical tests in the context of a draft board examination or personality tests in the context of occupational placement. They answer the question, "Will the examinee fit best in role A or role B or neither?" The "grades" assigned on the basis of tests conceived this way are shorthand messages to the effect that, "You ran the maze this well rather than that well." Examinees are thereby ticketed and set on different conveyor belts headed in different directions.

In this conception, schools are like horticultural stations that

* Reprinted from *The Urban Review*, a publication of the Center for Urban Education, Vol. 2, No. 5, April, 1968, 20-27, by permission of the author and publisher.

expose all varieties of plants to a standard treatment and sort them into those that had whatever it takes to thrive under those treatments and those that did not.

Conceived as nurturing structures, schools are more like horticultural stations that first sort plants into those that need one kind of treatment to maximize their growth and those that need another kind; and then tailor treatments to needs. The purpose of testing in such schools would be very different. It would be to discover what had been the result of the interaction between the individual and his experiences. What is commonly called "failure" on a test would be understood in very different terms; namely, as a signal that whatever had been the individual's experiences with a particular teaching style or pedagogical method or whatnot, they were not the experiences necessary to give him the qualities that would have resulted in a different score.

The relevant question about these tests would be their reliability and validity in providing diagnostic clues as to the effectiveness of the educational methods to which the particular student had been exposed. Tests would be opportunities for testers and test-takers to sit down and figure out what was wrong with the experiences of the test-taker and what remedy is suggested by the pattern of errors and the examinee's introspective accounts of how he made them. Tests in this context would be understood as being like tests for blood sugar in a *medical* setting, not a military recruitment or occupational placement setting. The difference can be enormous. Such an understanding of tests could mean freedom from the self-defeating sense of personal failure that often results from conventional interpretations of "low" test scores; and for both students and institutions it could serve as a built-in quality control mechanism leading to constant refinement of the educational procedures.

It seems clear that most current research is based on the assumption that the second view of schools is the one which at least *should* govern school practices. Otherwise, the question dominating the Coleman study, for example, is irrelevant; namely, "What school characteristics make a difference for students' test scores?" (Under the view of schools as sifting establishments, that question could not be raised; research would rather focus on such a question as, "What school characteristics produce the highest correlations between test scores and future success?"—a radically different matter.)

Although it starts out from the proper conception (in my view), current research does not, I want to argue, take that conception seriously enough, and in consequence it gives us information that is pragmatically meaningless. To make this point clear, let me review swiftly the findings of some recent research (including some of my own) that are at first glance surprising, and have been received as disconcerting.

Current Research in the Sociology of Education

1. Take the intellectual accomplishment of children and adolescents that seems most sensitive to variations in school characteristics—verbal skills. Find the average score of children at different grade levels on that ability, and then measure the variation of individual scores around that mean. Then ask yourself which school characteristics and which student characteristics are likely to account in varying degrees for some students being above the mean and for others being below it. Alternatively (though it is not too far from being the same thing), ascertain which school and student characteristics correlate with student scores. You will find that:

(a) The following school characteristics are associated with high test scores for middle-class students but are either associated with *low* scores for lower-class students or are not associated at all: small classes, small senior class, provision of study halls, number of books in the library, starting salaries of teachers.[1]

(b) Holding constant the background characteristics of the students and all other school characteristics, the following school characteristics contribute only minutely, if at all, to variations in students' scores: expenditures, books in library, science laboratories, extracurricular activities, presence of accelerated programs, comprehensiveness of curriculum, grouping or tracking practices, movement between tracks, size of school, extent of guidance programs, urbanism of the school.[2]

(c) Various measures of teacher quality are virtually unrelated to the scores of middle-class and white students, but *are* slightly related to those of lower-class and Negro children.[3]

(d) More important than all school characteristics and teacher quality for Negro students is the degree to which the *other* students in their schools have the following characteristics: Their families own encyclopedias, they do not transfer much, their attendance is regular, they plan to go to college, and they spend rather much time on homework.[4]

(e) For Negro students, but not for white students, a feeling that the environment will respond to reasonable effort is associated with high test scores; and there is some reason to suppose that such a feeling can be produced by school experiences.[5]

2. Compare the scores on tests of literature, social studies, and mathematical knowledge made by students when they were in the ninth grade with scores made on the same tests by the same students three years later, when they were in the 12th grade. Construct a "growth score"; and then ascertain which school and student characteristics account for student *growth* in ability, rather than simply for their scores at a point in time. You will find that there is virtually no relationship between student growth on the one hand, and on the other hand: teacher quality, school characteristics, students' initial intellectual ability, students' goals, the degree to which students embraced the role of student, student personality structure, or family backgrounds.[6]

3. Consider the hypothesis that different kinds of schools are *differentially* functional and dysfunctional for the growth of different kinds of students along different dimensions. In considering this hypothesis, continue to think of "kinds of schools" in the same terms as above, of student growth in the same terms, and of "kinds of students" in the same terms (initial ability, goal-orientations, personality structure, etc.). You will have to reject the hypothesis, which is to say that such things as class size, library books, double shifts, and per-pupil expenditures do not influence the relationship between growth and student predispositions, nor do such things as the percentage of teachers fully certified, the percentage teaching at least half-time in the area of their major preparation, the percentage with graduate training in the areas taught, starting salaries, etc.[7]

4. Classify low-income, predominantly Negro students according to their relative rates of growth and decline in reading ability between the third and sixth grades, and attempt to find family or other characteristics that are associated with different rates. You will find that family structures, eating habits, study habits, parental discipline, internal family relations, teacher characteristics, birth-place, or peer relations seem to make no difference.[8]

5. If you reduce the pupil-teacher ratio by about 50 per cent and double the per-pupil expenditures in schools serving disad-

vantaged students, you will make most teachers, parents, and students happier; but you will not make much difference in the students' functioning.[9]

6. If you allow the parents of students in deprived neighborhoods freely to choose schools outside their neighborhoods which are ethnically heterogeneous, you will probably select out of the sending schools the most able students, but you will not make much impact on their reading development.[10]

At first glance, these are surprising and unsettling findings. Second thought (which it is the major function of research to stimulate) produces a different reaction. In the first place, it should be obvious that such things as the number of books in a school library, the size of school classes, or the size of per-pupil expenditures *cannot as such* have anything to do with how much children know or how much they learn. When there are many books, most of them may be repellingly dull or incomprehensible; they may be kept in locked cases either literally or bureaucratically; and the librarian may be most of the time supervising study halls and the rest of the time ignored by the teachers. In the smallest of classes it is possible to teach the greatest nonsense in the densest way; and the cost of driver education and band instruments may skyrocket per-pupil expenditures, not to mention books that get locked up in the library.

In the second place, the issue of "which is more important— students' backgrounds or school characteristics?" is another version of the heredity-environment issue that we have learned not to raise because the question is put wrongly. The reasonable question is: under which school (environmental) circumstances do individuals with which characteristics (heredities) flourish best?

The fact of the matter is that it is useless to expect meaningful correlations between gross school characteristics such as library collections on the one hand and student performances on the other, because there is no reason to suppose any necessary mediating connection between the two. Correlatively, from a finding of no relationship, it cannot be inferred that a school characteristic is irrelevant to student achievement; everything depends on *what goes on between* students and e.g. libraries. "Environments" do not produce anything; the *interactions* between environing conditions and individual characteristics produce whatever products emerge.

Again, if one approaches the matter through analysis of variance, as Coleman and his colleagues did, it must be understood that any pattern of variation that might be observed could be produced by several different combinations of circumstances. What follows is that from any given pattern of the variation, one can infer nothing about what generated it. If we are to understand the implications of such research for educational improvement, it is important to understand this point; so I shall elaborate it a little further.

With respect to students' family, neighborhood, or, for that matter, genetic backgrounds, there are four major possibilities so far as educational policy is concerned: (1) There really are no "different kinds of children" in any respects that matter for education so far as learning is concerned; the *relevant* cognitive styles, personality structures, and so forth, are the same for all children in all schools. (2) There are relevant differences among children, but children with one set of relevant characteristics are in one set of schools and children with different relevant characteristics are in another set. That is, students are homogeneous within schools and heterogeneous between schools. (3) There are relevant differences, and all schools contain all types. (4) There are relevant differences, and some schools contain homogeneous students, while other schools contain heterogeneous students.

With respect to relevant *school* characteristics (the experience or vocabulary scores of teachers, for example, or libraries), three major possibilities may be distinguished: (1) All schools are alike so far as *relevant* educational treatments of students are concerned—that is, any observed differences are not in fact relevant to students' learning; and within schools, treatments of students are homogeneous. (2) Schools do differ in relevant respects from one to another, but any given school is internally homogeneous so far as its treatments of students are concerned. (3) Schools are internally heterogeneous with respect to relevant treatments. Within each of the last two possibilities, there are two sub-possibilities of concern to education: (a) the different kinds of educational treatments are appropriately matched to the different kinds of students; (b) they are not.

Now, if we cross-classify those *possible* circumstances about schools and about students, we get the logically possible combinations shown in Table 1. Suppose we then raise Coleman's question—How much variation is there in students' scores, and how much of that variation consists of variation in average *school* scores (that is, lies between schools), as compared to the amount lying *within* schools? Coleman's finding was that there is great variation, which surprised no one; and that most of it lies within schools, which surprised everyone.

But there are at least five sets of circumstances that could have generated that finding. In fact, any of the possible alternative findings (little variation, or variation lying mostly between schools) could have been generated by several different sets of circumstances. The findings to be expected from each combination are shown in the cells of Table 1. Only the five that could have produced the Coleman finding will be commented on here. (The numbers of the paragraphs that follow are keyed to the cell numbers in Table 1.)

Five. Students are alike in all schools with respect to any cognitive styles, motivations, self-images, and the like that are relevant to learning; but different teachers within schools teach differently in relevant respects, or teachers respond differently to students who (mistakenly) seem to *them* to be relevantly different from one another.

Ten. Students differ from one another, but all the students within any given school are like one another. (Schools are "segregated" in respects that actually are relevant to learning styles.) However, within each school, teachers vary in their pedagogy (or there are variations in class size, trackings, testing methods, etc.) in relevant ways, so that some students happen to get treatments matched to their needs and others do not.

Eleven. Students differ, and each school has a wide range of the different types; but in all respects that are relevant (never mind differences that educators only think are relevant), all students get the same sort of treatment. (Tests, for example, are here universally used as sorting devices and grades are used as rewards and punishments.)

Thirteen. Students differ and each school has a wide range of the different types, as in case 11; and schools do differ measurably from *one another* in terms of their overall possession of attributes that are educationally significant (*e.g.*, teachers' vocabulary scores). Still, there is variation *within* each school on those factors; and students are exposed to the differences in ways that do not match treatments to needs.

Table I. Pattern of variance expected from various combinations of heterogeneity—homogeneity of student backgrounds and school treatments.

	Treatments Homogeneous Between Schools	Treatments Homogeneous Within Schools but Heterogeneous Between		Treatments Heterogeneous Within Schools	
		Appropriate	Inappropriate	Appropriate	Inappropriate
Students alike in all schools	1 ○	2 ●	3 ◇	4 ●	5 ▼
Students Homogeneous Within Schools but Heterogeneous Between Schools	6 ◇	7 ○	8 ◇	9 ●	10 ▼
Students Heterogeneous Within Schools	11 ▼	12 ●	13 ▼	14 ○	15 ▼
Some Schools Homogeneous; Others Heterogeneous	16 ▼◇	17 ▼◇	18 ▼◇	19 ○	20 ▼◇

Legend:

- ○ Small Variance
- ◇ Large Variance Within
- ▼ Large Variance Between
- ▼◇ Large Variance Within and Between
- ● Not Applicable

Fifteen. Students differ as in cases 11 and 13; pedagogy is varied in relevant ways within each school; but the pedagogical variations are inaccurately matched with variations in students' needs.

The point of all this is that we have been studying the wrong things. We have started out on the right assumptions, or at least on useful assumptions: that "something about schools" probably makes a difference; that "something about children" probably does too; and that the business of schools is to nurture maximum growth rather than merely to run children through classificatory mazes. But we have focused on too gross characteristics of both schools and children, and have failed to explore properly the question of *matching* pedagogies with (relevant) student characteristics. I think it was necessary to make those "mistakes" in order to demonstrate their mistakenness; but now we are at a point where it is clear that a change of direction is in order.

To drive that point home, consider the attention we have paid to "family backgrounds" as a "source" of differential achievement.

Salient Background and Personal Characteristics

Whatever the influence of "family background" on children, it must in its relevant aspects show up in some characteristic of the student that is relevant to his school role. It may (or may not) be that having been read to when young, or having many books in the house, or having parents who talk a lot about school, affect in any invariant way a child's intellectual or emotional ability or motivation to play a given student role successfully. Such things probably do make a difference,[11] but the point to be emphasized is that they do so by affecting some observable intellectual or emotional ability or motivation. It is fairly obvious, in other words, that different children bring to school, and to any grade in school, different cognitive "schema" or styles;[12] different degrees of trust or mistrust, autonomy, or shame and doubt, initiative or guilt, industriousness or inferiority, identity or identity-diffuseness;[13] need-achievement, need-abasement;[14] activity or passivity, alienation or conformity orientation;[15] and so on.

My point is that it is some such characteristics as these that are *salient* for affecting children's embracement of or distance or alienation from the student role. They, then, are the student characteristics that need to be identified and measured. So far as "family backgrounds" are concerned, their relevance lies in their contribution to those salient student characteristics; and this is an area in which a great deal of research is needed before it makes sense to attempt to "account for" student performance in terms of family backgrounds. Even if we found very high correlations between family backgrounds and growth (which we do not), the knowledge would have no implications at all for the question of what to do now, in the schools. Such knowledge could be an answer to the question, "What historical or nonschool circumstances account for the fact that some students run these school mazes well and others do not?" But it would not be an answer to the question, "Under what present school circumstances do we maximize different students' growth?"[16]

The historical or current circumstances of family backgrounds could be *relevant* to the second question if it were found that certain family characteristics are associated with any salient student characteristics. The relevance would be twofold. First, knowledge of the family structure might be a useful basis for classifying students into those with certain treatment needs and those with other needs; and second, it might be possible to influence the facilitating or impeding features of families. Both of those potential relevances of family backgrounds, however, remain only potential until (1) linkages are established between family structures and salient student characteristics; and (2) linkages are established between those student characteristics and differential "treatment" needs.

In-School Treatments

To use my horticultural analogy again, it is not at all clear what are, in the cultivation of human intellectual potentials, the educational analogies of fertilizer, nitrogen, water temperatures, and so on. "Progressive" *vs.* "classical" education are too vague designations; and "alphabet learning" *vs.* "phonics" *vs.* "whole word learning" are usually debated in all or none terms without notice of the possibility that one method may be appropriate with one kind of student and another with another. Again, the "Dick and Jane" vs. "brown-faces-and-urban-scenes" controversy is too much freighted with speculative sentiment and ideology to be illuminating.

From the work of J. McV. Hunt, Erik Erikson, and Talcott Parsons cited earlier, and from the work of Jerome Bruner,[17] it should be possible to begin to distinguish systematically and relevantly among different pedagogical methods and techniques, which would be a first step to a rational association of methods with student needs.

The point is that, however important it is to ascertain the familial sources of various salient student characteristics in the hope of optimizing them, it is at least equally important to accept those characteristics, once present, as given; and then to ascertain *what their implications are* for children's embracement of or distance or alienation from *various structurings* of the student role. Do children with a high degree of initiative learn arithmetic under an approach that is lethal to children with a great deal of guilt, and vice versa? Is there a way of teaching reading that is functional for children who have the stored imagery of Dr. Seuss and that is dysfunctional for those who have "only" the stored imagery of Beatle lyrics? Do children who display "spoiled" characteristics learn better, regardless of the reading *method,* under teachers who are permissive, or under drill sergeants?

It is such questions as these, concerning educational techniques, teacher styles, and teacher-student transaction modes; and the impact of each on students with differing characteristics that need research emphasis now.

Research "versus" Immediate Action

Only to emphasize the "need for further research," however, is to insult, or at least to be useless to, both the children who are now being wasted in many schools and the educators who struggle daily *now.* I do not pretend to any solutions; it happens to be a *fact* that educators are being asked to perform functions for which the knowledge base is inadequate, and that the knowledge base has got to be improved before improved performances can be expected.

Still, it seems to me that those two needs—for more research and for action now—are not in this case such exclusive alternatives or so competitive for time and resources as they are often thought to be. On the contrary, the kind of research we need and the kind of immediate redirection of educational energies our present knowledge calls for can be mutually reinforcing. More precisely, the research we need is of a kind that can be carried out only in the schools by teachers, administrators, *and students,* who systematically and self-consciously adopt an experimental attitude toward their daily activities. I think the sheer adoption of such a "quality control" orientation toward their activities could revolutionize the climate, *esprit,* and effectiveness of the classroom.

I have alluded to one aspect of such in the discussion of "testing" above; but let me sketch out now a general orientation toward the research that is needed and indicate in doing so how administrators, teachers, and students would necessarily be active participants in it, in a way that (a) would make them investigators rather than "subjects" and (b) could inject a powerful dose of *élan* into the educational process.

Transactions in the School

Students and teachers are engaged, wittingly or not, in a series of transactions with one another in which teachers try to get students to accept certain things, try to resist their demands for certain other things, try to obtain certain things from them, and try to avoid accepting certain other things from them. Students are engaged in the same four kinds of activities. Students and teachers, in other words, make certain outputs to one another, seek certain inputs from one another, resist making certain other outputs, and resist accepting still other inputs. In this they are no different from workers and managers, husbands and wives, priests and parishioners, or any other set of inter-dependent role players.

When their respective demands, acceptances, willingnesses, and resistances exactly complement one another, their relations are in equilibrium. Departures from equilibrium take many forms: teachers or students feel over-demanded, under-demanded, surfeited, deprived, invaded, piratized, exploited, rejected, unappreciated, and so on, when their respective input-output needs are unbalanced in different ways.

Moreover, their transactions, whether balanced or imbalanced, take place under one or another set of rules of the game: a bargaining-market kind of structure may prevail, a legal-bureaucratic one, a solidaristic "Gemeinschaft" type, a team-cooperative kind, or a physically coercive type. Still further, there may or may not be consensus of various types[18] between teachers and students regarding which of those transactional modes the other actually is and normatively should be using.

The various kinds of possible disequilibrium and dissensus produce various adjustive and defensive reactions on the part of both teachers and students, which may spiral into various types of classroom and school conditions quite analogous to depressions and inflations in the economy—not to mention wars, acts of sabotage, secessions, and so on. These various kinds of imbalances undoubtedly have different sorts of consequences for student learning and growth, some disequilibrium being a necessary condition for growth to occur. (Which is to say that perfect equilibrium may be productive of great harmony, happiness, peace, and tranquility—but not of learning.)

The conditions under which disequilibrium and dissensus or equilibrium and consensus occur in schools, the conditions under which teachers and students respond in various ways to either state, the conditions under which those responses and the reaction-to-those-responses are functional or dysfunctional for the (different kinds of) growth of (different kinds of) students— these are among the issues that urgently need research and experimentation.

But who is in a position to know, or at least to find out, which demands are too much, which acceptances too little, and which defenses are being used with what effects on learning? I suggest that teachers, students, and administrators are. They are the persons any researcher would have to ask; and if they ask themselves and one another, they will be collecting the data we all need at the same time as they are transforming their relations into a team effort to explore the barriers to improved education.

We might start with some conception of what the theoretically relevant inputs and outputs of teachers and students from and to one another are, and inaugurate a running inventory of practitioners' conceptions of how relevant those are and of how "equilibrated" their exchanges are, with what results. For example, the critical outputs of teachers might initially be conceived as those delineated by Parsons, Hunt (following Piaget), and Erikson[19] as crucial for both "characterological" and intellectual development: Clear and consistent information, diffuse support, permissiveness, opportunities to express initiative and to express

or experience autonomy, "denial of reciprocity," rewards, opportunities to manipulate objects, corrective feedback, and so on.[20]
The relevant outputs of students to teachers may be conceived
as behaviors indicating the traits Erikson notes as optimum results of socialization (trust, initiative, autonomy, industry, identity), and such other cognitive and behavioral outputs as competence and "concrete" and "formal" operations.

Both teachers' and students' outputs and demands can be made
in a "too much" or "too little" fashion—"too much" and "too
little" for equilibrium and (separately) for student growth. To
focus first on the equilibrium issue, the questions for research
and for students and teachers to ask themselves and one another
would seem to be:

1. How much each "supplier" sees himself as supplying in the
case of each kind of output.

2. How satisfied the suppliers think the receivers are with
those rates and kinds of output.

3. How satisfied the receivers actually are.

4. How satisfied suppliers are with respect to receivers' acceptance of the outputs.

5. How the receivers handle the suppliers' over- or under-
supply of outputs.

6. How satisfied the receivers think the suppliers are with the
receivers' acceptance of suppliers' outputs.

Other Role Relations of Teachers

Teacher-student relations do not, obviously, exhaust the complexity of a school as a social system. Teachers have transactions
with principals, with other teachers, and with other persons in
their status-sets; they have various orientations to and identifi-
cations with their teacher role; and that role stands at a certain
point in each teacher's actual and anticipated status-sequence.
All of these factors help to comprise the total school environment
that is the social Skinner Box in which students learn either to
be "good students" or something else.

What teachers supply to and accept and demand from one
another would seem to be an important determinant of what
they are able and willing to supply to and demand or accept
from students. For example, it should theoretically make a dif-

ference how much personal support teachers get from one another in a profession in which the rewards from students and from parents, not to mention the public and taxpayers, may be less than munificent and are probably variable at best. Furthermore, in what interests the mutual support among teachers, if any, is harnessed would seem to be significant also—whether, for example, in the maintenance of a task-oriented climate, of intellectual stimulation, or of a kind of "us-against-them" mutual protection society against the "administration" and/or the students.

Each of these dimensions needs to be measured as part of a complete analysis of schools as social systems, and needs to be explored by the system's participants if they are to understand their own actions.

In addition, there are outputs by principals that probably affect teachers' embracements of their roles and hence their relations with students—and hence students' growth. And on the other side of the teacher-principal "market" are the things teachers may be expected (or may want) to supply to principals.

In addition, of course, the student-teacher relationship is no more the only significant one for students than it is for teachers. To one another, students supply or fail to supply what they seek from one another, with varying consequences of equilibrium and disequilibrium for growth and learning. Similar considerations apply to student-parent relationships.

The dynamics of the school as a system, in short, are to be understood in terms of the equilibrium and the level of the transactions among school personnel. These transactions are a joint product of the "needs" and adaptive modes of those personnel, and in turn affect the growth experiences of students. When we learn how to distinguish among schools in terms of their various patterns of transaction and their types and levels of equilibrium, using such indexes as those just briefly reviewed, we can then attempt to relate such dynamics to the differential growth of different kinds of students. This, I suggest, will throw considerably more light on the determinants of student development than can be thrown by the more "static" kinds of correlation of student achievement with gross and external school characteristics that were described in the first part of this paper. It can also be a self-correcting feedback process for the school activists themselves.

Students' Intellectual and Other Growth: Some Policy Issues

The concept of "growth" or "development," however, is itself a complex matter. Apart from methodological problems, which may be severe enough, there is the problem of delineating the purely cognitive dimensions along which it might be thought that students should grow. It should probably not be difficult to get consensus on the dimensions of mathematical competence, reading comprehension, understanding of history and of the operation of the student's society, and perhaps of the biological and physical worlds. But on the issues of *how much* or *what kind* of understanding and competence on those issues, consensus might be more difficult. It would probably be even more difficult on the issue of how much and what kind of competence in mathematics, for example, third graders should have as compared to sixth graders, sixth graders as compared to twelfth graders, and so on.

If consensus may be difficult to arrive at in the case of mathematics or reading comprehension, it may be staggeringly so in the case of history, "social studies," and "international affairs." For in those areas—and, in a somewhat different sense, in the areas of biology and physics—there are not only problems of sequence and approach, but also problems of the quantity and quality of content. Indeed, so far as sequence and approach are concerned in *any* area, it is an implication of the notion discussed above of "matching treatments to needs" that different kinds of students at the same chronological age might be mastering very different aspects of any subject matter, *even if all treatments were designed to bring nearly everyone to the same level of competence at some end point*—say, high school graduation.

When one turns to the other dimensions along which it might be considered the function of schools to help children grow, the problems become still more complicated. For one thing, it may often be the case that the most important function a school can perform for a child is to add to one or more of the "characteristics" that, in other children, are already facilitating their mastery of subject matter. That is, it may be that the transformation of self-doubt into autonomy, or the provision of Piaget's or Hunt's "concrete schemata" needs to take priority over subject-matter learning during several years' time, *in order* to optimize later cognitive growth.

For another thing, growth along such dimensions as "citizenship," "respect for the law-without-idolatry-of-it," "empathy," and the like obviously pose measurement problems of a very severe order.

None of these problems, however, is in principle insuperable. Perhaps the most important point to bear in mind in attacking them is that it is *growth* that is the major dependent variable, not point-in-time scores; and that there are probably many different paths to some common end point. If students of Type X, then, are found to diverge further and further from students of Type Y during their first through sixth or even ninth grades, there may be no inferences possible concerning the relative effectiveness of the two different educational treatments they may be receiving.[21] As with marriages, it is not how they begin but how they end that is the measure of their success.

Moreover, to engage in the kind of research advocated above would necessarily involve measuring students' growth along *all* dimensions—from Erikson's personality dimensions through Hunt's cognitive ones to subject-matter mastery. Students whose growth on one seemed to be occurring at the expense of growth on another would be detected at each testing point; and the question of whether this was a functional or a dysfunctional "detour" could be answered by comparative analysis at subsequent testing points.

So far as the dimensions of "citizenship" or "empathy" are concerned, our metrics leave much to be desired; but it is not at all likely that teachers' and peers' ratings and more "unobtrusive measures"[22] would be so clumsy as to be valueless.

An assumption (but not a necessary one) of some of the foregoing analysis has been that all students have the same potential ability to understand such things as arithmetic, literature, and social studies, and to develop initiative, autonomy, and so on, to the same degree. The assumption was conveyed in analogizing such "growth" to plants' development of "healthy" leaves. But the assumption may obviously be incorrect. Perhaps the better analogy is to compare different students' potentialities for growth along any of those dimensions—especially the cognitive ones—with different plants' potentialities for developing roses or lilacs.

Healthy Leaves and Student Achievement

Perhaps, in other words, it is at best a Procrustean enterprise to attempt to find those educational treatments with which student characteristics can be matched in such a way as to produce the same degree of mathematics understanding in everyone by late adolescence. Although there is no evidence to demonstrate conclusively that some students—or perhaps even some racial, ethnic, or sexual categories of students—have genetic characteristics, that *no* environmental treatments can turn into mathematical sophistication, there is, on the other hand, no evidence to demonstrate conclusively the opposite. Until the unlikely day that there will be such evidence, one way or the other, efforts to improve the quality of education will have to guard against two opposite dangers.

The danger of proceeding as if there are treatments which, if only they can be found, can turn students with any characteristic into competent mathematicians, for example, when in fact that is not so, is that both students and teachers will needlessly be frustrated. The danger of proceeding as if that were *not* the case, when in fact it is, is that students can be doomed to non-learning as the outcome of a self-fulfilling prophecy; and educators can be doomed to complacent ritualism.

Moreover, even apart from the possibility of genetic limitations, there are limitations on all students performing equally well on all tests imposed by differences in allocations of time. Dedicated young poets or dancers, for example, are hardly as likely to score as well on mathematics tests as dedicated young engineers, regardless of genes *or* treatments, any more than all students are going to run a four-minute mile, regardless of any kind of coaching *or* leg muscles and heart conditions.

In measuring the effectiveness of schools, then, it is going to be necessary to take into account a great variety of dimensions along which students can grow. There is a distinct sense in which a school whose students' *average* growth along any one or all dimensions is less than that of another school may still be performing an educational function more effectively. This is the sense that various subgroups of its student body may each be growing optimumly along different measured dimensions. If, to take an arbitrary example, one-tenth of School A's students were growing excellently on dimension 1, another tenth were growing excellently on dimension 2, and so on, whereas School B's students were all growing minimally on all ten dimensions, it is possible that the *average* score of School A's students on each of the ten dimensions would be less than that of School B's students. This, of course, would reveal something important about the two schools, but what it revealed would be apparent only if the information on which the schools were evaluated included comparisons between the fastest growing *segments* of the two schools on each dimension. A mere comparison of all-school averages would be seriously misleading.

It should be part of research policy, for this reason, to compare schools and school treatments not only with respect to their students' average growth on many different dimensions, but also with respect to the growth experienced by, say, the various thirds, quintiles, or deciles of growth-scorers in each school on each dimension. Only in this way will we be able to recognize that different schools may be effectively performing different kinds of educational functions for different kinds of students.

The "Jobs" of Teachers, Students, and Schools

I have so far tried to argue four points (1) we need to know what goes on between the various role players in a school, and the effects of these transactions on learning; (2) educators and students are those in a position to know those things; and an explicit effort on their part to keep aware of them would simultaneously improve our knowledge base and their functioning; (3) not all students can possibly grow at the same rate on all dimensions, and it is both cruel and undemocratic to try to force them to do so; (4) different students must take different paths to any given end, and comparisons of rates of progress must take into account the different paths being travelled.

Those points have important implications for educational practice and for public evaluation of the schools. One implication I dwelt on above, and will only restate here; namely, that schools should become places in which administrators, students, and teachers engage as a team in a perpetual self-analysis of their transactions, with "testing" becoming *hypothesis*-testing, not children-testing. (To take one final poke at the testing game, it should be, but appears not to be, self-evident that every test is *at least as* much a test of the effectiveness of the school treatments as it is of students, certainly below the college level.)

A second implication is that schools are not schools, teachers are not teachers, and students are not students, in any way that permits important generalizations. There need to be many different *kinds* of schools, experimenting with different kinds of approaches to different kinds of growth of different kinds of students. There cannot be one kind of effective teacher (hence, one kind of teacher training and certification); different kinds of teachers will be differentially functional and dysfunctional for different kinds of students' growth along different kinds of dimensions. And we must not expect students to be alike. At any age, they are at different points on different dimensions of different growth trends; and some learn one way, others another.

There should not, in other words, be "a" student role or "a" teacher role; there must be many different ones to accommodate the "matching" I spoke of earlier.

But a third implication cross-cuts the second and relates back to the first. The second suggests a policy of maximum flexibility, experimentation, decentralization, and a caution in evaluating all schools and teaching in any mechanically standardized way. The third, however, is that evaluation is essential. Whatever turns out to be the viable division of authority and autonomy among school boards, teachers' unions, teachers' associations, and parents, *no* solution to that problem must permit schools to be unaccountable for the success or failure of their processes. Schools and teachers must be permitted maximum freedom to say what their specific goals are and how they think their methods will achieve them for specified kinds of students; but freedom is not license. With maximum freedom must go maximum accountability, which means objective testing of how methods are working, and straight-forward publication of the results. Moreover, with freedom of schools to state special goals must go freedom of parents and children to choose among schools.

The job of schools is to arrange teaching so as to maximize student growth; the job of teachers is to maximize students' growth; and the job of students is to grow maximally. No one is in a position to tell any of them how to do it, which is why they must be permitted and encouraged (driven if necessary) to experiment in ways for which they must account. The ongoing practice of education must be tied constantly to research.

Which brings me to a final implication. There appears to be a renewed clamor for the abandonment of "methods" courses, or sometimes of whole departments of education and teachers' colleges, and the substitution for them of greater emphasis on "subject matter" and "liberal arts." This seems to me to be a fairly clear baby-and-bathwater case. We now have the anti-matter twin of educationist ritualism in the form of subject-matter magic. What is needed is something altogether different —namely, a recognition that, however necessary a condition for effective teaching is knowledge of the subject matter, a French *teacher* is as different from a French linguist as a physician is from a biologist.

What all of the research reviewed above adds up to is that we need more investments in education departments, not less. I have not read many complaints that college graduates with math majors do not know enough math; the complaint I hear (and share) is that they cannot *teach* math.

The "more" investments we need in education courses for teachers are not, it should go without saying, investments in more of what we have had. They are investments in departments that generate in teachers professional orientation toward re-search and that carry out the kinds of research discussed earlier.

NOTES

1. Harry C. Bredemeier, "The Differential Effectiveness of High Schools with Selected Characteristics in Producing Cognitive Growth in Different Kinds of Students," Final Report to U.S. Department of Health, Education, and Welfare, Office of Education, Project No. 6-8570, June 1967, p. 4.

2. James S. Coleman, *et al., Equality of Educational Opportunity* (Washington, D.C.: U.S. Government Printing Office, 1966), Table 3.24.2, p. 314.

3. *Ibid.*, Table 3.25.2, p. 318; Bredemeier, *op. cit.*, p. 7.

4. Coleman, *op. cit.*, p. 302. I assume that no one will infer from this that the "solution" is to put encyclopedias in everyone's home.

5. Bredemeier, *op. cit.*, pp. 13-16. See also Bernard Goldstein, *et al.*, "Social and Cultural Factors Related to School Achievement," Project No. 2071, U.S. Office of Education, June 1967, pp. D-4–D-6.

6. Bredemeier, *op. cit.*, pp. 18-31.

7. *Ibid.*, pp. 31-41.

8. Goldstein, *op. cit.*

9. David J. Fox, "Evaluation of New York City Title I Educational Projects 1966-67: Expansion of the More Effective Schools Program" (New York: The Center for Urban Education, 1967).

10. David J. Fox, "Evaluation of New York City Title I Educational Projects: Expansion of the Free Choice Open Enrollment Program" (New York: The Center for Urban Education, 1967).

11. See J. McV. Hunt, *Intelligence and Experience* (New York: The Ronald Press Co., 1961); Richard M. Wolf, "The Identification and Measurement of Environmental Process Variables Related to Intelligence," unpublished Ph.D. dissertation, University of Chicago, 1964; and Erik Erikson, "Identity and the Life Cycle," in George S. Klein, ed., *Psychological Issues* (New York: International University Press, Inc., 1959).

12. Cf. Hunt, *ibid.*

13. Erik Erikson, *op. cit.*

14. Henry A. Murray, *Explorations in Personality* (New York: Science Editors, Inc., 1962).

15. Talcott Parsons, *et al., Family, Socialization, and Interaction Process* (New York: Free Press of Glencoe, 1955).

16. I cannot resist the opportunity to point out that a similar confusion often vitiates the potential usefulness of psychoanalysis. To know what childhood experiences account for a given psychic state is to know nothing, without the addition of further premises, about what to do about it now.

17. Jerome Bruner, *Toward a Theory of Instruction* (Cambridge, Mass.: Harvard University, 1966).

18. See Thomas Scheff, "Toward a Sociological Model of Consensus," *Am. Soc. Rev.* 32: 32-46, February 1967.

19. See notes 13-17 above.

20. See Harry C. Bredemeier, "Proposal for An Adequate Socialization Structure," in Group for the Advancement of Psychiatry, *Urban America and the Planning of Mental Health Services* (New York: Group for the Advancement of Psychiatry, 1964). See also by the same author, "The Lower Class Family of Orientation," and "The Lower Class Family of Procreation," in Bernard Goldstein, *Low Income Youth in Urban Areas* (New York: Holt, Rinehart and Winston, 1967).

21. Cf. Hunt, *op. cit.*, pp. 275-277.

22. Eugene Webb, *et al., Unobtrusive Measures* (Chicago, Ill.: Rand, McNally & Co., 1966).

This selection, taken from the comprehensive Report of the National Advisory Commission on Civil Disorders, *aids considerably in illuminating the problems of the inner city, particularly that of the educational system. As noted earlier in the discussion on the socialization process (Introduction to the Second Division), the educational system is the primary socialization agency today. On this rests the future of urban life and its values. Whether as student or citizen, one cannot afford to ignore the information contained in this* Report.

XI

Recommendations for Action in Education: The Teacher. *Report of the National Advisory Commission on Civil Disorders*

Teachers

THE SCHOOLS ATTENDED BY DISADVANTAGED Negro children commonly are staffed by teachers with less experience and lower qualifications than those attended by middle-class whites.[1] For example, a 1963 study ranking Chicago's public high schools by the socio-economic status of surrounding neighborhoods found that in the 10 lowest-ranking schools only 63.2 per cent of all teachers were fully certified and the median level of teaching experience was 3.9 years. In three of these schools, the median level was one year. Four of these lowest ranking schools were 100 per cent Negro in enrollment and three were over 90 per cent Negro. By contrast eight of the ten highest ranking schools had nearly total white enrollments, and the other two were more than 75 per cent white. In these schools, 90.3 per cent of the teachers were fully certified and the median level of teaching experience was 12.3 years.

Testifying before the Commission, Dr. Paul Daniel Dodson, Director of the New York University Center for Human Relations and Community Services, stated that:

"Inner-city schools have not been able to hold teaching staff. Between 1952 and 1962 almost half the licensed teachers of New York City left the system. Almost two out of every five of the 50,000 teaching personnel of New York City do not hold regular permanent licenses for the assignments they have.

"In another school system in one of the large cities, it was reported of one inner-city school that of 84 staff members, 41 were temporary teachers, 25 were probationaries and 18 [were] tenure teachers. However, only one of the tenure teachers was licensed in academic subjects."

U.S. Commissioner of Education, Harold Howe, testified that many teachers are unprepared for teaching in schools serving disadvantaged children, "have what is a traumatic experience there and don't last." Moreover, the more experienced teachers normally select the more attractive schools in white neighborhoods, thereby relegating the least experienced teachers to the disadvantaged schools. This process reinforces the view of ghetto schools as inferior.

As a result, teachers assigned to these schools often begin with negative attitudes toward the students, and their ability and willingness to learn. These attitudes are aggravated by serious discipline problems, by the high crime rates in areas surrounding the schools, and by the greater difficulties of teaching students from disadvantaged backgrounds. These conditions are reflected in the Coleman Report's finding that a higher proportion of teachers in schools serving disadvantaged areas are dissatisfied with their present assignments and with their students than are their counterparts in other schools.[2]

Studies have shown that the attitudes of teachers toward their students have very powerful impacts upon educational attainment. The more teachers expect from their students—however disadvantaged those students may be—the better the students perform. Conversely, negative teacher attitudes act as self-fulfilling prophecies: the teachers expect little from their students; the students fulfill the expectation. As Dr. Kenneth Clark observed,

"Children who are treated as if they are uneducable invariably become uneducable."[3]

In disadvantaged areas, the neighborhood school concept tends to concentrate a relatively high proportion of emotionally disturbed and other problem children in the schools. Disadvantaged neighborhoods have the greatest need for health personnel, supplementary instructors and counsellors to assist with family problems, provide extra instruction to lagging students and deal with the many serious mental and physical health deficiencies that occur so often in poverty areas.

These conditions which make effective teaching vastly more difficult, reinforce negative teacher attitudes. A 1963 survey of Chicago public schools showed that the condition creating the highest amount of dissatisfaction among teachers was lack of adequate provision for the treatment of maladjusted, retarded and disturbed pupils. About 79 per cent of elementary school teachers and 67 per cent of high school teachers named this item as a key factor. The need for professional support for teachers in dealing with these extraordinary problems is seldom, if ever, met.

Although special schools or classes are available for emotionally disturbed and mentally handicapped children, many pupils requiring such help remain in regular classes because of negligence, red tape or unavailability of clinical staff. An example is provided by a National Education Association Study of Detroit:[4]

> Before a disturbed child can receive psychological assistance, he must receive diagnostic testing. But before this happens, the teacher must fill in a form . . . to be submitted . . . to a central office committee . . . If the committee decides that psychological testing is in order, the teacher must fill out a second form . . . to be submitted to the psychological clinic. The child may then be placed on the waiting list for psychological testing. The waiting period may last for several weeks, several months, or several years. And while he waits, he "sits in" the regular classroom . . . Since visiting teachers are scarce and special classes insufficient in number, the child who has been tested is usually returned to the regular classroom to serve more time as a "sit-in."

Teaching in disadvantaged areas is made more difficult by the high rate of student turnover. In New York City during 1963-1964, seven of ten students in the average, segregated Negro-

Puerto Rican elementary school either entered or left during the year.[5] Similar conditions are common to other inner-city schools. Continuity of education becomes exceedingly difficult—the more so because many of the students entering ghetto schools during the school year come from rural southern schools and are thus behind even the minimum levels of achievement attained by their fellow northern-born students.

Enrollments

In virtually every large American city, the inner city schools attended by Negroes are the most overcrowded. We have cited the vast population exchange—relatively affluent whites leaving the city to be replaced by Negroes—which has taken place over the last decade. The impact on public education facilities has been severe.

Despite an overall decrease in the population of many cities, school enrollment has increased. Over the last 15 years, Detroit has *lost* approximately 20,000 to 30,000 families. Yet during that same period the public school system *gained* approximately 50,000 to 60,000 children. Between 1961 and 1965, Detroit's Negro public school enrollment increased by 31,108, while white enrollment dropped 23,748. In Cleveland between 1950 and 1965, a population loss of 130,000 coincided with a school enrollment increase of 50,000. Enrollment gains in New York City and Chicago were even larger.

Although of lesser magnitude, similar changes have occurred in the public school systems of many other large cities. As white students withdraw from a public school, they are replaced by a greater number of Negro students. This reflects the fact that the Negro population is relatively younger, has more children of school age, makes less use of private schools, and is more densely concentrated than the white population.

As a result, Negro school enrollments have increased even more rapidly than the total Negro population in central cities. In Cincinnati, for example, between 1960 and 1965 the Negro population grew 16 per cent, while Negro public school enrollment increased 26 per cent.[6] The following data for four other cities illustrate how the proportion of Negroes in public schools has outgrown the Negro proportion of the total city population.[7]

TABLE 11-1—*Negro Population and Public School Enrollment*

	Negro % of Population			Negro % of Public School Enrollment		
	1950	1965	Change	1950	1965	Change
Atlanta	36.6	43.5	+ 6.9	39.1	53.7	+14.6
Milwaukee	3.5	10.8	+ 7.3	6.6	22.9	+16.3
Oakland	12.4	30.0	+17.6	14.0	45.0	+31.0
Washington	35.0	55.0	+20.0	50.1	89.4	+39.3

Negroes now comprise a majority or near majority of public school students in seven of the ten largest American cities, as well as in many other cities. The following table illustrates the percentage of Negro students for the period 1965-1966 in the public elementary schools of 42 cities, including the 28 largest, 17 of which have Negro majorities:

TABLE 11-2—*Proportion of Negro Students in Total Public Elementary School Enrollment, 1965-1966*

City	Per Cent Negro
Washington, D.C.	90.9%
Chester, Pa.	69.3
Wilmington, Del.	69.3
Newark	69.1
New Orleans	65.5
Richmond	64.7
Baltimore	64.3
East St. Louis	63.4
St. Louis	63.3
Gary	59.5
Philadelphia	58.6
Detroit	55.3
Atlanta	54.7
Cleveland	53.9
Memphis	53.2
Chicago	52.8
Oakland	52.1
Harrisburg	45.7
New Haven	45.6
Hartford	43.1
Kansas City	42.4
Cincinnati	40.3
Pittsburgh	39.4
Buffalo	34.6
Houston	33.9

Table 11-2—*continued*

City	Per Cent Negro
Flint	33.1
Indianapolis	30.8
New York City	30.1
Boston	28.9
San Francisco	28.8
Dallas	27.5
Miami	26.8
Milwaukee	26.5
Columbus	26.1
Los Angeles	23.4
Oklahoma City	21.2
Syracuse	19.0
San Antonio	14.2
Denver	14.0
San Diego	11.6
Seattle	10.5
Minneapolis	7.2

Source: U.S. Commission on Civil Rights, "Racial Isolation in the Public Schools."

Because this rapid expansion of Negro population has been concentrated in segregated neighborhoods, ghetto schools have experienced acute overcrowding. Shortages of textbooks and supplies have developed. Double shifts are common; hallways and other non-classroom space have been adapted for class instruction; and mobile classroom units are used. Even programs for massive construction of new schools in Negro neighborhoods cannot always keep up with increased overcrowding.

From 1951 to 1963, the Chicago Board of Education built 266 new schools or additions, mainly in all-Negro areas. Yet a special committee studying the schools in 1964 reported that 40 per cent of the Negro elementary schools had more than 35 students per available classroom, as compared to 12 per cent of the primarily white elementary schools. Of the eight Negro high schools, five had enrollments over 50 per cent above designed capacity. Four of the 10 integrated high schools, but only four of the 26 predominantly white high schools, were similarly overcrowded. Comparable conditions prevail in many other large cities.

The Civil Rights Commission found that two-thirds of the predominantly Negro elementary schools in Atlanta were overcrowded. This compared with 47 per cent of the white schools.

In 1965, all Atlanta Negro high schools were operating beyond their designed capacity; only one of three all-white high schools, and six of eight predominantly white schools were similarly overcrowded.[8]

Washington, D.C. elementary schools with 85-100 per cent Negro enrollments operated at a median of 115 per cent of capacity. The one predominantly white high school operated at 92.3 per cent, an integrated high school at 101.1 per cent, and the remaining schools—all predominantly Negro—at 108.4 per cent to 127.1 per cent of capacity.

Overcrowded and inadequately supplied schools have severe effects upon the quality of education, the most important of which is that teachers are forced to concentrate on maintaining classroom discipline, and thus have little time and energy to perform their primary function—educating the students.

NOTES

1. The Civil Rights Commission's survey found no major national differences in the educational attainment (years completed) of teachers in majority-Negro or majority-white schools. However, many large cities did not take part in the basic studies which supplied the data for this conclusion. It is precisely in these cities that teachers of disadvantaged Negro students tend to be the least experienced. Moreover, the Commission did conclude that Negro students, more often than whites, had teachers with non-academic college majors and lower verbal achievement levels.

2. Coleman Report, p. 12.

3. "Dark Ghetto," Dr. Kenneth Clark (1965), p. 128.

4. "Detroit, Michigan: A Study of Barriers to Equal Educational Opportunity in a Large City," National Commission on Professional Rights and Responsibilities of the National Education Association of the United States, March, 1967, p. 66.

5. The comparable rate in the white schools was four out of ten.

6. Cincinnati report for U.S. Commission on Civil Rights, pp. 8-9, 11.

7. Figures for Atlanta, Milwaukee and Oakland are from their reports to the Civil Rights Commission: Atlanta, pp. 2-3, 25; Milwaukee, pp. 19, 37, 42; Oakland, pp. 7, 11-15A; and the Bureau of the Census. Washington figures are from the District of Columbia Board of Education.

8. Atlanta report for Civil Rights Commission, pp. 32-34.

Karl Marx and others believed basically that the "working class" would eventually be the sole, undisputed spearhead for constructive transformation of human values. The following article helps clarify the complex reasons for the inaccuracy of Marx's oversimplified assertion.

XII

Democracy and Working-Class Authoritarianism*

SEYMOUR MARTIN LIPSET

GRADUAL REALIZATION THAT AUTHORITARIAN predispositions and ethnic prejudice flow more naturally from the situation of the lower classes than from that of the middle and upper classes in modern industrial society has posed a tragic dilemma for those intellectuals of the democratic left who once believed the proletariat necessarily to be a force for liberty, racial equality, and social progress. Ignazio Silone has asserted that "the myth of the liberating power of the proletariat has dissolved along with that other myth of progress. The recent examples of the Nazi labor unions, like those of Salazar and Peron . . . have at last convinced of this even those who were reluctant to admit it on the sole grounds of the totalitarian degeneration of Communism."[1]

* Reprinted from the *American Sociological Review*, Vol. 24, pp. 482-501, 1959, by permission of the author and the American Sociological Association.

An early version of this paper was written for a conference on "The Future of Liberty" sponsored by the Congress for Cultural Freedom in Milan, Italy in September, 1955. It has been extensively reworked since that time as part of a comparative study of the relationship between political behavior and social structure which has been supported by grants from the Committee on Comparative Politics of the Social Science Research Council and the Behavioral Sciences Division of the Ford Foundation. I am indebted to Robert Alford and Juan Linz for research assistance.

A slightly altered version of this article can be found in Professor Lipset's book, *Political Man,* published by Doubleday & Company, Inc., Garden City, New York (1959).

Dramatic demonstrations of this point have been given recently by the support of White Citizen's Councils and segregation by workers in the South, and by the active participation of many workers in the "race riots" in England. A "Short Talk with a Fascist Beast" (an 18-year-old casual laborer who took part in the beating of Negroes in London), appearing in the left Socialist *New Statesman*, portrays graphically the ideological syndrome which sometimes culminates in such behavior:[2]

> "That's why I'm with the Fascists," he says. "They're against the blacks. That Salmon, he's a Communist. The Labour Party is Communist too. Like the unions." His mother and father, he says, are strict Labour supporters. Is he against the Labour Party. "Nah, I'm for them. They're for y'know—us. I'm for the unions too." Even though they were dominated by Communists? "Sure," he says. "I like the Communist Party. It's powerful, like." How can he be for the Communists when the Fascists hate them?
>
> Len says, "Well, y'know, I'm for the Fascists when they're against the nigs. But the Fascists is really for the rich people y'know, like the Tories. All for the guv'nors, people like that. But the Communists are very powerful." I told him the Communist Party of Britain was quite small.
>
> "But," he says, "they got Russia behind them." His voice was full of marvel. "I admire Russia. Y'know, the people. They're peaceful. They're strong. When they say they'll do a thing, they do it. Not like us. Makes you think: they got a weapon over there can wipe us all out, with one wave of a general's arm. Destroy us completely and totally. Honest, those Russians. When they say they'll do a thing, they do it. Like in Hungary. I pity those people, the Hungarians. But did you see the Russians went in and stopped them. Tanks. Not like us in Cyprus. Our soldiers get shot in the back and what do we do? The Communists is for the small men."

The demonstrations of working-class ethnic prejudice and support for totalitarian political movements which have upset many leftist stereotypes parallel findings in such different areas of social science research as public opinion, religion, family patterns, and personality structure. Many studies suggest that the lower-class way of life produces individuals with rigid and intolerant approaches to politics. These findings, discussed below, imply that one may anticipate wide-spread support by lower-class individuals and groups for extremist movements.

This assertion may seem to be contradicted by the facts of political history. Since their beginnings in the nineteenth century, workers' organizations and parties have been a major force in extending political democracy and in waging progressive political and economic struggles. Before 1914, the classic division between the working-class left parties and the right was not based solely upon stratification issues, such as redistribution of income, status, and educational opportunities, but also rested upon civil liberties and international policy issues. The workers, judged by the policies of their parties, were often the backbone of the fight for greater political democracy, religious freedom and minority rights, and international peace. The parties backed by the conservative middle and upper classes in much of Europe, on the other hand, tended to favor more extremist political forms, resist the extension of the suffrage, back the established church, and support jingoistic foreign policies.

Events since 1914 have gradually eroded these patterns. In some countries working-class groups have proved to be the most nationalistic and jingoistic sector of the population. In a number of nations, they have clearly been in the forefront of the struggle against equal rights for minority groups, and have sought to limit immigration or to impose racial standards in countries with open immigration. The conclusion of the anti-Fascist era and the emergence of the cold war have shown that the struggle for freedom is not a simple variant of the economic class struggle. The threat to freedom posed by the Communist movement is as great as that once posed by Fascism and Nazism, and that movement, in all countries where it is strong, is based largely on the lower levels of the working-class or the rural population.[3] No other party has been as thoroughly and completely based on the working-class and the poor. Socialist parties, past and present, have secured much more support from the middle classes than have the Communists.

Some socialists and liberals have suggested that the fact of working-class backing for Communism proves nothing about authoritarian tendencies in the working-class, since the Communist Party often masquerades as a party seeking to fulfill the classic western-democratic revolutionary values of liberty, equality and fraternity; they argue that most Communist supporters, particularly the less educated, are deceived into thinking that the Communists are simply more militant and more efficient socialists. I would suggest, however, the alternative hypothesis that, rather than being a source of strain, the intransigent, intolerant, and demonological aspects of Communist ideology attract members from the lower class of low income, low-status occupation, and little education. In modern industrial societies such persons have made up a very large part of the working class.

The social situation of the lower strata, particularly in poorer countries with low levels of education, predisposes them to view politics in simplistic and chiliastic terms of black and white, good and evil. Consequently, other things being equal, they should be more likely than other strata to prefer extremist movements which suggest easy and quick solutions to social problems and have a rigid outlook rather than those which view the problem of reform or change in complex and gradualist terms and which support rational values of tolerance.

The "authoritarianism" of any social stratum or class, of course, is highly relative, as well as modifiable by organizational commitments to democracy and by individual cross-pressures. Thus the lower class in any given country may be more authoritarian than the upper classes, but on an "absolute" scale all the classes in that country may be less authoritarian than any class in another country. In a country such as Britain, where norms of toleration are well-developed and widespread in every social stratum, even the lowest class may be less authoritarian, more "sophisticated" in the sense of having a longer time-perspective and a gradualist political outlook, than the most highly educated stratum in an underdeveloped country, where immediate problems and crises impinge on every class and short-term solutions may be sought by all groups.[4]

Commitments to democratic procedures and ideals by the principal organizations to which low-status individuals belong may, however, influence their actual political behavior more than their underlying personal values, however authoritarian.[5] A working class which has developed an early (prior to the Communists) loyalty to a democratic political or trade-union movement which has successfully fought for the social and economic rights of that class will not easily change its allegiance.

Commitments to other values or institutions by individuals may also override the most established authoritarian predispositions. Thus a Catholic worker who is strongly anti-capitalist may still vote for a relatively conservative party in France, Italy, or

Germany because his ties to Catholicism are stronger determinants of his electoral choice than his resentments about his class status; a worker with a high authoritarian predisposition may defend democratic institutions against Fascist attack because his links to anti-Fascist working-class parties and unions affect his political behavior more than do his authoritarian values. Conversely, those who are not predisposed toward extremist political styles may back an extremist party because of certain aspects of its program and political role. Many persons supported the Communists in 1936 and 1943 as an anti-Fascist internationalist party.

The specific propensity of given social strata to support extremist or democratic political parties, then, cannot be derived or predicted from a knowledge of their psychological predispositions or from attitudes revealed by the survey data presented below.[6] Both evidence and theory suggest, however, that the lower strata are relatively more authoritarian, that (again, other things being equal) they will be more attracted toward an extremist movement than toward a moderate and democratic one, and that, once recruited, they will not be alienated by its lack of democracy, while more educated or sophisticated supporters will tend to drop away.

I shall first discuss basic lower-class attitudes toward civil liberties and non-economic liberalism in general and then examine certain parallels between religion and politics. After documenting some of the general patterns, I shall specify the elements in the general life-situation of lower class persons—the family patterns, typical educational experiences, characteristic tensions and insecurities, their isolated group existence and general lack of sophistication—which differentiate their life from that of the middle classes and make the poor receptive to authoritarian values and likely to support extremist movements.[7]

Democratic Values and Stratification

The distinction between economic and non-economic liberalism helps to clarify the relationship between class position and political behavior. Economic liberalism refers to the conventional issues concerning redistribution of income, status, and power among the classes. The poorer everywhere are more liberal or leftist on such issues; they favor more welfare state measures, higher wages, graduated income taxes, support of trade-unions, and other measures opposed by those of higher class position. On the other hand, when liberalism is defined in non-economic terms—so as to support, for example, civil liberties for political dissidents, civil rights for ethnic and racial minorities, internationalist foreign policies, and liberal immigration legislation—the correlation is reversed.[8]

Abundant data from almost every country in the world with competing political parties show that economic liberalism or leftism is inversely associated with socio-economic status. In Germany, for example, a study conducted by the UNESCO Institute at Cologne asked a systematic sample of 3,000 Germans: "Do you think that it would be better if there were one party, several parties, or no party?" The results analyzed according to occupational status indicate that the lower strata of the working class and the rural population were less likely to support a multi-party system (a reasonable index of democratic attitudes in westernized countries) than the middle and upper strata. (See Table 1.) Comparable results were obtained in 1958 when a similar question was asked of national or regional samples in Austria, Japan, Brazil, Canada, Mexico, West Germany, the Netherlands, Belgium, Italy, and France. Although the proportion favoring a multi-party system varied from country to country, within each nation low socio-economic status was associated with failure to support a multi-party system.[9]

TABLE 1.—*Responses of Different German Occupational Groups to Preferred Party System in Percentages (Males Only), 1953*[*]

Occupational Group	Several Parties	One Party	No Party	No Opinion	N
Civil Servants	88	6	3	3	111
Upper White-Collar	77	13	2	8	58
Free Professionals	69	13	8	10	38
Skilled Workers	65	22	5	8	277
Artisans	64	16	9	11	124
Lower White-Collar	62	19	7	12	221
Businessmen (Small)	60	15	12	13	156
Farmers	56	22	6	16	241
Semi-Skilled Workers	49	28	7	16	301
Unskilled Workers	40	27	11	22	172

[*] Computed from IBM cards supplied to author by the UNESCO Institute at Cologne from its 1953 survey of German opinion.

Somewhat similar findings were obtained in studies in Japan, Great Britain, and the United States in surveys designed to secure general reactions to problems of civil liberties or the rights of various minorities. In Japan, for example, the workers and the rural population tended to be more authoritarian and less concerned with civil liberties than the middle and upper classes.[10]

In England, Eysenck found comparable differences between "tough-minded" and "tender-minded" people in their general social outlook. The first group tended to be intolerant of deviations from the standard moral or religious codes, anti-Negro, anti-Semitic, and xenophobic, while the "tender-minded" in general were tolerant of deviation, unprejudiced, and internationalist.[11] In summing up his findings, based on attitude scales given to supporters of different British parties, Eysenck reports that "Middle-class Conservatives are more tender-minded than working-class Conservatives; middle-class Liberals are more tender-minded than working-class Liberals; middle-class Socialists are more tender-minded than working-class Socialists; and even middle-class Communists are more tender-minded than working-class Communists."[12]

The evidence from various American studies dealing with attitudes toward civil liberties, as well as such other components of non-economic liberalism as ethnic prejudice, is also clear and consistent—the lower strata are the least tolerant.[13] In the most systematic of these, based on a national sample of nearly 5,000 Americans, Stouffer divided his respondents into three categories, "less tolerant, in-between, and more tolerant," by using a scale based on responses to questions about the right of free speech for Communists, critics of religion, advocates of nationalization of industry, and the like. As the data presented in Table 2 demonstrate, tolerance increases with moves up the stratification lad-

TABLE 2.—*Proportion of Male Respondents Who Are "More Tolerant" With Respect to Civil Liberties Issues**

Professional and Semi-Professional	66%	(159)
Proprietors, Managers and Officials	51	(223)
Clerical and Sales	49	(200)
Manual Workers	30	(685)
Farmers or Farm Workers	20	(202)

* Source: Samuel A. Stouffer, *Communism, Conformity and Civil Liberties,* New York: Doubleday, 1955, p. 139. The figures for manual and farm workers were calculated from cards supplied by Professor Stouffer.

der. Only 30 per cent of those in manual occupations are in the "most tolerant" category, as contrasted with 66 per cent of the professionals and 51 per cent of the proprietors, managers, and officials. As in Germany and Japan, farmers are low in tolerance.

The findings of public opinion surveys in thirteen different countries that the lower strata are less committed to democratic norms than the middle classes are reaffirmed by the research of more psychologically oriented investigators, who have studied the social correlates of "authoritarian personality" structures as measured by the now famous "F scale."[14] The most recent summary of the research findings of the many studies in this area shows a consistent association of authoritarianism with lower class and status.[15] One survey of 460 Los Angeles adults reports that "the working class contains a higher proportion of authoritarians than either the middle or the upper class," and that among workers, those who explicitly identified themselves with "the working class" rather than "the middle class" were more authoritarian.[16]

Recent research within lower status groups suggests the possibility of a *negative* correlation between authoritarianism and neuroticism. This would be congruent with the hypothesis that those who deviate from the standards of their group are more likely to be neurotic than those who conform. Hence, if we assume that authoritarian traits are conventional reactions of low status people, then the lower class anti-authoritarian should be more neurotic.[17] As Davids and Eriksen point out, where the "standard of reference on authoritarianism is quite high," people may be well adjusted *and* authoritarian.[18] The absence of a relationship between authoritarian attitudes and neurotic traits among lower class groups reported by these authors is consistent with the hypothesis that authoritarian attitudes are "normal" and expected in such groups.[19]

Authoritarian Religion and Stratification

Many observers have called attention to a connection between low social status and fundamentalist or chiliastic religion. The liberal Protestant churches, on the other hand, almost invariably have been predominantly middle-class in membership. In the United States, this class division among the churches has created a dilemma for the clergy of the so-called liberal churches, who have tended to be liberal in their politics as well as in their religion and, hence, have often desired to spread their social and religious gospel among the lower strata. They have found, however, that the latter prefer ministers who preach of hell-fire and salvation, of a conflict between God and Satan, to those who advocate modern liberal Protestant theology.[20]

Writing in the early period of the socialist movement, Frederick Engels noted that early Christianity and the revolutionary workers' movement had "notable points of resemblance," particularly in their millenial appeals and lower-class base.[21] Recently, Elmer Clark has shown that small sects in contemporary America, sects resembling early Christianity, "originate mainly among the religiously neglected poor." He writes:

> [when] the revolts of the poor have been tinged with religion, which was nearly always the case until recent times, millenial ideas have appeared, and . . . these notions are prominent in most of the small sects which follow the evangelical tradition. Premillenarianism is essentially a defense mechanism of the disinherited; despairing of obtaining substantial blessings through social processes, they turn on the world which has withheld its benefits and look to its destruction in a cosmic cataclysm which will exalt them and cast down the rich and powerful.[22]

Troeltsch has characterized the psychological appeal of sectarian religion in a way that might as appropriately be applied to extremist politics:

> It is the lower classes which do the really creative work, forming communities on a genuine religious basis. They alone unite imagination and simplicity of feeling with a nonreflective habit of mind, a primitive energy, and an urgent sense of need. On such a foundation alone is it possible to build up an unconditional authoritative faith in a Divine Revelation with simplicity of surrender and unshaken certainty. Only within a fellowship of this kind is there room for those who have a sense of spiritual need, and who have not acquired the habit of intellectual reasoning, which always regards everything from a relative point of view.[23]

Jehovah's Witnesses is an excellent example of a rapidly growing sect which "continues to attract, as in the past, the under-privileged strata."[24] Their principal teaching is that the Kingdom of Heaven is at hand. "The end of the age is near. Armageddon is just around the corner, when the wicked will be destroyed, and the theocracy, or rule of God, will be set up upon the earth."[25] And as in the case of Communist political millenialists, the organization of the Witnesses, whose membership in the United States is many hundreds of thousands, is "hierarchical and highly authoritarian. There is little democratic participation in the management or in the formation of policies of the movement as a whole."[26]

Direct linkages between the social roots of political and of religious extremism have been observed in a number of countries. In Czarist Russia, the young Trotsky consciously recognized this relationship and successfully recruited the first working-class members of the South Russian Workers' Union (a revolutionary Marxist organization of the late 1890s) from adherents to religious sects.[27] In Holland and Sweden, recent studies have shown that the Communists are strongest in regions which once were centers of fundamentalist religious revivalism.[28]

These findings do not imply that religious sects supported by lower-class elements become centers of political protest; in fact, the discontent and frustration otherwise flowing into channels of political extremism are often drained off by a transvaluational religion. The point here is that rigid fundamentalism and chiliastic dogmatism are linked to the same underlying characteristics, attitudes, and predispositions, which find another outlet in allegiance to authoritarian political movements.

In his excellent study of the sources of Swedish communism, Sven Rydenfelt demonstrates the competitive relationship between religious and political extremism. He analyzed the differences between two northern counties of Sweden, Vasterbotten and Norrbotten, in an attempt to explain the relatively low Communist vote in the former (two per cent) and the much larger vote in the latter county (21 per cent), although both have comparable social and economic conditions. The Liberal Party, which in Sweden gives much more support than any other to religious extremism, was very strong in Vasterbotten (30 per cent) and correspondingly weak in Norrbotten (nine per cent). Rydenfelt concludes that a general predisposition toward radicalism existed in both counties, containing some of the poorest, most socially isolated, and rootless groups in Sweden, but that the expression of radicalism differed, taking a religious form in one county, and a Communist in the other. "The Communists and the religious radicals, as for instance the Pentecostal sects, seem to be competing for the allegiance of the same groups."[29]

The Typical Social Situation of Lower-Class Persons

A number of elements in the typical social situation of lower-class individuals may be singled out as contributing to authoritarian predispositions: low education, low participation in political organizations or in voluntary organizations of any type, little reading, isolated occupations, economic insecurity, and authoritarian family patterns. Although these elements are interrelated, they are by no means identical.

There is consistent evidence that degree of formal education, itself closely correlated with social and economic status, is also highly correlated with undemocratic attitudes. Data from Stouffer's study of attitudes toward civil liberties in America and from the UNESCO Research Institute's survey of German opinion bearing on a multi-party system presented in Tables 3 and 4 reveal this clearly.

These tables indicate that an increase in educational attainment has the effect of raising the proportion of democratic attitudes at each occupational level. Within each educational level, higher occupational status also seems to make for greater tolerance, but the increases associated with higher educational level are greater than those related to higher occupational level,

TABLE 3.—*The Relationship Between Occupation, Education, and Political Tolerance in the United States, 1955*[*]

Percentage in the Two "Most Tolerant" Categories

Occupation

	Low Manual		High Manual		Low White Collar		High White Collar	
Grade School	13	(228)	21	(178)	23	(47)	26	(100)
Some High School	32	(99)	33	(124)	29	(56)	46	(68)
High School Grad.	40	(64)	48	(127)	47	(102)	56	(108)
Some College	—	(14)	64	(36)	64	(80)	65	(37)
College Grad.	—	(3)	—	(11)	74	(147)	83	(21)

[*] Computed from IBM cards supplied by Samuel Stouffer from his study, *Communism, Conformity and Civil Liberties*, New York: Doubleday, 1955.

TABLE 4.—*The Relationship Between Occupation, Education, and Support of a Democratic Party System in Germany—1953*[*]

| | Per Cent Favoring the Existence of Several Parties Educational Level | |
Occupation	Elementary School	High School or Higher
Farm Laborers	29 (59)	—
Manual Workers	43 (1439)	52 (29)
Farmers	43 (381)	67 (9)
Lower White Collar	50 (273)	68 (107)
Self-Employed Business	53 (365)	65 (75)
Upper White Collar	58 (86)	69 (58)
Officials (Govt.)	59 (158)	78 (99)
Professions	56 (18)	68 (38)

[*] Source: see Table 1.

when the other factor is held constant.[30] It may be inferred that the quality of the educational experience is more highly associated with political tolerance than occupational experience *per se.* But both inferior education and low occupational position are highly intercorrelated, both are part of the complex making up low-status, and are associated with a lack of tolerance.[31]

Low-status groups also participate less in formal organizations, read fewer magazines and books regularly, possess less information on public affairs, vote less, and, in general, are less interested in politics.[32] The available evidence suggests that each of these attributes is related to democratic attitudes. Thus, an analysis of German data collected by the UNESCO Institute in 1953 found that at every occupational level those who belonged to voluntary associations were more likely to favor a multi-party than a one-party system.[33] American findings also indicate that authoritarians join fewer "community groups" than non-authoritarians.[34] A study of the determinants of economic and non-economic liberalism reports that on every occupational level the persons poorly informed on public questions are more likely to be both more radical on economic issues and less liberal on non-economic issues.[35] Non-voters and those less interested in political matters are much more intolerant and xenophobic than those who vote and have political interests.[36]

The authors of a study concerned with the "hard core" of "chronic know-nothings" suggest that such persons come disproportionately from the less-literate, lower socio-economic groups. These people are not only uninformed, but "harder to reach, no matter what the level or nature of the information." Here again is a hint at the complex character of the relations between education, liberalism, and status. Non-economic liberalism is not a simple matter of acquiring education and information; it must be considered at least in part a basic attitude which is actively discouraged by the social situation of lower-status persons.[37] As Knupfer has pointed out in her review of the literature bearing on the "underdog," "economic underprivilege is psychological underprivilege: habits of submission, little access to sources of information, lack of verbal facility. These things appear to produce a lack of self-confidence which increases the unwillingness of the low-status person to participate in many phases of our predominantly middle-class culture. . . ."[38]

These characteristics also reflect the extent to which lower-class persons are *isolated* from the activities, controversies, and organizations of democratic society, an isolation which prevents them from securing that sophisticated and complex view of the political structure which makes understandable and necessary the norms of tolerance. It is instructive to examine in this connection those occupations which are most isolated, in every sense, from contact with the world outside their own occupational group. We should expect that persons in these occupations will support extremist movements and exhibit low political tolerance. Such in fact is the case. Manual workers in "isolated occupations" which require them to live among their workmates in one-industry towns or areas—for example, miners, maritime workers, loggers, fishermen, and sheep shearers—all exhibit high rates of Communist support in most countries.[39]

Similarly, rural persons, both farmers and laborers, show high authoritarian predispositions. All public opinion surveys indicate that they oppose civil liberties and multi-party systems more than any other occupational group. Election surveys indicate farm owners to have been among the strongest supporters of Fascist parties, while farm workers and poor farmers and share-croppers have given even stronger backing to the Communists in Italy, France, and India, for example, than have manual workers.[40]

The same social conditions which are related to unsophistication and authoritarianism among workers are also associated with middle-class authoritarianism. The groups which have been most prone to support Fascist and other middle-class based extremist ideologies have been, in addition to farmers and peasants, the small businessmen of provincial communities. These groups are isolated from "cosmopolitan" culture and also rank far lower than any other non-manual occupational group in educational attainment.[41]

If elements which contribute to a lack of sophistication and detachment from the general cultural values constitute an important factor associated with lower-class authoritarian proclivities, a second and no less important factor is a relative lack of economic and psychological security. Economic uncertainty, unemployment, and fluctuation in total income all increase with moves down the socio-economic ladder. White collar workers, even those who receive no more pay than skilled manual workers, are less likely to suffer the tensions created by fear of loss of income. Studies of marital instability indicate clearly that family tension is closely correlated with low income and financial insecurity. Economic insecurity clearly affects the political and attitudinal responses of groups.[42] High states of tension encourage immediate alleviation through the venting of hostility against a scape-goat, the search for a short-term solution by support of extremist groups, or both. Considerable research indicates that the unemployed are less tolerant toward minorities than the employed, are more likely to be Communists if they are workers, and to be Nazis if they are middle class. Those industries with many Communists among their employees are also characterized by a large amount of economic instability.

The insecurities and tensions which flow directly from economic instability are reinforced by the particular patterns of family life associated with the lower strata. There is more direct frustration and aggression in the day-to-day lives of members of the lower classes, both children and the adults. A comprehensive review of the many studies made in the past 25 years of child-rearing patterns in the United States reports that their "most consistent finding" is the "more frequent use of physical punishment by working-class parents. The middle-class, in contrast, resorts to reasoning, isolation, and . . . 'love-oriented' techniques of discipline. . . . Such parents are more likely to overlook offenses, and when they do punish they are less likely to ridicule or inflict physical pain."[43] The link between such practices in lower-class families and adult hostility and authoritarianism is suggested by the findings of investigations in Boston and Detroit that physical punishments for aggression, characteristic of the working class, tend to increase rather than decrease aggressive behavior.[44]

The Perspectives of Lower-Class Groups

Acceptance of the norms of democracy requires a high level of sophistication and ego security. The less sophisticated and stable an individual, the more likely he is to favor a simplified and demonological view of politics, to fail to understand the rationale underlying the tolerance of those with whom he disagrees, and to find difficulty in grasping or tolerating a gradualist image of political change. Lack of sophistication and psychic insecurity, then, are basic "intervening variables" which clarify the empirical association between authoritarian attitudes and low status.

Several studies focusing on various aspects of working-class life and culture have emphasized different components of an unsophisticated perspective. Greater suggestibility, absence of a sense of past and future, inability to take a complex view, difficulty in abstracting from concrete experience, and lack of imagination each have been singled out as characteristic products of low status. All may be considered as interrelated indices of a more or less general lack of sophistication and ego stability, and also as part of the complex psychological basis of authoritarianism.

Suggestibility has been presented by one student of social movements as a major explanatory concept with which to account for participation in diverse extremist movements.[45] The two conditions for suggestibility are both characteristic of low-status persons: *lack* of an adequate mental context, and a *fixed* mental context (a term of Hadley Cantril's, meaning "frame of reference" or "general perspective"). A poorly developed mental context reflects a limited education: a paucity of the rich associations which provide a basis for critical evaluation of experience. A fixed mental context—in a sense, the opposite side of the coin—reflects the tendency to elevate whatever general principles are learned to absolutes which are difficult to correct by experience.

Richard Hoggart, with reference to Britain, notes the same point. Low-status persons, he explains, without rich and flexible mental context are likely to lack a developed sense of the past *and* future:

> Their education is unlikely to have left them with any historical panorama or with any idea of a continuing tradition. . . . A great many people, though they may possess a considerable amount of disconnected information, have little idea of an historical or ideological pattern or process. . . . With little intellectual or cultural furniture, with little training in the testing of opposing views against reason and existing judgments, judgments are usually made according to the promptings of those group-apophthegms which come first to mind. . . . Similarly, there can be little real sense of the future. . . . Such a mind is, I think, particularly accessible to the temptation to live in a constant present.[46]

This concern with the present leads to a concentration on daily activities, without much inner reflection, imaginative planning of one's future, or abstract thinking. One of the few studies of lower-class children utilizing projective techniques reports:

> . . . these young people are making an adjustment which is oriented toward the outside world rather than one which rests on a developing acquaintance with their own impulses and the handling of these impulses by fantasy and introspection. . . . They do not have a rich inner life, indeed their imaginative activity is meagre and limited. . . . When faced with a new situation, the subjects tend to react rapidly, and they do not alter their original impressions of the situation which is seen as a crude whole with little intellectual discrimination of components.[47]

Working-class life as a whole, and not merely the character of perception and imagination, has been seen as concrete and immediate. As Hoggart puts it, "if we want to capture something of the essence of working-class life . . . we must say that it is the 'dense and concrete' life, a life whose main stress is on the intimate, the sensory, the detailed and the personal. This would no doubt be true of working-class groups anywhere in the world."[48] Hoggart sees the concreteness of the perceptions of working-class people as a main difference from those of middle-class people, who more easily meet abstract and general questions. He identifies the sharp British working-class distinction between "Us" and "Them" as:

. . . part of a more general characteristic of the outlook of most working-class people. To come to terms with the world of "Them" involves, in the end, all kinds of political and social questions, and leads eventually beyond politics and social philosophy to metaphysics. The question of how we face "Them" (whoever "They" are) is, at last, the question of how we stand in relation to anything not visibly and intimately part of our local universe. The working-class splitting of the world into "Us" and "Them" is on this side a symptom of their difficulty in meeting abstract or general questions.[49]

Hoggart is careful to emphasize that probably most persons in *any* social class are uninterested in general ideas, but still "training in the handling of ideas or in analysis" is far more characteristic of the demands of middle-class parents and occupations.[50]

A recent discussion of variations in the conceptual apparatus of the different classes, which analyzes sources of variations in social mobility, also emphasizes the ways in which the different family patterns of the middle and working classes affect their authoritarianism. The author, B. Bernstein, points out that the middle-class parent stresses "an awareness of the importance between means and long-term ends, cognitively and affectually regarded . . . [and has] the ability to adopt appropriate measures to implement the attainment of distant ends by a purposeful means-end chain. . . . The child in the middle-classes and associated levels grows up in an environment which is finely and extensively controlled; the space, time and social relationships are explicitly regulated within and outside the family group."[51] But while the middle-class child is led to understand the need to defer immediate gratifications for long-term advantages, the situation in the working-class family is quite different:

The working-class family structure is less formally organized than the middle-class in relation to the development of the child. Although the authority within the family is explicit the values which it expresses do not give rise to the carefully ordered universe spatially and temporally of the middle-class child. The exercise of authority will not be related to a stable system of rewards and punishments but may often appear arbitrary. The specific character of long-term goals tends to be replaced by more general notions of the future, in which chance, a friend or a relative plays a greater part than the rigorous working out of connections. Thus present, or near-present activities, have greater value than the relation of the present activity to the attainment of a distant goal. The system of expectancies, or the time-span of anticipation, is shortened and this creates different sets of preferences, goals, and dissatisfactions. The environment limits the perception of the developing child of and in time. Present gratifications or present deprivations become absolute gratifications or absolute deprivations for there exists no developed time continuum upon which present activity can be ranged. Relative to the middle-classes, the postponement of present pleasure for future gratifications will be found difficult. By implication *a more volatile patterning of affectual and expressive behavior will be found in the working-classes.*[52]

This concern with the immediately perceivable, with the personal and concrete, is part and parcel of the short time-perspective and the inability to perceive the complex possibilities and consequences of actions which is referred to above as a lack of social sophistication. It is associated with some fundamental characteristics of low status, and often eventuates in a readiness to support extremist political and religious movements, and in a generally lower level of liberalism on non-economic questions.[53]

Within extremist movements, these differences in the perceptions and perspectives of working-class persons affect their experiences, ease of recruitment, and reasons for defecting. Almond's study of 221 ex-Communists in four countries provides some data on this point. He distinguishes between the "exoteric" (simple, for mass consumption) and "esoteric" (complex, for the inner circle) doctrines of the party. "Relatively few working-class respondents had been exposed to the esoteric doctrine of the party before joining, and . . . they tended to remain unindoctrinated while in the party," in contrast with the middle-class members.[54] Middle-class recruits who were potentially capable of absorbing a complex doctrine nevertheless "tended to come to the party with more complex value patterns and expectations which were more likely to obstruct assimilation into the party. . . . The working-class member, on the other hand, is relatively untroubled by doctrinal apparatus, less exposed to the media of communication, and his imagination and logical powers are relatively undeveloped."[55]

One aspect of the lack of sophistication and education of lower-class persons is their anti-intellectualism (a phenomenon noted by Engels long ago as a problem faced by working-class movements). While the complex esoteric ideology of Communism may have been a principal feature drawing middle-class persons to it, the fundamental anti-intellectualism of extremist movements has been a source of strain for their "genuine" intellectuals, who find it difficult to view the world in black or white terms. In the Communist Party, these class differences are reflected in the fact that the working-class rank-and-file are least likely to become disturbed by ideological shifts, and least likely to defect.[56] Their commitment, once established, cannot as easily be shaken by a sudden realization that the Party, after all, does not conform to liberal and humanistic values, as can the commitment of middle-class members, who usually joined for different reasons and values and maintain a more complex view both of their own lives and of politics.

Some evidence of the differential receptivity of leftist parties to middle- and working-class persons may be seen in the leadership composition of Socialist and Communist Parties. The former have been led by a higher proportion of intellectuals, in spite of an original ideological emphasis on maintaining a working-class orientation. The Communists, on the other hand, tend to alienate their intellectual leaders and to be led by those with preponderantly working-class occupations.[57] Almond's study of the *Appeals of Communism* concludes:

> . . . while the party is open to all comers, working-class party members have better prospects of success in the party than middle-class recruits. This is probably due both to party policy, which has always manifested greater confidence in the reliability of working-class recruits, and to the difficulties of assimilation into the party generally experienced by middle-class party members.[58]

The Main Findings Restated

To sum up, the lower-class individual is more likely to have been exposed to punishment, lack of love, and a general atmosphere of tension and aggression since early childhood, experiences which often produce deep-rooted hostilities expressed by ethnic prejudice, political authoritarianism, and chiliastic transvaluational religion. His educational attainment is less than that of men with higher socio-economic status, and his association as a child with others of similar background not only fails to stimulate his intellectual interests but also creates an atmosphere which prevents his educational experience from increasing his general social sophistication and his understanding of different groups and ideas. Leaving school relatively early, he is surrounded on the job by others with a similar restricted cultural, educational, and family background. Little external influence impinges on his limited environment to increase his connections with the larger world and to heighten his sophistication. From early childhood, he has sought immediate gratifications in favor of activities which might have long-term rewards. The logic of both his adult employment and his family situation reinforces this limited time-perspective. As North has well put it, isolation from heterogeneous environments, characteristic of low-status, operates to "limit the source of information, to retard the development of efficiency in judgment and reasoning abilities, and to confine the attention to more trivial interests in life."[59] All of these characteristics combine to produce a tendency to view politics, as well as personal relationships, in black-and-white terms, a desire for immediate action without critical reflection, impatience with talk and discussion, lack of interest in organizations which have a long-range gradualistic political perspective, and a readiness to follow leaders who offer a demonological interpretation of the presumably conspiratorial forces, either religious or political.[60]

It is interesting to note that Lenin saw the character of the lower classes and the tasks of those who would lead them in terms similar to those presented in this paper. He specified as the chief task of the Communist parties the leadership of the broad masses, who are "slumbering, apathetic, hidebound, inert, and dormant"—a picture borne out by the data presented here. These masses, said Lenin, must be aligned for the "final and decisive battle" (a term reminiscent of Armageddon) by the Party which alone can present an unequivocal, uncompromising, unified view of the world, and an immediate program for drastic change. In contrast to "effective" Communist leadership, Lenin pointed to the democratic parties and their leadership as "vacillating, wavering, unstable" elements, a characterization that is probably valid for any political group lacking ultimate certainty in its program and willing to grant legitimacy to opposition groups.[61]

The political outcome of these predispositions, however, as suggested above, is not determined by the multiplicity of factors bearing upon the development of authoritarian predispositions. Isolation, a punishing childhood, economic and occupational insecurities, and a lack of sophistication are conducive *both* to withdrawal, or even apathy, and to strong mobilization of hostile predispositions. The same underlying factors which predispose individuals toward support of extremist movements under certain conditions may result in withdrawal from political activity and concern under other conditions. Lack of information, social isolation, little participation in groups outside of one's immediate circle, a short-term time perspective, which generally characterize the lower strata, are associated both with low levels of political interest and involvement (while maintaining authoritarian attitudes) in "normal" non-crisis periods and with action in an extremist direction when those underlying predispositions are activated by a crisis and millenial appeals.[62]

Extremism as a Complex Alternative: a Test of an Hypothesis

Thus far this paper has been concerned with the authoritarian proclivities of lower-status groups. One proposition which has been drawn from the analysis is that the lack of a complex and rich frame of reference, a tendency to view events from a concrete and short-term perspective, is the vital intervening variable between low status and a predisposition toward transvaluational extremist religion or politics. The proposition, however, does not simply suggest that the lower strata will be authoritarian; it implies that other things being equal, they will choose the least complex alternative. If we can find situations in which extremist politics represents the more complex rather than the less complex form of transvaluational politics, we should expect low status to be associated with *opposition* to such movements and parties.

A situation in which an extremist movement is the more complex alternative exists wherever the Communist Party is a small party competing against a large reformist party, as in England, the United States, Sweden, and Norway. Where the Party is small and weak, it can not hold out the promise of immediate changes in the situation of the most deprived. Rather, such small extremist parties usually present the fairly complex intellectual argument that tendencies inherent in the social and economic system will strengthen them in the long run.[63] For the poorer worker, support of the Swedish Social-Democrats, the British Labor Party, or the American New Deal is a simpler and more easily understood way of securing redress of grievances or improvement of social conditions than supporting an electorally insignificant Communist Party.

The available evidence from countries such as Norway, Sweden, Canada, Brazil, and Great Britain suggests the validity of this interpretation. In these countries, where the Communist Party is small and a Labor or Socialist Party is much larger, the support of the Communists is stronger among the better-paid and more skilled workers than it is among the less skilled and poorer strata.[64] In Italy, France, and Finland, where the Communists are the largest party on the left, the lower the income level of workers, the higher their Communist vote.[65] A comparison of the differences in the relative income position of workers who vote Social-Democratic and those who back the Communists in two neighboring Scandinavian countries, Finland and Sweden, shows these alternative patterns clearly (see Table 5).[66]

These assumptions concerning the relationship between Communist strength, differential time perspective involved in support of the party, and variations in the social base of its electoral appeal hold up for all countries for which data exist.[67] Data from one other country, India, offer even better evidence for the hypothesis, however, because they permit a comparison of varia-

TABLE 5.—*The Income Composition of the Working-Class Support of the Social-Democratic and Communist Parties in Finland and Sweden*°

Finland—1956			Sweden—1946		
Income Class in Markkas	Social Democrats	Communists	Income Class in Kronen	Social Democrats	Communists
Under 100	8%	13%	Under 2,000	14%	8%
100–400	49	50	2,001–4,000	40	38
400–600	22	29	4,001–6,000	32	30
600+	21	8	6,001+	14	24
N	(173)	(119)		(5176)	(907)

° The Finnish data were secured from a special run made for this study by the Finnish Gallup Poll. The Swedish statistics were recomputed from data presented in Elis Hastad, *et al.*, editors, *"Gallup" och den Svenska Valjarkaren*, Uppsala: Hugo Gebers Forlag, 1950, pp. 175-176. Both studies include rural and urban workers.

tions in electoral strength within a single country, and also because these data were located after the hypothesis was formulated and thus can be considered an independent replication.

In India, the Communists are a major party, constituting the government or the major opposition (with 25 per cent or more of the votes) in two states, Kerala and Andhra. While it has substantial strength in some other states, it is much weaker in the rest of India. If the proposition is valid that Communist appeal should be relatively greater among the lower and uneducated strata where the Party is powerful, and proportionately stronger among the higher and better educated ones where it is weak, the characteristics of Party voters should vary greatly in different parts of India. This is precisely what Table 6 shows. Where the Indian Communist Party is small, its support, like that of the two small moderate Socialist Parties, comes disproportionately from relatively well-to-do and better educated strata. The picture shifts sharply in Kerala and Andhra, where the Communists are strong. The middle class provides only seven per cent of Com-

Table 6.—*Communist and Socialist Preferences in India, by Class and Education*[*]

| | Communist Party Preferences in | | |
	Kerala and Andhra	Rest of India	Preferences for Socialist Parties in All-India
Class			
Middle	7%	27%	23%
Lower Middle	19	30	36
Working	74	43	41
Education			
Illiterate	52%	43%	31%
Under-matric.	39	37	43
Matric. plus	9	20	26
N	(113)	(68)	(88)

[*] These figures have been computed from tables presented in the *Indian Institute of Public Opinion, Monthly Public Opinion Surveys,* Vol. 2, No. 4, 5, 6, 7 (Combined Issue), New Delhi, January–April, 1957, pp. 9–14. This was a pre-election poll, not a report of the actual voting results. The total sample consisted of 2,868 persons. The Socialist Party and the Praja-Socialist Party figures are combined here, since they share essentially the same moderate program. The support given to them in Andhra and Kerala was too small to be presented separately.

munist support there, with the working class supplying 74 per cent, showing the difference in the constituency of an extremist party when it becomes an effective political force.[68] Educational differences among party supporters show a similar pattern.

Historical Patterns and Democratic Action

Complex historical factors explain why, in the face of profoundly anti-democratic tendencies in lower class groups, their political organizations and movements in the more industrialized democratic countries have supported *both* economic and political liberalism. Economic liberalism or leftism flows from their situation, producing demands for redistribution of the wealth, but their situation neither produces nor calls for non-economic liberalism, support of ethnic tolerance, and democratic norms.[69] Of course, workers' organizations, trade unions, and political parties played a major role in extending political democracy in the nineteenth and early twentieth centuries. These struggles for political freedom by the workers, like those of the middle class before them, took place in the context of a fight for economic rights.[70] Freedom of organization and of speech, as well as universal suffrage, were necessary means in the battle for a better standard of living, social security, shorter hours, and the like. The upper classes resisted the extension of political freedom as part of their defense of economic and social privilege.

Few groups in history have ever voluntarily espoused civil liberties and freedom for those who advocate measures they consider despicable or dangerous. Religious freedom emerged in the western world because the contending powers found themselves unable to destroy the other group without destroying the entire society, and because the very struggle led many men to lose faith and interest in religion, and consequently lose the desire to suppress dissent. Similarly, universal suffrage and freedom of organization and opposition developed in many countries either as concessions to the established strength of the lower classes or as means of controlling the lower classes, a tactic advocated and used by such sophisticated conservatives as Disraeli and Bismarck.

Once in existence and although originating in a conflict of interests, however, democratic norms, like others, become part of an institutional system. Thus, the western labor and socialist movement has incorporated these values into its general ideology. But the fact that the ideology of the movement is democratic does not mean that its supporters actually understand its implications. The evidence seems to indicate that understanding of and adherence to these norms are highest among leaders and lowest among followers. The general opinions or attitudinal predispositions of the rank and file are relatively unimportant in predicting behavior as long as the organizations to which they are loyal continue to act democratically. In spite of the workers' greater authoritarian propensity, their organizations which are anti-Communist still function as better defenders and carriers of democratic values than parties based on the middle class. In Germany, the United States, Great Britain, and Japan, individuals who support the democratic left party are more likely to support civil liberties and democratic values than people *within* each occupational stratum who back the conservative parties. That is, workers who back the democratic left are more likely to have tolerant or non-authoritarian attitudes than workers who support the conservative parties. Similarly, middle-class Social-Democrats are more prone to support civil liberties than middle-class conservatives. It is probable that organized social-democracy not only supports civil liberties but influences its supporters in the same direction.[71]

Conservatism is especially vulnerable in a political democracy since there are more poor people than well-to-do and promises to redistribute wealth and to create a better life for the lower classes are difficult to rebut. Consequently, conservatives have traditionally feared a thorough-going political democracy and have endeavored in most countries—by restricting the franchise, or by manipulating the legislature through second chambers or overrepresentation of rural districts and small towns (traditional conservative strongholds)—to prevent a popular majority from controlling the government. The ideology of conservatism has often been based on élitist values which reject the idea that there is wisdom in the voice of the electorate. In addition, militarism and nationalism, often defended by conservatives, probably have an attraction for individuals with authoritarian predispositions.[72]

It would be a mistake to conclude from the data presented in this paper that the authoritarian predispositions of the lower-classes necessarily constitute a threat to a democratic social system; nor should similar conclusions be drawn about the anti-democratic aspects of conservatism. Whether or not a given class supports restrictions on freedom depends on a wide constellation of factors of which those discussed here are only a part.

The instability of the democratic process in general and the strength of the Communists in particular are closely related to national levels of economic development, including degrees of educational attainment.[73] The Communists represent a mass movement in the poorer countries of Europe and elsewhere, but are weak where economic development and educational attainment are high.[74] The lower classes of the less developed countries are poorer, more insecure, less educated, and possess fewer status symbols than those of the more well-to-do nations. In the more developed stable democracies of western Europe, North America, and Australasia the lower classes are "in the society" as well as "of it": their cultural isolation is much less than the isolation of the poorer groups in other countries, who are cut off from participation by abysmally low incomes and very limited, if any, schooling. Thus the incorporation of the workers into the body politic in the industrialized western world has greatly reduced their authoritarian predispositions, although in the United States, for example, McCarthy demonstrated that an irresponsible demagogue who combines a nationalist and anti-élitist appeal can still secure considerable support from the less educated.

While the evidence as to the effects of rising standards of living and education permits us to maintain hopeful expectations concerning working-class political values and behavior in those countries in which extremism is weak, the available data suggest pessimistic conclusions with regard to the less economically developed, unstable democracies. Where an extremist party has secured the support of the lower classes, often by stressing equality and economic security at the expense of liberty, it is problematic whether this support can be taken away from it through use of democratic methods. The Communists, in particular, combine the two types of politics which have a basic appeal to these classes, economic radicalism and a chiliastic view of the world. Whether democratic working-class parties able to demonstrate convincingly their ability to defend economic and class interests can be built up in the less stable democracies is a moot question.

NOTES

1. "The Choice of Comrades," *Encounter*, 3 (December, 1954), p. 25. Arnold A. Rogow, writing in the socialist magazine *Dissent*, even suggests that "the liberal and radical approach has always lacked a popular base, that in essence, the liberal tradition has been a confined minority, perhaps elitist, tradition." "The Revolt Against Social Equality," *Dissent*, 4 (Autumn, 1957), p. 370.

2. Clancy Sigal, in the *New Statesman*, October 4, 1958, p. 440.

3. The sources of variation in Communist strength from country to country are beyond the scope of this paper. For data and further discussion, see S. M. Lipset, "Socialism—Left and Right—East and West," *Confluence*, 7 (Summer, 1958), pp. 173-192; and Lipset, *Political Man: Essays on the Sociology of Democracy*, New York: Doubleday, 1959.

4. See Richard Hoggart, *The Uses of Literacy*, London: Chatto and Windus, 1957, pp. 78-79, 146-148, for a discussion of the acceptance of norms of toleration by the British working class. E. T. Prothro and Levon Melikian, in "The California Public Opinion Scale in an Authoritarian Culture," *Public Opinion Quarterly*, 17 (Fall, 1953), pp. 353-363, have shown, in a study of 130 students at the American University in Lebanon, that they exhibited the same association between authoritarianism and economic radicalism as is found among workers in the United States. A survey in 1951-52 of 1,800 Puerto Rican adults, representative of the entire rural population, found that 84 per cent were "somewhat authoritarian," as compared with 46 per cent for a comparable U. S. population; see Henry Wells, "Ideology and Leadership in Puerto Rican Politics," *American Political Science Review*, 49 (March, 1955), pp. 22-40.

5. The Southern Democrats were the staunchest opponents of McCarthy and his tactics, not because of any deep opposition to undemocratic methods, but rather because of an organizational commitment to the Democratic Party.

6. For a detailed discussion of the fallacy of attempting to suggest that political behavior is a necessary function of political attitudes or psychological traits, see Nathan Glazer and S. M. Lipset, "The Polls on Communism and Conformity" in Daniel Bell, editor, *The New American Right*, New York: Criterion Books, 1955, pp. 141-166.

7. The term "extremist" is used to refer to movements, parties, and ideologies. "Authoritarian" refers to the attitudinal predispositions of individuals (or of "groups," where a statistical aggregate of *individual* attitudes, and not group characteristics as such, are of concern). The term "authoritarian" has too many associations with attitudinal studies to be used safely to refer also to types of social organizations.

8. See G. H. Smith, "Liberalism and Level of Information," *Jour-*

nal of Educational Psychology, 39 (February, 1948), pp. 65-82; and "The Relation of 'Enlightenment' to Liberal-Conservative Opinions," *Journal of Social Psychology*, 28 (August, 1948), pp. 3-17.

9. Based on as yet unpublished data in the files of the World Poll, an organization established by International Research Associates which sponsors comparable surveys in a number of countries. The question asked in this survey was: "Suppose there was a political party here which corresponds to your own opinions—one you would more or less consider 'your' party. Would you wish this to be the only party in our country with no other parties besides, or would you be against such a one party system?" Similar correlations were found between low status and belief in the value of a strong leader.

10. See Kotaro Kido and Masataka Sugi, "A Report of Research on Social Stratification and Mobility in Tokyo (III), The Structure of Social Consciousness," *Japanese Sociological Review*, 4 (January, 1954), pp. 74-100; and National Public Opinion Institute of Japan, *Report No. 26, A Survey Concerning the Protection of Civil Liberties* (Tokyo, 1951).

11. H. J. Eysenck, *The Psychology of Politics*, London: Routledge and Kegan Paul, 1954, p. 127.

12. *Ibid.*, p. 137. For a severe critique of the methods used in this study see Richard Christie, "Eysenck's Treatment of the Personality of Communists," *Psychological Bulletin*, 53 (November, 1956), pp. 411-430.

13. See Arnold W. Rose, *Studies in Reduction of Prejudice*, Chicago: American Council on Race Relations, 1948, for a review of the literature bearing on this point prior to 1948. Several studies have shown the key importance of education and the independent effect of economic status, both basic components of low status. See Daniel J. Levinson and R. Nevitt Sanford, "A Scale for the Measurement of Anti-Semitism," *Journal of Psychology*, 17 (April, 1944), pp. 339-370; and H. H. Harlan, "Some Factors Affecting Attitudes Toward Jews," *American Sociological Review*, 7 (December, 1942), pp. 816-827, for data on attitudes toward one ethnic group. For a digest of recent research in the field of race relations in the United States, see Melvin M. Tumin, *Segregation and Desegregation*, New York: Anti-Defamation League of B'nai B'rith, 1957.

14. See Theodore Adorno, *et al.*, *The Authoritarian Personality*, New York: Harpers, 1950. This, the original study, shows less consistent results on this point than the many follow-up investigations. The authors themselves (p. 178) point to the inadequacy of their sample.

15. Richard Christie and Peggy Cook, "A Guide to Published Literature Relating to the Authoritarian Personality," *Journal of Psychology*, 45 (April, 1958), pp. 171-199.

16. W. J. McKinnon and R. Centers, "Authoritarianism and Urban Stratification," *American Journal of Sociology*, 61 (May, 1956), p. 618.

17. Much of contemporary psychological knowledge in this area has been gained from populations most convenient for the academic investigator to reach, university students. It is often forgotten that personality and attitude syndromes may be far different for this highly select group than for other segments of the total population.

18. See Anthony Davids and Charles W. Eriksen, "Some Social and Cultural Factors Determining Relations Between Authoritarianism and Measures of Neuroticism," *Journal of Consulting Psychology*, 21 (April, 1957), pp. 155-159. This article contains many references to the relevant literature.

19. The greater compatibility of the demands of Communist Party membership and working-class background as indicated by Almond's finding that twice as many of the middle-class party members as of the working-class group in his sample of Communists had neurotic problems hints again at the normality and congruence of authoritarian politics with a working-class background. See Gabriel Almond, *The Appeals of Communism*, Princeton: Princeton University Press, 1954, pp. 245-246.

20. See Liston Pope, *Millhands and Preachers*, New Haven: Yale University Press, 1942, pp. 105-116.

21. Frederick Engels, "On the Early History of Christianity," in K. Marx and F. Engels, *On Religion*, Moscow: Foreign Languages Publishing House, 1957, pp. 312-320.

22. Elmer T. Clark, *The Small Sects in America*, New York: The Abingdon Press, 1949, pp. 16, 218-219. According to Bryan Wilson, "insecurity, differential status anxiety, cultural neglect, prompt a need for readjustment which sects may, for some, provide. The maladjusted may be communities, or occupational groups, or dispersed individuals in similar marginal positions." "An Analysis of Sect Development," *American Sociological Review*, 24 (February, 1959), p. 8. See also Wilson's *Minority Religious Movements in Modern Britain*, London: Heineman and Sons, forthcoming.

23. Ernst Troeltsch, *The Social Teaching of the Christian Churches*, London: George Allen and Unwin, 1930, Vol. 1, p. 44.

24. Charles S. Braden, *These Also Believe. A Study of Modern American Cults and Minority Religious Movements*, New York: Macmillan, 1949, p. 384.

25. *Ibid.*, p. 370.

26. *Ibid.*, p. 363. It may be suggested that, as in authoritarian political movements, the intolerant character of most of the sects is an attractive feature and not a source of strain for their lower-class members. Although no systematic evidence is available, this assumption would help to account for the lack of tolerance of factionalism within

these sects, and for the endless schisms, with the new groups as intolerant as the old, since the splits usually occur over the issue of *whose* intolerant views and methods shall prevail.

27. See Isaac Deutscher, *The Prophet Armed, Trotsky, 1879-1921*, London: Oxford University Press, 1954, pp. 30-31.

28. Sven Rydenfelt, *Kommunismen i Sverige. En Samhallsvetenskaplig Studie*, Kund: Gleerupska Universitetsbokhandeln, 1954, pp. 296, 336-337; and Wiardi Beckman Institute, *Verkiezingen in Nederland*, Amsterdam: 1951, mimeographed, pp. 15, 93-94.

29. See W. Phillips Davison's extensive review of Rydenfelt, *op. cit.*, in the *Public Opinion Quarterly*, 18 (Winter, 1954-55), pp. 375-388; quoted at p. 382. Note that the total "extremist" vote in the two counties was almost identical, 30 and 32 per cent.

30. A study based on a national sample of Americans reported that education made no difference in the extent of authoritarian responses on an "authoritarian personality" scale among workers, but that higher educational attainment reduced such responses among the middle-class. The well-educated upper-middle class were least "authoritarian." Morris Janowitz and Dwaine Marvick, "Authoritarianism and Political Behavior," *Public Opinion Quarterly*, 17 (Summer, 1953), pp. 195-196.

31. The independent effect of education even when other social factors are least favorable has especial long-range significance in view of the rising educational level of the population. Kornhauser and his associates found that auto workers with an eighth grade education were more authoritarian than those with more education. See Arthur Kornhauser, A. L. Sheppard, and A. J. Mayer, *When Labor Votes*, New York: University Books, 1956, for further data on variations on authoritarianism *within* a working-class sample.

32. The research showing that such factors as education, status, and income (themselves components of an overall class or status index) are associated with political participation is summarized in Robert E. Lane, *Political Life*, Glencoe, Ill.: Free Press, 1959.

33. Data computed for this study.

34. F. H. Sanford, *Authoritarianism and Leadership*, Philadelphia: Stevenson Brothers, 1950, p. 168. See also Mirra Komarovsky, "The Voluntary Associations of Urban Dwellers," *American Sociological Review*, 11 (December, 1946), p. 688.

35. Smith, *op. cit.*, p. 71.

36. G. M. Connelly and H. H. Field, "The Non-Voter, Who He Is, and What He Thinks," *Public Opinion Quarterly*, 8 (Summer, 1944), p. 179; Samuel Stouffer, *op. cit.;* Sanford, *op. cit.*, p. 168; M. Janowitz and D. Marvick, *op. cit.*, p. 200.

37. See Herbert Hyman and Paul B. Sheatsley, "Some Reasons Why Information Campaigns Fail," *Public Opinion Quarterly*, 11

(Fall, 1947), p. 413. A recent survey of material on voluntary association memberships is contained in Charles L. Wright and Herbert Hyman, "Voluntary Association Memberships of American Adults: Evidence from National Sample Surveys," *American Sociological Review*, 23 (June, 1958), pp. 284-294.

38. Genevieve Knupfer, "Portrait of the Underdog," *Public Opinion Quarterly*, 11 (Spring, 1947), p. 114.

39. The greatest amount of comparative material is available on the miners. For Britain, see Herbert G. Nicholas, *British General Election of 1950*, London: Macmillan, 1951, pp. 318, 342, 361. For the United States, see Paul F. Brissenden, *The IWW, A Study of American Syndicalism*, New York: Columbia University Press, 1920, p. 74; and Harold Gosnell, *Grass Roots Politics*, Washington, D. C.: American Council on Public Affairs, 1942, pp. 31-32. For France, see François Goguel, "Geographie des elections sociales de 1950-1," *Revue Française de science politique*, 3 (April-June, 1953), pp. 246-271. For Germany, see Ossip K. Flectheim, *Die Kommunistische Partei Deutschlands in der Weimarer Republik*, Offenbach am Main: Bollwerk-Verlag, Karl Drott, 1948, p. 211. Data are also available for Australia, Scandinavia, Spain, and Chile.

Isolation has also been linked with the differential propensity to strike of different industries. Violent strikes having the character of a mass grievance against society as a whole occur most often in isolated industries, and probably have their origins in the same social situations producing authoritarianism. See Clark Kerr and Abraham Siegel, "The Interindustry Propensity to Strike: An International Comparison," in A. Kornhauser, R. Dubin, and A. M. Ross, editors, *Industrial Conflict*, New York: McGraw Hill, 1954, pp. 189-212.

40. According to Friedrich, agricultural groups are more emotionally nationalistic and potentially authoritarian politically because the "rural population is more homogeneous, . . . it contains a smaller number of outsiders and foreigners, . . . it has much less contact with foreign countries and peoples, and finally, . . . its mobility is much more limited." See Carl Friedrich, "The Agricultural Basis of Emotional Nationalism," *Public Opinion Quarterly*, 1 (April, 1937), pp. 50-51. See also Rudolf Heberle, *From Democracy to Nazism: A Regional Case Study of Political Parties in Germany*, Baton Rouge: Louisiana State University Press, 1945, pp. 32 ff., for a discussion of the appeal of Nazism to the German rural population; and K. Kido and M. Sugi, *op. cit.*, for similar findings in Japan. For references to materials on rural Communism, see Lipset, *Political Man, op. cit.*

41. Statistical data indicate that German and Austrian Nazism, contemporary Italian Neo-Fascism, French Poujadism, and American McCarthyism have all drawn their heaviest non-rural support from the less educated small businessmen of provincial small communities.

See "Fascism: Left, Right and Center," in Lipset, *Political Man, op. cit.*, Chapter 5.

42. In addition to the "normal" insecurity of lower-class existence, special conditions which uproot people from a stable community life and upset the social supports of their traditional values make them receptive to extremist chiliastic ideologies which help to redefine their world. I have discussed the evidence linking the *discontinuities* and rootlessness flowing from rapid industrialization and urbanization on the politics of workers in different countries in "Socialism: Left and Right," *op. cit.* Rydenfelt, in his study of Swedish Communism, suggests that "rootlessness" is a characteristic of individuals and occupations with high Communist voting records; see Davison, *op. cit.*, p. 378. It is interesting to note that Engels also called attention in the 1890s to the fact that chiliastic religions and social movements, including the revolutionary socialist one, attracted all the deviants, those without a place in society: e.g., "all the elements which had been set free, i.e., at a loose end, by the dissolution of the old world came one after the other into the orbit of [early] Christianity . . . [as today] all throng to the working-class parties in all countries." Engels, *op. cit.*, pp. 319-320. See also Almond, *op. cit.*, p. 236; and Hadley Cantril, *The Psychology of Social Movements*, New York: Wiley, 1941, Chapters 8 and 9.

43. Urie Bronfenbrenner, "Socialization and Social Class Through Time and Space," in E. E. Maccoby, T. M. Newcomb, and E. L. Hartley, editors, *Readings in Social Psychology*, New York: Henry Holt, 1958, p. 419.

44. Some hint of the complex of psychological factors underlying lower-class authoritarianism is given in one study which reports a relationship between overt hostility and authoritarianism. See Saul M. Siegel, "The Relationship of Hostility to Authoritarianism," *Journal of Abnormal and Social Psychology*, 52 (May, 1956), pp. 386 ff.

45. Cantril, *op. cit.*, p. 65.

46. Hoggart, *op. cit.*, pp. 158-159.

47. B. M. Spinley, *The Deprived and the Privileged*, London: Routledge and Kegan Paul, 1953, pp. 115-116. These conclusions are based on Rorschach tests given to 60 slum area children. The last point is related to that made by another British scholar that working-class persons are not as likely as those with middle-class backgrounds to perceive the *structure* of an object, involving thought on a more abstract level of relationships, but have an action-oriented reaction to the *content* of an object. For further discussion of this point, see B. Bernstein, "Some Sociological Determinants of Perception," *The British Journal of Sociology*, 9 (June, 1958), pp. 160 ff.

48. Hoggart, *op. cit.*, p. 88. This kind of life, as with other social characteristics, has different consequences for different areas of so-

ciety and social existence. It may be argued (contrary to my own views) that this capacity to establish personal relationships, to live in the present, may be more "healthy" (in a strictly mental-health sense) than a middle-class concern with status distinctions, one's own personal impact on one's life situation, and a preoccupation with the uncertain future. But in terms of political consequences, the problem of concern here, this same action-oriented, non-intellectualistic aspect of working-class life seems to prevent awareness of the realities of long-term social and economic trends simply because such awareness requires abstraction and generalization.

49. *Ibid.,* p. 86.

50. *Idem.*

51. Bernstein, *op. cit.,* pp. 161, 165.

52. *Ibid.,* p. 168 (italics added).

53. This hypothesis has suggestive implications for a theory of trade union democracy, and possible strains within trade union organizational life. Working-class union members may not be nearly as concerned with dictatorial union leadership as are middle-class critics who assume that the rank and file would actively form factions and critically evaluate union policies if they were not constrained by a monolithic structure imposed by the top leadership. On the other hand, the more educated, articulate staff members (on a union newspaper, for example) may desire to include more literate and complex discussions of issues facing the union but may be constrained by the need to present simple, easily understood propagandistic slogans for rank-and-file consumption. The "house-organ" type of union newspaper may not be due entirely to internal political necessities.

54. Almond, *op. cit.,* p. 244.

55. *Ibid.,* p. 177.

56. *Ibid.,* pp. 313 ff., 392.

57. For French data from 1936 to 1956 see Mattei Dogan, "Les Candidats et les élus," in L'Association Française de science politique, *Les Elections du 2 janvier,* Paris: Librairie Armand Colin, 1956, p. 462, and "L'origine sociale du personnel parlementaire Français," in Maurice Duverger, editor, *Parties politiques et classes sociales en France,* Paris: Librairie Armand Colin, 1955, pp. 291-329. For a comparison of German Social Democratic and Communist parliamentary leadership before Hitler see Viktor Engelhardt, "Die Zusammensatzung des Reichstage nach Alter, Beruf, und Religionsbekenntnis," *Die Arbeit,* 8 (January, 1931), p. 34.

58. Almond, *op. cit.,* p. 190. This statement is supported by analysis of the biographies of 123 Central Committee leaders of the Party in three countries, as well as by interviews with 221 ex-Communists (both leaders and rank-and-file members) in four countries, France, Italy, Great Britain, and the United States.

59. C. C. North, *Social Differentiation,* Chapel Hill: University of North Carolina Press, 1926, p. 247.

60. Most of these characteristics have been cited by psychologists as typical of adolescent attitudes and perspectives. Werner Cohn, in "Jehovah's Witnesses as a Proletarian Movement," *The American Scholar,* 24 (Summer, 1955), pp. 281-299, considers youth movements as a prototype of all such "proletarian" movements. Both "adolescence fixation and anomie are causal conditions" of their development (p. 297), and all such organizations have an "aura of social estrangement" (p. 282).

61. V. I. Lenin, *Left Wing Communism, An Infantile Disorder,* New York: International Publishers, 1940, pp. 74-75. Lenin's point, originally made in his pamphlet, *What Is to Be Done?,* that workers left to themselves would never develop socialist or class consciousness in place of economic "day to day" consciousness unless an organized group of revolutionary intellectuals brought them a broader vision, is similar to the generalizations presented here concerning the limited time perspective of the lower strata.

62. Various studies indicate that lower-class individuals in the United States who are non-voters and who have little political interest tend to reject the democratic norms of tolerance. See Stouffer, *op. cit.,* and Connelly and Field, *op. cit.,* p. 182. Studies of the behavior of the unemployed in countries in which extremist movements have been weak, such as the United States and Britain, indicate that apathy was their characteristic political response. See, e.g., E. W. Bakke, *Citizens Without Work,* New Haven: Yale University Press, 1940, pp. 46-70. On the other hand, German data indicate correlations between working-class unemployment and support of Communists and between middle-class unemployment and support of Nazis. In France, Italy, and Finland today, those who have been unemployed tend to back the large Communist parties. See S. M. Lipset, "Socialism: Left and Right," *op cit.,* p. 181; and Erik Allardt, *Social Struktur Och Politisk Aktivitet,* Helsingfors: Soderstrom and C: o Forlagsaktiebolag, 1956, pp. 84-85.

63. Recent research on the early sources of support for the Nazi Party challenges the hypothesis that it was the apathetic who came to its support prior to 1930, when it still represented a complex, long-range alternative. A negative rank-order correlation was found between the per cent increase in the Nazi vote and the increase in the proportion voting, in the German election districts between 1928 and 1930. Only after it had become a relatively large party did National Socialism recruit the previously apathetic, who then could see its immediate potential. For a report of this research, see Lipset, *Political Man, op. cit.*

64. For Norway, see Allen Barton, *Sociological and Psychological*

Implications of Economics Planning in Norway, Ph.D. thesis, Columbia University, 1957; and several surveys of voting behavior in Norway conducted by a Norwegian poll organization including the 1949 FAKTA Survey, and the February, 1954, and April, 1956, NGI Survey, the results of which are as yet unpublished. Data from the files of the Canadian Gallup Poll for 1945, 1949, and 1953 indicate that the Labor-Progressive (Communist) Party drew more support from the skilled than the unskilled sections of the working class. For Brazil, see A. Simao, "O voto operario em Sao Paulo," *Revista Brasilieras estudos politicos*, 1 (August, 1956), pp. 130-141.

65. For a table giving precise statistics for Italy and France, see S. M. Lipset, "Socialism: Left and Right, East and West," *op. cit.*, p. 182. In pre-Hitler Germany, where the Communists were a large party, they also secured their electoral strength much more from the less skilled sections of the workers than from the more skilled. See Samuel Pratt, *The Social Basis of Nazism and Communism in Urban Germany*, M.A. thesis, Michigan State College, 1948, pp. 156 ff.

66. In Finland, where the Communists are very strong, their support is drawn disproportionately from the poorer workers, while in Sweden, where the Communists are a minor party, they have considerably more success with the better paid and more skilled workers than they do with the unskilled and lowly paid. Or, to present the same data in another way, in Finland 41 per cent of all workers earning less than 100 markkas a month vote Communist, as compared with only 12 per cent among those earning over 600 markkas. In Sweden, 7 per cent of the workers earning less than 2,000 kronen a year vote Communist, as compared with 25 per cent among those earning over 8,000.

67. It may be noted, parenthetically, that where the Socialist Party is small and/or new, it also represents a complex alternative, and attracts more middle-class support proportionately than when it is a well-established mass party which can offer immediate reforms. On the other hand, when a small transvaluational group does *not* offer an intellectually complex alternative, it should draw disproportionate support from the lower strata. Such groups are the sectarian religions whose millenial appeals have no developed rationale. Some slight evidence on this point in a political context is available from a recent Norwegian poll which shows the composition of support for various parties. Only 11 persons supporting the Christian party, which appeals to the more fundamentalist Lutherans who are comparable to those in Sweden discussed earlier, were included in the total sample, but 82 per cent (nine) of these came from lower-income groups (less than 10,000 kronen per year). In comparison, 57 per cent of the 264 Labor Party supporters and 39 per cent of the 21 Communist supporters earned 10,000 kronen or more. Thus the small Communist

Party as the most complex transvaluational alternative drew its backing from relatively high strata, while the fundamentalist Christians appeared to have the economically poorest social base of any party in the country. See the NGI Survey of February, 1954, issued in December, 1956, in preliminary mimeographed form.

68. The hypothesis presented here does not attempt to explain the growth of small parties. Adaptations to major crises, particularly depressions and wars, are probably the key factors initially increasing the support for a small "complex" party. For an analysis of the change in electoral support of a Socialist party as it moved up to a major party status, see S. M. Lipset, *Agrarian Socialism*, Berkeley: University of California Press, 1950, esp. pp. 159-178.

69. There have been many exceptions to the generalization that democratic leftist parties based on the lower strata support non-economic liberalism. The Australian Labor party has been the foremost supporter of a "white Australia." Similarly, in the United States until the advent of the ideological New Deal, the lower-class based Democratic party has usually been the more anti-Negro of the two parties. For documentation of this point see "Classes and Parties in American Politics," in Lipset, *Political Man, op. cit.*, Chapter 9. The American labor movement has opposed non-white immigration, and much of it maintains barriers against Negro members. Even the Marxist Socialist movement of western Europe was not immune to anti-Semitism. Thus, before World War I there were several anti-Semitic incidents in which Socialists were involved, some avowedly anti-Semitic leaders connected with different socialist parties, and strong resistance shown to committing the socialist organization to oppose anti-Semitism. See E. Silberner, "The Anti-Semitic Tradition in Modern Socialism," *Scripta Hierosolymitana*, 3 (1956), pp. 378-396. In an article on the recent British "race riots," Michael Rumney notes the working-class base of anti-Negro sentiment and goes so far as to predict that "the Labor party will become the enemy of the Negro as time goes on." He reports that "while the Conservative party has been able to stand behind the police and take any means it feels necessary to preserve the peace, the Labor party has been strangely silent. If it speaks it will either antagonize the men who riot against West Indians, or forfeit its claim to being the party of equal rights." "Left Mythology and British Race Riots," *The New Leader* (September 22, 1958), pp. 10-11.

70. Similarities exist between the behavior of middle-class groups at the time when they were lowly ranked in a predominantly aristocratic and feudal society and working-class groups in newly industrialized societies. The affinities of both for religious and economic "radicalism," in the same sense, are striking. Calvin's doctrine of predestination, as Tawney points out, performed the same function for

the eighteenth century bourgeoisie as did Marx's theory of the inevitability of socialism for the proletariat in the nineteenth. Both "set their virtue at their best in sharp antithesis with the vices of the established order at its worst, taught them to feel that they were a chosen people, made them conscious of their great destiny . . . and resolute to realize it." The Communist Party, as did the Puritans, insists on "personal responsibility, discipline and asceticism," and although the historical contents differ, they may have the same sociological roots: in isolated, status-deprived occupational groups. See R. H. Tawney, *Religion and the Rise of Capitalism*, New York: Penguin Books, 1947, pp. 9, 99. For a similar point, see Donald G. MacRae, "The Bolshevik Ideology," *The Cambridge Journal*, 3 (December, 1950), pp. 164-177.

71. A striking case in point occurred in Australia in 1950. During a period of much agitation about the dangers of the Communist party, a Gallup Poll survey reported that 80 per cent of the electorate favored outlawing the Communists. Shortly after this survey, the conservative government submitted a proposal to outlaw the party to referendum. During the referendum electoral campaign, the Labor party and the trade-unions came out vigorously against the proposal. Considerable shifting took place thereafter, to the point that the measure to outlaw the Communists was actually defeated by a small majority, and Catholic workers who had overwhelmingly favored the measure when first questioned by the Gallup Poll eventually followed the advice of their party and unions and voted against it. See Leicester Webb, *Communism and Democracy in Australia, A Survey of the 1951 Referendum*, New York: Praeger, 1955.

72. A study of the 1952 elections in the United States reveals that at the grammar school, high school, *and* college levels individuals who scored high on an "authoritarian personality" scale were much more likely to vote for Eisenhower than for Stevenson. Robert Lane, "Political Personality and Electoral Choice," *American Political Science Review*, 49 (March, 1955), pp. 173-190. In Britain, a study of working-class anti-Semitism reports that the small number of Conservatives in the sample were much more anti-Semitic than the Liberals and the Laborites. James H. Robb, *Working-class Anti-Semite*, London: Tavistock Publications, 1954, pp. 93-94.

73. See S. M. Lipset, "Some Social Requisites of Democracy," *American Political Science Review*, 53 (March, 1959), pp. 69-105; and *Political Man, op. cit.*

74. "It is in the advanced industrial countries, principally the United States, Britain, and Northwestern Europe, where national income *has* been rising, where mass expectations of an equitable share in that increase are relatively fulfilled, and where social mobility affects ever greater numbers, that extremist politics have least hold." Daniel Bell, "The Theory of Mass Society," *Commentary*, 22 (July, 1956), p. 80.

Social institutions exist to transmit certain values and to meet certain social needs. The following article is a relevant illustration of these functions. It presents a lucid picture of the often persistent elements inherent in the origin, perpetuation or decline of religious and social movements.

XIII

Religion Among Ethnic and Racial Minorities*

J. OSCAR LEE

DURING THE PAST TWO DECADES the problem of race relations in the United States has moved into the forefront of the social problems confronting the nation. In spite of the numerous crises it has provoked, one of the most far-reaching social developments in the nation during the last ten years is the progress which has been achieved in eliminating the pattern of compulsory racial segregation. Moreover, we have been made aware by the mobility and urbanization of the Negro population that Negro-white relations are no longer a problem of the South alone. Increased awareness of the situation of Mexican Americans, Puerto Ricans, American Indians, and other ethnic and racial minority groups has caused the nation to recognize other dimensions of the problem. A third aspect of the problem which is gaining recognition is the international overtones of racial relationships in the United States vis-à-vis a world in which the achievement of human rights for all people is an increasingly important concern.

One cannot deal with religion among ethnic and racial minorities without seeing it in the context of the churches' concern about race relations. The churches have been especially preoccupied with this problem in the past twenty years. This interest

* Reprinted from the *Annals of the American Academy of Political and Social Sciences,* Vol. 332, November, 1960, 112-124, by permission of the author and publisher.

has included: an examination of the pattern of racial segregation in American society; a determination of the religious and ethical implications of racial segregation; and movement to eliminate racial segregation from the life and work of the churches. One result of this process is that an increasing number of Christians agree that racial segregation must be rejected since it is a violation of the spirit and the teaching of the Christian gospel. In fact, many religious leaders consider the elimination of segregation from religious institutions as probably the most crucial and urgent problem which the churches face today.

The problems of ethnic and racial minority groups are a concern of most of the churches in the nation. Mobility and urbanization, however, and other socio-economic changes which have affected the lives of people belonging to these ethnic and racial minority groups have special meaning for the churches of which they are members. They are important factors in determining the goals, functions, and programs of these churches. The changes in goals, functions, and programs which many of the churches have faced in the past twenty years are not only in response to demands for adjustments to new ways of life, but also may be indicative of changes in attitudes about the role of religion in meeting the needs of persons and groups.

The limitations of space and the specifications set forth for this article make it necessary to confine it to a consideration of the churches as religious institutions and how they have been affected by social changes.

The Negro Churches

The largest nonwhite minority group in the United States is the Negro-American group. In 1950, the United States Census indicated that there were 15,482,000 nonwhites in the United States and that Negroes constituted more than 95 per cent of this group. Negroes are mainly found in separate Negro denominations. These denominations are the National Baptist Convention, United States of America, Incorporated; the National Baptist Convention of America; the African Methodist Episcopal Church; the African Methodist Episcopal Zion Church, and the Christian Methodist Episcopal Church. While accurate membership figures for these denominations are not available, it is estimated that the five Negro denominations have approximately

ten million members.[1] Comparisons of this estimate with estimates made in previous years would seem to indicate that these
denominations are growing in membership. There are approximately 600,000 Negro members in the predominantly white Protestant denominations of which about 366,000 are in the Methodist
Church.[2] According to the *National Catholic Almanac* for 1960,
there were, as of January 1959, about 595,155 Roman Catholic
Negroes in the United States. This is an increase of 20,000 over
the preceding year.[3]

These figures indicate that a high proportion of the Negro
population are members of churches belonging to the five Negro
denominations. But they reflect more than this. They point to
the central place that the churches have occupied and continue
to occupy in the life of the Negro community. In a very real
sense, it is the Negro's own institution in that it is organized, led,
developed, owned, and controlled by Negroes.

Center of opportunity

Blocked as the Negro is by the pattern of racial segregation
from full participation in the total life of the community, the
Negro church affords him the opportunity for full participation
in an organized group. Charles Johnson has aptly described the
role of the Negro church.[4]

> It has provided a substitute for political organization and has
> furnished a channel for social as well as religious expression; it
> has been the center for face to face relations, for communication,
> for recreation and for physical as well as psychological escape
> from their troubles. It has been welcomed by Negroes even in
> areas where physical separation in worship was not demanded.

Even though Negro communities have developed many types
of organizations to serve various social, political, and civic purposes, the Negro church still occupies a central place. It is to
the churches that these organizations turn when they need to
communicate with the entire Negro community or desire mass
support for a program or project. The Negro churches are not
only composed of the masses of the people, but the churches are
also an important medium through which these masses shape
and express their aspirations. Moreover, the Negro minister has
the historic role of leader in the community. In the days after

slavery, he was the principal if not only leader in many communities. While this has changed as teachers, medical doctors, lawyers, and other professional and business people assume a share of the leadership burden, the Negro minister still occupies an important place of leadership. He still has direct contact with the masses of the people who are members of his congregation and who look to him for counsel and guidance on many problems.

Negro churches play an important role in the shaping and the expression of the aspirations of the masses of Negro people, and these aspirations are important in shaping the goals, functions, and programs of the churches which must attempt to meet the felt needs which confront people in a period of rapid social change.

Mobility and urbanization

The mobility and the urbanization of the Negro have been mentioned. These are probably the two most important factors affecting Negro life in the last twenty years. This movement of Negroes to urban areas first gained momentum during World War I and continued in the period between 1920 and 1930. In the depression years there was very little movement. During World War II it gained considerably greater momentum. According to data published by the United States Bureau of the Census in 1900, 77 per cent of the Negro population lived in rural areas and 23 per cent in urban areas. By 1950 this had changed radically; 37 per cent lived in rural areas and 63 per cent in urban areas. Also, much of this movement has been from the southern to the northern, midwestern, and western areas of the country. Indicative of this trend is the fact that the Negro population in the thirty largest cities of the North, Midwest, and West more than doubled in the decade 1940 to 1950. This trend appears to have continued in the decade 1950 to 1960.

The movement from rural to urban areas and from South to North has worked far-reaching changes in the status of Negroes. Eli Ginsberg points out in *The Negro Potential* that between 1940 and 1955 the number of Negroes in nonfarm civilian employment increased from about 3 million to about 5.5 million, a proportionately larger expansion than for the labor force as a whole. Although most of the nonfarm employment available to Negroes is unskilled or semiskilled, a higher income has become available to Negro families in urban areas than was available in the rural South. Ginsberg states that in 1954 the median money income of Negro farm families in the rural South was $742 annually. For Negro families in urban areas it was $2,876. The higher income was reflected in better living conditions, better health, and increased education. The status of Negroes has been affected and the economic opportunities for Negroes have been altered by social and political efforts in the past two decades to eliminate racial discrimination and segregation from public schools, higher education, employment, public transportation, and public accommodations. These changes have generally been accompanied by a clarification of the goals which Negroes seek. The racial church has, in many cases, been the only available channel through which the Negro could find social expression and could exercise leadership on the basis of character and ability.

In the movement from rural areas to urban areas, Negroes encounter a different group of social problems. Major problems are racial discrimination in housing and the slum conditions in city areas where most Negroes are forced to live. These are often accompanied by poor housing, poor schools, and poor community facilities and services. Another set of problems revolve around unemployment and underemployment. The rate of unemployment among Negroes continues higher than the national average. Involved in this is the fact that many of the better types of jobs are unavailable to Negroes and in the South many of the ordinary semiskilled and unskilled jobs in industry are unavailable. Also, there is increased recognition that major attention must be given to encouraging Negro youth to acquire skills. Still another set of problems centers around racial segregation and discrimination. These include the disenfranchisement of Negroes in the rural South; discrimination in the use of public accommodations and facilities; frequent instances of personal violence against Negroes; and a growing resolution to work for the elimination of discriminatory practices based upon race as soon as possible.

The changes and problems suggested above are relevant because the Negro church is confronted with them as it plays a role in the adjustment of Negroes to urban life. In this connection, these problems have affected the goals, functions, and programs of the Negro churches.

Mobility and urbanization have affected the rural Negro church. In 1947, Dr. Harry Richardson made the following observation:[5]

> Indeed, in sharp contrast to the increases reported were the cases of losses in membership, many of them so great as to reduce the size of some churches, and in a few cases, to close the churches completely. All the cases of extreme loss were due to migration or emigration from rural areas to urban centers. . . .

This movement has been accompanied by the growth of many existing urban churches and the establishment of many new ones. On the whole these urban churches are larger than the rural ones. Urban churches as a rule possess sufficient financial resources to employ full-time leadership which enables them to conduct a continuous program. This contrasts with the general pattern in the rural churches. The program of most of these churches is confined to conducting worship or preaching services one, two, or three Sundays a month, under the leadership of a pastor who lives in another community and who travels to the church for this particular purpose. Possibly this is a reason for the suggestion that the urban Negro church penetrates the community more than the rural one does and that its program is more practical in its community outreach.

Social relevance

Another important development seems to be an increasing interest in the integration of religious values into life. In the book, *Religion of Negro Protestants*, Ruby Johnston says:[6]

> Religious ideas are significant in action. The religious ideas and actions of the Negro reflect the "interests" of the collectivity. There is a close relation between the common value attitudes of the group and religious ideas.

There appears to be substantial agreement among many Negroes that in addition to worship and religious education the church should be active in promoting the social advancement of the race. There is an expectation among an increasing number of Negroes that the churches should be active in the improvement of the community, cooperate with community welfare and civic organizations, and engage in social action to correct injustice, particularly in race relations. Possibly the classic example of the realization of this expectation is the Montgomery, Alabama bus boycott which was led by ministers with the full and active support of their churches. This movement drew the admiration and support of Negroes nationally. These expectations have affected the programs of many churches which are including such activities as education in social and community problems, recreation, social service, and social action. Changes in the status of Negroes as well as the social problems which they confront in urban areas are factors in stimulating these expectations and this development.

Contrast of old and new

This is not to imply that the religious beliefs which are traditional in the Negro church have disappeared. There are still a substantial number of Negro church members who hold to religious concepts which emphasize personal salvation, pietistic individual living, and a better life after death. Also, there are many people who find escape in emotional expression. However, despite this, the emphasis on social concern and action may mean that such factors as the pressure of urban problems, increased education, and a better understanding of methods of group action are effective in changing the traditional attitudes of Negroes about the role of religion. Ruby Johnston in the book cited above presents an interesting discussion on the decline of traditional religion and emotionalism among Negroes.[7] While shouting and the use of the verbal expression "amen" continue to be practiced in many churches, the tendency appears to be that a smaller number of people, usually the older ones, engage in them.

Store-front churches

Emotional expression as a factor in the religious experience of the Negro raises the question of store-front churches and the movements of "personal saviors." Dissatisfaction about emotional expressions works two ways, and it is at least one index to class stratification in the churches. There are those people, usually members of the growing Negro middle class, who resent emotional expression in the church. Some of these people become members of churches with more restrained services. These churches usually emphasize a rational and action-oriented approach to religion under the leadership of a well-trained minister. At the other end of the spectrum are those who are dissatisfied with the restraint on emotional expression or who feel that the church does not provide the warmth of fellowship or who may have a doctrinal difference. These people withdraw to organize a church of their own. Many of these groups start as store-front churches.

Leadership appears to be a key factor in the destiny of these churches. Some are started for no other reason than that a person with some leadership capabilities decides to organize a church. The ministers of many of these churches have practical leadership capabilities but little academic or professional training. Some of these churches have a short span of existence because they are led by people who aim to exploit the members; others are quite permanent and still others grow into larger, established congregations. This is testimony to the practical leadership capabilities of some of the ministers who serve these small congregations. The people, usually of limited educational background and opportunity, who are members of these churches seem to find security by participating in a small group which emphasizes what is called the "old time religion." Some of these store-front churches may be affiliated with one of the five Negro denominational groups mentioned above, but the large group of them are identified as Holiness Pentecostal, Faith Healing, or Spiritualist.

Personal saviors

Many of the movements of the "personal saviors" are national in scope. Some of the better known examples are the United House of Prayer for All People, the Father Divine Peace Movement, and, more lately, the movement of Mr. Elijah Mohammad which calls itself "Muslim." It is difficult to summarize these movements because they vary greatly in purpose, organization, content of belief, and practices. Estimates of the number of people who belong to these various cult movements vary according to the source. While there are no reliable figures, it is apparent that the vast majority of Negroes do not belong to them. One has to be careful in making generalizations about these movements, but their centers of strength appear to be large urban centers. They are centered around strong leaders who have a unique appeal to masses of people. They seem to relieve and to release the psychological tensions of people who are extremely frustrated by the problems of urban life. Both their appeals and their activities are dramatic enough to attract considerable publicity. These movements appear to be closely knit organizations and to exercise a considerable degree of control over the personal lives of their adherents. It seems safe to say, however, that while these movements may serve the need of their adherents, they do not have a great influence in the Negro community as a whole.

Churches of Ethnic Groups

The great immigration from European countries prior to World War I made its impact upon the churches. The immigrants brought the religion of their home countries with them. In these immigrant churches the language of the homeland was spoken and some of the customs as well as traditions were maintained. As the children of these immigrant families grew older, they wished to be thought of as Americans; they spoke English and exhibited little desire to master the language of their parents. This made it necessary for the churches to hold some services in English. In effect, the churches became bilingual, but even this was temporary. The stoppage of the tide of European immigration, the depletion of the first generation by death, and the opposition of the second and third generations to the use of a foreign language have produced a gradual disappearance of the bilingual feature in many of these churches. In some cases these churches have had to close because the second and third generations have moved to other neighborhoods. In the cases in which these churches have made successful transitions, they have had to forego their preoccupation with European customs, traditions, and language in order to serve the current needs of their congregations. It is the judgment of many competent observers that when such a church fails to do this, its future is not promising.

This is only a part of the story of ethnic groups in the United States. Puerto Ricans, Spanish-speaking people of the Southwest, American Indians, Chinese Americans and Japanese Americans have churches with distinctive characteristics.

Spanish-speaking people

The Spanish-speaking population in the United States is a large one. This brief statement will deal with two groups, the Puerto Rican and the Spanish-speaking people of the Southwest. The latter group is defined to include naturalized immigrants from Mexico, native-born persons with parents or grandparents born in Mexico, alien Mexicans in the United States either on a temporary or permanent basis and Spanish Colonials largely concentrated in New Mexico and southern Colorado.[8] This definition is indicative of the difficulty of defining precisely the Spanish-speaking population of the Southwest. However, the bulk of this population is either Mexican by birth or the native-born descendants of persons born in Mexico.

The Migration Division of the Department of Labor of the Commonwealth of Puerto Rico estimated that the population of Puerto Rico as of July 1, 1958 was 2,317,000 and that as of December 31, 1958 there were 849,000 Puerto Ricans living on the mainland of which 77 per cent were living in New York City.[9] The 1950 United States Census reported that there were 2,448,977 white persons of Spanish surname in five Southwestern states and persons in other states born in Mexico or with one or more parents born in Mexico. Of this number 1,998,415 were native born and 450,562 were Mexican born. It is also reported that 1,519,812 of the Spanish surname population in 5 Southwestern states or 66 per cent were urban dwellers. The five Southwestern states are Arizona, California, Colorado, New Mexico, and Texas.

There are substantial differences between the Puerto Rican population and the Spanish-speaking population of the Southwest. For instance, one of these differences is that Puerto Ricans are citizens of the United States and movement within the country constitutes migration. On the other hand, the people of Mexican origin are immigrants 'from another country. There are some similarities. Many of the people of Mexican origin came from an agrarian society and some of the Puerto Ricans came from a similar type of society. Both groups came from societies in which the characteristics of Spanish culture and the traditions of the Roman Catholic Church are predominant. The majority of both groups have settled in urban areas. They speak Spanish and those who have not mastered English experience difficulty in communication. Both groups experience a lack of full acceptance in American society because of their ethnic background. Even though some people of Puerto Rican and Mexican background, because of education and skill, have gained a degree of acceptance, these groups are victimized by socio-economic disabilities.

These factors are reflected in the churches. The Spanish-speaking people of the Southwest come from a Catholic background. Catholicism was taken for granted in Mexico. There was little knowledge that other religious forms existed, and this was true of Protestantism, also. Religion was deeply interwoven into the life of the community. Thus those people coming into the country were predominantly of Roman Catholic background. Several competent observers have indicated that they were nominal Roman Catholics. It has also been pointed out that only a small proportion of those in this country are active members of the Roman Catholic Church. Possibly one of the reasons for this is that religion is not so fully integrated into community life in an urban-industrial society and is therefore unable to meet the needs of the people as it had done in an agrarian society.

Mexicans

Mexican Americans in the United States are attracted to Protestant churches, but the total number is small. Some attend English-language Protestant churches. It is reported, however, that few local Protestant churches in the border areas exhibit active interest in attracting Mexican Americans. The fear of not being accepted as well as difficulties of language may deter many Mexican Americans from joining these churches. Also, there are churches which serve Mexican Americans. A study of eighty-one Mexican churches in 1959 indicated that fifty-one claim less than one hundred members each. Sixty-three of these churches reported under one hundred in average attendance. Twenty-five of the churches reported using some English in the services and fifty-three used no English. The denominational distribution of these churches was as follows: Disciples—three; United Presbyterian, United States of America—twenty-one; Methodist—twenty-two; Congregational—three; American Lutheran—six; Church of God—two; Episcopal—five; American Baptist—nineteen.[10] These figures indicate that the Protestant churches serving Mexican Americans are small in size and that the total number of members involved is small.

Puerto Ricans

The fact that Puerto Rico is predominantly Roman Catholic in religious background is well known. It is reported that probably 80 per cent of the island population would say they were Catholic if pressed with the question of religious orientation. However, most recent observers note that perhaps 20 per cent or less actually practice the public and obvious manifestations of the Roman Catholic faith.[11] It is estimated that at least 10 per cent of the population of the island could be characterized as Protestant. Protestantism has been on the island for about fifty years. Protestant denominations are working in 522 areas of service on the island; 413 of these areas are identified as rural.[12]

Puerto Ricans bring their religious traditions to the mainland with them, but some observers believe that a larger proportion of Puerto Ricans in New York City than on the island do not have an active relationship with the Roman Catholic Church.[13] However, many Roman Catholic parishes serve the religious and social needs of Puerto Ricans. But the report *Midcentury Pioneers and Protestants* says:

> In summary, it would seem fair to say that few Protestant churches established in communities into which Puerto Ricans are moving have made an attempt to welcome the Protestant Puerto Ricans. Few churches have reached out to help the newcomers in their adjustment process. Even fewer have attempted to evangelize the Puerto Ricans.[14]

The few English-language Protestant churches that do serve Puerto Ricans offer activities designed to integrate them into the congregation, such as released time religious classes, Scout troops, athletic leagues, forums, and other types of leisure-time and recreational activities. Some churches conduct worship services in Spanish at various times and a few churches have Spanish-speaking staff members.

The report mentioned above established the existence of 181 non-Roman Catholic Spanish-speaking churches in New York City in 1953. Some information was gathered about 169 of these churches. Ninety-two of the 169 churches were identified as Pentecostal; thirty-eight were conducted by Protestant denominations; thirty-four were independent; and five were connected with New York City Mission Society. Ninety-six of the 169

churches which returned completed questionnaires reported
9,965 church members of which 8,239 were said to be active.
The average total number of members per church was about 103
and the total average attendance at the main Sunday Worship
Service was about 102. Seventy-one of the ninety-six churches
reported memberships of less than one hundred each and forty
of the seventy-one had memberships under fifty. It should be
pointed out that three of these churches had more than three
hundred members and three others had more than five hundred
members. However, seventy-nine of these churches are completely self-supporting and forty-five have full-time pastors. The
number of these churches appears to be growing. Seventy-one
of the ninety-six churches were organized between 1940 and the
first six months of 1953.[15] Most of these churches are small, but
they are self-reliant and active institutions.

The case of the Mexican Americans and the Puerto Ricans
seems to indicate that neither Roman Catholics nor Protestants
have developed an effective strategy for working with these
groups. Yet it must, in fairness, be said that there is awareness of
the need for such a strategy, and interested church groups are
grappling with the problem.

American Indians

Both Roman Catholic and Protestant churches have conducted
missionary activities among American Indians for a long period
of time. In 1951, thirty-six Protestant denominations were doing
mission work among these people. While there are no reliable
statistics, it is estimated that there are between 65,000 and 70,000
Protestants and about 95,000 Roman Catholics among American
Indians. In addition to meeting the spiritual needs of these people, this work has concerned itself with their social, material, and
economic problems. These missionary programs have been concerned with education, family life, land problems, economic development, health, and work with American Indians to achieve
responsible participation in community life on and off the res-
ervation. This has required a great deal of adaptability because
American Indians vary from those who occupy prominent places
of leadership in American society to those who lead a very
primitive tribal existence.

Of the 400,000 persons counted as Indians in the United States
about 300,000 live on or near reservations. Much of this land

has a low productive potential and with the increasing Indian population, it is unable to support the people who live on it. This suggests an important recent development among American Indians. Indians are leaving the reservations, some for work as agricultural migrants and others for jobs in urban centers. The movement of Indians to urban centers has become more pronounced since World War II. This movement flows into cities such as Minneapolis, Minnesota, Rapid City, South Dakota, Chicago, Illinois, Salt Lake City, Utah, and Los Angeles, California. Migration to urban centers confronts Indians who have lived in rural areas with the problems which are connected with adjustment to urban life. Problems such as employment, housing, and the use of community services and facilities are often compounded by the strangeness of the city and in some places by discrimination against American Indians.

The churches, both Roman Catholic and Protestant in many cities, have recognized the need to help American Indians adjust to and become a part of church and community life in urban centers. The result is that they have established programs to work with other interested community agencies to accomplish this.

Chinese

The United States Census of 1950 reported 117,629 Chinese in the United States. The estimated total for 1958 is 135,000. Rose Hum Lee says:

> The Chinese brought with them no organized religious system per se, but they imported a complex blend of traits selected from two ethical systems—Confucianism and Taoism—as well as some religious practices identified with Buddhism.[16]

The Protestant home missionary movement started work among Chinese about 1853. The Roman Catholics started work in San Francisco about 1900. San Francisco today is the largest center of Catholic activities among Chinese. Roman Catholic missions were organized in Philadelphia in 1939, Chicago in 1941, and New York in 1949. By 1952 there were sixty-two Protestant Chinese Churches and missions and six Catholic Churches and missions. It is estimated that there were about 6,000 members in the Protestant Chinese Churches and about 3,000 in the Catholic

Chinese Churches. This, of course, does not represent an accurate picture of the number of Chinese Christians because many Chinese attend churches which are predominantly white or interracial in membership.

In addition to religious services, the Roman Catholic centers conduct a social program to meet the needs of Chinese people— English classes for adults, parochial schools for children which sometimes supplement their courses with studies in Chinese culture.

A study of the sixty-two Protestant Chinese Churches in 1952 shows some of the characteristics of these churches.[17] Forty-three are denominational, five are interdenominational, and fourteen are independent. Twelve are self-supporting groups; twenty-six receive some aid from denominational mission boards; fifteen depend entirely upon, or receive the major part of their support from mission boards; and seven are small groups with limited programs. The average Chinese Church has 155 members with the range running from less than fifty members to over one thousand. The average budget is about $5,260. The data on membership indicate that some of these churches are growing in size and that there is a higher proportion of young people among Chinese church members than among non-Chinese church members.

The history of Protestant mission work among Chinese reveals continuing interest in the adjustment of Chinese to American life and in combating discrimination against Chinese. This interest continues. In addition to normal programs which are carried on by churches, the Chinese church appears to emphasize work with young people and pastoral counseling. Many of them maintain classes for those who wish to learn English as well as classes in Chinese language and culture. In this connection it might be mentioned that there is a trend toward the increased use of English in these churches. Possibly this might be due to the increasing influence of American-born Chinese.

Integration in the Churches

The previous discussion has considered the churches among racial and ethnic minorities. In a sense, this is testimony to the fact that these groups are separated in varying degrees from the main body of the churches. The concern about the elimination of segregation from religious institutions has been mentioned. The positive goal is the inclusion of persons in the congregation and the activities of the church or church-related institution on the basis of religious commitment without regard to race or ethnic origin. The churches are taking positive steps in this direction. Space does not permit more than mere mention of some of the highlights of this development.

The Roman Catholic Church has been clear and forthright in its policy that racial segregation is contrary to the teachings of the Church. On this basis it has moved forthrightly to eliminate it from the local parishes, parochial schools, and church organizations where it exists. Hundreds of Catholic parishes have members of all races in their membership. Catholic organizations, such as the Catholic Interracial Councils, the National Federation of Catholic College Students, and the National Catholic Welfare Conference have made major contributions toward improving race relations both within the Church and in the community.

The National Council of Churches and most of the major Protestant denominations have adopted statements either renouncing the practice of segregation in the churches or affirming a ministry which is inclusive of all people regardless of race or ethnic origin who desire to participate in a particular church or church-related institution.

These statements have provided the basis for the achievement of integration of national and regional church organizations. Significant integration has taken place in councils of churches. Racial minorities are integrated in the organization of the National Council of Churches. This is true also in state and city councils of churches, even in states where segregation is enforced by law. Several of the predominantly white denominations have moved to eliminate racial segregation from their national and regional organizations. Several are currently grappling with the problem. The Negro denominations face the problem of integrating white people into their organizations. A number of denominations with predominantly white membership are carrying on various types of programs aimed at the elimination of segregation in local churches and church-related institutions. While many Protestant church-related institutions have always been open without regard to race, there are numerous instances of others which have in recent years adopted and pursued policies of inclusive service to all people. However, it is widely acknowledged that much more progress must be made.

The local church has presented a difficult problem, but even here there is movement. While there are no reliable figures on the total number of Protestant churches which have members of more than one race, recent studies by denominations indicate they are increasing in number. While the figures of the denominational studies are not comparable, they would seem to indicate that possibly 10 per cent of the Protestant churches have members of more than one race and that most of these churches are located in urban communities where people of two or more races live together. To be sure, the percentage is small, but it involves hundreds of churches, and it is significant because movement among Protestant churches appears to be in the direction of integration.

Conclusion

It seems clear that a major function of the churches of ethnic and racial minorities is to serve the religious and social needs of their people. This function is shaped and reinforced by ethnic and racial discrimination, which is a dominant factor influencing every aspect of the lives of people belonging to these minority groups. Their aspirations are an influential factor in shaping the goals toward which these churches work. The church programs are determined to a large extent by the problems and needs which confront ethnic and racial minority peoples. These churches are dynamic in that they are affected by social changes such as mobility and urbanization as well as the increasing and imperative demand for full participation in community life on the basis of ability without regard to ethnic or racial background. There is evidence that this in turn has affected the expectations of people about the role or roles of the churches in meeting the needs of people who face the necessity of adjusting to these changes.

The very existence of churches which serve people belonging to a particular ethnic or racial minority group is, in a sense, a testimony to the pervasiveness of racial segregation in our society. It is clear that segregation based on ethnic or racial background is a major problem confronting the churches. At the same time, many people in the churches recognize that this is a basic contradiction of Christian principles and teaching. In recognition of this, there is a movement to eliminate segregation and to achieve inclusive practices in all areas of church life. While the churches face the responsibility of taking increasing initiative in accomplishing this, it must be recognized that desegregation and integration of the churches is related to desegregation and integration of the total community. For instance, many churches find that racial segregation in housing makes it extremely difficult, if not impossible, to achieve integration in fact in the churches. Therefore, the churches face the challenge to work for the elimination of segregation from every aspect of American society.

NOTES

1. *Yearbook of the American Churches, 1960* (New York: The National Council of Churches, 1960), pp. 253, 257.

2. "Proceedings of the General Conference of the Methodist Church, 1960," *Daily Christian Advocate,* Vol. 1, No. 3 (April 29, 1960), p. 105.

3. *National Catholic Almanac, 1960* (Garden City, N. Y.: Doubleday and Co., 1960), p. 473.

4. Charles S. Johnson, *A Preface to Racial Understanding* (New York: Friendship Press, 1936), pp. 153-54.

5. Harry V. Richardson, *Dark Glory* (New York: Friendship Press, 1947), p. 54.

6. Ruby Johnston, *The Religion of Negro Protestants* (New York: Philosophical Library, 1956), p. 33.

7. *Ibid.,* pp. 3-15.

8. Bureau of Research and Survey, *Spanish-Speaking Americans* (Unpublished manuscript by Blair, Lively, and Trimble; New York: National Council of Churches, 1959), p. 14.

9. *Ibid.,* p. 49.

10. Bureau of Research and Survey, *Missionary Opportunity Among Spanish-Americans, Report on Local Church Questionnaires* (Mimeographed; New York: National Council of Churches, September 1959), pp. 1, 6, 9.

11. *Midcentury Pioneers and Protestants—A Survey Report of the Puerto Rican Migration to the U. S. Mainland* and, in particular, *A Study of the Protestant Expression Among Puerto Ricans in New York City* (Mimeographed; New York: Protestant Council of the City of New York, March 1954), p. 3.

12. *Ibid.,* p. 2.

13. *Ibid.*, p. 10.

14. *Ibid.*, p. 14.

15. *Ibid.*, pp. 10-22.

16. Rose Hum Lee, *The Chinese in the United States of America* (Hong Kong: Hong Kong University Press, 1960), p. 278.

17. Horace R. Cayton and Anne O. Lively, *The Chinese in the United States and the Chinese Christian Churches* (New York: Bureau of Research and Survey, The National Council of Churches, April 1955), pp. 48-68.

*The author, in dramatic style, analyzes a contem-
porary social institution and the "entities" within
that institution. Through her unique presentation, the
American family scene with many of its membership
roles "leaps out" at the reader as an unending reminder of the ever-real theater that influences men's
lives.*

XIV

The Family As a Company
of Players*

ANNABELLE B. MOTZ

ALL THE WORLD'S A STAGE, AND WE ARE ALL PLAYERS.

Erving Goffman in his *The Presentation of Self in Everyday
Life* views our everyday world as having both front stage and
back. Like professionals, we try to give a careful and superior
performance out front. Back stage we unzip, take off our masks,
complain of the strain, think back over the last act, and prepare
anxiously for the next.

Sometimes the "on stage" performances are solos; sometimes
we act in teams or groups. The roles may be carefully planned,
rehearsed, and executed; or they may be spontaneous or impro-
vised. The presentation can be a hit; or it can flop badly.

Picture a theater starring the family. The "stars" are the husband, wife, and children. But the cast includes a wide range of
persons in the community—fellow workers, friends, neighbors,
delivery-men, shopkeepers, doctors, and everyone who passes by.
Usually husband and wife are the leads; and the appeal, impact,
and significance of their performances vary with the amount of
time on stage, the times of day and week, the circumstances of
each presentation, and the moods of the audience.

Backstage for the family members is generally to be found in
their homes, as suggested by the expression, "a man's home is
his castle." The front stage is where they act out their dramatic

parts in schools, stores, places of employment, on the street, in the homes of other persons; such as when entertaining guests, back in their own homes.

My aim is to analyze the performances of family members before the community audience—their *front stage* appearances. This behavior conforms to the rules and regulations that society places upon its members; perhaps the analysis of the family life drama will provide insights into the bases of the problems for which an increasing number of middle-class persons are seeking professional help.

Many years ago, Thorstein Veblen noted that although industrialization made it possible for the American worker to live better than at any previous time in history, it made him feel so insignificant that he sought ways to call attention to himself. In *The Theory of the Leisure Class,* Veblen showed that all strata of society practiced "conspicuous consumption"—the ability to use one's income for non-essential goods and services in ways readily visible to others. A man's abilities were equated with his monetary worth and the obvious command he had in the market place to purchase commodities beyond bare necessities. Thus, a family that lives more comfortably than most must be a "success."

While conspicuous consumption was becoming an essential element of front stage performance, the ideal of the American as a completely rational person—governed and governing by reason rather than emotion—was being projected around the world. The writings of the first four decades of this century stress over and over again the importance of the individual and individual opinion. (The growth of unionism, the Social Security program, public opinion polling, and federal aid to education are a few examples of the trend toward positive valuation of each human being—not to mention the impact of Freud and Dewey and their stress on individual worth.) The desirability of rule by majority and democratic debate and voting as the best means of reaching group decisions—all these glorified rationality.

As population, cities, and industry grew, so also did anonymity and complexity; and rationality in organizations (more properly known as bureaucratization) had to keep pace. The individual was exposed to more and more people he knew less and less. The face to face relationships of small towns and workshops declined. Job requirements, duties and loyalties, hiring and firing, had to "go by the book." Max Weber has described the bureaucratic organization: each job is explicitly defined, the rights of entry and exit from the organization can be found in the industry's manual, and the rights and duties of the worker and of the organization toward the worker are rationally defined; above all, the worker acts as a rational being on the job—he is never subject to emotional urges.

With the beams and bricks of "front" and rationality the middle-class theater is built; with matching props the stage is set.

There are two basic scenes. One revolves about family and close personal relationships. It takes place in a well-furnished house—very comfortable, very stylish, but not "vulgar." The actors are calm, controlled, reasonable.

The other scene typically takes place in a bureaucratic anteroom cluttered with physical props and with people treated like physical props. The actors do not want the audience to believe that they *are* props—so they attract attention to themselves and dramatize their individuality and worth by spending and buying far more than they need.

What does this mean in the daily life of the family stars?

Take first the leading lady, wife, and mother. She follows Veblen and dramatizes her husband's success by impressing any chance onlookers with her efficient house management. How does one run a house efficiently? All must be reasoned order. The wife-housekeeper plans what has to be done and does it simply and quickly. Kitchen, closets, and laundry display department store wares as attractively as the stores themselves. The house is always presentable, and so is she. Despite her obviously great labors, she does not seem to get flustered, over-fatigued, or too emotional. (What would her neighbors or even a passing door-to-door salesman think if they heard her screaming at the children?) With minimal household help she must appear the gracious hostess, fresh and serene—behind her a dirty kitchen magically cleaned, a meal effortlessly prepared, and husband and children well behaved and helpful.

Outside the home, too, she is composed and rational. She does not show resentment toward Johnny's teacher, who may irritate her or give Johnny poor marks. She does not yawn during interminable and dull PTA programs (what would they think of her and her family?). At citizen meetings she is the embodiment of civic-minded, responsible, property-ownership (even if the mortgage company actually owns the property). Her supermarket cart reflects her taste, affluence, efficiency, and concern. At church she exhibits no unchurchly feelings. She prays that her actions and facial expression will not give away the fact that her mind has wandered from the sermon; she hopes that as she greets people, whether interested in them or not, she will be able to say the "right" thing. Her clothes and car are extremely important props—the right make, style, finish; and they project her front stage character, giving the kind of impression she thinks she and the other members of the family want her to give.

Enter Father Center Stage

The male lead is husband, father, and man-of-affairs. He acts in ways that, he hopes, will help his status, and that of his family. At all times he must seem to be in relaxed control of difficult situations. This often takes some doing. For instance, he must be both unequal and equal to associates; that is, he is of course a good fellow and very democratic, but the way he greets and handles his superiors at work is distinctly, if subtly, different from the way he speaks to and handles inferiors. A superior who arrives unexpectedly must find him dynamically at work, worth every cent and more of his income; an inferior must also find him busy, demonstrating how worthy he is of superior status and respect. He must always be in control. Even when supposedly relaxing, swapping dirty jokes with his colleagues, he must be careful to avoid any that offend their biases. He has to get along; bigots, too, may be able to do him good or harm.

Sometimes he cannot give his real feelings release until he gets behind the wheel—and the savage jockeying which takes place during evening rush may reflect this simultaneous discharge by many drivers.

The scene shifts back to the home. The other stars greet him —enter loving wife and children. He may not yet be ready or able to re-establish complete emotional control—after all, a man's home is his backstage—and the interplay of the sub-plots begins. If his wife goes on with her role, she will be the dutiful spouse, listening sympathetically, keeping the children and her temper quiet. If she should want to cut loose at the same time, collision will probably still be avoided because both have been trained to restrain themselves and present the right front as parents to their children—if not to each other.

Leisure is not rest. At home father acts out his community role of responsible family head. The back yard is kept up as a "private" garden; the garage as a showroom for tools on display. He must exhibit interest—but not too much enthusiasm—in a number of activities, some ostensibly recreational, retaining a nice balance between appearing a dutiful husband and a henpecked one. Reason must rule emotion.

The children of old vaudevillians literally were born and reared in the theater—were nursed between acts by mothers in spangles, trained as toddlers to respond to footlights as other children might to sunlight. The young in the middle-class family drama also learn to recognize cues and to perform.

Since "front" determines the direction and content of the drama, they are supposed to be little ladies and gentlemen. Proper performances from such tyros require much backstage rehearsal. Unfortunately, the middle-class backstage is progressively disappearing, and so the children too must be prepared to respond appropriately to the unexpected—whether an unwanted salesman at the door who must be discreetly lied to about mother's whereabouts or a wanted friend who must not be offended. They are taught rationality and democracy in family councils—where they are also taught what behavior is expected of them. Reason is rife; even when they get out of hand the parents "reason" with them. As Dorothy Barclay says when discussing household chores and the child, "Appealing to a sense of family loyalty and pride in maturity is the tack most parents take first in trying to overcome youngsters' objections (to household chores). Offering rewards comes second, arguing and insisting third."

"Grown-up" and "good" children do family chores. They want the house to look "nice"; they don't tell family secrets when visitors are present, and even rush to close closet and bedroom doors when the doorbell rings unexpectedly.

The child, of course, carries the family play into school, describing it in "show and tell" performances and in his deportment and dress. Part of the role of responsible parenthood includes participation in PTA and teacher conferences, with the child an important player, even if offstage.

To the child, in fact, much of the main dynamic of the play takes place in the dim realm of offstage (not always the same as backstage)—his parents' sex activities, their real income and financial problems, and many other things, some of them strange and frightening, that "children are not old enough to understand."

They early learn the fundamental lessons of front stage: be prepared; know your lines. Who knows whether the neighbors' windows are open? The parent who answers a crying child with, "Calm down now, let's sit down and talk this over," is rehearsing him in stage presence, and in his character as middle-class child and eventually middle-class adult.

Often the family acts as a team. The act may be rehearsed, but it must appear spontaneous. Watch them file in and out of church on Sunday mornings. Even after more than an hour of sitting, the children seem fresh and starched. They do not laugh or shout as on the playground. The parents seem calm, in complete control. Conversations and postures are confined to those appropriate for a place of worship.

Audience reaction is essential to a play. At church others may say, "What nice children you have!" or, "We look forward to seeing you next Sunday." Taken at face value, these are sounds of audience approval and applause; the performers may bask in them. Silence or equivocal remarks may imply disapproval and cause anxiety. What did they really mean? What did we do wrong? Sometimes reaction is delayed, and the family will be uncertain of their impression. In any case, future performances will be affected.

Acting a role, keeping up a front, letting the impressions and expectations of other people influence our behavior, does result in a great deal of good. Organized society is possible only when there is some conformity to roles and rules. Also a person concerned with the impression others have of him feels that he is significant to them and they to him. When he polishes his car because a dirty one would embarrass him, when his wife straightens her make-up before answering the door, both exhibit a sense of their importance and personal dignity in human affairs. Those who must, or want to, serve as models or exemplars must be especially careful of speech and performance—they are always on stage. When people keep up appearances they are identifying themselves with a group and its standards. They need it; presumably it needs them.

Moreover, acting what seems a narrow role may actually broaden experience and open doors. To tend a lawn, or join a

PTA, social club, or art group—"to keep up appearances"—may result in real knowledge and understanding about horticulture, education, or civic responsibility.

For the community, front produces the positive assets of social cohesion. Well-kept lawns, homes, cars, clean children and adults have definite aesthetic, financial, and sanitary value. People relate to one another, develop common experiences. People who faithfully play their parts exhibit personal and civic responsibility. The rules make life predictable and safe, confine ad-libs within acceptable limits, control violence and emotional tangents, and allow the show to go on and the day's work to be done. Thus, the challenging game of maintaining front relates unique personalities to one another and unites them in activity and into a nation.

So much for the good which preoccupation with front and staging accomplishes; what of the bad?

First, the inhibition of the free play of emotion must lead to frustration. Human energies need outlets. If onstage acting does not allow for release of tension, then the escape should take place backstage. But what if there is virtually no backstage? Perhaps then the releases will be found in the case histories of psychiatrists and other counselors. Communication between husband and wife may break down because of the contrast between the onstage image each has of the other as a perfect mate and the unmasked actuality backstage. Perhaps when masks crumble and crack, when people can no longer stand the strain of the front, then what we call nervous breakdown occurs.

Growing Up With Bad Reviews

And how does the preoccupation with front affect the growth and development of the child? How can a child absorb and pattern himself after models which are essentially unreal? A mother may "control" her emotions when a child spills milk on her freshly scrubbed floor, and "reason" with him about it; she may still retain control when he leaves the refrigerator open after repeated warnings; but then some minor thing—such as loud laughter over the funnies—may suddenly blow off the lid, and she will "let him have it, but good!" What can he learn from such treatment? To respect his mother's hard work at keeping the house clean? To close the refrigerator door? Not to laugh loudly when reading the comics? That mother is a crab? Or, she's always got it in for him? Whatever he has learned, it is doubtful it was what his mother wanted! Whatever it was it will probably not clarify his understanding of such family values as pride in work, reward for effort, consideration of other people, or how to meet problems. Too, since the family's status is vitally linked with the maintenance of fronts, any deviance by the child, unless promptly rectified, threatens family standing in the community. This places a tremendous burden on a child actor.

Moreover, a concentration on front rather than content must result in a leveling and deadening of values and feelings. If a man buys a particular hat primarily because of what others may think, then its intrinsic value as a hat—in fact, even his own judgment and feelings about it—become secondary. Whether the judgment of those whose approval he covets is good or bad is unimportant—just so they approve. Applause has taken the place of value.

A PTA lecture on "The Future of America" will call for the same attentive front from him as a scientist's speech on the "Effects of Nuclear Warfare on Human Survival." Reading a newspaper on a crowded bus, his expression undergoes little change whether he is reading about nuclear tests, advice to the lovelorn, or Elizabeth Taylor's marital problems. To his employer he presents essentially the same bland, non-argumentative, courteous front whether he has just been refused a much deserved pay raise or told to estimate the cost of light bulbs. He seems impartial, objective, rational—and by so doing he also seems to deny that there is any difference to him between the pay raise and the light bulbs, as well as to deny his feelings.

The Price of Admission

What price does the community pay for its role as audience?

The individual human talents and energies are alienated from assuming responsibility for the well-being and survival of the group. The exaggerated self-consciousness of individuals results in diluted and superficial concern with the community at a time when deep involvement, new visions, and real leadership are needed. Can the world afford to have over-zealous actors who work so hard on their lines that they forget what the play is all about?

It is probable that this picture will become more general in the near future and involve more and more people—assuming that the aging of the population continues, that the Cold War doesn't become hot and continues to need constant checks on loyalty and patriotism, that automation increases man's leisure at the same time as it keeps up or increases the production of consumer goods, and that improved advertising techniques make every home a miniature department store. The resulting conformity, loyalty, and patriotism may foster social solidarity. It may also cause alienation, immaturity, confusion, and much insecurity when new situations, for which old fronts are no longer appropriate, suddenly occur. Unless people start today to separate the important from the tinsel and to assume responsibility for community matters that are vital, individual actors will feel even more isolated; and the society may drift ever further from the philosophy that values every person.

Tomorrow's communities will need to provide new backstages, as the home, work place, and recreation center become more and more visible. Psychiatrists, counselors, confessors, and other professional listeners must provide outlets for actors who are exhausted and want to share their backstage thoughts. With increased leisure, business men will probably find it profitable to provide backstage settings in the form of resorts, rest homes, or retreats.

The state of the world is such today that unless the family and the community work together to evaluate and value the significant and direct their energies accordingly, the theater with its actors, front stage, backstage, and audience may end in farce and tragedy.

*Both readable and revealing, this article stresses the
sociological, rather than psychopathological, dimensions that contribute to marital failure, emasculation
of spirit, and transitory sexual liaisons in the ghetto
area known as "Tally's Corner."*

XV

Husbands and Wives*

ELLIOT LIEBOW

A FEW OF THE STREETCORNER MEN expect to get married sooner
or later. A few are married. Most of the men have tried marriage
and found it wanting.

To be married is to be formally, legally married, to have a
marriage certificate, to "have papers." The rights and duties
conferred by marriage are clear-cut, unambiguous; they are those
rights and duties set forth in the marriage vows and by the
courts. Individuals may fail to exercise their rights or neglect
their duties but they do not deny them.

Men and women are careful to distinguish between marriage
on the one hand and "common law," "shacking up," "living with"
and other consensual unions on the other. There is, of course,
a large overlap. The rights and duties which attach to consensual
unions are patterned after those which attach to marriage and,
in practice, some consensual unions are publicly indistinguishable
from marriage. There are two principal differences. First, the
rights and duties of consensual unions generally have less public
force behind them. The result is that an act which violates both
the marital and consensual union invokes a stronger sanction in
the case of marriage. A second difference is that, in consensual
unions, rights and duties are less clearly defined, especially at
the edges. The result is that while everyone would agree that
a given act stands in violation of the marital relationship, there
could be—and frequently is—widespread disagreement as to

* Reprinted from *Tally's Corner*, by Elliot Liebow, copyright © 1967, by
Little, Brown and Company (Inc.), pp. 103-136, by permission of the
publisher.

whether the same act stands in violation of a consensual union.

The right to exclusive sexual access to one's spouse, for example, is freely acknowledged to be a right which attaches to marriage. But there is no consensus on sex rights in consensual unions. Some streetcorner men feel that a partner in a consensual union has a right to demand exclusive sexual access; others deny this. Perhaps the majority feel that one has a right to expect sexual exclusiveness but not to demand it. Indeed, this may be the chief distinction between rights in marriage and rights in consensual union. In marriage, one partner has a legal right to demand some kinds of behavior and the other has a legal duty to perform them. In consensual union, this relationship is watered down; one partner may come to expect some kinds of behavior but the other does not have a legal duty to perform them.[1]

The distinction between the demand rights of marriage and the privilege rights of the consensual union, as well as the absence of clearly defined rights in the consensual union, can be seen in the conflict between Stanton and Bernice. Shortly after they began living together, Stanton was arrested and jailed for thirty days. Upon his release, he went to their apartment where he discovered Bernice with another man. Over the next several weeks, Stanton refused to look for work. It was understood that he was "making Bernice pay" for what she had done by forcing her to "pay the rent and buy the groceries." Had Stanton and Bernice been married, some may have questioned the wisdom or efficacy or even fairness of Stanton's action but no one would have questioned his right to do this. But Stanton and Bernice were not married and there were both men and women who said that this was a "terrible" thing for Stanton to do, that maybe Bernice hadn't done the "right" thing but she had a right to do what she did because they weren't married and, because they weren't married, what she had done had not "hurt" Stanton, and even if it had, he had no right to make her "pay" for it.

A partner to a consensual union may explicitly point out the distinction between their own relationship and marriage in order to challenge the other's right or as justification for his own behavior. Thus, one woman walked away in a huff from a man who was trying to get her to accompany him with the reminder that "I'm your girl friend, not your wife." And Leroy, at a time when he had been living with Charlene for several months, conceded that his rights were compromised by the fact that they were not formally, legally married. They had had an argument which brought their relationship almost to the breaking point. Later the same day Leroy left a note for Charlene which concluded: "I have decided to let you think it over until 6 P.M. Sunday. Until then, you can go where you want to, do what you want to, because like you said, I don't have any papers on you yet."[2]

The distinction between marriage and consensual union is also carefully drawn in the labels one applies to the incumbents in the two relationships. The terms husband and wife, for example, are almost always reserved for formally married persons. Thus, Sea Cat explains that "Priscilla is my old lady. My wife lives over in Northeast." Tally explains to William that "Sara is Budder's old lady, they ain't married." When not used for contrastive purposes, however, "old man" and "old lady" and "man" and "woman" may also be used to label husband and wife. "My old man (lady)," then, may mean either "the man (woman) I am formally, legally married to," or "the man (woman) I am living with but whom I am not formally, legally married to." But "my husband (wife)" almost always means "the man (woman) I am formally, legally married to."

These labels and their usages reflect the overlapping relationship of marriage and the consensual union. The fact that "old man" and "old lady" are equally applicable in either relationship testifies to an equivalence between marriage and consensual unions; the fact that "husband" and "wife" are reserved for marriage and denied to persons in consensual union demonstrates the distinctiveness of the marriage relationship.

Thus marriage, as compared with consensual union, is clearly the superior relationship. Marriage has higher status than consensual union and greater respectability. Not only are its rights and duties better defined and supported with greater public force but only through marriage can a man and woman lay legitimate claim to being husband and wife.

But as the man on the streetcorner looks at the reality of marriage as it is experienced day in and day out by husbands and wives, his universe tells him that marriage does not work. He knows that it did not for his own mother and father and for the parents of most of his contemporaries. He knows that Lonny strangled his wife and almost paid with his own life as well. He sees Clarence trying to keep his wife from getting at the woman she has found him with while two of their four children look on in frightened silence. He knows that Tom Tom, whose busboy job did not pay enough to support his wife and children, moved away from his family so they would become eligible for ADC. He sees Leroy and Charlene circling slowly on the sidewalk, with Charlene holding a broken coke bottle thrust in front of her and Leroy pawing at her with his right arm wrapped in his jacket. He sees Tonk standing on the corner where his wife works as a waitress, afraid himself to take a job because the word is going around that she is "cutting out" on him. He sees Shirley bury her face in her hands and shudder, partly perhaps because the Christmas wind has again ripped away the blanket nailed across the window but mainly because she and Richard are trying to decide whether to send the children to Junior Village[3] or take them to the waiting room at Union Station for the night. And at two in the morning, he sees Leroy and Charlene, with Leroy holding their year-old son in his arms, anxiously looking for someone, anyone, to take them to Children's Hospital because their sleeping baby had just been bitten on the cheek by a rat.

These are the things he sees and hears and knows of streetcorner marriage: the disenchantment, sometimes bitter, of those who were or still are married; the public and private fights between husband and wife and the sexual jealousy that rages around them; husbands who cannot feed, clothe and house their wives and children and husbands who have lost their will to do so; the terror of husband and wife who suddenly find themselves unable to ward off attacks on the health and safety of their children. Nor is there—to redeem all this even in part—a single marriage among the streetcorner men and their women which they themselves recognize as a "good" marriage.

The talk that the streetcorner man is exposed to is uniformly antimarriage. On the corner, he hears Sea Cat proclaim that "I was married once and once was enough," and he hears a chorus of assent from the others: "I'll go along with that," they say. In the privacy of Richard's room, Richard, speaking quietly and with feeling, tells him that if his marriage to Shirley breaks up, "later for a marriage,[4] man, I don't want to get married again."

He hears others question whether Sea Cat or Richard or any other man really wanted to get married in the first place. They ascribe marriage to a variety of precipitating incidents and circumstances which are seen as pushing the man into marriage against his will. This presumption of coercion may apply to one's own marriage as well as to others. Richard usually claimed that he married Shirley only because his grandmother promised him fifty dollars if he would do so. The men generally agreed that if Leroy ever married Charlene (which he finally did), it would only be because Charlene had his baby and because Charlene's mother, Malvina, and her social worker were "getting behind him" (i.e., putting pressure on him). The men said that Robert married Siserene only to meet the competition from Lonny who had himself offered to marry her to get her away from Robert.

Where coercion cannot be presumed, the men claim not to understand the motive for marriage at all. When word reached the corner that Boley was to be married that weekend, Tonk shook his head and said he didn't understand why Boley was getting married since he was already shacking up with the girl anyway. No one else admitted to understanding it, either. Along with the others, Richard believed coercion to be an especially important element in early marriages.

> The average person you see at eighteen, he don't have nothing of his own and he gets out there [into the world]. And the average person you see now that gets married at eighteen, he gets married because they're gonna have a kid or something.

But the closer one looks at the individual cases, the more difficult it is to detect coercion. Robert was admittedly under no pressure at all. Siserene had, in fact, already decided against marrying Lonny and had gone back to living with Robert when Robert asked her to marry him. As for Leroy, it is true that he was under pressure from Malvina, her social worker, and the people at the clinic where Charlene went for prenatal care, but Charlene gave Leroy many opportunities to get out from under —had he chosen to do so—by saying she preferred to postpone the marriage until after the baby was born so that Leroy could make his decision free of external pressures.[5]

Thus, the contention that many men are, like Leroy, forced into marriage by premarital births or pregnancies is at best a half-truth for the men on the streetcorner, most of whom fathered one or more children before marriage by women other than those they subsequently married. It is true that the man usually feels a strong obligation to both the woman and the children she bears him and, on occasion, even an obligation to marry the woman if she's amenable to marriage. But if for any reason he is simply not ready to marry this woman, he does not. Like Tonk, he may take the child, give it to his mother, and contribute to its support; like Tommy, he may remain friends with the woman and help her financially whenever he can; like William, he may simply take off for parts unknown. If, like Wesley, he feels guilty about not marrying her, it is a guilt he can live with.

> The girl [mother of Wesley's child] . . . she's ready to get married any time I say so. . . . Right now, this girl—as long as this girl's single, I'm not going to get married. I don't want to marry her and I don't want to marry nobody else until she gets married. You see, when she gets married, I figure I'm free. You see, if I get married, I'd be inclined to think me awhile. I think about it now. I say, "I should go and marry this girl." But I don't want to.

Thus, the presumption of coercion in marriage is, in part at least, a public fiction. Beneath the pose of the put-upon male, and obscured by it, is a generalized readiness to get married, a readiness based principally on the recognition of marriage as a rite through which one passes into man's estate. For the young, never-married male, to get married is to become a man.

> It was a big deal when I got married. I didn't have to get married. We didn't have no children or nothing. But you know, I gonna be—try to prove I'm a man or something, and I jump up and get married. . . .

Richard said this softly, in a matter-of-fact tone, as he spoke to Wesley and me of his marriage.[6] Wesley nodded. He knew what Richard meant. He said he wanted to marry and settle down, too. He had the girl all picked out and was just waiting for the other girl by whom he had had a child to marry. Earl and Boley and the other young never-married men had not fixed on a girl or a time but privately they assumed they would be getting married soon, too.

The discrepancy between the private readiness to marry and the public presumption of coercion points up the discrepancy between what marriage is supposed to be and what it is, in fact. In theory, marriage is "a big thing"; it is the way to manhood with all its attendant responsibilities, duties, and obligations which, when discharged, bring one status and respectability. In fact, marriage is an occasion of failure in the critical area of manhood, and therefore leads to a diminished status and loss of respectability. The difference between what marriage offers in theory and what it delivers in fact can be as dust in one's mouth. It was in Richard's.

> A man [ready to get married], he's got big ideas. He thinks marriage is a big thing, you know. But you know, it's no big thing.

Men may want "to jump up and get married," "to be a man or something," but knowing, or strongly suspecting, that marriage is a poor risk, they hedge against probable failure by camouflaging their private readiness to marry with the public fiction of coercion. Hedging takes the edge off failure. The hedge asserts that the man does not enter fully and freely into the marriage contract; that he was forced into it, went into it reluctantly, or was merely "going along with the program." Thus, marriage becomes, in part, a hold that is not a hold. The hedge permits a more passive participation than the obligation that total public commitment carries with it. It gives the man a partial defense against those who would hold him strictly to the terms of the contract; and it somewhat lightens the onus attached to breaking up the marriage by permitting him to say, in effect, "I didn't really want to get married in the first place."

Why Marriage Does Not Work

The Theory of Manly Flaws—As the men look back on their broken marriages, they tend to explain the failure in terms of their personal inability or unwillingness to adjust to the built-in demands of the marriage relationship. Sea Cat, for example, admits to a group of men on the corner that his marriage broke up because he simply could not bring himself to subordinate his independence to the demands of a joint undertaking.

> I was married once and once was enough. I can't live that way, having someone tell me when to get up, when to eat, "go here," "go there." Man, I've got to be master. I've got to be kingpin.[7]

Stoopy blamed the failure of his marriage on his weakness for whiskey and would tell how angry his wife used to become when he got drunk and spent or gambled away the rent money. She put up with him longer than he had a right to expect her to, he said. Even now, when she comes on Saturday mornings to pick up money for the children, she says she is willing to try again if he will promise never to get drunk but he knows he could not stick to such a promise, even though he loves her and the children and would like them to get back together.

Stoopy, like Sea Cat, showed no rancor when his wife took him to court for nonsupport. Stoopy and Sea Cat had let their wives down; they were the ones who had violated the marital agreement and their wives were doing what they had a perfect right to do.

Tally felt much the same way. When he was living with his wife, his drinking and "bad language" rightly disturbed her. Also, he couldn't stay away from other women. But he still loved her and if she would give him another chance, he would "put down" all those things which come so easily to a man but which a wife is justified in refusing to accept in a husband.

> . . . I love my wife. When I go to bed at night [it's as if] she's with me, and my kids are, too. Deep down in my heart, I believe she's coming back to me. I really believe it. And if she do, I'm going to throw out all these other women. I'm going to change my whole life.

On close inspection, it is difficult to accept these self-analyses of marital failure at full face value. Quite apart from the fact that it seems to be the men who leave their wives, rather than the other way around, these public assumptions of blame express a modesty that is too self-serving to be above suspicion. In each instance, the man is always careful to attribute his inadequacies as a husband to his inability to slough off one or another attribute of manliness, such as independence of spirit, a liking for whiskey, or an appetite for a variety of women. They trace their failures as husbands directly to their weaknesses as men, to their manly flaws.[8]

Simple and self-serving, this theory of manly flaws to account for the failure of marriage has a strong appeal for the men on the streetcorner.[9] But the theory is too pat, too simple; one senses that it violates the principle of sufficient cause. The relational complexities of marriage and its breakdown want answers which touch on these complexities. A more detailed examination of sexual infidelity—the largest and most common manly flaw—suggests that these flaws are not too damaging in themselves but that each is rooted in a host of antecedents and consequences which reach into the very stuff of marriage.

Sexual Infidelity as a Manly Flaw—Tally's contention that he would "throw out all those women" if his wife would only return to him was acceptable as a declaration of good intentions, but none of the men on the streetcorner would accept it as a description of what would happen in fact. One of the most widespread and strongly supported views the men have of themselves and others is that men are, by nature, not monogamous; that no man can be satisfied with only one woman at a time.[10] This view holds that, quite apart from his desire to exploit women, the man seeks them out because it is his nature to do so. This "nature" that shapes his sex life, however, is not human nature but rather an animality which the human overlay cannot quite cover. The man who has a wife or other woman continues to seek out others because he has too much "dog" in him.

> Men are just dogs! We shouldn't call ourselves human, we're just dogs, dogs, dogs! They call me a dog, 'cause that's what I am, but so is everybody else—hopping around from woman to woman, just like a dog.

This pronouncement from Sea Cat met with unanimous agreement from the men on the corner. Another occasion brought forth similar unanimity. It was a Friday evening. Tally, Clarence, Preston, Wee Tom and I were sitting in a parked car and drinking. Tally cooed at the women as they walked by.

One woman, in response to Tally's "Where you going, baby?" approached the car and looked the five of us over carefully, each in turn. "Walking," she said, and turned away. We watched her saunter across the street, her hips lurching from side to side as if they were wholly independent of the rest of her body. "That's real nice," said Tally, "that's real nice." There was a chorus of yes noises from the others.

I wondered aloud at the paradox of the five of us, each with a good woman waiting for him to come home (although Tally was living alone at the time), sitting in a car, drinking, and ready to take on any woman who walked down the street. The answer came quickly, unanimously: we (men) have too much dog in us.

"It don't matter how much a man loves his wife and kids," said Clarence, "he's gonna keep on chasing other women. . . . A man's got too much dog in him." The others agreed with Clarence and remained in complete agreement throughout the discussion which followed.[11]

The dog in man which impels him to seek out an ever-expanding universe of sex is a push-pull affair. A "new" woman is, by common consent, more stimulating and satisfying sexually than one's own wife or girl friend. The man also sees himself performing better with "new meat" or "fresh meat" than with someone familiar to him sexually. Men in their late twenties or older pooh-pooh the suggestion that they are not as good sexually as they were in their late teens or early twenties, maintaining that their performance in any given sex encounter depends less on age or any other personal factor than on the woman they happen to be with. Variety is not only the spice of sex life, it is an aphrodisiac which elevates the man's sexual performance. The point is perhaps best made by a standard joke which frequently appeared when the subject of sexual competence came up. It was told more as a fact of life than as a subject of humor.

An old man and his wife were sitting on their porch, rocking slowly and watching a rooster mount one hen, then another. When the rooster had repeated this performance several times, the old woman turned to her husband and said, "Why can't you be like that rooster?"

"If you look close," the old man said, "you'll see that that rooster ain't knockin' off the same hen each time. If he had to stick with the same one, he wouldn't do no better than me."

In attempting to sustain simultaneous relationships with one's wife and one or more other women, it frequently happens that one such relationship compromises the other. The marriage relationship, in particular, may suffer sexual damage. The man who admits this is not thereby diminished. He does not have to —nor does he—boast of the frequency with which he can engage in sex nor of the number of times he can achieve an orgasm in any given encounter. In special circumstances, he can even admit to not being able to engage in sex and, in doing so, enhance his image as a man who is successful with women. This is the case, for example, when the men talk about coming home from an engagement with another woman and being unable or unwilling to meet the sexual demands of their wives or women they are living with.

This predicament is freely admitted to in an almost boastful manner. On the streetcorner, it is a source of great merriment, with each man claiming to have a characteristic way of dealing with it. Sea Cat claims that he usually feigns sleep or illness; Clarence insists on staying up to watch the late show on TV, waiting for his wife to give up and go to sleep; Richard manufactures an argument and sleeps anywhere but in bed with Shirley; others feign drunkenness, job exhaustion, or simply stay away from home until their wives are asleep or until morning when the household is up and beginning another day.

The damage inflicted on marriage by such avoidance behavior tends to be assessed one way by men, another by women. The man tends to look at the problem in simple terms: he has a flaw which leads him to run around with other women. He simply has too much dog in him. True, he has violated the marriage, but only in this one narrow area of sexual fidelity.

In fact, the damage is much wider and deeper, as suggested by the wife in one of the streetcorner marriages that was falling apart. In bitterness mixed with resignation, she told of how her husband had been running around with other women and avoiding her sexually. She could live with this, she said, but what made the situation intolerable was his determination to find fault with everything she did, such as the way she cared for the children or cleaned the room. What started out as a transparent attempt to create arguments as an excuse for avoiding sex with her had gotten out of hand.[12] The result, she said, was that all areas of their life, not only the sexual, were being poisoned.

Holding the narrow viewpoint implicit in the theory of manly flaws can lead to a false statement of the problem and to irrelevant solutions. Richard is a case in point. His marriage to Shirley was going badly. Almost nothing was right. The problem, as he saw it, was a simple one. "I'm a sport. I'll always be a sport. I was born that way. I got a lot of dog in me." Being a sport, he said, drove him to seek out other women. Being a "walking man" (because he had no car) forced him to confine his amorous adventures to within walking distance of home and this, in turn, led to repeated discovery by Shirley and to a home life characterized by chronic fights and arguments. Now if he had a car, he argued, he would have women outside the area. Shirley wouldn't know where he was—at least, she wouldn't catch him at it—and the fights and arguments would stop.[13]

Another Point of View—Not all the men hold to the theory of manly flaws in accounting for the failure of their marriage. Sometimes, even those who do may give alternate explanations. In general, those who do not blame themselves for the failure of their marriage blame their wives, rather than family, friends, marriage itself, or the world at large. Even Richard, a prominent exponent of the theory of manly flaws, once shifted his ground. His marriage to Shirley had deteriorated to the point that it was barely recognizable as such. "I'm going to cut out," he said. "I can't take no more of her shit. She's getting under my skin."

One older man recalls in detail how his marriage ended.

> Me and my wife separated May 31, 1940, Friday night. I came home from work and right away she started nagging me. She said the landlord wanted his rent money and the insurance man, he was there too. I was tired of all that nagging. I said I had some money and she could pay the insurance man tomorrow when I went to work. I was real drunk and she hit me with brass knuckles. Then I got mad and cut her . . .[14]

Sweets's explanation was along the same lines.

> From now on, I'm playing the field. A man's better off in the field. I lived with her five years and every day, as soon as I walked in the house, I'd hear nothing but nagging. Mostly money. I got tired hearing all that shit.

Explanations such as these appear to stand up better than those which emphasize manly flaws. They are more solid on several counts. First, they suggest that it is the husband who does the leaving, which seems most often to be the case in fact. Second, they are not self-serving. True, they do place the blame on the wife but no special advantage accrues to the man thereby; neither his public nor private self is materially enhanced. And third, unlike the appeal to manly flaws, these explanations are compatible with the way in which women look at the same events. Both agree that the man quits, and quits under the pressure of the marriage relationship. To the man, the pressure is generated by his wife's expectations of him as a husband. Importantly, he avoids the "why" of her nagging behavior and complains of the "how." He does not deny the legitimacy of her expectations but objects to their insistent repetition and the unrelieved constancy of it all. "Getting under my skin" and nagging behavior give flesh-and-blood expression to his wife's unmet legitimate expectations for herself and her children. This, it seems, is what he finds so intolerable, for his wife's unmet expectations are a standing reminder of his failure as husband and father.

The foregoing quotations point clearly to the importance of money in the wife's expectations. To pay the rent, buy the groceries, and provide for the other necessary goods and services is the sine qua non of a good husband. There are, of course, several possible alternate sources of financial support—the wife herself, friends or relatives, or public or private agencies—but it remains peculiarly the (good) husband's responsibility, not anyone else's.[15]

The primacy ascribed to financial support derives from two analytically separable sources of value: the simple use value, in and of itself, of supporting and maintaining the lives of one's wife and children; and the expressive or symbolic value associated with providing this support.[16] Men and women both agree that providing financial support has a weightiness that goes beyond its simple use value. One of the men was talking to several others, derogating someone he didn't particularly care for. "But one thing you got to say," he conceded, "when he was living with her, he stone[17] took care of her and the children."

By itself, the plain fact of supporting one's wife and children defines the principal obligation of a husband. But the expressive value carried by the providing of this support elevates the husband to manliness. He who provides for his wife and children has gone a long way toward meeting his obligations to his family as he sees them. Drinking, gambling, or seeing other women may detract from but cannot, by themselves, nullify his performance. Both as husband and father, he has gone a long way toward proving himself a man.

Few married men, however, do in fact support their families over sustained periods of time. Money is chronically in short supply and chronically a source of dissension in the home. Financial support for herself and her children remains one of the principal unmet expectations of the wife. Moreover, although providing such support would be, so far as the husband is concerned, necessary and sufficient, the wife—who seldom gets even this much—wants more, much more.

She wants him to be a man in her terms, a husband and father according to her lights. It is not enough that he simply give money for her and the children's support, then step away until the next time he shares his pay day with them. She wants him to join them as a full-time member of the family, to participate in their affairs, to take an active interest in her and the children, in their activities, in their development as individuals. She wants his ultimate loyalty to be to her and the children, and she wants this loyalty to be public knowledge. She wants the family to present a united front to the outside world.

Most important of all, perhaps, she wants him to be *head of the family,* not only to take an interest and demonstrate concern but to take responsibility and to make decisions. She wants him to take charge, to "wear the pants," to lay down the rules of their day-to-day life and enforce them. She wants him to take over, to be someone she can lean on. Alas, she ends up standing alone or, even worse perhaps, having to hold him up as well.

Wryly, and with a bitterness born of experience, Shirley smiles to herself and says,

> I used to lean on Richard. Like when I was having the baby,
> I leaned on him but he wasn't there and I fell down. . . . Now,
> I don't lean on him anymore. I pretend I lean, but I'm not leaning.

Shirley had not always surrendered with quiet resignation. Like Lorena and other women, she too had tried to cajole, tease, shame, encourage, threaten, or otherwise attempt to make her man a man. Lorena said that in the beginning of her marriage, she used to pray to God, "Make John a good husband and father." Then she realized that "that's not God's job, that's my job," and she changed her prayers accordingly: "Lord, this is Lorena Patterson. You know all about me. You know what I need."

So Lorena took on herself the job of making John a good husband and father, but it didn't work. She blames herself for the failure of her marriage but she blames John, too. John was a boy, she said, not a man. He wasn't the "master."

I want the man to wear the pants but John made me wear the pants, too. His pants had a crease in them, mine had a ruffle, but I was wearing the pants, too.

Lorena's desperate gambits to force John to assert himself as man of the house ended disastrously, leaving her with mixed feelings of contempt, indignation, pity, and failure.

After we got married, I used to push him to see how far I could go. Once, I told him to kiss my ass. He laid my lip open and I stayed in the room till the scar healed up. For the next two weeks, he didn't do anything, no matter what I did, so I tried again. I called him an s.o.b. His family used to say that those were fighting words to John. They said he couldn't stand to hear anyone say something about his mother. So I called him an s.o.b. You know what he did? He sat down in a chair and cried. He just sat down and cried!

The husband who sometimes responds to this testing and challenging by slapping his wife's face or putting his fist in her mouth is frequently surprised at the satisfactory results. He does not understand—or does not admit to understanding—the woman's motives and may attribute them to some vague impulse to masochism latent in women. Leroy, for example, was getting ready to take his leave from the streetcorner. He said he was going home to see what "Mouth" (Charlene) wanted. She probably wanted a whipping, he said; she seems to beg him to beat her. Afterwards, she's "tame as a baby, sweet as she can be."

Then he told of how, the day before, Charlene beat on him with a broomstick, daring him to slap her, but he simply walked out because he knew this would hurt her more than a whipping. Doubtless, it did. For Charlene, like Lorena, wanted some tangible evidence that her husband cared about her, about them as a family, and that he was willing to fight to establish and protect his (nominal) status as head of the family. She openly envied Shirley who, when things were going tolerably well for her and Richard, took pleasure in boasting to Charlene, Lorena and other women that Richard pushed her around, insisted she stay off the street, and enforced the rule that she be up early every morning, dress the children and clean the house. For evidence of this kind of concern, Charlene would gladly pay the price of a slap in the face or a pushing around. All too often, however, Leroy declined to accept the challenge or, accepting it, was himself reduced, like John, to tears of shame, helplessness and defeat.

Richard and Shirley, whom Leroy and Charlene lived with for several months, were frequent observers—or rather over-hearers—of these tearful denouements to Leroy and Charlene's domestic quarrels. Richard was contemptuous of Leroy. No one had ever seen Richard cry. Leroy must be "weak" or "lame" to let Charlene make him cry like that. As for himself, he cried, too, he admitted, but he always cried "on the inside."

Thus, marriage is an occasion of failure. To stay married is to live with your failure, to be confronted by it day in and day out. It is to live in a world whose standards of manliness are forever beyond one's reach, where one is continuously tested and challenged and continually found wanting. In self-defense, the husband retreats to the streetcorner. Here, where the measure of man is considerably smaller, and where weaknesses are somehow turned upside down and almost magically transformed into strengths, he can be, once again, a man among men.

NOTES

1. In the language of Wesley Newcombe Hohfeld, the difference is between demand right—duty in one relationship, and privilege right —no demand right in the other. See E. Adamson Hoebel, *The Law of Primitive Man: A Study in Comparative Legal Dynamics,* pp. 48ff.

2. The time of this episode (October 1962) is especially significant. Charlene was then in her ninth month with Leroy's child but even the imminence of parenthood could not elevate their respective rights and duties to those of husband and wife.

3. Washington, D.C.'s home for neglected and dependent children.

4. "Later for [something]" means roughly, I do not want anything to do with or I am not concerned with that something, at least for the present.

5. In fact, they did not get married until July 1964 when their son was a year and a half old and Charlene was several months pregnant with their second child.

6. This time, there was no boastful reference to his grandmother and the fifty dollar bribe—an omission which suggests that the bribe served mainly as an enabling mechanism for his own readiness to marry.

7. Women, too, want the man to be "master," but the word means one thing to husbands, another to wives. See p. . . . [304].

8. ". . . people do not simply want to excel; they want to excel as a man or as a woman, that is to say, in those respects which, in their culture, are symbolic of their respective sex roles. . . . Even when they adopt behavior which is considered disreputable by conventional standards, *the tendency is to be disreputable in ways that are characteristically masculine and feminine.*" (Emphasis added.) Albert K. Cohen, *Delinquent Boys*, p. 138.

9. In an imaginative discussion of adaptations to failure in the evolution of delinquent subcultures, Cloward and Ohlin hypothesize that "collective adaptations are likely to emerge where failure is attributed to the inadequacy of existing institutional arrangements; conversely, when failure is attributed to personal deficiencies, solitary adaptations are more likely." Richard A. Cloward and Lloyd E. Ohlin, *Delinquency and Opportunity: A Theory of Delinquent Gangs*, p. 125. The "theory of manly flaws," when seen as an adaptation to failure in marriage, does not appear to fit this hypothesis, or at least suggests another possibility: a collective adaptation in which the participants agree to attribute failure to themselves as individuals.

10. "In lower social levels there is a somewhat bitter acceptance of the idea that the male is basically promiscuous and that he is going to have extramarital intercourse, whether or not his wife or society objects." Alfred C. Kinsey, Wardell B. Pomeroy, and Clyde E. Martin, "Social Level and Sexual Outlet," p. 307.

11. But a few minutes later, when the question arose as to whether women have as much dog in them as men, the men were less sure of their answers and disagreed among themselves. One said that women have as much dog in them as men but that a good woman also has a lot of pride and that's what keeps her from acting the same way men do. Another said that women have less dog in them, hence their more conservative sexual behavior. A third opinion held that women had more dog than men but that this was obscured by the double standard which inhibited women's freedom of action. And still another held that some women have less dog than men, some more, and that this accounted for the division of women into "good" and "bad."

12. One need not be a specialist in intrapsychic processes to recognize the snowballing effect of guilt on the one hand, and self-justifying behavior to relieve the guilt, on the other. They feed on one another. One starts with "wrong" behavior, feels guilty for it, attempts to create, post facto, conditions which justify the original behavior, and feels guilty all over again, and so on and on.

13. Richard repeated this argument at different times, each time in complete seriousness. It is an appealing argument. If access to an automobile does indeed confer stability on marriage, then, other things being equal, working- and middle-class marriages have a better

chance for survival than marriages among the lower, unpropertied classes. At best, however, it is a highly debatable point. When Richard did manage to acquire an automobile for a few brief weeks, the deterioration of his marriage to Shirley was dramatically accelerated.

14. Together with other references to violence between husband and wife, this quotation is, in my opinion, clear supporting evidence for the insightful observation that "rolling pins and pots are more often preludes to the disintegration of marriage than the basis on which a balance of power is worked out." Robert O. Blood and Donald M. Wolfe, *Husbands and Wives: The Dynamics of Married Living*, p. 12. Thus, the widespread violence between streetcorner husbands and their wives seems to be more a product of persons engaged in an always failing enterprise than merely the "style" or "characteristic feature" of streetcorner husband-wife relationships.

15. Providing financial support is so intimately associated with the husband that, on one curious occasion, financial support was argued to be one of two paramount considerations in defining sex and kinship roles. Charlene was pregnant but she and Leroy were not yet married when Leroy got into a heated argument with Beverly, the bull-dagger (Lesbian) who was living with Charlene's mother, Malvina. They cursed one another and Leroy took out his knife. Beverly was indignant, and pointed out that Leroy should be more respectful because she, Beverly, was his stepfather-in-law! Her argument rested on the twin assertions that she was sleeping with Malvina and supporting her.

Beverly should have left well enough alone. Leroy was willing to acknowledge some merit in her argument but when Beverly claimed she was even more of a man than Leroy, this was too much. Laughing about it the next day, Leroy recalls what followed: "I said, 'If you're more of a man than I am, pull your meat out and lay it on this rail.' I put mine on the rail and she said, 'I'm not that common. I don't do my lovin' that way.'"

16. Studies of a variety of lower-class populations emphasize that, for the man, self-respect, status, self-esteem, etc., is intimately bound up with the ability to support one's family: "The man's role is financial and his status in the household depends rather stringently on his ability as a breadwinner: his self-respect is closely tied to his financial independence." Josephine Klein, *Samples from English Cultures*, Vol. I, p. 164; "A man who . . . is unable to carry out his breadwinning role . . . falls a great distance in the estimation of himself, his wife and children, and his fellows." J. H. Robb, *Working-Class Anti-Semite*, quoted in *Samples from English Cultures*, Vol. I, p. 164; "The Negro man . . . cannot provide the economic support that is a *principal male function* in American society. As a result, the woman becomes the head of the family, and the man a marginal appendage who deserts or is rejected by his wife . . ." Herbert J. Gans, "The Negro Family: Reflections on the Moynihan Report," p. 48.

17. An intensive, in this case meaning "really took care . . ."

The French novelist, Balzac, very succinctly articu-
lated the problem of human sexual behavior when
he said that sex is the topic most thought about but
least talked about. In an attempt to bridge that gap,
the following article, with its developed methodologi-
cal technique, assists in shedding light on at least
one aspect of the problem—namely, the existence of
a "cultural relativism of premarital sexual intimacy."

XVI

Value-Behavior Discrepancies Regarding Premarital Coitus in Three Western Cultures*

HAROLD T. CHRISTENSEN
GEORGE R. CARPENTER

IN AN EARLIER ARTICLE, it was shown that premarital pregnancy and its consequences are in certain respects related to the general culture of the society involved. A "record linkage" comparison of samples from three modern Western societies—the sexually restrictive Mormon culture of Utah, the more typical United States culture as found in Indiana, and the sexually permissive Scandinavian culture of Denmark—revealed that the last named had not only the highest incidence of premarital pregnancy, but also the least negative effects therefrom. In Denmark there was found to be less pressure than in the American samples to either hasten into marriage or to dissolve the marriage as a consequence of premarital pregnancy.[1]

This report has been prepared as a companion piece to the work just cited. Whereas the first publication was based upon official registration data and was restricted to the phenomenon of premarital pregnancy, the present analysis was built from

* Reprinted from *American Sociological Review*, Vol. 27: 66-74, 1962, by permission of the authors and the American Sociological Association.

questionnaire responses of university students and it deals with: (1) attitudes respecting premarital sexual intimacy, (2) actual rates of premarital coitus, and (3) comparisons between the two. Nevertheless, both articles are concerned with the same three general cultures and both focus upon the problem of cultural relativism applied to premarital sex norms. By the use of complementary data, this second article attempts to retest and to further complete the theory suggested in the first.[2]

Samples and Procedures

Though university populations cannot be considered as cross-sections of the societies in which they are located, students are perhaps the most accessible and cooperative of all possible subjects for research purposes. For this reason, and since cross-cultural research involves some unusual difficulties at best, it was decided to use college students and thereby minimize the problem of achieving uniformity in the data gathering procedures. In line with this decision, our samples were drawn from a Danish university, from a university in Midwestern United States, and from a university of the Intermountain region of the United States having a high proportion of Mormons in its student body.[3]

A questionnaire was constructed, translated into Danish, pretested on both sides of the Atlantic, and exposed to criticism and revised several different times.[4] It was finally revised after a Danish draft had been translated back into English by a person not previously involved, and the translation then compared with the previous English draft so that discrepancies could be discovered and eliminated. These extreme precautions were used in an attempt to get rid of as many of the subtle differences in language as possible, so that the questions would have identical meanings in all three of the cultures. We believe that this aim was accomplished to a reasonable extent.[5]

The questionnaires were administered in university classes during regular class hours from late February through early May, 1958. Brief verbal instructions were generally given stressing the importance of the research and the voluntary and anonymous nature of participation. Response was almost one hundred per cent.

Prior to analysis, all questionnaires were carefully checked for completeness of answers and for internal consistency. This resulted in the elimination of thirty-three cases. Since the analysis was confined to persons under thirty years of age, an additional sixty-one cases were eliminated. The resulting samples consisted of 149 males and 86 females (total 235) from the Danish university, 213 males and 142 females (total 355) from the Midwestern university, and 94 males and 74 females (total 168) from the Intermountain university.

An Intimacy Permissiveness Scale. As a first step in analysis, it was desired to test the original assumption of intercultural variability regarding sexual permissiveness-restrictiveness. A Guttman type scale was constructed for this purpose, thereby permitting us to represent each respondent's attitude concerning premarital intimacy with a single numerical symbol.[6]

We started with twenty-one different items, but tests for unidimensionality reduced this number to ten. These are: agreeing with the statement, "I would prefer marrying a non-virgin"; disagreeing with the statement, "I would prefer marrying a virgin"; approving of petting any time before marriage for oneself; approving of petting any time before marriage for the daughter; approving of coitus any time before marriage for the daughter; approving of coitus on random or casual dates; approving of coitus when a couple is in love and going steady; approving of coitus when a couple is in love and formally engaged to be married; agreeing that premarital pregnancy is nothing to be ashamed of or to hide providing the couple is in love and later gets married; and agreeing that it is best not to try to prohibit erotic and obscene literature and pictures by law, but rather to leave people free to follow their judgments and tastes in such matters.[7]

All ten items were stated in terms of permissiveness, and, therefore, the higher the resulting scale value the greater the permissiveness of the respondent being considered. The range of possible scores was from zero through ten.

Tests of reproducibility were applied separately to each male and female group in each culture, and then to the combination of all. Resulting coefficients ranged from .90 to .96, showing that the scale meets acceptable standards.

Intimacy Permissiveness

In Table 1 are presented mean intimacy permissiveness scores for males and females, and then for the total, in all three cultures. (1) The most striking thing to be observed is the very great and consistent decreases in scores as one moves from left to right. Danish scores are almost twice as large as the Midwestern, and Midwestern scores are almost twice as large as the Intermountain—which is practically a geometric decline. Furthermore, the comparison holds for males and females considered separately, as well as for the total, and in all cases the differences are statistically significant.[8] (2) A second observation is that the Midwestern scores are closer to the Intermountain than to the Danish. These two findings give further support to the hypothesis, partially tested by record linkage data in our earlier article, that Danish culture is sexually permissive, Intermountain Mormon culture sexually restrictive, and Midwestern culture somewhere in between but closer to the restrictive norms. (3) Thirdly, males are shown to have higher scores than females in all three cultures, indicating that they are more permissive regarding sexual matters. However, these differences were found to be statistically significant in the Midwestern sample only.

The sequence of Danish-Midwestern-Intermountain on the permissive-restrictive continuum is clear for every type of attitude test that has been run. Statistically significant differences in this direction were found, not only for totals and when sex as a variable was controlled, as shown in Table 1, but when two factors were controlled simultaneously (sex combined one at a time with each of the following factors: age, educational level, religious participation, social class, happiness of parents' marriage, and courtship-marriage status), and even when three factors were controlled simultaneously (sex, age, and religious participation; and sex, age, and social class). It was the most consistent and significant relationship revealed in the entire study.

TABLE 1.—*Mean Intimacy Permissiveness Scores by Sex and Culture*

Sex	Danish	Midwestern	Inter-mountain
Males	8.4	4.8	2.7
Females	8.2	3.4	2.0
Total	8.3	4.1	2.4

Patterns of Premarital Coitus

Responses to our query on most advanced stage of intimacy revealed varying percentages who had experienced premarital coitus, as shown in Table 2. The points to be observed, as might have been expected, are similar to those of Table 1 for Intimacy Permissiveness scores: (1) Danish respondents show the highest percentages, with Midwestern intermediate and Intermountain lowest.[9] This is true for males and females alike (especially the latter) and for totals. All three sets of differences were found to be statistically significant. (2) For the females at least, Midwestern percentages are closer to the Intermountain than to the Danish. Male percentages, however, show approximately equal intercultural gaps. (3) In all three cultures, significantly higher percentages of males than females had experienced premarital coitus. It can be observed, however, that in the Danish sample the rates are within four percentage points of each other whereas in both the Midwestern and Intermountain samples the rates are approximately thirty points apart. Furthermore, all six tests wherein other factors (age, educational level, courtship-marriage status, religious participation, social class, and happiness of parents' marriage) were controlled, one at a time, revealed non-significant male-female differences for the Danish sample but significant differences for the Midwestern and Intermountain samples.

When the cross-cultural analysis is refined by controlling other factors, two and three at a time,[10] the picture remains essentially the same as above described—for females *but not for males.* For females, all tests but one (age, sex, and religious participation

TABLE 2.—*Percentage Having Experienced Premarital Coitus, by Sex and Culture*

Sex	Danish (N-228)*	Midwestern (N-351)*	Inter-mountain (N-168)
Males	63.7	50.7	39.4
Females	59.8	20.7	9.5
Total	62.3	38.8	26.2

* Three males and 4 females in the Danish sample, and 2 males and 2 females in the Midwestern sample, failed to answer the question on most advanced stage of intimacy prior to marriage.

controlled simultaneously) showed significance at the five per cent level. But for males, only two (sex with social class and sex with courtship-marriage status) out of eight tests of cross-cultural differences showed significance. The major intervening variable for males was age. The fact that advanced age is related to higher rates of premarital coitus, together with the fact that the Danish sample has disproportionately more older males, suggest that for males part of the higher coital rate in Denmark is due to the different age distribution there.

Additional aspects of premarital coitus, for those who had experienced it, are presented in Table 3. Following are some relevant observations. (1) The Danish males and females had their first coital experience about a year and a half later in life than did the Midwestern and Intermountain males and females. The former were about nineteen and one-half years of age whereas the latter were approximately eighteen. These cross-cultural differences were found to be statistically significant. In the Danish and Midwestern samples, females at first coitus were slightly older than males at first coitus, whereas Intermountain males and females were the same age. (2) Not only did males tend to start coitus earlier but they tended to be more promiscuous; that is, more of them had had more than one sexual partner. This was true in all three cultures, but especially in the Midwestern and Intermountain. Here is another example of males and females being more similar in behavior in Denmark than in the United States (though none of these intersex differences were statistically significant). (3) Still another example of the point just made is demonstrated by the percentage having first coital experience with either a "steady" or a fiance(e). Here, also, are the Danish males and females rather close together in their responses while the males and females of the other two samples are extremely far apart. By this measure, the Danish males were less promiscuous and the Danish females more promiscuous than the respective males and females of the other two samples.[11] In all three cultures, however, more females than males had their first coital experience under conditions of relative stability and commitment; that is, with a steady or a fiance(e). Intersex differences were significant for the Midwestern and Intermountain samples but not for the Danish sample. Intercultural differences fell a little short of the five per cent significance level. (4) In the majority of cases, first coitus was claimed

TABLE 3.—*Selected Responses by Persons Having Had Premarital Coital Experience, by Sex and Culture*

Items	Males			Females		
	Danish	Mid-western	Inter-mountain	Danish	Mid-western	Inter-mountain
Number of persons having had premarital coitus*	93	107	37	49	29	7
Median age at first coital experience	19.5	17.9	17.8	19.9	18.6	17.8
Percentage having had only one coital partner	40.9	33.7	35.1	42.9	65.5	57.1
Percentage where first coitus was with a "steady" or fianc(e)	64.5	42.1	46.0	71.4	75.9	100.0
Percentage where first coitus was voluntary because of desire	95.6	90.7	86.5	64.4	62.1	57.1
Percentage having "pleasant" feelings on day after first coitus†	71.4	44.8	33.3	72.9	34.5	14.3

* In a few instances, the statistical bases for averages and percentages to follow were slightly lower than those shown here because some respondents didn't answer every question, or answered ambiguously.

† Responses classified as "pleasant" were happiness, relaxation, and conquest. "Unpleasant" responses, which together made up the complements of the percentages shown here, included: tenseness, remorse, guilt, disgust, fear of others knowing, fear of religious punishment, fear of pregnancy, and fear of disease.

to have been voluntary because of desire; and the percentages claiming this were highest for the Danish sample, next highest for the Midwestern sample, and lowest for the Intermountain sample. Though more males than females in every culture gave "desire" as their reason for first coitus,[12] the intercultural pattern for both sexes turned out in the expected direction. However, neither the intersex nor the intercultural differences were significant. (5) Finally, a majority of the Danish respondents but only minorities of the Midwestern and Intermountain respondents had "pleasant" reactions on the day after first coitus. As might be expected, pleasant reaction percentages were lowest in the Intermountain sample. Also as might be expected, pleasant reaction percentages were lower for females than males—except for the Danish sample where the familiar pattern of greater male-female similarity held. Only the intercultural differences were statistically significant.

Attitude-Behavior Comparisons

The two points just made are suggestive of an important cross-cultural relationship. If coitus *by desire*, and also *pleasant feelings* the day after first coitus, both decrease in relative magnitude from Denmark to the Midwest to the Intermountain, as has been shown, there must be a reason. Perhaps the reason is that in sexually permissive societies there is less guilt and hence more desire and pleasure, while in sexually restrictive societies there is more guilt and hence less desire and pleasure —the restrictions being aim-inhibiting.[13] To further test this hunch, we have attempted an analysis of attitude-behavior discrepancies within each of the three samples.

It already has been observed that the variations of Table 1 and Table 2 are substantially the same. Thus, premarital coital experience was found to be more likely in those categories showing the highest Intimacy Permissiveness scores; attitudes and behavior tended to line up.

Another approach was to compare *individual* score values on the Intimacy Permissiveness scale with the presence or absence of premarital coital experience. When this was done a positive relationship was found. In other words, the higher the permissiveness score, the larger the per cent having had premarital coitus.

The relationship held in all three cultures and differences were found to be statistically significant.

By considering for each sex and culture the percentage who approved of coitus before marriage, and then superimposing upon this the percentage who had actually experienced premarital coitus, we were able to study the several patterns of discrepancy between attitude and behavior in this regard. Comparisons are given in two ways: first, by showing numerical ratios of approval to experience; and second, by picturing graphically for each subdivision both the per cent approving and the per cent experiencing the phenomenon. (See Figure 1.) The following points stand out: (1) First and most important, both males and females in the Danish sample gave greater approval than actual experience whereas those of the other two samples indicated more experience than approval. Apparently, in the Danish sample, there were a number of both sexes who had not experienced premarital coitus but thought they would do so later on.[14] Obviously, where there has been premarital coitus by more people than approve, some of these will be harboring guilt feelings about their behavior. Both Midwestern and Intermountain students (especially the latter) fell into this category. In the Intermountain—where guilt over premarital sex may be presumed to be the greatest—a larger percentage of total males than total females experienced coitus without approving it, but of the sexually experienced the situation was the reverse of this (compare graph bars with approval-experience ratios). (2) As with previous comparisons, females showed up more conservative than males. This may be observed in all three cultures and for both approved behavior and actual coital experience. Furthermore, all of the female approval-experience ratios were lower than the corresponding ones for males. Thus, of the sexually experienced, proportionately more females than males apparently had compromised their standards.[15] Statistical significance was found for the intercultural differences of Figure 1, but not the intersex differences.

The Measurement of Effects

From the beginning, it has been our contention that premarital sexual behavior is related to the general culture in which it occurs: first, in respect to the attitudes or values which people

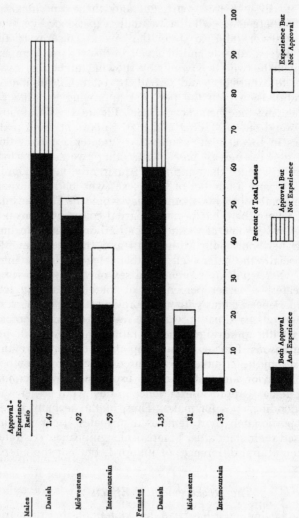

FIGURE 1. COMPARISONS OF APPROVAL WITH EXPERIENCE IN PREMARITAL COITUS

hold; second, in respect to the actual overt behavior which takes place; but third, *in respect to the consequences or effects of this behavior.* Specifically on this last point, it has been hypothesized that the most permissive culture would have the least negative effects from premarital sexual intimacy, because behavior there would be in line with accepted values, while the most restrictive culture would show the greatest negative effects, since in that situation behavior would tend to be in violation of the values held. Therefore, in considering the three cultures dealt with in this study, we have expected the Danish sample to show the least and the Intermountain sample the greatest negative effects from premarital coitus.

One important measure of effects was provided by the senior author's earlier analysis of these three cultures by the method of record linkage. It was shown that premarital pregnancy in Denmark does not cause either the hurried up marriage or the same pressure for divorce later on as it tends to do in America.[16]

Another clear indication of effects was suggested above by three different but complementary findings: first, that the percentages of respondents who said their first premarital coitus was "voluntary because of desire" were highest for Denmark and lowest for Intermountain (Table 3); second, that the percentages of respondents who had "pleasant" reactions the day after first premarital coitus were highest for Denmark and lowest for Intermountain (Table 3); and third, that the Danish respondents indicated greater approval of premarital coitus than they had actually experienced, whereas both the Midwestern and Intermountain respondents indicated the reverse of this (Figure 1). Thus, the Danish respondents had a margin of tolerance in which they could feel relatively comfortable, whereas many Midwestern and Intermountain respondents (especially the latter) had overstepped the moral bounds of their groups and so must have been experiencing some guilt. Actually, the guilt expressed for the day after first coitus was greatest for the Intermountain sample and least for the Danish sample, which bears out the claim just made (see footnote 13). The probable explanation for these cross-cultural differences in sexual desire at first coitus, and pleasant feelings the day following first coitus, seems to be the relative lack of inner conflict over sexual matters in the permissive culture as against the presumed inner conflict in the more restrictive cultures due to the value-behavior discrepancies existing there.

A final test of effects, which the data permit, has to do with indications of satisfaction or lack of satisfaction over present courtship-marriage status. Respondents had been asked to give their present relationship with the opposite sex and then to tell whether they estimated this to be "very satisfactory or happy," "moderately satisfactory or happy," "moderately unsatisfactory or unhappy," or "very unsatisfactory or unhappy." Correlation tests between the two sets of data revealed a positive relationship; that is, greater satisfaction in the more advanced statuses (differences significant for males but not for females).

We were interested in the possibility of a relationship between satisfaction over courtship-marriage status and the presence or absence of coital experience. A preliminary test with undifferentiated data revealed, for all three cultures, higher coital rates in the "satisfied" as compared with the "unsatisfied" groups (differences significant for males but not for females). However, since both coital experience and status satisfaction were known to increase with level of courtship-marriage status, it seemed necessary to control the latter variable for purposes of the analysis. In order to accomplish this, the "never date" and "married" categories were discarded entirely, and the "frequent dating" was combined with the "steady dating" category and the "informally engaged" with the "formally engaged" category. Even so, some of the cells remained too small for reliable comparisons. Nevertheless, the results are presented in Table 4, so that the reader may judge for himself.

Though differences were non-significant in the statistical sense, nine out of the twelve comparisons showed lower satisfaction rates for those who had experienced premarital coitus as compared with those who had not. The exceptions were Danish males and Intermountain females in the "Frequent or Steady Dating" category, and Danish females in the "Informally or Formally Engaged" category. Cross-cultural differences in this suggested relationship are not too clear. Nevertheless, the smallness of numbers in some of the cells, together with the fact that two out of three of the exceptions to the suggested relationship were in the Danish sample, leaves us wondering if our hypothesis of smaller negative effects in the more permissive culture (Denmark) does not hold here also. Certainly such a relationship has

TABLE 4.—*Comparisons of Presence or Absence of Premarital Coital Experi-ence with Satisfaction Over Present Courtship Status, by Sex and Culture*

Satisfaction Over Courtship Status	Danish Premarital Coitus		Midwestern Premarital Coitus		Intermountain Premarital Coitus	
	Yes	No	Yes	No	Yes	No
Frequent or Steady Dating						
Males						
Total cases	31	24	49	56	20	22
Percentage answering						
"Very satisfactory"	29.0	25.0	38.8	41.1	30.0	31.8
Females						
Total cases	13	16	13	68	3	42
Percentage answering						
"Very satisfactory"	23.1	37.5	15.4	50.0	33.3	19.1
Informally or Formally Engaged						
Males						
Total cases	25	7	25	22	3	9
Percentage answering						
"Very satisfactory"	60.0	100.0	64.0	72.7	66.7	77.8
Females						
Total cases	15	5	9	33	3	13
Percentage answering						
"Very satisfactory"	87.7	80.0	66.7	84.9	66.7	76.9

not been established, but neither has it been disproved. Conclu-sive evidences for either this assumed relationship, or for the possibility of premarital coital experience being accompanied by dissatisfaction in courtship, are lacking; yet our data are high-ly suggestive of both.

Summary and Conclusions

This paper is the complement of an earlier one dealing with the cultural relativism of premarital sexual intimacy. Three cul-tures have been analyzed by means of both governmental record data and university questionnaire data. The cultures involved are Denmark with its rather permissive sex norms, Midwestern United States with its somewhat typically American sex norms, and the Mormon culture of the Intermountain West with its rather restrictive sex norms. No claim is made for precise representativeness of the samples or for exact comparability of the data. Yet, it is believed that the data are reasonably qualified in these respects. Furthermore, the fact that both sets of data present the same general cross-cultural pattern, tends to increase one's confidence in the results.

The general pattern revealed is as follows: (1) Denmark has the most permissive and Intermountain the most restrictive *attitudes* regarding premarital sexual intimacy. This was shown through citations from the literature and by means of an Intimacy Permissiveness Scale. (2) Likewise, Denmark has the most permissive and Intermountain the most restrictive *behavior patterns* in the area of premarital sexual intimacy. This was shown by means of indices for premarital coitus and premarital pregnancy. (3) But when it comes to *negative effects* resulting from premarital intimacy, Denmark has the least and Intermountain the most. The effects analyzed in this regard were lack of sexual desire at first coitus, unpleasant feelings on the day following first coitus, lack of satisfaction with present courtship status, tendency to hurry the marriage after discovery of pregnancy, and tendency to terminate the marriage by divorce. (4) In most of the above comparisons, Midwestern United States is intermediate, though closer to the Intermountain Mormon culture than to the Danish culture. The largest gap, in other words, was found to be between the Danish and the United States cultures.

It must be remembered that, for males, the higher coital rate in Denmark may be accounted for in part by the larger percentage of older males in the Danish sample.

Also to be kept in mind are the facts that larger percentages of Danish men had only one sexual partner and had their first coitus with a steady or fiancée, which means that they are *less promiscuous,* and that Danish men and women had their first sexual experience at a later age than was true in the United States. In other words, sexual intimacy in Denmark is more a part of the marriage process; the culture there is actually less permissive of intimacy for its own sake; in this sense, the Danish pattern is the more conservative. This closer association of sexual intimacy with the marriage process in Denmark may help account for the greater likelihood of pleasant feelings accompanying first coital experience there.

There is some evidence that sexual restrictiveness tends to converge male and female *attitudes,* perhaps by idealizing the male; while sexual permissiveness tends to converge male and female *behavior,* perhaps by liberalizing the female.[17] Apparently, a possibly stronger male sex drive causes males more than females in the restrictive cultures to "break over the traces"; so that—in regards to behavior but not in regards to attitude—cross-cultural differentials are less for males than for females.

But, though the male in the restrictive culture seems to have the greater discrepancy between what he believes and how he behaves sexually, both sexes within such cultures experience some discrepancy in this direction. And it seems probable that it is this discrepancy that causes the guilt feelings, the dulled sexual experiences, the lack of satisfaction in courtship-marriage status, the higher rate of divorce, and possibly other negative effects which seem to be highest in restrictive cultures. In other words, it may be the *value-behavior discrepancy,* as much or even more than the behavior itself, that is causing the difficulty.

NOTES

1. Harold T. Christensen, "Cultural Relativism and Premarital Sex Norms," *American Sociological Review,* 25 (February, 1960), pp. 31-39.

2. Logically, the order of appearance of these two articles might have been reversed—since in sequence of time attitudes come first, coitus next, and pregnancy last. Explanation for the actual order of publication lies in the fact that the record linkage data were collected and analyzed first. Actually, in two of the cultures the record linkage analyses had been completed a number of years before the present cross-cultural research began.

The first article also compared attitudes (expressed as cultural norms) with sexual behavior (premarital pregnancy). However, there the norm differences among the samples were merely described, whereas here an attempt is made to measure them.

Although we also have data bearing upon the other levels of premarital sexual intimacy, space limitations require that our present analysis be confined to the phenomenon of premarital coitus. However, this is not a serious limitation for present purposes, since a preliminary examination made clear that intercultural differences tend to stand out most clearly when the most intimate type of behavior (coitus) is considered.

3. So as to maintain anonymity, the three samples will be referred to throughout this work simply as Danish, Midwestern, and Intermountain.

Seventy-nine per cent of the students in our Intermountain sample were Latter-day Saint, or "Mormon," in religious affiliation.

4. The senior author was living in Copenhagen at the time (1957-58) as a Fulbright Research Scholar. He took the lead in research design and questionnaire construction, and gathered all of the data from the University of Copenhagen. The junior author assisted from the American side and gathered all of the data from the two universities located there. He also analyzed substantial portions of the data for his Ph.D. dissertation at Purdue University, completed in June, 1960.

5. Additional approaches to questions of reliability and validity will be briefly mentioned: Responses were compared among pretests, and between pretests and the final questionnaire, and were found to be very similar. In each of the Danish and Midwestern samples, approximately two dozen respondents were interviewed and then certain of the interview data were compared with the questionnaire data on a matched case basis; correspondence was almost one hundred per cent—on presence or absence of premarital coital experience it *was* one hundred per cent. Completed schedules were studied for internal consistency and the inconsistent ones were then discarded.

It must nevertheless be recognized that more of the respondents from the conservative samples (Midwestern and especially Intermountain) *may* have covered up on their most intimate behavior because of the greater cultural disapproval of this behavior. However, since anonymity was always carefully assured, we do not believe this potential tendency actually expressed itself to any significant extent.

6. See Louis Guttman, "A Basis for Scaling Qualitative Data," *American Sociological Review,* 19 (April, 1944), pp. 139-150.

7. Though the last item named does not refer to intimacy between the sexes, but rather the public display of intimate sexual portrayals, it nevertheless tested in as part of our unidimensional scale.

8. The five per cent level of significance is used throughout this paper. However, in the tests just cited, significance was well beyond the one per cent level.

9. A separate analysis of percentages who stopped their premarital intimacy with petting showed the reverse order; that is, Intermountain high and Danish low. This opposite cross-cultural relationship for petting would suggest that in the United States, as compared with Denmark, the tendency is to preserve the chastity norm by substituting petting for coitus.

10. Space limitations precluded any detailed reporting of these intracultural tests.

11. Not reported here are data which show a smaller percentage of Danish males but a larger percentage of Danish females, than the males and females of the other two samples, having first coitus with either an "unmarried stranger," an "unmarried casual acquaintance," an "unmarried friend," or "a person married to someone else."

12. In all three samples, many more females than males indicated that the first coital experience was either forced upon them or was voluntary on their part because of a felt obligation.

13. Actually, responses concerning feelings the day after first coitus showed only 2.2 per cent of the combined male and female sample from Denmark feeling guilt, as compared with 12.7 per cent from Midwestern, and 25.6 per cent from Intermountain. This, of course, supports our hypothesis.

14. The reader will recall that the Danish students with coital experience were initiated about one and one-half years later than their American counterparts.

15. Cf. footnote 12 and the next to the last item in Table 3. It should be pointed out that there is no contradiction between the claim (1) that, *of the sexually experienced,* more females than males compromise their standards, and (2) the suggestion soon to be made (see footnote 17) that, in the restrictive Intermountain culture, more males than females *of the total sample* compromise their standards.

16. Christensen, *loc. cit.*

17. Table 1 shows males and females to be close together in attitude in *both* Denmark and Intermountain, whereas Table 2 and parts of Table 3 show the behavior of the two sexes to be close together in Denmark but strikingly far apart in Midwestern and especially in Intermountain. Furthermore, Figure 1 shows the Intermountain—and especially the Intermountain male—to have the greatest excess of experience over approval. Nevertheless, this "evidence" we speak of is suggestive only.

THE FOURTH DIVISION

COLLECTIVITIES and CHANGE

COLLECTIVITIES and CHANGE

IF THERE IS ONE GOAL to which the sociologist is dedicated, it is his desire to conquer chaos. More specifically, he tries to extract from group activity the recurring patterns of behavior. Thus, instead of writing in detail about a particular revolution, a particular religion, or a particular family, he attempts to find certain features or directions common to *all* revolutions, religions, and families.

In his generalizing about human behavior he knows that the economically and emotionally impoverished of large urban centers (America's bourgeoning "underclass") have often been attracted to sectarian movements, most of which convey a radically new identity to the individual. These sects in their pristine form are often distinguished by the fact that they have a values system which conflicts with or almost totally rejects the existing social order. The joiner will have little difficulty in accepting the sect's values if one or both of the following general conditions are present: either the existing social order does not accommodate the individual's need for recognition and security (at least in his own opinion); or else the order is undergoing change or questioning of its own traditional values. It is when these conditions are present that radical groups have their appeal —communal religious groups, the Ku Klux Klan groups in the changing South, and the proliferation of fascist and communist factions in post World War I Germany.

A basic objective of the sociologist is to investigate the phenomenon of change, and to see whether or not he can perceive in the changing situations similar social conditions which, regardless of differences in time or place, tend to produce in men the same intrapersonal and social reactions. Sociology endeavors to understand the individual's behavior in relation to the statuses, roles, norms, values, and groups of which he is a member. A knowledge of these factors tends to enable the social scientist to understand why the individual acts—or prefers to act—in a certain way.

Nevertheless, it appears that sporadic, very short-lived situations arise which are devoid of the prerequisites for organized group behavior. Scientists refer to such phenomena as examples of collective behavior. Although this type of human interaction is unplanned, unexpected, and seemingly unpredictable, if one steps back and reflects on the processes of behavior that occur during such situations, he can still arrive at some generalizations, whether tentative or enduring, concerning these happenings. In the articles that follow, the reader will perhaps perceive that amidst diversity or disorder there are often threads of unity and order.

*As suggested in the title, the small towns are begin-
ning to experience their demise. Some automatic
explanations come readily to mind—the probable
existence of more "action," employment opportunities, and income offered by the city. In this article,
the authors attempt to analyze how and why the
different small towns are reacting and surrendering
to the challenge offered by the urbanization process.*

XVII

The Decline and Fall of the
Small Town*

WILLIAM SIMON
JOHN H. GAGNON

IT IS A FACT OF OUR TWENTIETH CENTURY LIFE that as the centers
of economic, social, and political power have shifted from farm
and countryside to city and suburb, those small communities that
are not absorbed by some metropolitan complex come under
threat (if not actual sentence) of decline and decay. But why
do some small towns wither and not others? And is there long
term hope for any?

Actually, this Darwinian life and death struggle of American
small towns is not confined to modern times. During the nineteenth century the petering out of natural resources or the demand for them (gold in California, coal in parts of the Midwest)
and the considerations that determined whether a railroad went
through one area rather than another often determined whether
a village would prosper or become a ghost town. Today, decisions about where to place highways, intersections, dams, or
where to move an industry can have similar effects—revitalizing
or building one community, sentencing another to senescence.

* Copyright © 1967 by Washington University, St. Louis, Mo. Reprinted
from *Trans-Action* Magazine, April, 1967, 42-51, by permission of the
authors and publisher.

But in the nineteenth century decline or vitalization were considered to result from the natural workings of *laissez-faire*. The fittest survived. The economic success grew and the failure faded away—a process that was not to be interfered with and that made for progress. Today the state and federal governments are actively intervening to try to maintain the small town —which they perceive to be a useful way of life, a balancing force against the rise of megalopolis.

But is it enough to simply inject redevelopment funds into a community to assure its health? For that matter, what do we learn from using medical terms to describe a town's economic vitality—a robust community, a sick or moribund community? What really determines a town's viability? Is it different with each town?

This article attempts detailed analyses of three neighboring rural towns in southern Illinois, to determine why, despite many similarities in location, economic problems, and history, they developed differently after World War II.

The three communities—which we will call East Parrish, Clyde, and Spiresburg—are in an area distinctly "Southern" in many characteristics and values. It was originally settled in the first half of the nineteenth century by migrants from the southern hill country. They rapidly exhausted a land as inhospitable, if not more so, than what they had originally left. Its barren, clay-ridden soil did not, and will not in the future, support more than meager subsistence farming.

At the turn of the century coal was discovered in the area, and large-scale mining brought a new, unprecedented, and profoundly uncertain prosperity. Coal camps appeared, and rail lines connecting them to each other and to the outside world began to crisscross the region. Typical of the influence of the railroads, in a very few years entire town sites moved to the nearby rail lines.

The growing coal industry brought in a few Negroes and many immigrants, largely from Eastern Europe. Though farming continued, it increasingly became a part-time venture, and everything became tied to a highly unstable, single industry—coal. Typical of coal mining areas, a culture full of strong contrasts developed (as Herman Lantz described it in his *The People of Coaltown*). Side by side there was violence and resignation, Bible-belt religion and hard-drinking, serious gambling, and (at least historically) no small amount of whoring. All three communities are within 40 miles of what has, with full justification, become known as "Bloody Williamson County."

By the mid-1920's, the local coal boom reached its peak, and from then on, except for a brief period during World War II, went into continuous decline. East Parrish, the largest of the three towns, declined from almost 25,000 to its present 9,000. From 1950 to 1960 East Parrish declined by 21 per cent, Clyde by 11 per cent, and Spiresburg by 6 per cent. People continue to leave in large numbers—primarily the younger, healthier, and better educated. Nor has there been (especially as far as mining is concerned) any substantial leveling off of employment. Between 1950 and 1960 the number of persons employed in mining in East Parrish decreased by 71 per cent, in Clyde by 72 per cent, and in Spiresburg by 61 per cent. And there were substantial, if smaller, declines in such things as railroad carloadings. All during the preceding decade the immediate area has been defined by government agencies as "chronically depressed" and "surplus labor."

By the early 1950's people in all three communities began to realize that the very survival of their towns was at stake. Responding to this realization, and prodded by federal and state governments and a nearby state university, community leaders became very adept at the rhetoric of community redevelopment.

But the consequences of both rhetoric and action have been markedly different among the three. East Parrish (population 9,000) has had virtually no change or improvement—nor does any appear even remotely likely. Clyde (population 7,000) has been able to check its decline somewhat and expects in the near future to derive the benefits of a federal water and land redevelopment project. Spiresburg, the smallest (population 3,000), has in the last six years attracted four new industries and thereby largely reconstituted its economic base.

East Parrish

East Parrish first recognized its problem openly in the early 1950's when the East Parrish Industrial Fund was created with working capital of $100,000 raised from over 2,000 public contributors. This fund was deposited in the local bank where it remained untouched for eight years. Its first expenditure was to rebuild a dress factory that had burned down. This factory, typical of industry attracted by such communities, is "labor-intensive," paying low wages and primarily employing women.

But while the basic fund was put to restricted use, the accumulated interest was more freely available. Much of it went to subsidize the local Chamber of Commerce; and this in turn strengthened the hold of the community conservatives over the Chamber.

Rarely was any money used in realistic scouting for new industry. As one member of the development board put it:

> We didn't run around like some of the towns around here wining and dining company officials or taking junkets around the country looking for companies. And we weren't going to offer the moon to some of these companies. Industry that you get that way either won't stay or won't pay off. Sure, there are companies that we might have looked at, but they are out for what they can get. They don't want to pay taxes, want free water, gas, and free land. It is just like raping a community. And then they move on. If you can get them on this basis, so can another town get them from you on the same basis. Hell, they have no ties to the community; they could move tomorrow. Besides, our real problem is labor. For all the talk around here, most of the people really don't want to work—they're content on public assistance. And those that do want to work have been spoiled by the unions; they won't work for wages that the kind of industry that would come here would pay—they [the workers] think that they can only work for the $16 and $17 a day they used to make when the mines were running.

The next big economic event was the discovery of exploitable oil within the corporate limits of the community. However, the oil industry is highly automated. The oil ownership was concentrated among a very few, and additional employment was barely noticeable. To this day the endlessly see-sawing, black, squat pumps constantly remind the population of still another disappointment.

To date no federal funds have been requested—except for some public housing and clearance—and on at least two occasions they were rejected by community leaders when offered.

When we look at East Parrish's formal political structure one thing stands out: Since 1947, no mayor of the community succeeded himself (although two tried), and only two city commission members won re-election. This would suggest considerable political instability. Curiously, however, as one makes inquiries of community residents about community events during this period, one finds that essentially the same names appear. These names virtually never appear in contests for major political office (mayor or city commission), although roughly half of them have participated in one or more public commissions. Formal government apparently became the target for the expression of the frustrations of community residents, but rarely the framework within which serious solutions for community problems could be approached.

What, then, is the political life of East Parrish? Of the three communities, East Parrish is the only one with a strong tradition of working-class involvement in politics. This probably developed out of the high level of social solidarity characteristic of coal mining communities.

There is a basic cleavage going back for a number of decades between the miners (for whom the merchants remain those "bastards on Main Street") and the professional merchant group (for whom the miner remains the hillbilly or hunkie to whom they once sold silk shirts at highly inflated prices). As the medical director of the United Mine Workers Association hospital remarked, it was still almost impossible to get a Main Street merchant to serve on the hospital board. One effect of this cleavage was a historic pattern of miner representation in city government. One mayor, deposed in a recent election, was employed as a miner concurrently with his occupancy of the mayor's office.

The effects of this traditional cleavage became intensified because the middle-class elite (if this term is at all applicable) is itself badly split. Among the merchants a split occurs between those whose operations serve a broad area market (there are 14 furniture stores in the community), and those whose business centers entirely upon local retail trade. One cost of this second cleavage has been the inability—despite successive attempts—to have Main Street broadened and repaved with state funds and turned over to state maintenance because the local retail merchants refuse to surrender angle parking.

Typical of self-centered communities, there is no local industrial elite—even in the heyday of the coal boom most operations were absentee owned.

With the decline of mining, its importance to the community and the number of people it employs, the effectiveness of the miners and their ability to organize has lessened. In addition, a relatively high proportion of miners or their families are on welfare. In towns like East Parrish, welfare is handled very informally through the township supervisor, a very political office. Further, people generally know who is on relief. Both these factors make welfare recipients feel very vulnerable, and this tends to undermine their political participation. Also, the more promising young people, potential political leaders, leave in large numbers.

This does not mean that working-class politics has eroded in East Parrish. There has been considerable miner participation. In 1959, for instance, three of four city commissioners were miners, and one of these was later appointed mayor upon the death of the incumbent. But it does mean that their effectiveness and independence has been undermined. Election rhetoric centers heavily on class politics—but the election of miners has not given rise to working-class programs. The miners in politics have been largely coopted by the "politicos" of the community.

Between the larger, more affluent merchants and the lower-class community a small but crucial group of professional, or near professional, politicians has developed—a group whose basic constituency is greatly enhanced by a large number of dependent and chronic welfare recipients. As with government in an underdeveloped country, an amazing amount of money can be made by manipulating the local political structure, particularly in playing with taxes and land speculation, even where land itself is not worth much.

Significantly absent from political life are the community's hired professionals—schoolteachers and ministers. Local school systems, because they are small and split among several authorities, are highly vulnerable. Moreover, the staff in such school systems—either women tied to families that in turn are tied to the community, or men of rather low competence—are not likely to seek involvement. Ministers, at least Protestant ministers, move around a great deal and are at the mercy of lay leaders who are primarily drawn from the community conservatives. They tend to avoid speaking out on community issues because there is rarely a community issue that would not find competing factions within the same church, and it is a rare minister who, in the context of East Parrish's long history of community conflicts, would invite such a conflict into his church.

While churches seem to be nearly totally estranged from power and community decision-making in all three communities, in East Parrish the social and fraternal organizations have also tended to withdraw. A recent reform movement has taken control of city hall, and it reflects primarily the needs of local merchants. Ostensibly it is committed to industrial renewal, but little is expected to come of it. The professional politicians know all too well that they, despite this temporary setback, control access to county and state politicians, without whom little can be done.

As a result, the recent political history of East Parrish is one of apathy and distrust punctuated by episodes of scandal and conflict. Where decisions have to be made—such as providing a new library or even something as trivial as paying for a local production of an opera produced by a nearby university—they are made by a very small number of citizens operating in a completely nonpublic way. This nonpublic process—which turns out to be the only way to get something done because it does not invoke some form of community cleavage—only further feeds community paranoia and resentment. During our interview with one of the city fathers who showed us the drawings for a projected new library, he turned to his secretary and jokingly asked: "How much have we made on it so far?"

Clyde

Economically, Clyde, aside from its new dress factory, has seen no substantial change. Its biggest step forward came when a small group of community leaders, in the mid-1950's, created a tax-raising administration with special bond-issuing powers under some long obscure state law. About $250,000 were raised in taxes that went into a local water development based on a nearby lake. After considerable lobbying, the federal government took over the project. The leaders hope that this development will attract new industry, and lead to expanded development of Clyde and environs into a prosperous and pleasant recreation center and resort.

Politically, Clyde differs considerably from East Parrish. It has no real tradition of lower-class action. As a county seat, it has a higher proportion of middle-class people working for, or involved in, county and courthouse activities. This is also the reason why the main political focus in Clyde is on county, rather than civic, affairs. It does not even have the same "coal-camp" appearance of East Parrish. To the innocent urban eye it looks very much like any small town in Illinois; one has to go to the unincorporated fringe, or to a tavern in an obscure alley off the square, to see what almost 20 years of poverty will do to human beings. Of the three towns, only in Clyde does one hear frequent and almost compulsive talk of "white trash."

Also, probably because it is a county seat, a number of industry executives live there. The town's previous mayor was a retired railroad vice president; its present mayor is a retired coal company president—in manner and style very much resembling his famous brother who led the miner's union. One of the last major coal companies—the one reputed to be the most ruthlessly exploitative—maintains offices in Clyde. This small executive group has left its mark on the politics of Clyde.

If the politics of East Parrish resemble in a strange way the politics of France before DeGaulle, the politics of Clyde resemble the politics of DeGaulle. There have been a series of strong mayors who have not "sought" public office, but who have demanded that the community offer it to them. The present mayor in his first election cautioned supporters that, if campaign posters were put up, he would decline the office. These strong mayors have given the community its neat, clean appearance; they have also sapped the political vitality of the people.

The present upper-middle class, which might ordinarily have been expected to provide considerable leadership, will obviously bring little change. It has split into two elements. The more conservative element was described by one citizen:

> There is definitely a group of inheritors—doctors, lawyers, those running insurance agencies, stores, garages. For the most part a very unaggressive lot. . . . These people are in no great hurry to see things change.

One conservative spoke about his group this way:

> True, we might lack some spirit. For most of us, it is a matter of getting out of school and inheriting your father's business. This is what happened in my case. I'm not sure I really wanted to come back. . . . But, as I say, it is a life with many compensations.

To the extent that they take an interest in politics, they are Republican and concentrate on town affairs.

The other element mostly consists of the recently prosperous —including those who rose from Italian or Slavic coal mining families. They—with a few mavericks from the older elites—tend to dominate county politics which are largely Democratic. They are more concerned with the decline of the community than the older group, possibly because they are more vulnerable—yet they accept, with little quibble, the present structure of control.

Clyde has experienced none of the turbulence of East Parrish politics—but that is probably because it has not evinced as much interest as East Parrish—the interest caused by frustration. It developed no new community organizations, engaged in no campaigns to raise funds from community residents, and rarely did economic redevelopment become a political issue.

It is thus not unexpected that Clyde's major bid for renewal came not from some broad, popular campaign, but from an administrative unit of government; that it did not seek funds through public appeal, but through taxation. Despite the fact that, as one resident put it, "for years the merchants have been hanging on by their teeth hoping for a miracle to save them," and that the pressures of poverty are such that the state's attorney (the Illinois name for county prosecutor) complains that he "can only do a small part of what the state requires because I spend 90 per cent of my time doing social work," this community feels it can afford to take the long view. But even at this point, the brightest estimate of the transformations to be wrought by the new lake development offers a promise for only a small section of the community.

The only public opposition, an angry typographer employed by the community's daily newspaper, can be seen on occasional Saturdays parading around the town square, carrying now familiar sandwich boards that decry the community's domination by a small and selfish group and that challenge the community to undertake its own program of revival. And just as this single, isolated figure is accepted with good humor but not much thought by the residents of Clyde, so there appears to be a somewhat thoughtless and casual acceptance of an unchanging drift.

Spiresburg

Spiresburg clearly has been the most successful of the three towns. In a sense, the crisis caused by the decline of the coal industry came to it first. Spiresburg lost its two major mines during the early years of the great depression and, while it retained a number of persons employed in mining, it served essentially as a dormitory for miners of the general area.

Like Clyde, it is a county seat and the core of the community is located around the courthouse. Also, like Clyde, Spiresburg is a second city in its county, subordinate in industry, retail, and service activity to a nearby town.

In these respects, as well as in general location, types of industry, natural resources and so on, it has some similarity to the other two. If anything, it has more disadvantages. It has not been nearly as successful as Clyde in attracting potentially prominent, capable, and educated people to live there. It is markedly smaller than either—less than half the population of Clyde, a third that of East Parrish. But it is the character and activity of the political and community leaders of Spiresburg that is most dramatically different.

They are a fairly well-integrated group of small merchants and independent professionals and semiprofessionals. Even schoolteachers and ministers, in contrast to Clyde and East Parrish, are included. Reading a roster of offices for social clubs, official and semiofficial boards, and local government offices for a period of years, one quickly detects an interweaving and recurrence of names that suggests nothing so much as a well-rehearsed square dance. To the middle class, high or low, a lot of sociability is most of what is required for access to community life. The pattern of integrated community leadership is so great that lower-class participation is all but impossible. (Its dormitory status, which meant a dispersal of its workers over the countryside, obviously weakened class solidarity, unlike East Parrish where residential and work populations overlapped.)

Social contacts among Spiresburg's upper group is the highest

for all three communities—while social participation for its workers and reliefers is the lowest for all three. The frequent and easy
contacts among influentials are facilitated by Spiresburg's size
—it is small enough so that its community leadership can take
a collective daily coffee break. While sitting in a restaurant in
early afternoon for less than an hour with the mayor, the senior
author met most of the town's leading merchants, a local insurance agent, the police chief, postmaster, state senator, optometrist, and the newspaper publisher.

In three of the cases of successful plant relocation in Spiresburg government aid was sought and utilized; in the fourth the
community provided its own resources. The wages in all four
plants are at best marginal, and there are few white collar or
managerial positions.

However, the limits of Spiresburg's recovery have been set by
the shopkeeper mentalities of its leadership. By these standards
the town has recovered. But in Spiresburg's lower class there
is a continuing, if ineffectual, discontent. And in the upper class
the most promising young people leave, usually for college, and
seldom return. Spiresburg's situation is best symbolized by the
contrast between its four almost brand-new factories—on its outskirts—and its town square which looks today much as it must
have about 1925.

The Issue of Leadership

From this comparison of the three towns it seems obvious
that the quality of community leadership—particularly political
leadership—is a crucial determinant of the course of development. The picture is amazingly consistent with that thesis. And
it is also reflected in the feelings and attitudes of the citizens
of each town.

The depressed spirit in East Parrish and Clyde, and the un-
realistic attitudes toward their problems, is revealed by the
answers people had to questions about events that had occurred
recently. (For example, what was "the biggest thing that happened in the community during the last year?") The ones they
emphasized were on the horizon rather than of immediate importance. Very prominent were a major interstate highway due
to pass close to both towns and the federal lake resort project
—both due for completion well in the future. Seventy-three per

cent of the citizens of Clyde, the town most directly involved, mentioned one or the other. Even though East Parrish was not as closely concerned, 27 per cent also referred to them.

Similar results came from the more specific question that asked people to describe the "most important problem facing the community." Almost 80 per cent of Clyde's respondents spoke of unemployment or poor business conditions, as did 66 per cent from East Parrish. (The continuing political conflict in East Parrish, not present in Clyde, accounted for 17 per cent, and so kept the score for economic depression from being even higher.) Spiresburg, too, registered a 47 per cent vote for unemployment and poor business which indicated that its recovery was also far from complete. On the other hand, 36 per cent of Spiresburg's respondents listed problems associated with growth—the taxing of existing community facilities or the financing of improvements —as being the "most important."

Would the picture get "better or worse in the next few months?" Fifty per cent of East Parrish votes went for worse; in Clyde 26 per cent felt this way; but in optimistic Spiresburg, only 12 per cent.

How attached the respondents were to their communities and how they felt about them are described in the table.

Spiresburg is the easiest to single out. Its economic improvement has had an effect on (and perhaps also was affected by) the attitude of its citizens. A majority thought it no place for a young man just starting out (63 per cent); but that is considerably lower than the 78 and 83 per cent who felt that way about East Parrish and Clyde. They also show the highest community identification and commitment—68 per cent selected it as their ideal community of residence; 84 per cent felt their fellow residents "really care" about it.

The differences between the depressed communities, Clyde and East Parrish, were not great; but such as they were, they emphasized the greater magnitude of East Parrish's decline.

Change—But Don't Upset Anything

In these three towns different traditions and different political structures have led to three essentially different modes of adjustment to similar crises. What these modes do have in common however—despite a prevailing rhetoric of community

Perception of and Attachment to Community

Items:	East Parrish	Clyde	Spires-burg
Most of the important decisions in .... are made by a small group of people who are on "the inside."	82%*	72%*	78%*
There have been so many changes in .... that it is hardly the same town.	24	12	15
Most people in .... really care about what happens to the community.	68	62	84
.... is no place for a young man just starting out.	78	83	63
It is better to live in a small town than a big city.	80	88	90
Per cent selecting present community in free choice of ideal community in which to live.	58	53	68

* *Per cent agreeing.*

renewal—is a deep-seated resistance to social change of any real significance. And in this respect they resemble hundreds of other declining communities too far from urban centers in an urban society.

This resistance to change has many causes. Most important perhaps, community leaders do not really believe enough in the futures of their towns to be willing to commit their own children to them. (The lower classes have little choice.) There was only one professional or semiprofessional in all those we interviewed in all three communities who did not sometime boast about how well his children were doing somewhere else. The only middle-class group whose children, generally, did not leave, are the marginal retail merchants who often had little to bequeath except their businesses.

And it is precisely this element, notably in East Parrish, that is most committed to community renewal. The mayor of Spiresburg talked—as most people did—about the loss of young people to the community; each new plant was referred to as having taken care of the graduating class of the community high school of this year or that year. But the reference was not to the entire graduating class, only that part of it primarily, if not exclusively, lower class. That is, that portion not going on to college. The son of the mayor himself, obviously, had no future in a plant with few managerial or professional jobs.

Since the leaders are not really committed to the future of the towns—except in the most abstract way—there is little incentive to undertake community renewal that might rock their boats; and any genuine community renewal would have to rock it. The president of East Parrish's only bank was most explicit:

> This community has lost population and it may have to lose more. But things have settled down quite nicely and everything operates smoothly. East Parrish has a pretty stable economy. Of course there are no new industries. But when I started this bank in 1943 there was a mine payroll of over one million dollars a month, now it is down to one hundred and fifty thousand. Then there were three banks with combined assets of about four million, now there is only one (his), but it has assets of over twelve million. . . . The town may get smaller instead of bigger. For a community, like a man, things have to balance out.

The town might die, but he was doing nicely. Things balanced out.

This banker was a leading member of the East Parrish Industrial fund; it is easy to see why it was so cautious about spending its $100,000 to attract new industry. Even in Spiresburg, though everyone was in favor of prosperity in general, some did not want too much—too much being defined as the point at which it might bring competition to established businesses and established allocations of power.

The present high level of integration of leadership in Spiresburg is sustained by systematic back-scratching. For example, the town's optometrist makes it perfectly clear that none of the town's four practicing physicians would dream of giving an eye examination. Unfortunately, economic back-scratching cannot survive where there is extensive economic and social growth, vital to community renewal. You can't have everything. Despite the rhetoric, the choice has been made.

Further, whether as rationalization or compensation, or because those who might think otherwise have already flown to the cities, a strongly anti-urban system of values has emerged. One community resident observed:

When I or my wife want to take a walk we can do it without being robbed or assaulted. You can't say that in St. Louis or Chicago.

This is an overstatement, but not without some truth. However, he does not ask what the young people of the community ask continually: Where in town is there anything to walk to?

Since for most the money lies in the cities, those who stay must believe, or profess, a rejection of purely mercenary values. A young returnee to East Parrish commented:

This is a friendly town. I know 'most everyone. When I walk down the street, everyone says hello. Here I am my own boss. I make less, but I also worry less. In St. Louis, at GM, everyone was worried that the guy at the next desk would get a promotion before you did—I could have stayed, they called from Flint and offered me a promotion. You have to grow up sometimes, a person has to learn to walk a straight road.

Or a young publisher in Clyde:

You might say that we here in Clyde have learned to settle for second best. But I prefer to think that we just value things differently. . . . I have ten minutes from my house what the big city businessman has to travel hundreds of miles to get and then for only a few days a year.

The lessons are plain. First, superficial indicators are not the accurate predictors of community health they are often conceived to be. Whether a town will climb, slow its decline, or go under altogether is determined often very largely by the character and activity of its middle and upper-middle class political leadership.

But there is an even more important lesson hovering ominously in the background. The economic progress of each of the three southern Illinois towns studied is different, and they have responded differently to crisis; but none represents a substantial —certainly not permanent—comeback in the face of increased urbanization.

Their approach to the future is one of improvisation. Their horizons must remain limited—for redevelopment is not only a promise but a threat to the ideologies of small town life. They must lose their best people and business concerns to the larger towns because of greater opportunities, education, and satisfactions there. Those who return will be failures—or be willing, for whatever reason, to settle for what represents second-best in our competitive society.

It is impossible for any similar small town to maintain a first-rate school system—and the children, and the future, must suffer for it. The fundamental character of the leadership of these communities will limit the nature and direction of growth—because they do not want to face real competition. If they had been willing and prepared to face it, they would have moved out long before. They cannot be expected to deliberately make their own worst fears come true.

The land and the economy of the United States will not support as many small towns as they did before. It is very difficult not to see the future as a long drawn-out struggle for community survival, lasting for half a century, in which some battles may be won but the war will be lost. A future in which most such towns will become isolated or decayed, in which the local amenities must deteriorate, and in which there will finally be left only the aged, the inept, the very young—and the local power elite.

How does the group react to deviance in its ranks?
What functions are served in the acts of deviance?
The authors look at how the structure of a social
system determines the kinds of acts that occur and
the kinds of reactions they receive.

XVIII

The Functions of Deviance
in Groups*

ROBERT A. DENTLER
KAI T. ERIKSON

ALTHOUGH SOCIOLOGISTS HAVE REPEATEDLY NOTED that close similarities exist between various forms of social marginality, research
directed at these forms has only begun to mark the path toward
a social theory of deviance. This slow pace may in part result
from the fact that deviant behavior is too frequently visualized
as a product of organizational failure rather than as a facet of
organization itself.

Albert Cohen has recently attempted to specify some of the
assumptions and definitions necessary for a sociology of deviant
behavior (3). He has urged the importance of erecting clearly
defined concepts, devising a homogeneous class of phenomena
explainable by a unified system of theory, and developing a
sociological rather than a psychological framework—as would
be the case, for example, in a central problem which was stated:
"What is it about the structure of social systems that determines
the kinds of criminal acts that occur in these systems and the
way in which such acts are distributed within the systems?"
(3, p. 462). Cohen has also suggested that a theory of deviant
behavior should account simultaneously for deviance and conformity; that is, the explanation of one should serve as the explanation of the other.

* Reprinted from *Social Problems*, Vol. 7, No. 2, 1959, 98-107, by permission of the authors and the Society for the Study of Social Problems.

In this paper we hope to contribute to these objectives by presenting some propositions about the sources and functions of deviant behavior in small groups. Although we suspect that the same general processes may well characterize larger social systems, this paper will be limited to small groups, and more particularly to enduring task and primary groups. Any set of propositions about the functions of deviance would have to be shaped to fit the scope of the social unit chosen for analysis, and we have elected to use the small group unit in this exploratory paper primarily because a large body of empirical material dealing with deviance in groups has accumulated which offers important leads into the study of deviance in general.

With Cohen, we define deviance as "behavior which violates institutionalized expectations, that is, expectations which are shared and recognized as legitimate within a social system" (3, p. 462). Our guiding assumption is that deviant behavior is a reflection not only of the personality of the actor, but the structure of the group in which the behavior was enacted. The violations of expectation which the group experiences, as well as the norms which it observes, express both cultural and structural aspects of the group. While we shall attend to cultural elements in later illustrations, our propositions are addressed primarily to the structure of groups and the functions that deviant behavior serves in maintaining this structure.

Proposition One

Our first proposition is that *groups tend to induce, sustain, and permit deviant behavior.* To say that a group *induces* deviant behavior, here, is to say that as it goes through the early stages of development and structures the range of behavior among its members, a group will tend to define the behavior of certain members as deviant. A group *sustains* or *permits* this newly defined deviance in the sense that it tends to institutionalize and absorb this behavior into its structure rather than eliminating it. As group structure emerges and role specialization takes place, one or more role categories will be differentiated to accommodate individuals whose behavior is occasionally or regularly expected to be deviant. It is essential to the argument that this process be viewed not only as a simple group adjustment to individual differences, but also as a requirement of group formation, analogous to the requirement of leadership.

The process of role differentiation and specialization which takes place in groups has been illuminated by studies which use concepts of sociometric rank. Riecken and Homans conclude from this evidence: "The higher the rank of a member the closer his activities come to realizing the norms of the group . . . and there is a tendency toward 'equilibration of rank' " (11, p. 794). Thus the rankings that take place on a scale of social preference serve to identify the activities that members are expected to carry out: each general rank represents or contains an equivalent role which defines that member's special relationship to the group and its norms. To the extent that a group ranks its members preferentially, it distributes functions differentially. The proposition, then, simply notes that group members who violate norms will be given low sociometric rank; that this designation carries with it an appropriate differentiation of the functions that such members are expected to perform in respect to the group; and that the roles contained in these low-rank positions become institutionalized and are retained in the structure of the group.

The most difficult aspect of this proposition is the concept of *induction* of deviance. We do not mean to suggest that the group creates the motives for an individual's deviant behavior or compels it from persons not otherwise disposed toward this form of expression. When a person encounters a new group, two different historical continuities meet. The individual brings to the group a background of private experience which disposes him to certain patterns of conduct; the group, on the other hand, is organized around a network of role priorities to which each new member is required to conform. While the individual brings new resources into the group and alters its potential for change and innovation, the group certainly operates to rephrase each member's private experience into a new self-formula, a new sense of his own needs.

Thus any encounter between a group and a new member is an event which is novel to the experience of both. In the trial-and-error behavior which issues, both the functional requirements of the group and the individual needs of the person will undergo certain revisions, and in the process the group plays an important part in determining whether those already disposed toward deviant behavior will actually express it overtly, or whether those who are lightly disposed toward deviating styles will be encouraged to develop that potential. *Inducing* deviance, then, is meant to be a process by which the group channels and organizes the deviant possibilities contained in its membership.

The proposition argues that groups induce deviant behavior in the same sense that they induce other group qualities like leadership, fellowship, and so on. These qualities emerge early and clearly in the formation of new groups, even in traditionless laboratory groups, and while they may be diffusely distributed among the membership initially they tend toward specificity and equilibrium over time. In giving definition to the end points in the range of behavior which is brought to a group by its membership, the group establishes its boundaries and gives dimension to its structure. In this process, the designation of low-ranking deviants emerges as surely as the designation of high-ranking task leaders.

Proposition Two

Bales has written:

> The displacement of hostilities on a scapegoat at the bottom of the status structure is one mechanism, apparently, by which the ambivalent attitudes toward the . . . "top man" . . . can be diverted and drained off. These patterns, culturally elaborated and various in form, can be viewed as particular cases of mechanisms relevant to the much more general problem of equilibrium (2, p. 454).

This comment provides a bridge between our first and second propositions by suggesting that deviant behavior may serve important functions for groups—thereby contributing to, rather than disrupting, equilibrium in the group. Our second proposition, accordingly, is that *deviant behavior functions in enduring groups to help maintain group equilibrium*. In the following discussion we would like to consider some of the ways this function operates.

Group performance. The proposition implies that deviant behavior contributes to the maintenance of optimum levels of performance, and we add at this point that this will particularly obtain where a group's achievement depends upon the contributions of all its members.

McCurdy and Lambert devised a laboratory task which required full group participation in finding a solution to a given problem (7). They found that the performance of their groups compared unfavorably with that of individual problem-solvers, and explained this by noting the high likelihood that a group would contain at least one member who failed to attend to instructions. The group, they observed, may prove no stronger than its weakest member. The implication here, as in the old adage, seems to be that the group would have become correspondingly stronger if its weakest link were removed. Yet this implication requires some consideration: to what extent can we say that the inattentive member was acting in the name of the group, performing a function which is valuable to the group over time? To what extent can we call this behavior a product of group structure rather than a product of individual eccentricity?

As roles and their equivalent ranks become differentiated in a group, some members will be expected to perform more capably than others; and in turn the structure of the group will certainly be organized to take advantage of the relative capabilities of its members—as it demonstrably does in leadership choice. These differentials require testing and experimentation: the norms about performance in a group cannot emerge until clues appear as to how much the present membership can accomplish, how wide the range of variation in performance is likely to be, and so on. To the extent that group structure becomes an elaboration and organization of these differentials, certainly the "weak link" becomes as essential to this process as the high-producer. Both are outside links in the communication system which feeds back information about the range of group performance and the limits of the differentiated structure.

As this basis for differentiation becomes established, then, the group moves from a state in which pressure is exerted equally on all members to conform to performance norms, and moves toward a state in which these norms become a kind of anchor which locates the center of wide variations in behavior. The performance "mean" of a group is of course expected to be set at a level dictated by "norms"; and this mean is not only achieved by the most conforming members but by a balance of high and low producers as well. It is a simple calculation that the loss of a weak-link, the low producer, would raise the mean output of the group to a point where it no longer corresponded to original norms unless the entire structure of the group shifted as compensation. In this sense we can argue that neither role differentiation nor norm formation could occur and be maintained without the "aid" of regular deviations.

Rewards. Stated briefly, we would argue that the process of distributing incentives to members of the group is similarly dependent upon the recurrence of deviant behavior. This is an instance where, as Cohen has urged, an explanation of conformity may lead to an explanation of deviance. Customarily, conformance is rewarded while deviance is either unrewarded or actively punished. The rewards of conformity, however, are seen as "rewarding" in comparison to other possible outcomes, and obviously the presence of a deviant in the group would provide the continual contrast without which the reward structure would have little meaning. The problem, then, becomes complex: the reward structure is set up as an incentive for conformity, but depends upon the outcome that differentials in conformity will occur. As shall be pointed out later, the deviant is rewarded in another sense for his role in the group, which makes it "profitable" for him to serve as a contrast in the conventional reward structure. Generally speaking, comparison is as essential in the maintenance of norms as is conformity: a norm becomes most evident in its occasional violation, and in this sense a group maintains "equilibrium" by a controlled balance of the relations which provide comparison and those which assure conformity.

Boundaries. Implicit in the foregoing is the argument that the presence of deviance in a group is a boundary maintaining function. The comparisons which deviance makes possible help establish the range in which the group operates, the extent of its jurisdiction over behavior, the variety of styles it contains, and these are among the essential dimensions which give a group identity and distinctiveness. In Quaker work camps, Riecken found that members prided themselves on their acceptance of deviations, and rejected such controls as ridicule and rejection (10, pp. 57-67). Homans has noted that men in the Bank Wiring Group employed certain sanctions against deviant behavior which were felt to be peculiar to the structure of the group (5). A group is distinguished in part by the norms it creates for handling deviance and by the forms of deviance it is able to absorb and contain. In helping, then, to give members a sense of their group's distinctiveness, deviant behavior on the group's margins provides an important boundary-maintaining function.

Proposition Three

Kelley and Thibault have asserted:

> It is common knowledge that when a member deviates markedly from a group standard, the remaining members of the group bring pressures to bear on the deviate to return to conformity. If pressure is of no avail, the deviate is rejected and cast out of the group. The research on this point is consistent with common sense (6, p. 768).

Apparently a deviating member who was *not* rejected after repeated violations would be defined as one who did not deviate markedly enough. While there is considerable justification to support this common-sense notion, we suggest that it over-attends to rejection and neglects the range of alternatives short of rejection. The same focus is evident in the following statement by Rossi and Merton:

> What the individual experiences as estrangement from a group tends to be experienced by his associates as repudiation of the group, and this ordinarily evokes a hostile response. As social relations between the individual and the rest of the group deteriorate, the norms of the group become less binding for him. For since he is progressively seceding from the group and being penalized by it, he is the less likely to experience rewards for adherence to . . . norms. Once initiated, this process seems to move toward a cumulative detachment from the group (8, p. 270).

While both of the above quotations reflect current research concerns in their attention to the group's rejection of the individual and his alienation from the group, our third proposition focuses on the common situation in which the group works to prevent elimination of a deviant member. *Groups will resist any trend toward alienation of a member whose behavior is deviant.* From the point of view of the group majority, deviants will be retained in the group up to a point where the deviant expression becomes critically dangerous to group solidarity. This accords with Kelley and Thibault's general statement, if not with its implication; but we would add that the point at which deviation becomes "markedly" extreme—and dangerous to the group—cannot be well defined in advance. This point is located by the group as a result of recurrent interaction between conforming members who respect the central norms of the group and deviating members who test its boundaries. This is the context from which the group derives a conception of what constitutes "danger," or what variations from the norm shall be viewed as "marked."

From the point of view of the deviant, then, the testing of limits is an exercise of his role in the group; from the point of view of the group, pressures are set into motion which secure the deviant in his "testing" role, yet try to assure that his deviation will not become pronounced enough to make rejection necessary. Obviously this is a delicate balance to maintain, and failures are continually visible. Yet there are a great many conditions under which it is worth while for the group to retain its deviant members and resist any trend which might lead the majority membership and other deviant members to progressive estrangement.

Illustrations of Propositions

Each of the authors of this paper has recently completed field research which illuminates the propositions set forth here. Dentler studied the relative effectiveness of ten Quaker work projects in influencing conformity with norms of tolerance, pacifism, democratic group relations, and related social attitudes (4). One interesting sidelight in this study was the finding that while all ten groups were highly solidary, those with relatively higher numbers of sociometric isolates exhibited higher degrees of favorable increased conformity.

Case study of five of the ten groups, using interviews and participant observation, revealed that the two groups achieving the greatest favorable changes in tolerance, democratism, pacifism, and associated attitudes not only had the highest proportions of social isolates, but some of the isolates were low-ranking deviants. Of course none of the groups was without at least one isolate and one deviant, and these roles were not always occupied by the same member. But in the two high-change groups low-rank deviants were present.

In one group, one of these members came from a background that differed radically from those of other members. Although these were cooperative living and work projects, this member insisted upon separately prepared special food and complained loudly about its quality. Where three-fourths of the group members came from professional and managerial families, and dressed and acted in conformity with upper-middle-class standards, this deviant refused to wear a shirt to Sunday dinner and often came to meals without his shoes. He could not hold a job and lost two provided by the group leader during the first two weeks of the program.

His social and political attitudes also differed radically from group norms, and he was often belligerently assertive of his minority perspectives. He had no allies for his views. In an interview one of the group leaders described the group's response to this deviant:

> At first we didn't know how to cope with him though we were determined to do just that. After he came to Sunday dinner in his undershirt, and after he smashed a bowl of food that had been fixed specially for him—as usual—we figured out a way to set down certain firm manners for him. There were some rules, we decided, that no one was going to violate. We knew he was very new to this kind of life and so we sought to understand him. We never rejected him. Finally, he began to come to terms; he adapted, at least enough so that we can live with him. He has begun to conform on the surface to some of our ways. It's been very hard to take that he is really proud of having lost his first two jobs and is not quiet about it. Things have gone better since we made a birthday cake for him, and I feel proud of the way our group has managed to handle this internal problem.

The same group sustained another deviant and even worked hard to retain him when he decided to leave the group. Here a group leader discusses group relations with this member:

> X left our group after the first four weeks of the eight-week program. He had never been away from home before although he was about 21 years old. He couldn't seem to adjust to his job at the day camp, and he just couldn't stand doing his share of the housework and cooking. This lack of doing his share was especially hard on us, and we often discussed privately whether

it would be good for him to relieve him of any household chores. We decided that wouldn't be right, but we still couldn't get him to work. Funny, but this sort of made housework the center of our group life. We are proud that no one else has shirked his chores; there is no quibbling now. . . . Anyway, X kept being pressured by his mother and brother to come home, but we gave him tremendous support. We talked it all out with him. We let him know we really wanted him to stay. This seemed to unify our group. It was working out the problem of X that seemed to unify our group. It was working out the problem of X that seemed to help us build some group standards. He began to follow some of our standards but he also stayed free to dissent. His mother finally forced him to come home.

In the second high-change group, there were also two extreme deviants. Here a group leader comments on one of them:

I've never got over feeling strongly antagonistic toward K. K has been a real troublemaker and we never really came to terms with him or controlled him significantly. He is simply a highly neurotic, conflicted person as far as life in our group goes. Personally, I've resented the fact that he has monopolized Z, who without him would have been a real contributor but who has become nothing more than a sort of poor imitation of K. After we had been here about half the summer, incidentally, a professional came out from staff headquarters and after observing our meetings he asked why K hadn't been dismissed or asked to leave the group early in the summer. But K didn't leave, of course, and most of us wouldn't want him to leave.

Finally a group leader described the reaction to the departure of its second deviant, who was repeatedly described in interviews as "kind of obnoxious":

On the night N was upstairs talking with your interviewer, the group got together downstairs suddenly to talk about getting up a quick party, a farewell party for him. In 15 minutes, like a whirlwind, we decorated the house and some of the fellows wrote a special song of farewell for N. We also wrote a last-minute appeal asking him to stay with the group and people ran about asking, "What are you doing for N?" There seemed to be a lot of guilt among us about his leaving. We felt that maybe we hadn't done enough to get him more involved in the life of our group. I think there was some hidden envy too. After he had left, a joke began to spread around that went like this: If you leave now maybe we'll have a party for you.

The group with the lowest amount of change during the summer contained two low-ranking members, one of whom deviated from the group's norms occasionally, but no evidence came to light to indicate that this group achieved the same intensity in social relationships or the same degree of role differentiation as did groups with more extremely deviant members. Members of this low-change group reflected almost without exception the views expressed in this typical quotation:

> Objectively, this is a good, congenial group of individuals. Personally they leave me a little cold. I've been in other project groups, and this is the most congenial one I've been in; yet, I don't think there will be any lasting friendships.

All these quotations reflect strong impressions embodied in our observational reports. Taken as a whole they illustrate aspects of our three postulates. While this material does not reveal the sense in which a group may induce deviance—and this is perhaps the most critical proposition of all—it does show how groups will make great efforts to keep deviant members attached to the group, to prevent full alienation. By referring to our findings about attitude change we have hoped to suggest the relevance of deviance to increasing conformity, a functional relationship of action and reaction.

In 1955-6, Erikson participated in a study of schizophrenia among basic trainees in the U.S. Army, portions of which have been published elsewhere (1). Through various interview and questionnaire techniques, a large body of data was collected which enabled the investigators to reconstruct short histories of the group life shared by the future schizophrenic and his squad prior to the former's hospitalization. There were eleven subjects in the data under consideration. The bulk of the evidence used for this short report comes from loosely structured interviews which were conducted with the entire squad in attendance, shortly after it had lost one of its members to the psychiatric hospital.

The eleven young men whose breakdown was the subject of the interviews all came from the north-eastern corner of the United States, most of them from rural or small-town communities. Typically, these men had accumulated long records of deviation in civilian life: while few of them had attracted psychiatric attention, they had left behind them fairly consistent records of job failure, school truancy, and other minor difficulties in the community. Persons in the community took notice of this behavior, of course, but they tended to be gently puzzled by it rather than attributing distinct deviant motives to it.

When such a person enters the service, vaguely aware that his past performance did not entirely live up to expectations current in his community, he is likely to start negotiating with his squad mates about the conditions of his membership in the group. He sees himself as warranting special group consideration, as a consequence of a deviant style which he himself is unable to define; yet the group has clear-cut obligations which require a high degree of responsibility and coordination from everyone. The negotiation seems to go through several successive stages, during which a reversal of original positions takes place and the individual is fitted for a role which is clearly deviant.

The first stage is characteristic of the recruit's first days in camp. His initial reaction is likely to be an abrupt attempt to discard his entire "civilian" repertoire to free himself for adoption of new styles and new ways. His new uniform for daily wear seems to become for him a symbolic uniform for his sense of identity: he is, in short, overconforming. He is likely to interpret any gesture of command as a literal moral mandate, sometimes suffering injury when told to scrub the floor until his fingers bleed, or trying to consciously repress thoughts of home when told to get everything out of his head but the military exercise of the moment.

The second stage begins shortly thereafter as he fails to recognize that "regulation" reality is different from the reality of group life, and that the circuits which carry useful information are contained within the more informal source. The pre-psychotic is, to begin with, a person for whom contacts with peers are not easy to establish, and as he tries to find his way into these circuits, looking for cues to the rhythm of group life, he sees that a fairly standard set of interaction techniques is in use. There are ways to initiate conversation, ways to impose demands, and so on. Out of this cultural lore, then, he chooses different gambits to test. He may learn to ask for matches to start discussion, be ready with a supply of cigarettes for others to "bum," or he may pick up a local joke or expression and repeat it continually. Too often, however, he misses the context in which these interaction cues are appropriate, so that his behavior, in its over-literal simplicity, becomes almost a caricature of the sociability rule he is trying to follow. We may cite the "specialist" in giving away cigarettes:

> I was out of cigarettes and he had a whole pack. I said, "Joe, you got a smoke?" He says "yes," and Jesus, he gave me about twelve of them. At other times he used to offer me two or three packs of cigarettes at a time when I was out.

Or the "specialist" in greetings:

> He'd go by you in the barracks and say, "What do you say, Jake?" I'd say, "Hi, George, how are you?" and he'd walk into the latrine. And he'd come by not a minute later, and it's the same thing all over again, "What do you say, Jake?" It seemed to me he was always saying "hi" to someone. You could be sitting right beside him for ten minutes and he would keep on saying it.

These clumsy overtures lead the individual and the group into the third stage. Here the recruit, almost hidden from group view in his earlier over-conformity, has become a highly visible group object: his behavior is clearly "off beat," anomalous; he has made a presentation of himself to the squad, and the squad has had either to make provisions for him in the group structure or begin the process of eliminating him. The pre-psychotic is clearly a low producer, and in this sense he is potentially a handicap. Yet the group neither exerts strong pressures on him to conform nor attempts to expel him from the squad. Instead, he is typically given a wide license to deviate from both the performance and behavior norms of the group, and the group in turn forms a hard protective shell around him which hides him from exposure to outside authorities.

His duties are performed by others, and in response the squad only seems to ask of him that he be at least consistent in his deviation—that he be consistently helpless and consistently anomalous. In a sense, he becomes the ward of the group, hidden from outside view but the object of friendly ridicule within. He is referred to as "our teddy bear," "our pet," "mascot," "little brother," "toy," and so on. In a setting where having buddies is highly valued, he is unlikely to receive any sociometric choices at all. But it would be quite unfortunate to assume that he is therefore isolated from the group or repudiated by it: an accurate sociogram would have the deviant individual encircled by the interlocking sociometric preferences, sheltered by the group structure, and an important point of reference for it.

The examples just presented are weak in that they include only failures of the process described. The shell which protected the deviant from visibility leaked, outside medical authorities were notified, and he was eventually hospitalized. But as a final note it is interesting to observe that the shell remained even after the person for whom it was erected had withdrawn. Large portions of every squad interview were devoted to arguments, directed at a psychiatrist, that the departed member was not ill and should never have been hospitalized.

Discussion

The most widely cited social theories of deviant behavior which have appeared in recent years—notably those of Merton and Parsons (8; 9)—have helped turn sociologists' attention from earlier models of social pathology in which deviance was seen as direct evidence of disorganization. These newer models have attended to the problem of how social structures exert pressure on certain individuals rather than others toward the expression of deviance. Yet the break with the older social disorganization tradition is only partial, since these theories still regard deviance from the point of view of its value as a "symptom" of dysfunctional structures. One aim of this paper is to encourage a functional approach to deviance, to consider the contributions deviant behavior may make toward the development of organizational structures, rather than focusing on the implicit assumption that structures must be somehow in a state of disrepair if they produce deviant behavior.

Any group attempts to locate its position in social space by defining its symbolic boundaries, and this process of self-location takes place not only in reference to the central norms which the group develops but in reference to the *range* of possibilities which the culture makes available. Specialized statuses which are located on the margins of the group, chiefly high-rank leaders and low-rank deviants, become critical referents for establishing the end points of this range, the group boundaries.

As both the Quaker and Army illustrations suggest, deviant members are important targets toward which group concerns become focused. Not only do they symbolize the group's activities, but they help give other members a sense of group size, its range and extent, by marking where the group begins and ends in space. In general, the deviant seems to help give the group structure a visible "shape." The deviant is someone about whom something should be done, and the group, in expressing this concern, is able to reaffirm its essential cohesion and indicate what the group is and what it can do. Of course the character of the deviant behavior in each group would vary with the group's general objectives, its relationship to the larger culture, and so on. In both the Quaker groups and Army squads, nurturance was a strong element of the other members' reaction to their deviant fellow. More specifically in the Army material it is fairly sure that the degree of helplessness and softness supplied by the pre-psychotic introduced emotional qualities which the population—lacking women and younger persons—could not otherwise afford.

These have been short and necessarily limited illustrations of the propositions advanced. In a brief final note we would like to point out how this crude theory could articulate with the small group research tradition by suggesting one relatively ideal laboratory procedure that might be used. Groups composed of extremely homogeneous members should be assigned tasks which require group solution but which impose a high similarity of activity upon all members. If role differentiation occurs, then, it would be less a product of individual differences or the specific requirements of the task than a product of group formation. We would hypothesize that such differentiation would take place, and that one or more roles thus differentiated would be reserved for deviants. The occupants of these deviant roles should be removed from the group. If the propositions have substance, the group—and this is the critical hypothesis—would realign its members so that these roles would become occupied by other members. While no single experiment could address all the implications of our paradigm, this one would confront its main point.

This paper, of course, has deliberately neglected those group conditions in which deviant behavior becomes dysfunctional: it is a frequent group experience that deviant behavior fails to provide a valued function for the structure and helps reduce performance standards or lower levels of interaction. We have attempted here to present a side of the coin which we felt was often neglected, and in our turn we are equally—if intentionally—guilty of neglect.

Summary

This paper has proposed the following interpretations of deviant behavior in enduring primary and task groups:

1. Deviant behavior tends to be induced, permitted, and sustained by a given group.

2. Deviant behavior functions to help maintain group equilibrium.

3. Groups will resist any trend toward alienation of a member whose behavior is deviant.

The substance of each proposition was discussed heuristically and illustrated by reference to field studies of deviant behavior in Quaker work projects and Army basic training squads. A laboratory test was suggested as one kind of critical test of the paradigm. The aim of the presentation was to direct attention to the functional interdependence of deviance and organization.

REFERENCES

1. Artiss, Kenneth L., ed., *The Symptom as Communication in Schizophrenia* (New York: Grune and Stratton, 1959).

2. Bales, Robert F., "The Equilibrium Problem in Small Groups," in *Small Groups,* A. Paul Hare, *et al.,* eds. (New York: Knopf, 1955), 424-456.

3. Cohen, Albert K., "The Study of Social Disorganization and Deviant Behavior," in *Sociology Today,* Robert K. Merton, *et al.,* eds. (New York: Basic Books, 1959), 461-484.

4. Dentler, Robert, *The Young Volunteers* (Chicago: National Opinion Research Center Report, 1959).

5. Homans, George W., *The Human Group* (New York: Harcourt, Brace, 1950).

6. Kelley, Harold H., and John W. Thibault, "Experimental Studies of Group Problem Solving and Process," in *Handbook of Social Psychology,* Vol. II, Gardner Lindzey, ed. (Cambridge: Addison-Wesley, 1954), 759-768.

7. McCurdy, Harold G., and Wallace E. Lambert, "The Efficiency of Small Human Groups in the Solution of Problems Requiring Genuine Cooperation," *Journal of Personality,* 20 (June, 1952), 478-494.

8. Merton, Robert K., *Social Theory and Social Structure*, rev. ed. (Glencoe: Free Press, 1957).

9. Parsons, Talcott, *The Social System* (Glencoe: Free Press, 1951), 256-267, 321-325; and Talcott Parsons, Robert F. Bales and Edward A. Shils, *Working Papers in the Theory of Action* (Glencoe: Free Press, 1953), 67-78.

10. Riecken, Henry, *Volunteer Work Camp* (Cambridge: Addison-Wesley, 1952), 57-67.

11. Riecken, Henry, and George W. Homans, "Psychological Aspects of Social Structure," in *Handbook of Social Psychology*, Vol. II, Gardner Lindzey, ed. (Cambridge: Addison-Wesley, 1954), 786-832.

Reflecting on the processes of change in modern society, and on the themes of force, speed, and violence characteristic of American culture, the author warns his fellow social scientists that they must transform their knowledge into social action. The possible consequences of the absence of such action are clearly presented in this article.

XIX

Kapow!!: An Argument and a Forecast*

ROY G. FRANCIS

An Argument

THE THEMES WHICH CHARACTERIZE the American culture scene include force, speed, and violence. These themes appear in virtually every aspect of public life. Brutal murders which arouse public indignation are but one evidence of these themes; most of them are regarded as being quite appropriate to the times.

Whether news accounts of violence simply reflect the culture or the profit-making motives of the publisher is a common enough argument. We need observe only that both take place: acts of violence and the reporting of them. Newspapers thrive on wars, rumors of wars, murders, rapes, arson, and traffic accidents. An anxious person pushed to act out his part in life's drama on a window ledge attracts great interest. And modern television certainly achieved its highest peak in the instant reporting of a murder done live on camera.

Few TV news accounts are without some accounting of force and violence. If a good labor dispute is unavailable; if the police haven't used firehoses or dogs on civil rights demonstrators—note how unbelievable is the theme of "passive resistance" in that movement—then the news can at least show the tangled mess of steel that once was an automobile capable of generating 300 horsepower, capable of hurtling down the street at speeds in excess of a hundred miles an hour. If the station is lucky, they

* Reprinted from *Social Problems*, Vol. 12, No. 3, Winter, 1965, 328-335, by permission of the author and the Society for the Study of Social Problems.

can show the tangled forms of the occupants to demonstrate the simple laws of physics involving the contact of moving and stationary bodies.

Our mass media of literary expression, including the paperbacks that sell widely, as well as television, characteristically employ the three themes. The force may take the form of political or military power, or even economic power. The explosion may simply be the fist of a private detective hitting the chin of a deserving hood. The violence may simply be one of the dozen murders incorporated in the story. It may only be the emotional outburst of a keyed-up doctor. But violence is there.

It may be debatable whether one ought include "comics" as a form of literary expression. Literary or not, they are sold by the millions. And even in the few designed to win parental approval, some justification of violence is manifest. The plot may be that the bad guys are on the verge of hurting the good guys (or simply, the wolf is about to eat the little pig); the good guys are therefore required to meet violence with violence. And the worse the bad guys, the greater the justification of violence. Indeed, without the appeal to violence, nothing in the comic book makes sense. "Zap!" and "Kapowee!!," fairly well within the phonetic range of our slow reading citizens, are merely signs of the times.

Sports, too, carry out this theme. The argument of speed is thoroughly justified in anything that involves racing—track meets, horse races, and car races. In the latter area, the use of jalopies in crash contests, to see which car obviously trying to bump others can survive the longest time, combines the imagery of racing and violence. Car shows, in which automobiles speed up ramps to sail through the air to another ramp, or run through walls, are modern mechanical evidences of the preference for violence. Wrestling, whether as a show or some real physical contest, employs the theme of violence both in reference to the action and to the rules; the bad guys do violence to the rules. Roller skating team contests seem to make a similar appeal. The skaters of course attempt considerable speed: Bumping body contacts and outbursts of violent temper tantrums, however, entertain the crowd more thoroughly.

Professional hockey seems to have legitimized the display of temper. It is true that penalties are invoked, but they simply serve to emphasize the "reality" of the display of anger. In any case, hockey without fighting seems unable to attract sufficient crowds to make it a worthwhile economic venture. And when the fighting is not going on, the tamer elements of speed and power are continuously on display.

In baseball, the stylistic game of base-running, the squeeze play, the hit-and-run have given way to a "power game." Today any muscular man, by virtue of being able to move his brawny shoulders in such a way as to make the ball fly over the fence 40 or more times a year, is paid from three to five or ten times as much as a professor of sociology. Similarly, designers of golf equipment and golf courses have turned that game into one which favors the power player. The crowd adores the one who can get a maximum drive, who hits a long ball. A precision game is too methodical and dull, and out of keeping with the times.

It has been said that football is taking over the position of our national game from baseball. One can hardly fail to observe the contact element in football. As far as the number of seconds that the ball is actually being moved during play, football comes close to baseball in accumulated tedium. The point of the game is, of course, the violent charging of twenty-two well conditioned and very large physical specimens. As though the long pass was not quite violent enough to fit the preferred image of football, the sports writers named it a "bomb." When the tag of violence was attached to the forward pass, it had a legitimate place in our ritual of speed, force and violence.

Areas generally thought of as being effeminate or non-masculine (for violence seems to be identified with masculinity), such as music and graphic arts, are beginning to show their presentation of these themes. We need only think of the cacophony of sound that does violence to our traditional image of concert music, of those composers who incorporate urban sounds of the jackhammer in their musical scores. The artist who throws paint at the canvas or smashes a musical instrument, carefully gluing its several parts in the proper place, is simply applying the theme of violence to his manner of expression. Not only is the resulting composition violent in character; its method of execution is violent also. The viewer who "takes the role of the artist" to share, if only vicariously, the moment of creation must also be violent in his imagination.

The purpose of the arts at any moment in time is to show what it is like to be a human being at that time. Today's artists, like all artists, are products of their time. They can only show that a human being today acts out a life in a matrix of speed, force, and violence. The number of poems that reveal this commitment are so numerous as to tempt one into a quantitative analysis. No simple minded chi-square would be necessary, however.

The intellectual world is much the same. The themes of war and power in history scarcely need comment. Geological studies of such violent happenings as earthquakes and volcanic eruptions are not entirely impelled by the force of an outside world. The sociologist's concern with the distribution of power or his enormous interest in public manifestations of violence in a criminal setting are not mere mirrorings of the world. The psychologist's new found power in the experimental setting in which he can violently reorient the actors of a situation, or the psychiatrist's approval of the use of electric shock treatment in which the painful writhings of the patient are viewed with interest if not compassion, are, of course, evidences of the place of violence in these disciplines.

In the queen of all sciences, physics, the themes are blatantly paraded. The speed of light, moving particles, accelerators, the violent consequence of atomic collision, are modern manifestations of a classic interest in force. Not only are these the things physics is made of, the physicist is committed to creating mechanisms to make the power available virtually fantastic.

In the good old days, an accelerator could be constructed of a size that one man could move it about. Today, there is one about two miles long; and the unit of measurement has become the billion-electron volt (Bev). We are no longer concerned about disrupting the composition of an atom with its accompanied release of incredible energy.

The empirical investigations of scientists in action—instead of the normative writings called "methodology" or "philosophy of science"—find that few scientists enjoy either reading or writing scientific papers. Instead of conceiving of science to be the written paper, or even the process by which it is written, the scientists I interviewed at the Oak Ridge National Laboratory more frequently thought of it as that moment of discovery when, *in their presence*, the particle attained the predicted speed and the predicted collision occurred. Intellectually separated by great distances from the rabid wrestling fan, emotionally the modern physicists share the love of violent contact.

From the huckster who writes the automobile ad emphasizing speed, to the reporter who describes its ideal termination in collision, to the physicist who watches small worlds collide, we live in a time characterized by the three themes of speed, force and violence. Small wonder that the strivers for peace and harmony seem so out of joint as to be morally suspect. It is not enough to hope that violence is a preface to harmony. For conciliatory themes to become part of the visible world, those acting out the themes of harmony must in some way be accorded legitimate social validation. Otherwise, we can only expect to continue to read about those areas of disapproved violence called "social problems."

A Forecast

Assuming that the ultimate use of violence, thermo-nuclear war, will be avoided, certain implications of my description seem to follow. The themes of speed, force, and violence do not complete the description of modern society. They do seem to be the major modes of action that will shape the emerging society. Whatever adaptations man makes in the immediate future will be made because of and in terms of violent reaction. The spread of violence into areas of life not previously violent in character can easily be predicted. The utilization of violence by minorities is already becoming common-place news; the formation of reaction groups, as the Maccabees in some Jewish communities, will soon lose their journalistic value.

The speed with which social relations are now changing does violence to the rule of tradition and custom over human behavior. Nowhere before has man lived in megopolis. No generation, no ethnic group, no social class has experienced the kind of world we are creating. Attempts to use analogies to the emergence of the truly industrial city of the early 20th century are failing— witness the pathetic attempts to appeal to the mass transportation theories of the 1920's in modern city life.

Speed of change is characteristic of the growth of modern knowledge. I refer in part to the exponential growth of scientific publications and the proliferation of disciplines and fields within disciplines. But I am referring to more than that. With the perfection of experimental techniques in psychology and sociology, we are learning more about controlling human behavior than Comte could imagine. More important, however, we are willing to use this knowledge and, consequently to destroy a previous image of man's relation to man.

At one time, one could imagine a man learning at least the fundamental ideas in all the arts and sciences. That is no longer possible. We are today committed to a society of experts and we don't know how experts are to relate to each other. We don't know, for example, how a road-building expert is to relate to a vote-getting expert (or to a clothing-selling expert, for that matter). The consequence is that we are witnessing the destruction of traditional ways of societal decision making. The old processes are gone. Instant news makes it mandatory that we recognize the demise of the past; the spectre of "knowing" the outcome of an election before the polls close does something to the voting process.

Now, as I have noted, not all forms of violence are acceptable —only those that serve "my" ends. Other forms of violence are to be defined as illegal and, failing that, to be removed from our minds. I say this because we have witnessed a strategy in our society of removing unpleasant scenes from view. With Urban Renewal, we get rid of dilapidated buildings and leave the social relations torn asunder. Generally, the process by which areas are de- and re-populated is a violent one. Life dreams, as pitiful as they may be when manifest in slum property, are torn apart with only monetary recompense. Neighborhood relations and friendship patterns are shattered as though they either do not exist or do not matter. New structures are created and the remaining social and economic poverty is partially camouflaged by such devices as the one-way street. These not only aid the sense of speed in modern transportation but render invisible less desired segments of the city. Part of the emerging view will be to render invisible those forms of violence good people find distasteful.

One further characteristic of our society, before we begin to draw the inferences I think I see, is the success-orientation fundamental to our behavior. We *are* a striving, competitive people. Various segments of the work force may have various schemes for measuring success. Yet, in one way or another, we all manage to render our pattern of consumption into a continuous potlatch ceremony. The painter may not use the banker's criterion of success; but he is concerned with success by those who count to him. Few categories are as competitive as the faculties of our universities in their frenzied attempt to increase research projects, foundation monies, or publication lists. The physician, the attorney, the businessman, the politician are all acting out the cultural dictate to succeed, and to succeed as fast as possible.

Success implies failure. The suave, sophisticated playboy may carefully plan his sexual conquest. But, for the failures, there is always the strategy of rape. The hard-headed businessman may plan an economic empire, with penthouse offices. The failures can always leap from the 13th floor of any office building. Yet not all failures result in violent disavowal. There are some socially approved strategies for meeting with failure. Those failing in medicine can try for dentistry; those failing at the Met can become pop singers; those failing in the chorus line can become strippers.

Numerically, these are trivial. I am concerned about the vastness of the impending failures in the near future. With the economy rapidly destroying old identities by making jobs obsolete and rapid changes in urban residential patterns, resulting from dramatic changes in building strategies and requiring immense modifications of old living arrangements, it seems to me that we are on the verge of separating our society into the visibly successful and the invisible failures. We will couple this, I think, with strategies for localizing various forms of violent behavior.

Given the connections ecological studies imply between class, area, and family, and the implications this has for opportunity for the education and training which makes sense in the modern world, I think we are going to create an enormous pattern of ghettoes for our failures. Our failures may be of a variety of sorts, but they will be mostly economic and social in character. Those with inadequate incomes will find residence in restricted areas of the metropolitan area. These areas will have minimal education, medical, and police services. During the period of transition, before areas achieve a final definition by the public, there will be moments in which certain residents will make claims for better schools, better services in general. These claims will fade and pass.

Two processes are already at work to achieve these ends. First, in the areas for the dispossessed, those who achieve a modicum of success are induced to migrate—and they do. Those who could provide leadership leave. Second, those residing in these areas have no real spokesmen. Public welfare workers and probation officers, for example, do not support them vis-à-vis the state or county. Indeed, they are officers of and paid for by the "greater community." As demographic changes send more and more voters to the periphery, the political value of these pockets of disenchantment decreases until they will have no spokesman except for the alderman whose ward encompasses them. Those citizens with economic establishments in these areas are more and more likely to live elsewhere. In short, ecological isolation wards are already being established.

From time to time, those who live out their lives in these concentrations of violent behavior will be in contact with those in the "nice" areas. At times, the "nice folk" will go slumming, and encounter considerable violence. On other occasions, the contact will be at the instigation of the displaced. We must recall the selective process will not be simply on the dimension of "intelligence," but on the social dimension of "failure." From time to time, then, leaders will emerge who cannot escape since they will have been completely submerged in the pattern of economic and social depravity characteristic of the area. Gangs will likely operate in a situation of a quasi-guerilla war, wreaking havoc if not vengeance upon those with power and status. Since these contacts will be violent ones, the nice people will be induced to return violence for violence.

Individuals from the "nice society" will not direct personal violence against selected individuals. Rather, the police structure will be justified in violent reactions. For the most part, these incidents will be "contained" and unnoticed. When, on occasion, they are brought into public view, they will be justified on the grounds that the victims are deserving of their fate. After all, if a people in a state which denies capital punishment can invest a police officer with the decision to kill a youngster violating a speed law, they can justify other types of violence as long as the recipient of it is seen as "deserving" the violence.

Of course, part of my argument depends upon the premise that contemporary assumptions of individual worth will largely be negated. I think this is precisely what is now occurring. The privacy of the individual and his personal integrity are now being assaulted on a variety of fronts. Social scientists are in the vanguard of this assault. We lie to our subjects and, through various schemes, misrepresent our studies and invade the privacy of the individual. Subliminal stimuli are obvious examples of an assault on the psyche of an individual. Recent experiments have indicated new and, in a sense, exciting ways to invade the individual's private world. The study demonstrating how people may be persuaded to change their minds by presenting arguments in a situation distracting the person from the point of the argument lends weight to the possibility of real control by outside agencies. Our studies seem to sanction the manipulation of what were once private and personal processes. The premises of "1984" will emerge. With the technological advances in snooping—the devices for eavesdropping, telescopic lenses permitting a camera to cross considerable distances, and the like—no individual is certain any more that his personal and private life is not publicly available for scrutiny. With judicial acceptance of the post office "scanning" mail, with the Attorney General pleading for the legalization of wiretapping and other invasions of the person, we can scarcely conclude that the process is not now underway. With the advent of scientific knowledge about how to use the data now obtainable by surreptitious means to control the outcome of interaction, the stage for "1984" seems to be set.

I also envisage the extension of violence into an area until recently quite peaceful, namely, national politics. At this writing, Senator Goldwater appears to have sufficient delegate strength to get the Republican nomination on the first ballot. He may be induced to make certain "moderate" utterances in order to legitimize support by "Liberal Republicans"; or he may not. In any event, he will have gone far in establishing the argument that the voting public must be given "a clear choice" between an obvious conservative and an obvious liberal. Whether that would or would not be possible with the present arrangement of political leaders, the implication of his argument is quite clear. He is calling for a polarization of political sentiment, around the greatest political prize we have to offer. Many people of both parties seem to agree on this point.

As views get polarized, the differences (by definition) become more and more distinct. As our politics now stand, both major parties are hodge-podges of compromise. There are conservatives in both groups, and liberals in both. In neither group can an extreme point of view dominate. If political thinking does indeed get to be polarized, we will find it easier for extreme points of view to dominate both parties.

Some research indicates that the intensity by which one holds a point of view is a U-shaped function of the belief held. This implies, at least to me, that the polarization of political thinking will necessarily be accompanied by increased intensity of conviction. It implies, moreover, an increased disappointment at the loss of an important election.

Given our cultural commitment to violence, one inference must be that our political decisions will be increasingly marked by violence. Physical violence will occur to alter voting patterns. Voters will be intimidated and reprisals will occur. Voting machines probably will be destroyed to prevent either a count or a recount of opposition votes. Voting places will be attacked and, in general, candidates and their supporters will be subject to various kinds of assault.

Should this occur, some political victor will be able to use our scientific knowledge to induce "harmony" and to "restore order." There are, of course, some existing premises implying a national community even now. Few localities are able to make significant decisions. National industries need scarcely take local interests into account; many decisions already occur on the basis of national interests. Both mass media of communication and recent political events have tended to remove the consequences of regional and local history. During a period of reconstruction, the victor would have these forces going in his behalf.

At that time, the population could be convinced that our culture is too violent in character, and that this violence is disruptive of an orderly life. The nice people living in what is now suburbia, yearning to have the predictable life success should bring, will find the argument overwhelming. The failures will find the wastebaskets called "slums" already existing and waiting for them. Then the gulf between the successes and the failures will widen and major forms of communication between them will become inoperative. Controlled by the use of scientific knowledge of human behavior, the nice people will be unaware of what happens to the failures. According to an old sociological law, "out of sight, out of mind." The deprived will be ignored; for, as another sociological law asserts, "ignorance is bliss."

Of course, projections of this kind are not the consequence of logical necessity. They are "possible," and concerned people can concertedly work to prevent their occurrence. Just as "ecological areas" can be redefined as "de facto segregation," so can other sociological findings be redefined by the society which generated the original study. In particular, I think, those of us who study social problems have a unique set of responsibilities to the society of which we are a part.

If we can have any faith in psychometrics at all, we must admit that there are a class of *aments* properly labelled *idiots*. Because of their constitutional deficiencies, we do not expect them to contribute to the solution of social problems. We expect them neither to study problems, propose courses of action, nor engage in action programs. It seems to me, then, that those of us who have knowledge about our society, especially if we are aware of processes which we find threatening to that part of society we would prefer to perpetuate, must engage in social action. For if we do not so engage ourselves, we take the social role of the idiot.

The previous generation of social scientists pushed a value-free orientation to the point of inquiry being value-less. If we continue this ignorance of values, we can hasten the sort of processes I think are now underway. But by becoming a part of the world, we may change their direction or otherwise contribute to man's appreciation of man as human being. With effort, and by taking some risks, we may prevent the emergence of my dire predictions. But if we fail—"KAPOW"—right in the collective kisser.

The following article is an excerpt from a full case study that was reported in Progressive Architecture, entitled, "Urban Planning and Urban Revolt." The editors would like to point out that the Green and Cheney work that is quoted is a journalistic and impressionistic account of urban unrest. "Diary" is being republished here so that the reader can view this important phenomena in a sociological framework. It is hoped that in this new intellectual setting, these skillfully written observations can be carefully studied.

The many dynamics that can be found in a riot or riot-like situation are recorded in this work: the highly charged feeling that is generated in the progression of events; the changing roles; and the possibility of a communications breakdown. One can also observe from this quick account the effect of rumor in a highly urbanized setting.

XX

The Diary of a Riot*

NEW HAVEN, CONNECTICUT
Saturday, August 19, 1967:

5:55 P.M.—The white owner of Tony's Snack Bar on Congress Avenue, in the predominantly Negro section called the Hill, shoots Julio Diaz, a Puerto Rican, as crowds mill around outside.

6:30 P.M.—Reports reach police headquarters that small gangs of youths are running up and down Congress Avenue smashing store windows.

7:30 P.M.—Fairly large crowds—demonstrators and by-standers —plus police, begin to accumulate around the headquarters of the Hill Parents Association (HPA), a neighborhood organization. Everyone is jumpy, and HPA leaders try to calm them

---

* Reprinted through the courtesy of *Progressive Architecture*, January, 1968.

Editor's note: This poignant "blow-by-blow" account of the August, 1967, disturbance in New Haven, Conn., has been compiled by Associate Editor Peter M. Green and Assistant Editor Ruth H. Cheney.

down. The leaders talk with police and help try to pull back the more militant demonstrators. Scattered incidents of looting are reported.

8:30 P.M.—About 20 young Negroes, yelling and laughing but unarmed, approach a large group of policemen. The two groups yell back and forth at each other. The police then drop seven or eight canisters of tear gas in front of the Negroes, who retreat back down the street, now clearly angry at the unexpected police move.

Soon violence erupts a few blocks away on Washington Avenue. Fred Harris, President of HPA, goes there with police and succeeds in halting the trouble. But Harris reports to a friend that he was clubbed in the chest with a rifle butt and shot at. He says, "I've had it helping the police. I'm losing my own guys in helping, and then the cops go after me. You can't do nothing. They deserve whatever's going to happen. There's no talking or reasoning with them."

Harris, in these first few hours, asks the city for 100 brooms and two sanitation trucks, and promises to clean up the broken glass on the street in a few hours—providing that no more police are sent in. Neighborhood feeling is still optimistic that the few demonstrators can be controlled. Police are viewed as antagonists.

The city sends the trucks and brooms, but the police do not let them through their barricades. Mayor Richard C. Lee calls in the state police.

9:00 P.M.—A loud crash near Congress Avenue; seconds later, the entire front of Ciociola Clothing Store erupts in flames. Police ring firemen to protect them from thrown objects.

9:30 P.M.—Yelling, clapping, fire-bombing, singing, fist-throwing packs of angry young black men roam the streets of New Haven, the most model of modern major "urban renewal" cities.

Rampaging youths attack a free-lance photographer angling for a better shot of two burning buildings—a small department store and a tenement in the Hill, a bare half-mile from Yale.

Mayor Lee, dubbed "King Richard the Little-Hearted" by some Negroes, receives news that the trouble has spread to the city's three other low-income sections: Newhallville, Fair Haven, and Dixwell. All are integrated, but predominantly Negro and Puerto Rican.

One, the Dixwell section adjacent to Yale, has been a major focus of urban renewal programs during the past 10 years; the

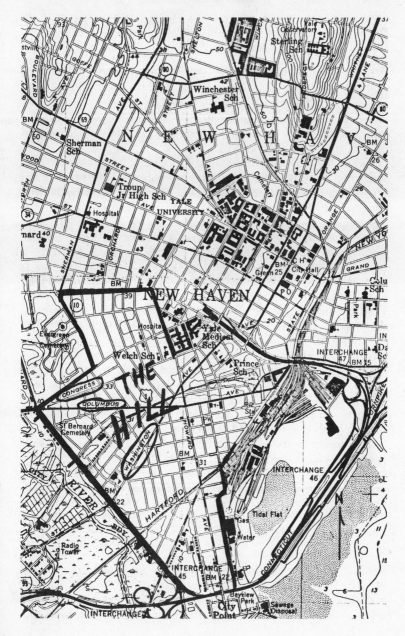

other three are still in the planning stage. Lee says: "I seriously thought that something like this wouldn't happen here . . . although I would never leave the city during summer." He calls the National Guard.

10:00 P.M.—Police Chief Francis McManus drives through the Hill urging people to go home. He is answered with obscenities. Well-prepared police (New Haven is one of the few cities to equip local police with Mace spray cans, a chemical inducing temporary paralysis) continue to put up barricades around the main areas of violence.

Sightseers arrive. White vigilante groups converge on Hill residents. In most reported instances, police try to break them up. A white citizen marches down Congress Avenue with a shotgun. He tells the police: "I'll help you kill the niggers."

Later, as *The New Haven Register* noted, "a sense of numb fear, helplessness, and defiance could be felt on the sidewalks throughout the smoke-filled area Saturday night." Many residents, mainly women and children, flee the Hill, an area that is currently under study for urban renewal in the office of architect Louis I. Kahn. A young white woman is seen sitting in her white Ford holding the back of her bleeding head. She is driven to the nearby Yale-New Haven Medical Center by the police.

11:00 P.M.—As the night wears on, the tempo of violence increases in some areas and continues to spread. Rampaging gangs break windows, throw fire-bombs, and attack reporters. About 350 policemen are on duty, attempting to break up groups with tear gas and Mace. The main office of the Elm Haven low-income housing project in the Dixwell section is broken into. All the white-owned stores in the section are "hit."

The action in the Hill is stalled for awhile as everyone waits for Fred Harris and his aide, Ronald Johnson, to come back from downtown. Police stand on one side of the street, facing Negro men on the other; there is occasional shouting and mutual provocation. Harris finally returns, angry and disappointed. Action begins again. A serious fire is reported in the Dwight section, next to the Hill.

SUNDAY

Early Morning—Harris is sprayed with Mace and arrested just after he helps a crippled woman in a wheelchair out of a burning building. Police begin making wholesale arrests in the Hill section. Scattered reports of looting come in from Dixwell.

In the Hill, the air hangs heavy with tear gas, smoke, and a stifling humidity. People's eyes fill with tears.

A small army of police, wearing powder-blue riot helmets and equipped with shotguns, carbines, and automatic weapons, scours the panicked city for troublemakers. Some of the police wear gas masks, others handle dogs. Small supply trucks stand ready to provide more ammunition and tear-gas bombs. Nearly all residents are openly hostile or indifferent to the police—even those who disapprove of the rioters.

10:30 A.M.—Traffic on Congress Avenue, the most widely publicized area of violence, is jammed solid with sightseers. Police with drawn rifles are stationed along the avenue.

1:00 P.M.—Mayor Lee meets with HPA leaders, representatives from the Redevelopment Agency, the clergy, and Community Progress, Inc., the New Haven anti-poverty agency. The Mayor agrees to give HPA leaders the names of people in jail, to have the police keep their shotguns out of sight in the trunks of their cars, to pull back some of the police in order to cut down the visible force that apparently antagonizes Hill residents, to put four Negro policemen (selected by HPA because of their rapport with the community) in charge of the police in the Hill, and to allow Fred Harris and other Hill leaders to work with these policemen in cooling things off.

As they leave this meeting, HPA leaders witness the arrival of the state police. Wondering now about the mayor's sincerity in the meeting they have just left, they return to the Hill to see if the Negro policemen arrive. They don't. Police shotguns are bared on Congress Avenue. HPA decides it will now be impossible to stop or control the violence.

4:00 P.M.—Groups of teen-agers and young men begin to form again on Congress Avenue. Mayor Lee reacts strongly—some think too strongly—when he calls in 225 state police and imposes an 8 P.M. curfew on the entire city.

Lee, no longer surprised that violence has come to New Haven, says: "There are no outside influences involved in the ferment; what happened here is part of urban America, 1967. It can happen regardless of the city or state, anywhere in the nation."

6:00 P.M.—Lee announces a state of emergency. State police cars with four or five men, followed by city patrol cars with an equal number of local police, prowl through the four hardest hit sections. Later, many describe this show of mass force by the city as uncalled for, and a further incitement to already angered area residents. A National Guard unit of 250 men stands ready for action at the Fire Department Training Center. Meanwhile, white sightseers are being "pelted" by Negroes in the Hill.

8:30-11:00 P.M.—Half-a-dozen fires are set, several automobiles are put to the torch. As police converge on one area, violence erupts in another. Spotlights flash against buildings; police warn people to stay away from their windows. Fear and rumors spread. Platoons of police march down the streets. Armored tracked vehicles appear.

Sometimes, incidents occur simultaneously in different areas. On the other side of the city, in fabled Wooster Square, Negroes in Farnum Court (a pre-Lee, low-income housing project separated by Interstate Route I-91 from the rest of Wooster Square) invade grocery stores, smashing windows and looting. Incidents are reported in the sparkling new business district; a jewelry store and a clothing store are looted on Chapel St. Even in Westville, an affluent white neighborhood, vandals and looters break into a jewelry store.

The city rents 50 rooms at the newly opened Park Plaza Hotel —a showplace of downtown renewal—for police and officials working overtime. Police patrols rush from one incident to another in scattered neighborhoods as complaints of violence pour in from all over the city. Newspaper photographs later show that many young white citizens are arrested, along with the Negroes and Puerto Ricans. Many are vigilantes; some are demonstrators. A woman shouts frantically from a second-floor window; a dozen police run up to get her, bring her down, and put her in the wagon with other prisoners. Some claim she is beaten by police.

At some locations, a carnival atmosphere prevails, as determined looting begins. Negro and white looters help themselves and each other to liquor and food. Photographs show smiling children not older than 9 or 10 helping themselves, parents, and friends.

In an interview with P/A, one young Negro told how he had been away from New Haven on Saturday, and returned on Sunday not knowing about the curfew. He claims he saw several policemen beating the heads of two youths against a brick wall in the Dixwell section. No one else was on the street, so he stopped his car and went over to find out what was going on.

He is a city worker, and showed the police his ID card. They refused to look at it. To mask their own identity, they wore no shields. When the Negro began taking down their license plate number, the police took him and the two victims to jail.

When P/A questioned this same man about newspaper reports and the word of city officials that "not a single shot had been fired by the police," he replied, "Bull."

Elsewhere, Lee paces the floor in his map-lined basement command post, tears filling his eyes, asking, "Why? Why? Why?"

HPA headquarters discovers that its telephone line is broken.

MONDAY

9:00 A.M.—Fred Harris and Ronald Johnson request Mayor Lee to remove police and barricades from the Hill, and to lift the 8 P.M. curfew. The Mayor refuses.

10:00 A.M.—Lee, called by some Negroes the "Great White Father," holds a series of talks with city officials. He grants interviews to three television networks, which question him largely on New Haven's national image as a model city. Lee believes that there are ". . . no organized efforts or organized group" behind the "disturbances."

12:30 P.M.—Lee explains to a large group of HPA representatives and other community leaders that he has no control over the state police, that it was his decision to put them on the alert, but that it was a local police decision actually to call them into riot areas. Community groups now wonder whether the situation has passed from municipal to police control.

They feel the Mayor is under enormous pressure from many other groups besides their own, and that these other groups are pressuring for precisely the opposite of what they feel is needed —less police action. One misunderstanding they clarify is that many Puerto Ricans do not understand what "curfew" means and are being arrested for violating it.

Officials state that "the disturbances have taken on a different light, with many more vicious and violent acts aimed at policemen and firemen."

2:00 P.M.—Amid persistent rumors that the entire Hill will be burned down on Monday night by its inhabitants, hundreds of women and children seek help from HPA in leaving the area. Many leave on their own.

HPA asks Yale University for the use of its vacant dormitories to house fleeing Hill residents. After conferring with university officials, Sam Chauncey, President Brewster's top aide, gives Yale's final answer—no. Harris contacts the Connecticut Bus Company, and hundreds of families are sent to the suburbs for the next two nights. Other families seek shelter at the nearby Connecticut Mental Health Center.

Harris says that no one has control in the riot areas. "The guys that are supposed to be in charge look like they're the worst racists around."

6 P.M.-2 A.M.—Violence starts earlier than on preceding evenings. Fire-bombs ignite buildings in Wooster Square, hallmark of New Haven renewal programs; the Dwight area, which is fully integrated; the Yale University area; downtown; and in Fair Haven, a low-income area; and again in Dixwell. The Hill is relatively quiet. Many incidents of violence occur in and around the Elm Haven housing project in Dixwell, for the third straight night.

Police, patrolling in small groups, are working 16- and 20-hour shifts.

A meeting of New Haven's 40 Negro leaders is held at the Zion Lutheran Evangelical Church. They proclaim that their meeting "puts the white community on notice that from now on it must work exclusively with our unified black leadership." They draw up a manifesto calling for an apology from the police for brutality.

Police rigidly enforce the curfew only in black and Puerto Rican neighborhoods. Gangs of white men gather in some troubled areas; not all of them are dispersed by police.

HPA discovers that the electric power in their headquarters has been turned off.

TUESDAY

12:00 P.M.—After a conference with police officials, Mayor Lee announces that the curfew will not be lifted today. He states that the ". . . incidents were not racially motivated: they are wanton acts of violence and disregard for the law."

Fred Harris says, "Something meaningful had better happen soon. Things are getting out of control. There is no trust in Lee or the police. I don't know how it will be established. There's no dialogue between the black community and downtown."

He says he thinks the situation would be helped if the police would get ". . . all their rifles out from under the noses" of the rioters, and remove dogs and tear gas. These things are bitterly resented, he states.

Lee comments: "I wish there were some way of getting across to the people in the neighborhoods involved that the police and fire departments represent law and order, and are the first line of defense for all the people."

Residents of Congress Avenue feel that removal of the curfew and most of the police would bring things back to normal more quickly than any other measure.

A Negro walks over to a policeman with a rifle and asks him why he has it, since an agreement was made with Mayor Lee that rifles would be withdrawn. The cop answers, "It's not loaded, boy, but it can be loaded in a second." (In New Haven, the police call adult Negroes "boy," as in the South.)

2:00-6:00 P.M.—Isolated and sporadic incidents of looting and fire-bombing occur during daylight hours. Police begin patrolling at 3 P.M.

It is estimated that insured losses in the town will total close to $1 million; uninsured and incalculable losses will boost the final total to several million dollars. One incalculable loss is that business in downtown stores is way down, due to suburban shoppers' reluctance to drive into New Haven along the only existing routes, which go straight through the heart of the riot areas that ring the downtown district.

7:00 P.M.—More families from low-income areas are bused out to the suburbs. About 650 city and state police again penetrate all riot areas, armed with rifles, shotguns, riot guns, gas masks, riot sticks, and Mace. Everyone is ordered off the streets. Those who refuse are arrested.

Again, persistent rumors spread that the Hill is going to be burned down during the night. Hundreds of whites and Negroes leave New Haven for the suburbs after warnings by HPA. "They told us to leave," says a young woman, "because there might be violence tonight. . . . I don't have any faith in the police."

8:00 P.M.-1:00 A.M.—A man is arrested for carrying a bull-horn after the curfew. Residents in the Hill and Dixwell monitor police calls with stolen receivers.

A Negro woman says, "I think the violence should stop, especially by the police. The violence of the people is only against property; the violence of the police is against people."

Police spirits rise when they are given a free hand to make

wholesale arrests and seal off Dixwell, Hill, Fair Haven, and Newhallville areas.

Most areas are quieter throughout the night. A policeman says, "They know we aren't kidding this time." Groups of police are seen laughing and joking among themselves.

WEDNESDAY

7:00 A.M.—Police discover a cache of 16 Molotov cocktails on the roof of an apartment building on Congress Avenue in the Hill section. As they attempt to leave, they find the door locked. They break the lock and leave amid a stream of obscenities, threats, and curses hurled from nearby apartments. Several people are arrested as they tack up posters announcing an evening meeting in the Hill.

10:00 A.M.—After meeting with police officials, Lee announces that, despite a relatively quiet night on Tuesday, the curfew will go into effect at 11 P.M. "The state police will remain in New Haven until such time as [local police] are satisfied that the elements of unrest have ebbed to the point where the local police can assume complete jurisdiction. . . . Police patrols will remain on a saturation basis, however."

Insurance field-men enter riot-torn areas for the first time. Whole blocks of storefronts are covered with plywood. Glass is strewn over the streets in the Wooster Square and Dwight neighborhoods, in addition to the four main areas.

8:00 P.M.—The mood on Congress Avenue in the Hill has changed from heated tension to light-heartedness. Children play horseshoes in the neighborhood-built park.

Police are less visible, although guns are still drawn.

Several fire-bombings occur in Hill and Dixwell. Many whites are arrested for carrying knives and violating the curfew.

THURSDAY

On Thursday, August 24, although heavy police patrols continue for another day, Mayor Lee lifts the curfew. The state of emergency that has lasted 111 hours since Saturday night is over. New Haven breathes a collective sigh of relief, and most people go about their normal business.

That night, Lee attends the biennial celebration that takes place when he is nominated for yet another term—this time an unprecedented eighth.

That rumor is a universal phenomenon, as are many of the techniques used in its diffusion, is discussed in this pertinent study of collective behavior in present day Nationalist China.

XXI

The Phantom Slasher of Taipei: Mass Hysteria in a Non-Western Society*

NORMAN JACOBS

I

DESCRIPTION AND ANALYSIS OF INSTANCES of mass hysteria have been well documented in western societies.[1] Do such affairs also occur in non-western societies and, if so, are they different from their counterparts in western society?

While I was teaching in a university in the city of Taipei, Taiwan (Formosa), China, during 1956 an instance of mass hysteria occurred. Although, for political reasons (to be discussed subsequently), I was prevented from interviewing the major participants and gaining the necessary information upon which to make a personal, psychological field study as, for example, Johnson was able to do, I was able to follow the affair carefully in the daily press and to discuss the affair in sociologically meaningful terms with many individuals in the local society. Consequently, although I concede obvious limitations, I feel the case study adds something to the general literature on mass hysteria.

The narrative of the case study follows the affair as it was unfolded in the local press. I have selected three newspapers, each of which is representative of a particular point of view (to be discussed in the conclusions); namely, the (Chinese) ver-

* Reprinted from *Social Problems*, Vol. 12, No. 3, Winter, 1965, 318-328, by permission of the author and the Society for the Study of Social Problems.

nacular *China Daily News,* the English language daily *China Post* (both published in Taipei) and the Hong Kong *Tiger Standard,* an English language daily printed in that city but distributed among non- and anti-Communist Chinese throughout Southeast Asia, including Taiwan.

II

The incident made the press on May 4, 1956 with a simultaneous announcement in many Taipei city newspapers that a number of children of both sexes from the ages of six months to eight years had been the victims of slashings with what appeared to be razor blades or similar weapons. The slashings apparently had been occurring for a considerable time prior to the May 4 report date, although the newspapers did not agree as to precisely when the first case had happened. Claims ran from as late as about a month previous[2] to as early as three months previous[3] to May.

The newspapers clearly differentiated between those cases based upon hard evidence and those cases which had been reported without supporting evidence, although the number of alleged authenticated cases varied from a low of eight[4] to a high of more than thirty.[5] The slashings were reported as having occurred to various parts of the body and under varied social circumstances. For example, one account described a youngster being cut on the left arm while he was being carried, Chinese style, on the back of his mother.[6] Another report described the infliction of two cuts on the back of a hand and one on a shin while one child was waiting to board a public bus.[7] A gash across the back (interestingly, reported elsewhere as across the head[8]) was stated to have occurred to a child playing in the vicinity of its home. Even a case of castration, resulting in the death of a victim, was recorded.[9]

There was general agreement that the attacks had originated in a single district in the northwest sector of the city, although one newspaper claimed that incidents also had occurred elsewhere in the city further to the east and south.[10] There was some disagreement as to who first reported the incidents to the proper authorities, i.e., the municipal police. Although the papers agreed that attending physicians in hospitals and eager reporters were the primary source, it was disputed whether or not any of the parents of the victims had added to that knowledge. One paper suggested that parents would not readily report a case since this would be an admission of carelessness on their part, with a consequent loss of prestige (or "face"), a serious matter in China.[11]

Opinions varied on the reasons for the slashings. In addition to the obvious possibility of sex sadism, certain unusual reasons were advanced: for example, to facilitate theft by drawing the attention of potential victims away from the true motive of the offenders, since loss of bracelets and other articles were reported to have accompanied the infliction of the cuts in several cases.[12] One source offered the possibility of blood ritual. This apparently was prompted by the old local superstition that the drawing of blood from a given number of small children brings good luck.[13]

Who had committed such foul deeds? Neither the parents, the victims, or anyone else for that matter, was able to offer any positive identification. The interviewed talked vaguely of a "teenager with a sad smile" and "suspicious looking men and women" as having been "around" at the time of the incidents. But since all the victims under questioning admitted that they had not actually seen the slashings being inflicted, they were unable to state positively who the slashers might be.

By the morning of May 3, the police considered the affair serious enough to investigate it formally, which brought the matter to the attention of the press. Hence the first newspaper report on May 4. The Director of the Taipei City Police Bureau charged the Director of the (Northwest) Sub Police Bureau to carry out a thorough investigation and to make every effort to apprehend the unknown slasher or slashers. The effort was to be pursued around the clock, an approach, the press noted, that was very unusual for such a matter. The police requested the press to caution the populace not to believe unfounded stories and to reserve judgment until an official report could be made on the case. Nevertheless the press reported that the people were aroused over the incidents and that children were being kept indoors as a self-protective measure.[14]

On the morning of May 3 the police found a "hysterical" woman with knife in hand wandering about in the center of the city. When the police questioned her, she claimed that she carried the knife for self-defense because she recently had been in an argument with a pedicab driver who had threatened to beat her. Her neighbors corroborated her story. However, since the woman was an aboriginal Taiwanese from a tribe which, in the good old days before "pacification," had been noted for head-hunting and other strange ways that *might* conceivably have included blood ritual (which had been suggested as a possible motive for the slashings), the police held her for further questioning.[15]

The next day, May 4 (as recorded in the press on May 5), an incident was reported outside the northwest sector of the city. An eleven-year-old in the southern part of the city reported receiving a cut on his left arm without knowing how or when it had been inflicted. In addition, a two-year-old boy, the son of a farmer, living in a northern suburb of Taipei also was reported as cut in the leg while playing in the front of his house. Stories of widespread slashings at a number of girls' primary schools around the city were claimed, but the police could only authenticate one case. It was obvious that parents were becoming more and more nervous over the safety of their children. The smaller ones increasingly were being kept indoors, while those of school age were being accompanied to and from school by adults.[16] In consequence, the newspapers were asked by the Director of the Taipei Bureau of Education to record that he had sent an investigator to the various primary schools in the city who had reported that very few students were absent from class and that nervous parents should not believe rumors that the schools were being emptied of pupils and thus add to the hysteria by removing their youngsters from school.

The police became more active in the affair with the entrance of the *Provincial* (Taiwan) Department of Police, and especially of its Criminal Investigation Division (CID) into the case. These agencies appealed to the populace to remain calm, assuring the people that all the victims were being visited and questioned carefully and that a full report would be issued shortly. The police were visibly annoyed at what were referred to as "unfounded rumors and absurd stories" built upon the superstitions of ignorant people who were spreading ridiculous stories in the streets. The police chief himself called in the members of the press and demanded that they "clarify" the previous day's claim that some of the victims had died. But, when questioned, the chief refused to state officially that deaths had not occurred. Police service was increased with the dispatch of a number of plain-clothes detectives to market places, theaters, schools and other such places where numbers of people congregated and which conceivably might be tempting to the slashers,[17] and six mobile police jeeps were ordered out on a constant alert throughout the city.[18] The Taipei City Council discussed the incidents and passed a resolution to urge the harassed police authorities to "solve the mystery as soon as possible."

Two aspects of press reportage of this date are worth noting. First, the vernacular press referred to the affair as a "terror," but the English language press did not. The paper far removed from the location persisted in its claim that all victims had died, in spite of local press coverage to the contrary. Second, the pictures of the victims appeared for the first time on this date in the English language press, while the Chinese press had published portraits in its columns the previous day. And to sum the progress of the affair on this date, new incidents were being reported now throughout the city and even in the suburbs and various authorities up to the provincial level were becoming interested and involved in the affair.

May 5 (reported in the press on May 6) may be characterized as a day of government discussion, reports, and action. The Commissioner of the Provincial Police Department met with the mayor of Taipei. As a result of this meeting, the mayor appropriated Taiwan $10,000 (then approximately U.S. $250) as an extra fund for use of the city police to carry out its investigation.[19] The Chief Public Prosecutor of the Taiwan Supreme Court held a conference with the Taipei City Police Commissioner. It was decided at this meeting that the police would report all cases immediately to the Prosecutor's office for further investigation.[20] The chief of the city police, who had been engaging in an intensive inquiry of the affair for the previous few days, made public the results and conclusions of his study. He emphasized that he was aware of the necessity of investigating all reports of slashings as soon as possible and that his office was hard at work to this end. But after close examination and investigation, he could report that a number of alleged cases were due to accident, innocent misrepresentation or deliberate hoax. For example, it had been proven beyond doubt that the cuts of three of the children had been due to objects other than that of a razor; namely, a silver pin, a twig, and a tin plate respectively. That is, objects children were apt to be cut with while at play. He also pointed out that most of the wounds reported in this and in other cases were on exposed parts of the body, especially the hands, legs and faces, also to be expected of children at play. However, he did admit that there still were under investigation ten cases of alleged slashing for which no adequate explanation could be given at that time. Of the cases attributable to deliberate falsification, one example was the case reported on the previous day involving the seventeen-year-old male which proved to be an instance of a self-inflicted injury while resting an elbow on a piece of broken counter-glass. Rather than face a mother's admonition for carelessness, the youth, impressed by the affair, had reported the source as a razor slash. However, someone who had seen the cutting taking place, reported the facts to the police when he read the false account in the newspapers. (Presumably the police hoped that this would encourage similar reactions in the future.) It is interesting to note that although the tale obviously was false and the boy was fined for falsely reporting a crime, the newspapers, along with the official version, once again presented an account of the lad explaining how he had suffered the injury, with appropriate photos!

An obvious case of innocent misrepresentation due to hyper-suggestibility was the case of a middle-aged man who had reported to a doctor that he had been slashed by a male of about thirty years who was carrying a mysterious black bag. The doctor who examined the wound concluded that it had been caused by some dull object and could not possibly have been the result of a razor slash. Under intensive questioning the victim admitted he did not know how or when the cut had been made but he had assumed it had been by a razor because of all the talk going around about razor slashings. Also reported was a case of a boy who had been reported by a neighbor as having been slashed by a razor while at play. When the police arrived, the mother of the boy supported the razor story of the neighbor, embellishing it considerably. When, upon intensive examination, it was proven that the boy inadvertently had been cut by a waste can, the mother was forced to admit the hoax. The Commissioner also described the case of an old man who came to a doctor with a bleeding wrist. The man was advised by the doctor to report the case to the police after the man casually mentioned that a suspicious stranger had touched him about the time that the bleeding began. The police, upon examination of the victim, concluded that the wound in fact was an old one that had probably opened by innocently scratching it. Finally, a report was made on a waste collector who had been dragging a cart containing a crying girl. The people in the vicinity immediately assumed that she was a razor victim and the man was the much sought after slasher. They hauled the man, the girl, and the cart to the police station. The man readily admitted that the child was not his and that he had picked her off the street, but he vehemently denied that he had done any bodily harm to her. It appeared that the police once again had lost a potential suspect in the razor case, although it had obtained custody of a kidnapper who might otherwise have escaped the law but for the public's concern over the razor affair.

In concluding his report, the Commissioner promised continued vigilance, but in the light of his disclosures, he suggested that the people were being unnecessarily frightened by baseless stories and he cautioned them about spreading false rumors which might add to the hysteria.[21] He hinted that certain mysterious rascals might be behind all these happenings, perhaps even Communist agents who might be trying to create an atmosphere of confusion and uneasiness in connection with the (Communist) May Day season. Yes, it was true that ten suspects were taken into custody that very day, including some who were found to have razors on their person, but it was wrong to assume that any necessary connection existed between this fact and the still unsolved razor cases.[22] Nor, he stated, were these arrests to be connected with the case of an eleven-year-old girl in the city of Keelung (*forty* miles north of Taipei) who had been reported as being wounded in both legs soon after a man who had been hanging around her for a while passed her very closely. It was true that the man had been described in great detail, but the case was still being investigated.[23] It is to be noted that in spite of a decline in the number of reported cases on this date and the official police report, the local English language press for the first time referred to the affair as a "terror," following the vernacular press in this description by one day.[24]

On May 6 (as presented in the press on May 7), the police were able to report that an alleged cutting on May 3 had been disproved as the result of an on-the-spot investigation. The victim, an eight-year-old girl, in fact had only suffered a bruise on her ankle which she had acquired while playing with an iron

rod in her father's shop.[25] The publication of this and other investigations, however, apparently had not dampened down the
affair. Three new cases claimed to have taken place in Keelung
on May 5 were brought to the attention of the police officially
on this date. Three youngsters individually asserted that they
had received razor-blade cuts from assailants unknown while
on the way home from school. The police, as usual, promised
to check out the reports.[26]

A bizarre incident occurred on May 6. Sometime during the
very early hours of the morning, a pedicab driver who resided
in the northwest district of the city where the first incidents had
been reported noticed, upon arising to go to work, a sheet of
Chinese style letter paper fastened to the wall of his house.
Scrawled in blue ink across the top of the paper was a representation of the pirate skull and crossbones with a legend (in
Chinese) "A notice—a good knife." The driver's first reaction to
the paper was that it was part of a practical joke played on him
by his granddaughter. But upon learning of her innocence, he
reported the incident to the police, thinking, perhaps, that it
was connected with the razor incidents he had been hearing so
much about. The police refused comment, pending investigation.[27]

The Chief Prosecutor of the Taiwan Supreme Court continued
to be active in the case. He ordered ". . . the police and court
authorities *all over the island* (my italics) to conduct an extensive and thorough investigation into alleged cuts inflicted by
unknown assailants on young victims from unknown motives."
Though the incidents seem to have been more or less contained
to certain areas of Taipei and Keelung, news and rumors of incidents apparently had brought "terror" to communities all over
the island. Hence, the Chief Prosecutor urged the people not to
get excited, and to await the presentation of the facts by the
authorities.[28]

In the May 8 press, it was reported that the Chief of the
Criminal Investigation Section and the Deputy Director of the
Taiwan Police Department had held a news conference the previous evening at nine o'clock. The two officials stated that, as of
that date, only twenty-one authenticated reports of slashings had
occurred, regardless of the recording of "scores" of slashings in
the press. Of these twenty-one cases, seventeen had originated
in Taipei, one in a suburb (Peitou), and three in Keelung. Of

all these, five already had been proven false (and so reported in the press) and seven more now could be reported as false. Of the remaining, one individual could not be located and doubt was expressed as to his very existence let alone his slashing and eight still were under investigation. Of the seven cases that now could be reported as false, the alleged razor assaults, as in other cases, had been found to be the result of such causes as cuts while playing or self-inflicted wounds on glass.[29] As the lesson to be learned from the affair, the officials suggested that the press be more responsible in its reporting so as not to create "uneasiness" in the minds of the public. The officers revealed that the seventeen-year-old youth who had previously been reported on had been turned over to the Taipei District Court for prosecution according to that section of the criminal code which applied to the spreading of rumors under conditions of martial law, a very serious offense in wartime Taiwan.[30]

The vernacular press of May 9 described a May 8 police report of a second strange note incident. It seems that the day before (May 7) the police were attracted by a crowd reading a note attached to the fence of a house. The note contained a drawing of three pairs of knives, each pair in the shape of a cross, followed by a signature and an address in the city of Keelung. The police became aware of the presence of a suspicious looking youth loitering about. In the course of interviewing the boy, his family, and his teacher, the police discovered that the boy's handwriting matched that on the note. Confronted with this evidence, the youth broke down and admitted his crime, stating that he had written the note in order to avenge an insult. The name on the note was that of an acquaintance with whom he had quarreled while playing cards and whom he hoped to involve with the authorities through the latter's interest in the razor cases. It may be noted that all the May 8 press coverage was that of the vernacular press alone.[31]

No further mention of the affair occurred in any newspaper until May 12. On that date it was reported that a spokesman of the Provincial Police Department had announced the previous day that, as a result of a thorough investigation, all twenty-one cases reported officially to the police had been proven false. Of these cases, five were innocent false reports, seven were self-inflicted cuts, eight were due to cuts other than razors, and one was a complete fantasy. The self-inflicted wounds and the wounds due to other than razor cuts were described in detail. For example, the baby who was wounded while waiting for a bus, in one of the cases described previously, turned out only to have been scratched by an umbrella. It seems that it was raining the day of the incident and many umbrella peddlers were out attempting to sell their products at the bus depot, and one such peddler inadvertently had scratched the baby. The police hoped the people would finally realize that the spreading of unconfirmed rumors was an unnecessary disturbance of the peace. And so once again they appealed to the populace to cooperate and not spread sensationalism.[32]

But on the very day that the razor blade case was being clarified by the police and the affair was being (hopefully) officially closed, the most sensational incident occurred. Significantly it was not reported in the press until May 13 and May 14. On May 11 a mysterious "woman in red" was arrested in the now familiar northwest part of the city. The woman was accused of cutting a nine-month-old baby girl with a razor blade. It seems that a mother and baby in arms were on the street. Suddenly the baby cried. Looking about, the mother noticed that a girl in a red jacket was immediately behind her. The mother cried out, whereupon the strange girl fled, and the mother chased after her. People began to collect about the mother to help her in pursuit of the girl. As the pursuers and the pursued passed a theater, a bystander shouted "get the girl in red." The girl, aware of her tell-tale red coat, dropped it on the road and attempted to lose herself in the crowd as the swelling mob continued to chase her. The girl discarded a small packet which was retrieved by someone in the crowd in pursuit. Eventually a police officer joined the pursuers and succeeded in stopping the girl and taking her to a police station. The retrieved parcel was found to contain a razor blade. The milling crowd which had followed the policeman and the girl to the police station became increasingly angry and threatening, as the investigation proceeded inside. Upon being interrogated the girl stated that, as it was about to rain, she had opened her umbrella, and in so doing, had innocently caught hold of the baby's sleeve. When the mother suddenly cried out, the girl panicked and fled. Fearing that she might be taken for the razor slasher, she decided to throw away the parcel with the potentially incriminating razor blade. The mother, however, contradicted the girl's testimony. She claimed that the girl had held her daughter's arm and did not release it until she (the girl) was conscious of the fact that the mother was aware of her presence. The mother denied that it was raining at the time of the incident. She further stated that the girl had the umbrella and a basket in one hand and another object in the other hand. The girl denied that she had taken the baby's hand, but stated that she only was trying to loosen the iron frame of the umbrella which had caught in the baby's sleeve. The girl further stated that she had told this to the woman when the latter had turned around and discovered her near the child. Then why did the girl run if she was innocent? Because she became fearful of the woman and did not know what to do. What of the razor blade? She was a seamstress and used it in her work. She reminded the police that the razor blade had been discovered wrapped in a piece of paper and hence could not have been used as claimed. Her only "weapons" were her long finger nails and her umbrella, which, as she had already stated, probably had accidentally caused the cuts. Then why had so many believed that she had slashed the baby? She didn't know. A doctor who was called in to examine the child stated that the wound could not have been made by a razor, and that the umbrella story seemed reasonable to him. The girl was released and the irate mob was dispersed. As the papers had wisely noted in their account, the incident had nearly revived the "terror" but fortunately the fever was short-lived.[33]

I am aware of only one further reference in the press after the "lady in red" incident. On May 17, the local English language press carried a report that the *National* Control Parliament (the "watchdog" branch of the Chinese national government) had decided to review the razor affair. Other than the statement that this august body considered the incident "serious" no rationale for the discussion was provided. To the best of my knowledge no report was ever issued of the discussion.[34] In any case after this date, the phantom razor-slasher(s) never appeared again on the streets of Taipei, or anywhere else in Taiwan for that matter.

III

The Taipei affair exhibited most of the salient characteristics which have been noted in mass hysteria case studies in western societies, namely:

(1) The action profile may be characterized by (a) a rapid and steady buildup in the number of reported incidents and a growing intensity in the uncritical and hyper-suggestible nature of the cases reported; (b) a period of stock-taking and sober analysis with a consequent decline in reported incidents; but then (c) a spectacular but short-lived revival of interest; and (d) finally, a rapid cessation of the affair.

(2) The major participants predominantly were drawn from those elements in the society most susceptible to hyper-suggestibility, namely, the lower income, lower educated stratum, and within that stratum, women and children.

(3) The motives of those who claimed to be the affair's victims were varied. Some individuals were well aware that their claims were conscious hoaxes, born of a desire for personal publicity or for personal advantage. But others were the victims of innocent error or psychogenic hallucination, brought about by the heightened suggestibility during the affair.

(4) The victims' descriptions of the actual infliction of the wounds under alleged mysterious circumstances by allegedly mysterious individuals acting out of allegedly mysterious motives were both a product of, and helped further to intensify, the hyper-suggestibility and mass hysteria so characteristic of the affair. The assimilation of all potentially related incidents (that is, any cutting, no matter how innocent) that occurred during the time of the affair into the mainstream of the affair may also be noted.

(5) Rumor-mongering which played such a vital part in spreading the hysteria and heightening suggestibility was carried on (a) by gossiping in centers where people, especially women and children of low income, low education stratum of the society were apt to congregate; that is, at the market, at the entertainment centers, and at public transportation centers, which spread the affair *within confined areas* of the city, especially in the northwest part of the city, and (b) by the mass media—in this society the newspapers—which were instrumental in spreading the affair *from one confined area to another;* successively to the whole city of Taipei, to the suburbs, to other cities on the island, and ultimately to a Chinese community outside the island. Significantly, as elsewhere, face-to-face rumor spreading was a negligible factor in maintaining the affair.

(6) The press reflected the respective social affiliations of the

various audiences, although exceptions can be noted; as for example, in the initial May 4 reportage. The vernacular press which catered to the low-income groups was the most sensational, was most apt to describe the mythical incidents, was the most complete in its coverage (both in details and in number of incidents recorded), and was the most prone to carry contradictory reports without later retraction. The local (Taipei) English language press whose audience primarily was either the well-educated Chinese or the foreigner was the most conservative in reporting the number and character of the incidents and was more apt to report the details of the police investigations and the appeal of the authorities for calm and the dampening down of rumor-mongering. Finally the English language Hong Kong newspaper, removed from the immediate situation, reported fewer incidents and fewer details over a briefer time span, but made up for this deficiency by presenting the most sensational, garbled and far-fetched version of the affair.

(7) The affair continued after, and in spite of, all the efforts that responsible members of the society were taking to discount the rumors and alleged incidents. The final incident of the "lady in red" occurred even after the newspapers obviously had been "persuaded" by the authorities to play down or even ignore reporting new incidents. It can be said then that any affair of this sort, since it is one of mass hysteria which may be exaggerated further by an existing situation of social and psychological insecurity (to be discussed below) has to spend itself regardless of the weight of so-called counter forces of reason operative in the society at that time.

IV

Apart from these general social and psychological characteristics, the specific patterning of this affair is a reflection of the specific societal and cultural influences of the Taiwanese situation which may be contrasted with those influences bearing on other mass hysteria affairs in other social or cultural contexts.

(1) The low-income and poorly-educated stratum of Taiwan society, is made up almost exclusively of the local-born Chinese, or as they have come to be termed, the Taiwanese. During the Japanese occupation of Taiwan (1895-1945) the Taiwanese, as

colonial subjects, were given for the most part disproportionately less access to the privileges of the society, especially to the organs of political, economic, and social security. The situation, although it improved especially for the well-educated and for the rising generation, with the return of the island to Chinese control in 1945, did not drastically change the status and prerogatives of the uneducated, lower-income mass of adult Taiwanese. This was especially true for the urban Taiwanese, when (with the Communist take over of the mainland in 1949) over a million essentially urban refugees swarmed into Taiwan and claimed the desirable positions in the society. However, even before that date, in 1947, a particularly ugly incident occurred between mainlanders and local-born, which made it clear to the latter that the former were willing and able to enforce their desires on the Taiwanese, if need be through violence. In brief, within Taiwan society, the insecurities and frustrations of the locals, especially the urban, lower-stratum locals, make them especially susceptible to mass hysteria. And not surprisingly, it is in the area(s) of the cities of Taipai and Keelung in which these individuals predominantly reside that most of the incidents originated.

(2) Taiwan in 1956 was the nominal seat of the government-in-exile of the (Nationalist) Republic of China (as it has been since 1949). Technically, this government has been at war with the mainland (Communist) People's Republic of China since 1949. Consequently, the island of Taiwan simultaneously is both a staging area for a claimed potential Nationalist reconquest of the mainland and also is under constant siege in defense against any invasion threat from the mainland. Through the various media of mass communication the people are continually reminded of these two possibilities. The government, in order to stir the people (especially the mass of locals who have no *obvious* loyalty to a program of reconquest of the mainland, whatever their feelings about a local Communist conquest) to greater economic and political support of the present regime and its goals, has from time to time circulated reports of impending action in both directions, keeping the people's nerves on edge in the international political game of confrontation. Such a campaign of mass mobilization existed at the time of the Taipei incident.

(3) Significantly, although the government is ever conscious

of the value of maintaining a state of heightened suggestibility among the populace to serve its own political purposes, it simultaneously recognized the need to control mass-hysteria movements that might get out of its control or be used by its enemy across the Taiwan Strait toward its destruction. For obviously if the population is placed perpetually in a psychological state in which it is tuned to receiving and accepting incidents of heightened suggestibility from official Nationalist sources, it also might be tuned potentially to receiving and accepting Communist inspired mass hysteria campaigns. But perhaps even more dangerous would be incidents which, although ostensibly innocent of Communist influence, still functioned to destroy confidence in the regime's ability to overcome enemies and to continue to provide security to the island. I believe this hypothesis helps to explain the unusual interest and concentration of the political apparatus and its counterintelligence agencies in the affair, as noted in the case study. Significantly the unusual interest was to some degree self-defeating, as it only incited the imagination of the uninformed that something was up to which they were not privy.

(4) The razors and other cutting objects which played the key role in this incident form part of the general Chinese pattern of using physical mutilation as outlet for frustration and aggression. Various acts of mutilation are periodically reported in the press, as for example, the incident of a young lover who threw nitric acid in the face of the girl who spurned him.[35] The association of blood-letting with certain local, aboriginal (pre-Chinese) inhabitants has been mentioned in the body of the study.

V

In summation and conclusion I would say that at least this incident seems to bear out the hypothesis that the basic circumstances which give rise to mass hysteria movements and the trends that they take appear to be similar regardless of the specific social and cultural contexts in which they occur. However, the social and cultural contexts are most important in defining why they take place when they do and where they do, and the specific media which they use.

NOTES

1. See, for example, Donald M. Johnson, "The Phantom Anesthetist of Matoon: A Field Study of Mass Hysteria," *The Journal of Abnormal and Social Psychology*, XL (April 1945), pp. 175-186.

2. China Post, May 4, 1956.

3. China Daily News, May 4, 1956.

4. *Ibid.*

5. China Post, May 4, 1956.

6. China Daily News and China Post, May 4, 1956.

7. Hong Kong Standard, May 4, 1956.

8. China Post, May 4, 1956.

9. China Post and Hong Kong Standard, May 4, 1956.

10. China Post, May 4, 1956.

11. Compare the China Post and the China Daily News, May 4, 1956.

12. China Post, May 4, 1956.

13. Hong Kong Standard and China Post, May 4, 1956.

14. China Daily News, May 4, 1956.

15. *Ibid.*

16. China Post, May 5, 1956.

17. China Daily News, May 5, 1956.

18. Hong Kong Standard, May 5, 1956.

19. China Post, May 6, 1956.

20. China Daily News, May 6, 1956.

21. *Ibid.*

22. China Post, May 6, 1956.

23. China Daily News, May 6, 1956.

24. China Post, May 6, 1956.

25. China Post, May 7, 1956.

26. *Ibid.*

27. China Daily News, May 7, 1956.

28. China Post, May 7, 1956.

29. China Daily News, May 8, 1956.

30. China Post, May 8, 1956; Hong Kong Standard, May 9, 1956.

31. China Daily News, May 9, 1956.

32. China Daily News, May 12, 1956; China Post, May 12, 1956.

33. China Daily News, May 13, 1956; China Post, May 13 and May 14, 1956.

34. China Post, May 17, 1956.

35. China Post, March 24, 1956.

The author, a one-time noted Broadway producer, relates here an aspect of his partnership with the celebrated actor-producer, Orson Welles, during the time of the latter's unique radio dramatization in the Autumn of 1938. It was this radio program which virtually paralyzed the emotions of countless numbers of listeners. Picture, if you will, an invasion of our planet by a superior form of life from Mars. How will you, your family, and others react? See what happened when others believed this situation to exist. Collective behavior in its most dramatic form is the subject of "The Men from Mars."

XXII

The Men from Mars*

JOHN HOUSEMAN

III

ON SUNDAY, OCTOBER 30, AT 8:00 P.M., E.S.T., in a studio littered with coffee cartons and sandwich paper, Orson [Welles] swallowed a second container of pineapple juice, put on his earphones, raised his long white fingers and threw the cue for the Mercury theme—the Tchaikovsky Piano Concerto in B Flat Minor #1. After the music dipped, there were routine introductions—then the announcement that a dramatization of H. G. Wells' famous novel, *The War of the Worlds*, was about to be performed. Around 8:01 Orson began to speak, as follows:

WELLES

We know now that in the early years of the twentieth century this world was being watched closely by intelligences greater than man's and yet as mortal as his own. We know now that as human beings busied themselves about their various concerns they were scrutinized and studied, perhaps almost as narrowly

as a man with a microscope might scrutinize the transient crea-
tures that swarm and multiply in a drop of water. With infinite
complacence people went to and fro over the earth about their
little affairs, serene in the assurance of their dominion over this
small spinning fragment of solar driftwood which by chance or
design man has inherited out of the dark mystery of Time and
Space. Yet across an immense ethereal gulf minds that are to our
minds as ours are to the beasts in the jungle, intellects vast,
cool, and unsympathetic regarded this earth with envious eyes
and slowly and surely drew their plans against us. In the thirty-
ninth year of the twentieth century came the great disillusion-
ment.

It was near the end of October. Business was better. The war
scare was over. More men were back at work. Sales were pick-
ing up. On this particular evening, October 30, the Crossley
service estimated that thirty-two million people were listening
in on their radios. . . .

Neatly, without perceptible transition, he was followed on the
air by an anonymous announcer caught in a routine bulletin:

ANNOUNCER

. . . for the next twenty-four hours not much change in temperature. A slight atmospheric disturbance of undetermined origin
is reported over Nova Scotia, causing a low pressure area to
move down rather rapidly over the northeastern states, bringing
a forecast of rain, accompanied by winds of light gale force.
Maximum temperature 66; minimum 48. This weather report
comes to you from the Government Weather Bureau. . . . We
now take you to the Meridian Room in the Hotel Park Plaza in
downtown New York, where you will be entertained by the
music of Ramon Raquello and his orchestra.

At which cue, Bernard Herrmann led the massed men of the
CBS house orchestra in a thunderous rendition of "La Cumparsita." The entire hoax might well have exploded there and
then—but for the fact that hardly anyone was listening. They
were being entertained by Charlie McCarthy—then at the height
of his success.

The Crossley census, taken about a week before the broadcast,
had given us 3.6 per cent of the listening audience to Edgar
Bergen's 34.7 per cent. What the Crossley Institute (that hire-
ling of the advertising agencies) deliberately ignored, was the

healthy American habit of dial-twisting. On that particular evening, Edgar Bergen in the person of Charlie McCarthy temporarily left the air about 8:12 P.M., E.S.T., yielding place to a new and not very popular singer. At that point, and during the following minutes, a large number of listeners started twisting their dials in search of other entertainment. Many of them turned to us—and when they did, they stayed put! For by this time the mysterious meteorite had fallen at Grovers Mill in New Jersey, the Martians had begun to show their foul leathery heads above the ground, and the New Jersey State Police were racing to the spot. Within a few minutes people all over the United States were praying, crying, fleeing frantically to escape death from the Martians. Some remembered to rescue loved ones, others telephoned farewells or warnings, hurried to inform neighbors, sought information from newspapers or radio stations, summoned ambulances and police cars.

The reaction was strongest at points nearest the tragedy—in Newark, New Jersey, in a single block, more than twenty families rushed out of their houses with wet handkerchiefs and towels over their faces. Some began moving household furniture. Police switchboards were flooded with calls inquiring, "Shall I close my windows?" "Have the police any extra gas masks?" Police found one family waiting in the yard with wet cloths on faces contorted with hysteria. As one woman reported later:

> I was terribly frightened. I wanted to pack and take my child in my arms, gather up my friends and get in the car and just go north as far as we could. But what I did was just sit by one window, praying, listening, and scared stiff, and my husband by the other sniffling and looking out to see if people were running. . . .

In New York hundreds of people on Riverside Drive left their homes ready for flight. Bus terminals were crowded. A woman calling up the Dixie Bus Terminal for information said impatiently, "Hurry please, the world is coming to an end and I have a lot to do."

In the parlor churches of Harlem evening service became "end of the world" prayer meetings. Many turned to God in that moment:

I held a crucifix in my hand and prayed while looking out of my open window for falling meteors. . . . When the monsters were wading across the Hudson River and coming into New York, I wanted to run up on my roof to see what they looked like, but I couldn't leave my radio while it was telling me of their whereabouts.

Aunt Grace began to pray with Uncle Henry. Lily got sick to her stomach. I don't know what I did exactly but I know I prayed harder and more earnestly than ever before. Just as soon as we were convinced that this thing was real, how petty all things on this earth seemed; how soon we put our trust in God!

The panic moved upstate. One man called up the Mt. Vernon Police Headquarters to find out "where the forty policemen were killed." Another took time out to philosophize:

I thought the whole human race was going to be wiped out— that seemed more important than the fact that we were going to die. It seemed awful that everything that had been worked on for years was going to be lost forever.

In Rhode Island weeping and hysterical women swamped the switchboard of the Providence *Journal* for details of the massacre, and officials of the electric light company received a score of calls urging them to turn off all lights so that the city would be safe from the enemy. The Boston *Globe* received a call from one woman "who could see the fire." A man in Pittsburgh hurried home in the midst of the broadcast and found his wife in the bathroom, a bottle of poison in her hand, screaming, "I'd rather die this way than that." In Minneapolis a woman ran into church screaming, "New York destroyed this is the end of the world. You might as well go home to die I just heard it on the radio."

The Kansas City Bureau of the AP received inquiries about the "meteors" from Los Angeles, Salt Lake City, Beaumont, Texas, and St. Joseph, Missouri. In San Francisco the general impression of listeners seemed to be that an overwhelming force had invaded the United States from the air—was in process of destroying New York and threatening to move westward. "My God," roared an inquirer into a telephone, "where can I volunteer my services, we've got to stop this awful thing!"

As far south as Birmingham, Alabama, people gathered in churches and prayed. On the campus of a Southeastern college—

> The girls in the sorority houses and dormitories huddled around their radios trembling and weeping in each other's arms. They separated themselves from their friends only to take their turn at the telephones to make long distance calls to their parents, saying goodbye for what they thought might be the last time. . . .

There are hundreds of such bits of testimony, gathered from coast to coast.

IV

At least one book* and quite a pile of sociological literature has appeared on the subject of "The Invasion from Mars." Many theories have been put forward to explain the "tidal wave" of panic that swept the nation. I know of two factors that largely contributed to the broadcast's extraordinarily violent effect. First, its historical timing. It came within thirty-five days of the Munich crisis. For weeks, the American people had been hanging on their radios, getting most of their news no longer from the press, but over the air. A new technique of "on-the-spot" reporting had been developed and eagerly accepted by an anxious and news-hungry world. The Mercury Theater on the Air by faithfully copying every detail of the new technique—including its imperfections—found an already enervated audience ready to accept its wildest fantasies. The second factor was the show's sheer technical brilliance. To this day it is impossible to sit in a room and hear the scratched, worn, off-the-air recording of the broadcast, without feeling in the back of your neck some slight draft left over from that great wind of terror that swept the nation. Even with the element of credibility totally removed it remains a surprisingly frightening show.

Radio drama was taken seriously in the thirties—before the Quiz and the Giveaway became the lords of the air. In the work of such directors as Reis, Corwin, Fickett, Welles, Robson, Spier, and Oboler there was an eager, excited drive to get the most out of this new, all too rapidly freezing medium. But what happened that Sunday, up on the twentieth floor of the CBS

---

* *The Invasion from Mars* by Hadley Cantril, Princeton University Press, from which many of the above quotations were taken.

building was something quite special. Beginning around two, when the show started to take shape under Orson's hands, a strange fever seemed to invade the studio—part childish mischief, part professional zeal.

First to feel it were the actors. I remember Frank Readick (who played the part of Carl Phillips, the network's special reporter) going down to the record library and digging up the Morrison recording of the explosion of the Hindenburg at Lakehurst. This is a classic reportage—one of those wonderful, unpredictable accidents of eyewitness description. The broadcaster is casually describing a routine landing of the giant gasbag. Suddenly he sees something. A flash of flame! An instant later the whole thing explodes. It takes him time—a full second—to react at all. Then seconds more of sputtering ejaculations before he can make the adjustment between brain and tongue. He starts to describe the terrible things he sees—the writhing human figures twisting and squirming as they fall from the white burning wreckage. He stops, fumbles, vomits, then quickly continues. Readick played the record to himself, over and over. Then, recreating the emotion in his own terms, he described the Martian meteorite as he saw it lying inert and harmless in a field at Grovers Mill, lit up by the headlights of a hundred cars—the coppery cylinder suddenly opening, revealing the leathery tentacles and the terrible pale-eyed faces of the Martians within. As they begin to emerge he freezes, unable to translate his vision into words; he fumbles, retches—and then after a second continues.

A few moments later Carl Phillips lay dead, tumbling over the microphone in his fall—one of the first victims of the Martian Ray. There followed a moment of absolute silence—an eternity of waiting. Then, without warning, the network's emergency fill-in was heard—somewhere in a quiet studio, a piano, close on mike, playing "Clair de Lune," soft and sweet as honey, for many seconds, while the fate of the universe hung in the balance. Finally it was interrupted by the manly reassuring voice of Brigadier General Montgomery Smith, Commander of the New Jersey State Militia, speaking from Trenton, and placing "the counties of Mercer and Middlesex as far west as Princeton and east to Jamesburg" under Martial Law! Tension—release—then renewed tension. For soon after that came an eyewitness account of the fatal battle of the Watchung Hills; and then, once again, that lone piano was heard—now a symbol of terror, shattering the dead air with its ominous tinkle. As it played, on and on, its effect became increasingly sinister—a thin band of suspense stretched almost beyond endurance.

That piano was the neatest trick of the show—a fine specimen of the theatrical "retard," boldly conceived and exploited to the full. It was one of the many devices with which Welles succeeded in compelling, not merely the attention, but also the belief of his invisible audience. "The War of the Worlds" was a magic act, one of the world's greatest, and Orson was just the man to bring it off.

For Welles is at heart a magician whose particular talent lies not so much in his creative imagination (which is considerable) as in his proven ability to stretch the familiar elements of theatrical effect far beyond their normal point of tension. For this reason his productions require more elaborate preparation and more perfect execution than most. At that—like all complicated magic tricks—they remain, till the last moment, in a state of precarious balance. When they come off, they give—by virtue of their unusually high intensity—an impression of great brilliance and power; when they fail—when something in their balance goes wrong or the original structure proves to have been unsound—they provoke, among their audience, a particularly violent reaction of unease and revulsion. Welles' flops are louder than other men's. The Mars broadcast was one of his unqualified successes.

Among the columnists and public figures who discussed the affair during the next few days (some praising us for the public service we had rendered, some condemning us as sinister scoundrels) the most general reaction was one of amazement at the "incredible stupidity" and "gullibility" of the American public, who had accepted as real, in this single broadcast, incidents which in actual fact would have taken days or even weeks to occur. "Nothing about the broadcast," wrote Dorothy Thompson with her usual aplomb, "was in the least credible." She was wrong. The first few minutes of our broadcast were, in point of fact, strictly realistic in time and perfectly credible, though somewhat boring, in content. Herein lay the great tensile strength of the show; it was the structural device that made the whole illusion possible. And it could have been carried off in no other medium than radio.

Our actual broadcasting time, from the first mention of the

meteorites to the fall of New York City, was less than forty minutes. During that time men traveled long distances, large bodies of troops were mobilized, cabinet meetings were held, savage battles fought on land and in the air. And millions of people accepted it—emotionally if not logically.

There is nothing so very strange about that. Most of us do the same thing, to some degree, most days of our lives—every time we look at a movie or listen to a broadcast. Not even the realistic theater observes the literal unities; motion pictures and, particularly, radio (where neither place nor time exists save in the imagination of the listener) have no difficulty in getting their audiences to accept the telescoped reality of dramatic time. Our special hazard lay in the fact that we purported to be, not a play, but reality. In order to take advantage of the accepted convention, we had to slide swiftly and imperceptibly out of the "real" time of a news report into the "dramatic" time of a fictional broadcast. Once that was achieved—without losing the audience's attention or arousing their skepticism, if they could be sufficiently absorbed and bewitched not to notice the transition—then, we felt, there was no extreme of fantasy through which they would not follow us. We were keenly aware of our problem; we found what we believed was the key to its solution. And if, that night, the American public proved "gullible," it was because enormous pains and a great deal of thought had been spent to make it so.

In the script, "The War of the Worlds" started extremely slowly—dull meteorological and astronomical bulletins alternating with musical interludes. These were followed by a colorless scientific interview and still another stretch of dance music. These first few minutes of routine broadcasting "within the existing standards of judgment of the listener" were intended to lull (or maybe bore) the audience into a false security and to furnish a solid base of realistic time from which to accelerate later. Orson, in making over the show, extended this slow movement far beyond our original conception. "La Cumparsita," rendered by "Ramon Raquello, from the Meridian Room of the Hotel Park Plaza in downtown New York," had been thought of as running only a few seconds; "Bobby Millette playing 'Stardust' from the Hotel Martinet in Brooklyn," even less. At rehearsal Orson stretched both these numbers to what seemed to us, in the control room, an almost unbearable length. We ob-

jected. The interview in the Princeton Observatory—the clock-
work ticking monotonously overhead, the woolly-minded professor mumbling vague replies to the reporters' uninformed
questions—this, too, he dragged out to a point of tedium. Over
our protests, lines were restored that had been cut at earlier re-
hearsals. We cried there would not be a listener left. Welles
stretched them out even longer.

He was right. His sense of tempo, that night, was infallible.
When the flashed news of the cylinder's landing finally came—
almost fifteen minutes after the beginning of a fairly dull show
—he was able suddenly to spiral his action to a speed as wild
and reckless as its base was solid. The appearance of the Martians; their first treacherous act; the death of Carl Phillips; the
arrival of the militia; the battle of the Watchung Hills; the destruction of New Jersey—all these were telescoped into a space
of twelve minutes without overstretching the listeners' emotional
credulity. The broadcast, by then, had its own reality, the reality of emotionally felt time and space.

V

At the height of the crisis, around 8:31, the Secretary of the
Interior came on the air with an exhortation to the American
people. His words, as you read them now, ten years later, have
a Voltairean ring. (They were admirably spoken—in a voice just
faintly reminiscent of the President's—by a young man named
Kenneth Delmar, who has since grown rich and famous as
Senator Claghorn.)

THE SECRETARY

Citizens of the nation: I shall not try to conceal the gravity of
the situation that confronts the country, nor the concern of your
Government in protecting the lives and property of its people.
However, I wish to impress upon you—private citizens and public officials, all of you—the urgent need of calm and resourceful
action. Fortunately, this formidable enemy is still confined to a
comparatively small area, and we may place our faith in the
military forces to keep them there. In the meantime placing our
trust in God, we must continue the performance of our duties,
each and every one of us, so that we may confront this destructive adversary with a nation united, courageous, and consecrated
to the preservation of human supremacy on this earth. I thank
you.

Toward the end of this speech (*circa* 8:32 E.S.T.), Davidson Taylor, supervisor of the broadcast for the Columbia Broadcasting System, received a phone call in the control room, creased his lips, and hurriedly left the studio. By the time he returned, a few moments later—pale as death—clouds of heavy smoke were rising from Newark, New Jersey, and the Martians, tall as skyscrapers, were astride the Pulaski Highway preparatory to wading the Hudson River. To us in the studio the show seemed to be progressing splendidly—how splendidly Davidson Taylor had just learned outside. For several minutes now, a kind of madness had seemed to be sweeping the continent—somehow connected with our show. The CBS switchboards had been swamped into uselessness but from outside sources vague rumors were coming in of deaths and suicides and panic injuries.

Taylor had requests to interrupt the show immediately with an explanatory station-announcement. By now the Martians were across the Hudson and gas was blanketing the city. The end was near. We were less than a minute from the Station Break. The organ was allowed to swirl out under the slackening fingers of its failing organist and Ray Collins, superb as the "last announcer," choked heroically to death on the roof of Broadcasting Building. The boats were all whistling for a while as the last of the refugees perished in New York Harbor. Finally, as they died away, an amateur shortwave operator was heard, from heaven knows where, weakly reaching out for human companionship across the empty world:

> 2X2L Calling CQ
> 2X2L Calling CQ
> 2X2L Calling CQ
> Isn't there anyone on the air?
> Isn't there anyone?

Five seconds of absolute silence. Then, shattering the reality of World's End—the Announcer's voice was heard, suave and bright:

ANNOUNCER

You are listening to the CBS presentation of Orson Welles and the Mercury Theater on the Air in an original dramatization of *The War of the Worlds,* by H. G. Wells. The performance will continue after a brief intermission.

The second part of the show was extremely well written and most sensitively played—but nobody heard it. It recounted the adventures of a lone survivor, with interesting observations on the nature of human society; it described the eventual death of the Martian Invaders, slain—"after all man's defenses had failed by the humblest thing that God in his wisdom had put upon this earth"—by bacteriological action; it told of the rebuilding of a brave new world. After a stirring musical finale. Welles, in his own person, delivered a charming informal little speech about Halloween, which it happened to be.

I remember, during the playing of the final theme, the phone starting to ring in the control room and a shrill voice through the receiver announcing itself as belonging to the mayor of some Midwestern city, one of the big ones. He is screaming for Welles. Choking with fury, he reports mobs in the streets of his city, women and children huddled in the churches, violence and looting. If, as he now learns, the whole thing is nothing but a crummy joke—then he, personally, is coming up to New York to punch the author of it on the nose! Orson hangs up quickly. For we are off the air now and the studio door bursts open. The following hours are a nightmare. The building is suddenly full of people and dark blue uniforms. We are hurried out of the studio, downstairs, into a back office. Here we sit incommunicado while network employees are busily collecting, destroying, or locking up all scripts and records of the broadcast. Then the press is let loose upon us, ravening for horror. How many deaths have *we* heard of? (Implying they know of thousands.) What do *we* know of the fatal stampede in a Jersey hall? (Implying it is one of many.) What traffic deaths? (The ditches must be choked with corpses.) The suicides? (Haven't you heard about the one on Riverside Drive?) It is all quite vague in my memory and quite terrible.

Hours later, instead of arresting us, they let us out a back way. We scurry down to the theater like hunted animals to their hole. It is surprising to see life going on as usual in the midnight streets, cars stopping for traffic, people walking. At the Mercury the company is still stoically rehearsing—falling downstairs and singing the "Carmagnole." Welles goes up on stage, where photographers, lying in wait, catch him with his eyes raised up to heaven, his arms outstretched in an attitude of crucifixion. Thus he appeared in a tabloid that morning over the caption, "I Didn't

Know What I Was Doing!" The *New York Times* quoted him as saying, "I don't think we will choose anything like this again."

We were on the front page for two days. Having had to bow to radio as a news source during the Munich crisis, the press was now only too eager to expose the perilous irresponsibilities of the new medium. Orson was their whipping boy. They quizzed and badgered him. Condemnatory editorials were delivered by our press-clipping bureau in bushel baskets. There was talk, for a while, of criminal action.

Then gradually, after about two weeks, the excitement subsided. By then it had been discovered that the casualties were not as numerous or as serious as had at first been supposed. One young woman had fallen and broken her arm running downstairs. Later the Federal Communications Commission held some hearings and passed some regulations. The Columbia Broadcasting System made a public apology. With that the official aspects of the incident were closed.

As to the Mercury—our new play, "Danton's Death," finally opened after five postponements. Not even our fantastic publicity was able to offset its generally unfavorable notices. On the other hand, that same week the Mecury Theater on the Air was signed up by Campbell Soups at a most lavish figure.

Of the suits that were brought against us—amounting to over three quarters of a million dollars for damages, injuries, miscarriages, and distresses of various kinds—none was substantiated or legally proved. We did settle one claim however, against the advice of our lawyers. It was the particularly affecting case of a man in Massachusetts, who wrote:

"I thought the best thing to do was to go away. So I took three dollars twenty-five cents out of my savings and bought a ticket. After I had gone sixty miles I knew it was a play. Now I don't have money left for the shoes I was saving up for. Will you please have someone send me a pair of black shoes size 9B!"

We did.

Written by one of the most prolific writers of 20th-century social thought, this article, though in edited form, clearly attempts to point out how any tendency on the part of a culture to strongly emphasize either "individualism" or "communism" is harmful to the interest of the common good. Sorokin asserts that only a constructive synthesis of both modes of thought can provide the way to peace and self-fulfillment. During his early years in his native Russia, this man enjoyed the dubious distinction of being considered the number one enemy by both tsarists and Communists.

XXIII

Reflections on the Mutual Convergence of the United States and the U.S.S.R.*

PITIRIM A. SOROKIN

1. THREE PROGNOSES Leaders of the West assure us that the future belongs to the capitalist ("free enterprise") type of society and culture. In contrast, leaders of the Communist nations confidently expect a Communist victory in the coming decades. Differing from both of these predictions I am inclined to think that if mankind avoids new world wars and can overcome today's grave emergencies, the dominant type of the emerging society and culture is likely to be neither capitalistic nor communistic, but a type *sui generis* which we can designate as an *integral type*. This type will be intermediary between the capitalist and Communist orders and ways of life. It is going to incorporate most of the positive values and to be free from the serious defects of each type. Moreover, the emerging integral order in its full development is not likely to be a mere eclectic mixture of the features of both types but a unified system of

* Reprinted, by permission of the publisher, from *The Basic Trends of Our Times*, pp. 78-89, copyright © 1964 by College and University Press, New Haven, Conn.

integral cultural values, social institutions, and of the integral type of personality essentially different from those of the capitalist and the Communist patterns. If mankind does not avoid new world wars and cannot mitigate today's grave emergencies, then its future becomes problematic and dark. Such in brief is my prognosis about the alternative future of mankind.

My main reasons for this prognosis are three: First, in their pure or extreme form, both the capitalist and the Communist orders are very defective and cannot meet the needs of a good, creative life for future mankind. Second, both orders are serviceable only under specific conditions for specific periods. In different conditions and periods both become disserviceable and therefore unneeded. Third, progressively both orders in the Western and the Soviet blocs of nations[1] for the last three decades have been increasingly losing their specific features and "borrowing" and incorporating in themselves each other's characteristics. In this sense, both types have been withering more and more and are becoming more and more similar to each other in their cultures, social institutions, systems of value, and ways of life. This means that both types, exemplified by the United States and Soviet Russia, have been increasingly converging to the intermediary type, different from communism and capitalism. This intermediary type, for the time being, represents an eclectic mixture of the characteristics of both orders. However, given the necessary time for its peaceful development, it eventually will grow into a unified integral social, cultural, and personal order in the human universe.

2. THE DECAY OF REAL CAPITALISM In this chapter I am not going to discuss in detail the first two reasons of my prognosis. For my purposes it suffices to say that if capitalism were able to meet successfully the urgent needs of contemporary humanity, it would not have decayed as it has in the leading capitalist countries and would not have met an increasing resistance to its development in so-called "backward countries." Any country, and mankind in general, rarely, if ever, discards any important value, or institution—be it political, economic, or other—as long as this value or institution renders a real service in meeting the urgent needs of a given society. If, in our case, the capitalist sociocultural order is increasingly abandoned even in the previously capitalist nations and replaced by the Communist, the Socialist, the welfare state, the guided democracy, the Fascist,

the Nazi, the "corporative," and other orders, this means that it has become increasingly unserviceable and obsolete. This conclusion becomes particularly evident in the cases of formerly capitalist countries like Germany, England, France, the United States, and most of the Western countries where the withering of capitalism had already begun at the end of the nineteenth century, was often initiated by the leaders of capitalism itself (especially by those who introduced "the corporation economy"), and has progressed from that time "naturally," immanently, gradually, without being overthrown by violent revolutions or by military coercion of foreign armies. At the present time, this withering of capitalism has already progressed so far that in all Euro-American countries, including the United States, the genuine, "full-blooded" capitalist or "free-enterprise" system of economy has become only a sector in the total economy of these countries and not always the major one. For the last few decades, especially since 1914, side by side with this "full-blooded" capitalist system, based upon "full-blooded" private property, there emerged and have grown "the corporation economy" and "the governmentally managed economy"—both essentially different from the capitalist system. And with some fluctuations, these two systems of economy have been replacing more and more the genuine capitalist economic order. To understand properly this last statement, one has to be reminded of the fact that "full-blooded," classical capitalism is based upon "full-blooded" private property, which means the right to possess, to use, to manage, and to dispose of the owned thing. In the governmentally managed economy, the officials are not the owners of the national property they control; the owner is the nation and the government is only the manager of the nation's property. Similarly, in the corporation economy the board of directors that manages it is not the owner of the total property of a big corporation; in some two-hundred of the biggest corporations in the United States, none of the directors owns even five per cent of the property of the corporation. The owners are tens and hundreds of thousands of holders of the shares of stocks of these corporations. An overwhelming majority of these owners neither manages nor disposes of the corporation's property. These functions are discharged by the board of directors of each corporation who, like the government officials, are not its owners. In the governmentally managed and the corporation economy we have a basic split of "full-blooded" property; those who own do not manage, those who manage do not own. This basic difference from the classical type of full ownership upon which the capitalist system was based makes the governmentally managed and the corporation economies fundamentally different from classical capitalism (with which—intentionally or not—the corporation economy is still mistakenly identified, especially by corporation bosses who speak of it as "free enterprise," or "the capitalist economy").

As in practically all Western countries in recent decades, governmentally managed and corporation economy have been systematically growing at the cost of "full-blooded" capitalism; and as this capitalism is already a minor sector in the total economy of the United States and of several other Western countries, this fact clearly testifies to the decay of the true capitalist system, as pointed out above.

3. THE SOCIAL LAW OF FLUCTUATION OF TOTALITARIANISM AND FREEDOM   In a somewhat different way, the same can be said of the totalitarian-Communist system of economy. By it is meant the system of economy in which private property is abolished; the total economy of the country is "nationalized" and in its entirety is managed by the government. It is "centralized," "planned" economy in which the government decides all matters concerning the production, the distribution, the exchange, and the consumption of economic goods. The Communist system is a mere variety of this totalitarian system of economy.

Under different governmental regimes and different ideologies this system of economy emerged long ago and has occurred many times in human history: in several periods of Ancient Egypt, especially in the Ptolemaic period; in Ancient Sparta and Lipara; in Rome, especially after 301 A.D.; in some periods of the Byzantine Empire; in Ancient Peru; in several periods in China, India, and many other countries—to mention but a few outstanding cases. It was initiated and introduced by all sorts of governments and under all kinds of "beautifying," "rationalizing," and "sanctifying" ideologies; by the Egyptian pharaohs, the Roman and Byzantine emperors, the Incas of Peru, the Chinese or European autocratic kings, the host of military conquerors, the religious authorities like the Jesuits in America and many monarchist, republican, democratic, military, Socialist, and Communist governments. No less diverse have been the "ideologies" that justified, supported, rationalized, and beautified this totalitarian system of economy and government; all sorts of ideologies—religious, moral, political, utilitarian, "nationalistic," "economic," "sociological," and others, beginning with the traditional Egyptian religious beliefs and cult of the Pharaoh as God and ending with the recent Communist, Socialist, Nazi, Fascist, Labor Party, Pentagon, welfare state, and many "dictatorial" ideologies—have performed this role.

This means that the Communist system of economy and ideology is only one of many varieties of the totalitarian systems of economy, ideology, and political regime. In diverse forms they have been predominant in the past and have frequently appeared in recent times.

The types of economies, governments, and ideologies of all countries are not something constant but continuously fluctuate between the poles of the totalitarian and the strictly free regimes of the *laissez passer, laissez faire* type with a minimum of government control of social life, relations, and behavior of the citizens. During a particular period the governmental control of the economic, political, and other sectors of social life of the citizens may increase and the respective systems of economy, government, and ideologies experience a totalitarian conversion (in various degrees); at another period in the same society the amount and severity of governmental regimentation may decrease and its economy, government, ideologies, and whole way of life undergo a process of detotalitarianization or reconversion toward a free economy, government, ideology, and way of life.

As a matter of fact today's sociology has even a generalized formula that satisfactorily accounts for the how, when, and why of these fluctuations. In a simplified form the formula runs as follows: Every time when in a given society there appears an important emergency in the form of war or threat of war, or great famine, or great economic depression, or devastating epidemic, or earthquake, or flood, or anarchy, unrest and revolution, or any other big emergency, the amount and severity of governmental regimentation invariably increase, and the society's economy, political regime, way of life, and ideologies experience a totalitarian conversion; and the greater the emergency the greater the totalitarian transformation. Conversely each time the important emergency of a society decreases, the amount and severity of its governmental regimentation begin to decrease and the society's economic, political, ideological, and cultural systems undergo a detotalitarian reconversion toward less regimented and freer ways of life; and the greater the decrease of the emergency, the greater the free reconversion. I can add to this that these fluctuations—or the totalitarian conversions and the detotalitarian reconversion to freedom—depend little upon the wishes of the governments involved and take place as regularly as do mercury fluctuations in thermometers in accordance with the factor of temperature.[2]

In the light of this "social uniformity" or "social law" it is comprehensible why governmental control of practically all areas of social life invariably increases with the outbreak of war or pestilence or earthquake or famine or social unrest or any other emergency. Among other things the uniformity accounts also for a regular and often very sharp totalitarian conversion of the "free, democratic" economy and government in times of war or other emergencies. Further on, the formula shows that various totalitarian transformations of the systems of economy, government, and ideologies are not something rare but on the contrary are quite frequent in the history of practically all nations.

Finally, this "social law" also explains my statement of why the Communist-totalitarian variety of economy, government, and the way of life cannot meet successfully the vital and creative needs of a good life, free from desperate emergencies, if tomorrow's mankind is destined to have such a good life. The Communist and other varieties of the totalitarian economy, government, and way of life are the children of emergency-parents. They are the dangerously strong "medicine" applied to counteract the desperate "emergency sickness." Under the conditions of this "sickness" they are sometimes (though not always) helpful in overcoming the "illness" and in recovering the normal "health" of the sick body-social. As soon as its health is improved, this "medicine" becomes unneeded, even harmful to the society. For this reason it is progressively abandoned and replaced by the "normal" regime of social, cultural, and personal life free from an excessive governmental regimentation and other totalitarian features. Hence, we have the detotalitarian reconversion that regularly takes place with the mitigation of emergency conditions, as indicated in the outlined "social law" or the "formula of the uniformity."

The conclusion of this analysis in regard to today's Communist, "the military" (Pentagon), "Nazi," "pseudo-democratic," and all sorts of other "dictatorial" varieties of the totalitarian order is as follows: If in the near future today's desperate emergencies (of cold and hot wars, of great social unrest, of extreme poverty in a large portion of mankind, of deadly radiation, of overpopulation, and others) are going to decline, the greater the recovery of mankind from these emergencies, the greater decline of totalitarianism is to be expected. If instead of a notable decline the great emergencies of our time are going to last or to increase for a long time, then the Communist and other varieties of totalitarianism are bound to grow for as long as the emergencies last or grow. Eventually the lasting emergencies with their totalitarian offsprings may lead to a fatal catastrophe of the human race and may terminate for a long time, if not forever, the creative history of Homo sapiens on this planet. Great lasting emergencies like a grave sickness increasingly undermine the healthy and creative vitality of the bodies-social; and, if not "cured" in time, they can harm it fatally beyond the point of recovery and eventually lead the gravely sick organisms of nations, or even of all mankind, to inglorious death or to the incurable chronic agony of "the uncreative life in death." If we assume that today's grave emergencies are going to be mitigated by "normal," "noncritical" ways and means, then all forms of contemporary totalitarianism are going to decline; if the emergencies are going to last or to increase, then the immediate future will bring victory to the Communist and other forms of totalitarianism. If, after their victory, their "dangerously strong medicine" does not cure the grave emergencies of our age, then chronic "life in death" looms as the destiny of the surviving, disillusioned and gravely sick, part of mankind.

4. MUTUAL CONVERGENCE OF THE UNITED STATES AND SOVIET RUSSIA Nobody can predict with certainty which of these alternatives will take place in the future. If mankind can avoid the catastrophe of a world war, then other emergencies can be mitigated or eliminated to a great extent. In these conditions the eventual decline of all forms of totalitarianism appears to be probable. If the emergency of such a war cannot be abolished, then there is no chance to eliminate other emergencies. In these conditions the temporary triumph of various forms of totalitarianism is to be expected. So far the international policies of the governments of both blocs of nations have been unsuccessful in

abolishing the threat of a new world war and in establishing lasting peace. And there is no guarantee these policies can abolish this emergency in the future. If our hopes in this matter were dependent entirely upon the policies of the existing governments, then the future of mankind would be dark and uncertain.

Fortunately for all of us, the course of human history is only partially dependent upon the policies of governments. In a much greater degree it is determined by the collective, anonymous forces of humanity—by the totality of actions and reactions of every human being, every human group, and, ultimately, of the whole of mankind. If the policies of governments contradict the course of history which these collective, anonymous forces consciously and unconsciously, in planned and unplanned, and in organized and unorganized forms endeavor to realize, then in due time such governmental policies are "cancelled" and replaced by the policies promoted by these collective forces. Under these conditions, often the governments themselves are "dismissed" and replaced—in an orderly or violent way—by governments that are willing and capable of realizing the demands of the collective forces of humanity or, if you prefer, of the forces of historical destiny or of guiding Providence.

The discordancy between the course of history required by the interests of mankind and the course of the governmental policies of the United States and Soviet Russia for the last forty years, and especially since the Armistice, gives a good example of this sort of historical situation. While the politicians of both countries have been feverishly carrying on the policies of mutual vituperation, enmity, cold and hot war; while they have been madly engaged in the armament race and in preparation for a suicidal world war; while both governments have been trying to discredit, to hurt and destroy each other by all means available; while for this purpose in their propaganda they have been extolling their own virtues and magnifying the vices of the other government and fantastically exaggerating the irreconcilability of the values and of the biological, social, and cultural differences between the two governments and the two nations; while the governments have been promoting this policy of war, the collective forces of both nations, of mankind, and of history have been engaged in a different kind of work and have been performing a task opposed to the policies of both governments, of their politicians, and of their "power-elites."

Instead of a magnification of the allegedly irreconcilable differences in the system of values, in social institutions, in culture and in the ways of life of both countries, these forces have been mitigating and decreasing these differences and making both countries more similar to each other in all these fields. Often silently but relentlessly, these collective forces have been progressively eliminating the irreconcilability of the values and the real interests of both nations and have been building a bridge for their peaceful coexistence and cooperation. Instead of separating both countries from each other, these forces have been converging them toward the intermediary type different from the pure capitalistic as well as from the extreme communistic type. Both countries have been increasingly borrowing and adopting the values, institutions, and cultural features of each other. This convergence has already progressed so far that at the present time both nations are much more similar to each other—socially, culturally, and in practical ways of life—than they were at the beginning of the Russian Revolution.[3]

The net result of this convergence is a progressive mitigation and elimination of practically all the justifiable reasons for continuing cold or hot wars, the mad armament race, and the policies of armed conflict. The convergence has already progressed so far that at the present time there is no justifiable reason for these policies and relationships between the two nations. If the belligerent policies continue and if they eventually result in a new world war, the only reasons for this sort of catastrophe will be the inexcusable stupidity, greediness, power-lust and poorly understood tribal interests of the governments, power-elites, and of "the brain-washed" masses of both countries. There is no certainty that these blind and irrational forces will not temporarily prevail in the future, but if such a catastrophe occurs, its reasons or motives cannot be qualified as justifiable, rational, and excusable.*

---

* Editors' Note

Professor Sorokin documents this thesis in detail in a lengthier statement found in his book, *Basic Trends of Our Times* (College and University Press, 1964). In Chapter III of that text he investigates the "trend of increasing similarity and mutual convergence of both countries toward a mixed intermediary type."

NOTES

1. In this article I limit my analysis to the Euro-American continent concentrating on the changes for the last forty years in the United States and Soviet Russia. In regard to China, where the Communist system is still largely in its first, coercive phase, I simply can state that, if the Chinese Communist order is given the peaceful conditions for its free development, in due time it also will experience a transformation essentially similar to that of Soviet Russia. The first phase of any violent revolution, and especially of the Communist revolution, is always predominantly destructive, coercive, and inhumanly cruel. Eventually, if the revolution is not suppressed, it passes from this destructive into an increasingly constructive phase. The predominantly destructive phase of the Russian Revolution is already over and it has now entered into its constructive phase (unfortunately interrupted by World War II and greatly hindered in its progress by the subsequent cold and hot wars), while the Chinese revolution is still at the end of its destructive phase and is just entering its constructive stage of development. See on these phases in the development of practically all great revolutions P. Sorokin, *Sociology of Revolution* (Philadelphia, 1924) and P. Sorokin, *Society, Culture and Personality* (New York, 1962), Ch. 31. A Spanish edition of this work is entitled *Sociedad, Cultura y Personalidad* (Madrid, 1960).

2. Compare for a detailed formula of this uniformity and for the vast body of evidence supporting it P. Sorokin, *Social and Cultural Dynamics* (New York, 1962), Vol. 3, Ch. 7; abridged, one-volume edition of the *Dynamics*, chs. 29-30; P. Sorokin, *Man and Society in Calamity* (New York: E. P. Dutton & Co., 1942), Ch. 7.

3. One of the gross blunders committed daily by the belligerent politicians is their assumption that neither the USSR nor the U.S. has changed for the period of forty-six years since the beginning of the Russian Revolution in 1917. American politicians still talk about Russia in terms of the Russian Revolution of 1917-20 and Russian politicians talk about the United States as it was some forty or fifty years ago. If these politicians had studied the enormous changes which the United States or France or England had forty-six years after the beginning of the American, great French and Cromwellian revolutions, the politicians would have understood the big error they commit daily in their silly utterances. Their criticism applicable to either of the two countries forty-six years ago is quite inapplicable to each of the nations, as it is today.